The poetics of mind

The poetics of mind

Figurative thought, language, and understanding

RAYMOND W. GIBBS, JR.

University of California, Santa Cruz

CAMBRIDGE
UNIVERSITY PRESS

Published by the Press Syndicate of the University of Cambridge
The Pitt Building, Trumpington Street, Cambridge CB2 1RP
40 West 20th Street, New York, NY 10011-4211, USA
10 Stamford Road, Oakleigh, Melbourne 3166, Australia

First published 1994

Printed in the United States of America

Library of Congress Cataloging-in-Publication Data
Gibbs, Raymond W.
The poetics of mind : figurative thought, language, and
understanding / Raymond W. Gibbs, Jr.
p.   cm.
Includes bibliographical references and index.
ISBN 0-521-41965-4 (hardback). – ISBN 0-521-42992-7 (pbk.)
1. Psycholinguistics. 2. Figures of speech. 3. Thought and
thinking. 4. Poetics. I. Title
P37.5.F53G5   1994
401'.9 – dc20   93-38232

A catalog record for this book is available from the British Library.

ISBN 0–521–41965–4 hardback
ISBN 0–521–42992–7 paperback

Contents

Contents

Acknowledgments

I am indebted to a large number of colleagues and friends who have contributed to my development as a cognitive scientist. I want first to thank David Rumelhart, Herb Clark, and George Lakoff for acting as wonderful, yet very different, mentors over the past 15 years. My intellectual and personal debt to these fine people is enormous.

Many other people influenced my thinking during the writing of this book. Although I list them together, each person's contribution is individually appreciated: Larry Barsalou, Christina Cacciari, Dedre Gentner, Richard Gerrig, Sam Glucksberg, Mark Johnson, Boaz Keysar, Barbara Malt, Greg Murphy, Andrew Ortony, Yeshayahu Shen, Gerard Steen, Eve Sweetser, and Mark Turner. Special thanks to Larry Barsalou, Richard Gerrig, and Sam Glucksberg for their helpful comments on an earlier draft of this book.

Support for some of the work described in this book came from the National Institute of Mental Health and the Academic Senate of the University of California, Santa Cruz. I thank my colleagues at the University of California, Santa Cruz, for all their support. My undergraduate and graduate students deserve special notice for their intelligence, hard work, and enthusiasm in collaborating with me on some of the research discussed in this book. My gratitude goes to Tamiko Azuma, Dinara Beitel, John Bolton, Darin Buchalter, Cooper Cutting, Suzanne Delaney, Bill Farrar, Gayle Gonzales, Mike Johnson, Melissa Keppel, Jeff Kishner, Sachi Kumon-Nakamura, Julia Kushner, Rob Mills, Jessica Moise, Rachel Mueller-Lust,

Acknowledgments

Annette Nagaoka, Solange Nascimento, Nandini Nayak, Jennifer O'Brien, Kerry Pfaff, David Smith, Michael Spivey, Lise Strom, and Jeff Sykes.

Many thanks to Julia Hough for her advice and support during the writing of this book. Her reading of an earlier draft substantially improved the final product. The entire staff at Cambridge University Press have been wonderful throughout the preparation of this book. A special tip of the hat to Julie Holloway for her assistance in proofreading the manuscript.

Finally, I must express my appreciation and affection to my parents, Raymond and Dorothy Gibbs, and to Guy Van Orden and Lydia Kearney. Fuzz the cat has been a constant source of encouragement.

PERMISSION ACKNOWLEDGMENTS

"Metaphors," from *Crossing the Water*, by Sylvia Plath, © Ted Hughes 1960, is reprinted by permission of HarperCollins Publishers, Inc.

"I Taste a Liquor Never Brewed," by Emily Dickinson, is reprinted by permission of the publishers and the Trustees of Amherst College from *The Poems of Emily Dickinson*, ed. Thomas H. Johnson, Cambridge, Mass.: The Belknap Press of Harvard University Press, © the President and Fellows of Harvard College 1951, 1955, 1979, 1983.

"The Phenomenology of Anger," from *The Fact of a Doorframe: Poems Selected and New, 1950–1984*, by Adrienne Rich, © Adrienne Rich 1984, © W. W. Norton & Company, Inc., 1975, 1978, is reprinted by permissions of the author and W. W. Norton & Company.

"I Need You" (David Stewart/Annie Lennox), © D'N'A' Ltd. 1987, administered by BMG Songs, Inc., is used by permission.

"The Road Not Taken," from *The Poetry of Robert Frost*, ed. Edward Connery Lathem, © Robert Frost 1944, © Henry Holt and Company, Inc., 1916, 1969, is reprinted by permission of Henry Holt and Company, Inc.

"Messenger," from *Goshawk, Antelope: Poems*, by David Smith, © University of Illinois Press 1979, is reprinted by permission.

"This is Just to Say," from William Carlos Williams, *Collected Po-*

Acknowledgments

ems, 1909–1939, vol. 1, © New Directions Publishing Corp. 1938, is reprinted by permission.

"The Mind Is an Ancient and Famous Capital," by Delmore Schwartz, is reprinted from *Last and Lost Poems of Delmore Schwartz*, ed. R. Phillips (New York: Vanguard Press, 1979), by permission of Robert S. Phillips, literary executor for the Estate of Delmore Schwartz.

Chapter 1

Introduction and overview

Why should poetic imagination matter to cognitive science? An old but still prevailing view among students of mind holds that thought and language are inherently literal. Even though people can and do speak figuratively, the ability to think, imagine, and speak poetically has historically been seen as a special human trait, requiring different cognitive and linguistic skills than those employed in ordinary life. This traditional conception of mind has imposed serious limitations on both the scholarly study of mental life in cognitive science and the humanities and on everyday folk conceptions of human experience. We see the mind as a mirror of some God-given reality that can be best described in simple, nonmetaphorical terms, language that more closely reflects underlying "truths" about the world. Figurative or poetic assertions are distinct from true knowledge, a claim first made by Plato in his famous critique of poetry. To think or speak poetically is to adopt a distorted stance toward the ordinary world, one that is held in disdain by most philosophers, scientists, and educators.

This book advances the idea that the traditional view of mind is mistaken, because human cognition is fundamentally shaped by various poetic or figurative processes. Metaphor, metonymy, irony, and other tropes are not linguistic distortions of literal mental thought but constitute basic schemes by which people conceptualize their experience and the external world. Since every mental construct reflects an adaptation of the mind to the world, the language that expresses these constructs attests to the continuous process of poetic thinking.

My emphasis in this book is on how figurative aspects of language reveal the poetic structure of mind.

Most discussions of figurative thought and language concern the interpretation of literature and poetry. Literary texts in particular are accepted as the most appropriate arena for the calculated risk of speaking figuratively. Sylvia Plath implicitly acknowledges this in a poem titled simply "Metaphors."

> I'm a riddle in nine syllables,
> An elephant, a ponderous house,
> A melon strolling on two tendrils.
> O red fruit, ivory, fine timbers!
> This loaf's big with its yeasty rising.
> Money's new-minted in this fat purse.
> I'm a means, a stage, a cow in calf.
> I've eaten a bag of green apples,
> Boarded a train there's no getting off.

This poem mocks the familiar link between the physical state of pregnancy and the poet's art of analogy. The numerous quick-shifting metaphors emphasize different aspects of a pregnant woman's size, shape, fertility, value, the inevitability of her fate. At another level, these metaphors herald not just the impending birth of a child but the emergence of Plath's own poetic voice, noting that the female body is of literary interest as it continually gives birth to new relationships between the things in the world and the I of the poem. Together the metaphors in this poem form a riddle for the reader to interpret and appreciate. The risk for the poet or any producer of figurative language is that the audience may be unable to recognize what is meant from what is said. But when a poem is understandable, when it conveys new poetic insights about human experience, we credit its author with possessing special intellectual gifts. We praise writers such as Plath for their creative genius to think and express themselves figuratively.

It is a mistake, though, to think that using figurative language requires a special cognitive ability or that such language is encountered only in literary texts. Traditionally viewed as the tool of poets and politicians, figurative language is found not only in the treasured pages of literature but throughout ordinary speech and writing. The language of great poets is clearly more creative, or poetic, than that employed by most ordinary speakers. But both poets and ordinary people make use of the same figurative schemes of thought in saying what they do. Much of our everyday talk reflects people's ability to think in ways that go beyond the literal.

The merits of figurative thought and language have been fiercely debated since the time of the ancient Greeks. Even though the study of figurative thought and language is now a respectable topic in the humanities, arts, and cognitive sciences, there remains on the part of many scholars a deep mistrust toward all things figurative ("tropophobia," or fear of tropes). Scientists, philosophers, educators, and psychologists have each, on occasion, rallied their forces against the supposed evils of figurative thought and language. For instance, some contemporary textbooks on writing and rhetoric warn that figurative language is at odds with clarity and literal thought and therefore must be repressed in the interest of making meaning transparent. As stated in one college textbook:

> Figurative language . . . is tricky as it is useful. When you intend an abstract meaning, you must make sure that your metaphors stay good and dead. And when you wish to be figurative, see whether you are getting the necessary vividness and consistency. If not, go back to literal statement; it is better to make plain assertion than litter your verbal landscape with those strange hulks. (*Crews, 1984: 233*)

Such warnings about the misuse of figurative language might seem reasonable, given the often-noted mixed metaphors and twisted tropes that "litter" writing and speech. The *New Yorker* magazine often publishes amusing examples of misspun metaphors under the title "Block That Metaphor." Two such examples, both originally published in newspaper editorials, are:

> (*Mobile, Ala.*) – In the dwindling twilight of a storm tossed Thursday, Charlie Graddick grabbed the burnished levers of

political demagoguery to whip up a hometown crowd and breathe life into a bid for governor that has seen more switchbacks than a snaky mountain road. (*Oct. 27, 1986, p. 115*)

(*Montgomery, Ala.*) – The mayor has a heart as big as the Sahara for protecting "his" police officers, and that is commendable. Unfortunately, he also often strips his gears by failing to engage the clutch when shifting what emanates from his brain to his mouth. The bullets he fires too often land in his own feet. (*Nov. 16, 1987, p. 146*)

Most writing teachers tremble with horror at the sight of these twisted examples of figurative speech. Even though we understand what the original speakers must have intended with each of these examples, it seems perfectly reasonable to admonish students to be careful about mixing their metaphors.

Yet the problem of mixed metaphors is not the main reason why many scholars warn against the use of figurative speech in everyday and academic discourse. There are other significant, deeply entrenched reasons why figurative thought and language have been held in such suspicion throughout history. These reasons stem directly from the long-standing assumption, still in fashion in many areas of the cognitive sciences, that language is independent of cognition and that figurative language is only an embellishment of ordinary literal language with little cognitive value of its own. These beliefs are evident in two central philosophical commitments (G. Lakoff, 1990).

The first is the *Objectivist Commitment*: the commitment to the view that reality is made objectively of determinate entities with properties and relations holding among those entities at each instant. This is a commitment to a view that reality comes with a preferred description, and it is a commitment as to what reality is like. The second commitment is the *Fregean Commitment* (following Frege, 1892/1952): the commitment to understand meaning in terms of reference and truth, given the objectivist commitment. Semantics consists of the relationship between symbols and the objective world independent of the minds of any beings. In addition, the Fregean commitment views semantics as independent of pragmatics. That is, semantics (the relationship between symbols and things in the world) is defined so as not to take into account how those symbols and their interpretations might be used by people. Pragmatics (the relations between signs and their users) is viewed as the study of meaning in context. Both the Objectivist and Fregean commitments underlie the idea that literal meaning best reflects the objectively determined external world and is the primary mode for the description of truth. For this reason, semantics is still viewed in linguistics, logic, and philosophy as the study of literal meaning, whereas figurative meaning is relegated to the "wastebasket" of pragmatics.

Thinking of figurative language as a strictly pragmatic phenomenon perpetuates the traditional view that such speech is deviant or, at best, ornamental. Pragmatic accounts suggest that figurative language understanding is separate from "normal" or "ordinary" linguistic processing because of its heavy reliance on contextual, real-world knowledge. But there is now much research showing that our linguistic system, even that responsible for what we often conceive of as literal language, is inextricably related to the rest of our physical and cognitive system. Recent advances in cognitive linguistics, philosophy, anthropology, and psychology show that not only is much of our language metaphorically structured, but so is much of our cognition. People conceptualize their experiences in figurative terms via metaphor, metonymy, irony, oxymoron, and so on, and these principles underlie the way we think, reason, and imagine.

Consider the idea of love. Many of the creative uses of language that talk about love and other difficult concepts are themselves based on a much smaller set of cognitive models that constrain the way individuals think about and express their experiences. American speakers often talk of love in the following ways: *He was burning with love, I am crazy about her, We are one, I was given new strength by her love, The magic is gone, Don't ever let me go, She pursued him relentlessly,* and so on (Kovecses, 1986; G. Lakoff & Johnson, 1980). Each of these expressions reflects particular ways that we think of love. For instance, *I was given new strength by her love, I thrive on love,*

5

He's sustained by love, and *I'm starved for your affection* reflect the metaphorical concept of love as some kind of nutrient. The LOVE AS NUTRIENT conceptual metaphor has as its primary function the cognitive role of understanding one concept (love) in terms of another (nutrients). Conceptual metaphors arise when we try to understand difficult, complex, abstract, or less delineated concepts, such as love, in terms of familiar ideas, such as different kinds of nutrients.

Poetic verse about love often embellishes on more mundane ways of speaking of our love experiences (Gibbs, 1992a). One of my favorite examples comes from Emily Dickinson, who writes of love in a poem titled "I Taste a Liquor Never Brewed":

> I taste a liquor never brewed
> From tankards scooped in pearl.
> Not all the Frankfort berries
> Yield such an alcohol.
>
> Inebriate of air am I
> And debauchee of dew,
> Reeling through endless summer days
> From inns of molten blue.
>
> When landlords turn the drunken bee
> Out of the foxglove's door,
> When butterflies renounce their drams,
> I shall but drink the more,
>
> Til seraphs swing their snowy hats
> And saints to windows run
> To see the little tippler
> From the manzanilla come!

Dickinson's poetic description of love as a *liquor never brewed* is an embellishment of the idea that love is a kind of nutrient, the same metaphorical mapping that motivates conventional expressions like *I'm drunk with love, He's sustained by love, I'm starved for your affection,* and so on. Creative individuals will often provide unique artistic instantiations of conceptual metaphors that partially structure our experiences.

But do metaphors *create* new insights into human experience? Or is it more accurate to say that metaphors reflect underlying schemes of thought that themselves are based on fundamental processes of figuration? My claim is that much of our conceptualization of experience is metaphorical, which both motivates and constrains the way we think creatively (G. Lakoff, 1987; G. Lakoff & Johnson, 1980; G. Lakoff & Turner, 1989). The idea that metaphor constrains creativity might seem contrary to the widely held belief that metaphor somehow liberates the mind to engage in divergent thinking. Yet it is misleading to assert that a creative poet like Dickinson has actually created a new metaphorical mapping between dissimilar domains when she has only made manifest some of the possibilities about love that are suggested by the conceptual metaphor LOVE IS A NUTRIENT. Providing new ways of looking at the entailments of conceptual metaphor is itself a creative act. But the fundamental conceptualizations of experience that provide the grounds for these creative acts reflect the conventional metaphors we ordinarily live by.

Consider another metaphorical concept that structures part of our experience in the mundane world: ANGER IS HEATED FLUID IN A CONTAINER. This conceptual metaphor is actually one of the limited number of ways that people in Western cultures conceive of anger. Our understanding of anger (the source domain) as heated fluid in a container (the target domain) gives rise to a number of interesting entailments (Gibbs, 1990a; Kovecses, 1986; G. Lakoff, 1987). For example, when the intensity of anger increases, the fluid rises (*His pent-up anger welled up inside him*). We also know that intense heat produces steam and exerts pressure on the container (*Bill is getting hot under the collar* and *Jim's just blowing off steam*). Likewise, intense anger produces pressure in the container (*He was bursting with anger*). When the pressure in the container becomes too high, the container explodes (*She blew up at me*). Each of these metaphorical entailments is a direct result of the conceptual mapping of anger onto our understanding of heated fluid in a container.

What poets primarily do, again, is not create new conceptualizations of experience but talk about the metaphorical entailments of ordinary conceptual mappings in new ways. Consider this fragment from a poem titled "The

Phenomenology of Anger," by Adrienne Rich.

> Fantasies of murder: not enough:
> to kill is to cut off from pain
> but the killer goes on hurting
>
> Not enough. When I dream of meeting
> the enemy, this is my dream:
>
> white acetylene
> ripples from my body
> effortlessly released
> perfectly trained
> on the true enemy
>
> raking his body down to the thread
>
> of existence
> burning away his lie
> leaving him in a new
> world; a changed
> man.

Rich specifies the heated fluid representing anger as acety-lene that she can focus as a weapon upon the object of her emotion. Her verse is beautifully poetic yet makes use of the same figurative modes of thought that motivate such common idioms as *blow your stack, flip your lid,* or *hit the ceiling* as well as such conventional expressions about anger as *His pent-up anger welled up inside him.* Rich's poem has great intuitive appeal for us precisely because she refers to, and elaborates upon, a common metaphorical view of anger.

My argument in this book is that our basic metaphorical conceptualizations of experience constrain how we think creatively and express our ideas in both everyday and literary discourse. The way we ordinarily speak, the way creative writers compose, is not unlimited. Yet the constraints on how we speak and write are not imposed by the limits of language but by the ways we actually think of our ordinary experiences. We do not, for example, arbitrarily talk about getting angry in terms of mowing lawns or buying apples but in terms such as blowing stacks, getting hot under the collar, exploding, and

8

so on, because we metaphorically conceptualize our anger experiences (e.g., ANGER IS HEATED FLUID IN A CONTAINER). In this way, metaphor does not just help us see things in new ways. Metaphor constitutes much of our experience and helps constrain the way we think and speak of our ordinary lives. Many linguists, philosophers, literary theorists, and psychologists miss this important point because they fail to acknowledge the systematic conceptual underpinnings of the vast number of linguistic expressions that are metaphorical and creative. What is frequently seen as a creative expression of some idea is often only a spectacular instantiation of specific metaphorical entailments arising from a small set of conceptual metaphors shared by many individuals within a culture. Some of these entailments are products of highly divergent, flexible thinking. But the very existence of these entailments of concepts is motivated by underlying metaphorical schemes of thought that constrain, even define, the ways we think, reason, and imagine.

The metaphoric nature of everyday thought is not only seen in the work of great poets and in the mundane expressions of ordinary speakers but is also found in the ways people attach meanings to individual words. Take the phenomenon of polysemy, in which a single word has many related meanings. For instance, the word *stand* has many related senses, as seen in *The house stands in the field, He couldn't stand the pressure of his job, The law still stands, The barometer stands at 29.56.* Some of these meanings are based on the physical act of standing; others extend this central sense, sometimes metaphorically, to convey ideas about verticality (*She stood six feet tall*), resistance (*He stood up to the verbal attacks against his theory*), and endurance (*The law still stands*).

Traditional accounts in lexical semantics assume that some highly abstract set of features unifies all of a polysemous word's different meanings. According to this view, there must be some set of features that underlies each use of the word *stand*. However, for many polysemous words lexical semantics has failed to specify exactly what these abstract meanings are. On the other hand, new work in lexical semantics suggests that the meanings of many polysemous words can be explained in terms of basic metaphors that motivate, among other things, the transfer of English vocabulary from the domain of physical motion and object manipulation and location (*stand* in its physical sense) to various social and mental domains (*stand* in *He took a stand on the matter*).

To take another example, consider the common English word *see*, as in *I see the plane in the sky, I see what you're doing,* or *I see your point.* The *Oxford English Dictionary* lists numerous meanings for this word, ranging from "to perceive by the eye" to "to meet a bet in poker or to equal the bet." Most theories of word meaning suggest that *see* is a classic example of a dead metaphor. That is, speakers may at one time have metaphorically extended the literal meaning of *see*, meaning "to perceive by eye," to other meanings, such as "to know or understand." This metaphorical relationship between these two senses of *see* has presumably been lost over time, and speakers now understand the various meanings of *see* as being related to some highly abstract set of features.

But there is now good evidence in cognitive linguistics to suggest that many words that appear to be classic examples of dead metaphors actually have vitally alive metaphorical roots. For instance, in Indo-European languages, words meaning "see" regularly acquire the meaning "know" at various times and places (Sweetser, 1990). The dead-metaphor view of word meaning provides no explanation of why the same kinds of meaning change recur in the history of Indo-European languages. Yet one can easily explain such changes in terms of conceptual metaphors (ibid.). In the case of *see* words, there is a widespread and ancient conceptual metaphor KNOW-ING IS SEEING, which is part of the more general MIND AS BODY metaphor. Because this metaphor exists in the conceptual systems of Indo-European-speakers, the conceptual mapping between seeing and knowing defines a "pathway" for semantic change, so that as new words for seeing develop, they eventually extend their meanings to knowing. The metaphor KNOW-ING IS SEEING, like most other conceptual metaphors, actually shows why many words acquire multiple meanings that make sense to us as contemporary speakers. The recognition that polysemy is partly motivated by our metaphorical structuring of experience is a significant development for theories of lexical semantics. But this work most significantly provides additional evidence of the inextricable link between the figurative nature of everyday thought and the ordinary use of language.

Metonymy is another figurative mode of thought that is reflected in both literary and everyday language (G. Lakoff, 1987; G. Lakoff & Turner, 1989). Consider the following section of the book *E. M. Forster: A Life*, by P. N. Furbank (1978). This short paragraph provides an innovative personal account of Forster's daily life, represented almost entirely by metonyms.

> . . . fine eyes, in steel-rimmed glasses, and a most expressive and sensitive mouth, by turns tremulous, amused, morally reproving or full of scorn. It was the mouth, one felt, of a man defending the right to be sensitive. Physically he was awkward, limp and still at the same time. He would stand rather askew, as it were, holding himself together by gripping his left hand in his right. By contrast his gestures were most graceful. (*pp. 292–93*)

This passage reflects the general cognitive principle of metonymy, or how people use one well-understood aspect of something to stand for the thing as a whole or for some other aspect of it. Forster's eyes, mouth, and gestures are contiguously presented, but we picture the entire man as unified through our ability to think metonymically.

Literary texts rely extensively on metonymy as a source of realism, exactness, and detail. A particular form of metonymy, called synecdoche, exchanges the name of the part for the whole. For example, at one point in Shakespeare's *Othello*, Iago pledges total loyalty to Othello. He calls upon the stars to

> Witness, that here Iago doth give up
> The execution of his wit, hands, heart,
> To wrong'd Othello's service! (*III. iii. 465–67*)

Wit, hands, and *heart* are metonyms that stand for the familiar tripartite division of the self often expressed as mind, body, and soul. Synecdoches like these are so common as to verge on invisibility. But like realistic novelists or biographers, poets like Shakespeare rely heavily on synecdochic detail to evoke scene, characters, and cultural experience. The poet Philip Larkin, to take another example, evokes the past glories of racehorses in the following stanza from "At Grass."

> Silks at the start: against the sky
> Numbers and parasols: outside,
> Squadrons of empty cars, and heat,
> And littered grass: then the long cry
> Hanging unhushed till it subside
> To stop-press columns on the street.

Our understanding and appreciation of this poem depends on our ability to think metonymically: to recognize, for example, that *Silks at the start* refers to jockeys atop their mounts at the starting gate.

Although metonymy is primarily studied as a mode of discourse in literature and poetry, metonymy is a ubiquitous feature of everyday speech. Consider the following mundane examples (from G. Lakoff & Johnson, 1980).

> Washington has started negotiating with Moscow.
> The White House isn't saying anything.
> Wall Street is in a panic.
> The Kremlin agreed to support the boycott.
> Hollywood is putting out terrible movies.

These examples are not isolated figures but all relate to the general metonymic principle by which a place may stand for an institution located at that place. Thus, a place like Hollywood stands for an institution located at that place, namely, the major motion picture studies. *The White House* stands for the president and the executive branch of the U.S. government.

There are a variety of conventional metonymic models that are quite common in ordinary discourse. We conceptualize AN OBJECT USED FOR THE USER (*The sax has the flu today, We need a better glove at third base*), THE CONTROLLER FOR THE CONTROLLED (*Nixon bombed Hanoi, Ozawa gave a terrible concert last night*), THE PLACE FOR THE EVENT (*Watergate changed our politics, Let's not* let *El Salvador become another Vietnam*), and THE AUTHOR FOR THE WORK (*Have you ever read any Hemingway?*). These metonymic models involve only one conceptual domain, in that the mapping or connection between two things is done within the same domain. Thus, referring to the movie industry by the place where movies are made maps a salient characteristic of one domain (its location) as representing the entire domain (the movie industry). In metaphor, on the other hand, there are two conceptual domains, and one is understood in terms of the other (e.g., love is understood as a kind of nutrient). Despite these differences in the kinds of mappings invoked, both metaphor and metonymy can be conventionalized, that is, made part of our everyday conceptual system. The fact that people easily use and understand metonymic expressions attests to the automatic, effortless, and unconscious way that people structure their experiences in terms of metonymic relations.

Metaphor and metonymy are two of the major figurative modes whereby people conceptualize their experience. Another figurative mode of thought, one that has been widely studied as a rhetorical figure but not as a fundamental aspect of our conceptual system, is irony. Speakers use irony frequently in their everyday speech, often in the form of sarcasm. For example, one person might say to another *A fine friend you are* after the addressee did something harmful to the speaker. We use sarcasm and irony for a variety of important interpersonal reasons (e.g., to be polite, to avoid responsibility for what we are saying). But we also speak ironically as often as we do because of a fundamental ability to conceptualize situations as being ironic. When someone says *It's a lovely day* in the midst of a rainstorm, the speaker signals his or her recognition of the incongruity between an expectation that the day will be nice and the reality of rain. In the same way, we judge some event as ironic because of an awareness of the incongruity between expectation and reality, even though other participants in the situation might be blind to what is really happening (often called dramatic irony). A wonderful example of this incongruity comes from the classic O. Henry short story "The Gift of the Magi." Each of a pair of newlyweds wanted to give the other a special gift for Christmas, but neither had any money. The only thing of value the wife owned was her beautiful long hair; the only valuable possession the husband had was a fine watch. To obtain funds to buy the present each wanted to give the other, the husband sold his watch to buy an ornate comb for his wife's hair, and the wife sold her hair to buy her husband a gold chain for his watch.

The ironic twist in this story is common to many situations in life. We conceptualize such situations as ironic and often comment on them in everyday discourse by speaking ironically. Writers have throughout history written in an ironic manner to convey their understanding of ironic situations. Consider the following recent example of the lyrics for a song titled "I need you," by the Eurythmics. The song is a ballad in which the singer Annie Lennox states:

> I need you to pin me down
> Just for one frozen moment.
> I need you to pin me down
> So I can live in torment.
> I need you to really feel
> The twist of my back breaking.
> I need someone to listen
> To the ecstasy I'm faking.
> I need you you you
>
> I need you to catch each breath
> That issues from my lips
> I need someone to crack my skull
> I need someone to kiss.
> So hold me now
> And make pretend
> That I won't ever fall
> Oh hold me down
> I'm gonna be your baby doll
>
> I need you you you . . .
> Is it you I really need?
> I do I do I do
> I really do

Introduction and overview

I need you . . .

As is the case with many ironic compositions, it is momentarily difficult to assess whether the speaker is being serious in saying what she does. But the singer Lennox, despite her heartfelt, sincere tone of voice, seems to be adopting the pretense of actually needing someone to treat her badly in the ways described in the song to show that she, and women in general, don't need such men in their lives. We understand the ironic message in the Eurythmics song precisely because we recognize the incongruity between some reality and our expectations.

These observations about metaphor, metonymy, and irony illustrate some of the ways our use of everyday and poetic language reflects common schemes of figurative thought. This book describes in greater detail how people naturally think in poetic ways to make sense of their ordinary experiences and how poetic thought gives rise to the language we employ to express our thoughts, feelings, and experiences. My strategy in exploring the ubiquity of figurative thought in everyday experience and language adopts what might be called the *cognitive wager* (cf. H. Clark & Malt, 1984):

> It is highly likely that most language universals are a result not of linguistically autonomous constraints but of constraints general to other cognitive functions. It is therefore appropriate a priori to assume that language universals are derived from general cognitive constraints and to leave it to others to prove otherwise.

This wager constrains me to adhere to two primary commitments: (a) a commitment to seek general principles governing all aspects of human language (the generalization commitment) and (b) a commitment to make my account of human language consistent with what is generally known about human cognition (the cognitive commitment) (G. Lakoff, 1990). I seek to explore the possibility that how we speak about our experiences is closely tied to ways we figuratively conceptualize our lives. This approach differs from that adopted by many cognitive scientists, who seek generalizations that are often thought to reflect underlying linguistic universals. These scholars work from what might be called the *generative wager* (cf. H. Clark & Malt, 1984):

> It is highly likely that most aspects of language that are universal are a result not of general cognitive constraints but of constraints specific to language functions – specific to an autonomous language faculty. It is therefore appropriate a priori to assume autonomous psychological constraints and to leave it to others to prove otherwise.

The generative wager seems unsound because it encourages investigators not to look for structure-independent explanations of language universals but to be satisfied with a purely linguistic description of a universal, assuming that it is also a description of a feature of the human language faculty. Advocates of the generative wager will often miss cognitive/functional explanations of linguistic structure because they assume a priori that linguistic constructs are autonomous of general conceptual knowledge (Gibbs, in press). In many instances, however, the cognitive motivation for linguistic structures will rest on specific kinds of figurative knowledge.

My adoption of the cognitive wager as a working strategy leads me to present a different picture of human thought and language from the one traditionally assumed in many disciplines in the humanities and social sciences. This new view of the poetics of mind has the following general characteristics:

The mind is not inherently literal.

Language is not independent of the mind but reflects our perceptual and conceptual understanding of experience.

Figuration is not merely a matter of language but provides much of the foundation for thought, reason, and imagination.

Figurative language is not deviant or ornamental but is ubiquitous in everyday speech.

Figurative modes of thought motivate the meanings of many linguistic expressions that are commonly viewed as having literal interpretations.

Metaphorical meaning is grounded in nonmetaphorical aspects of recurring bodily experiences or experiential gestalts.

Scientific theories, legal reasoning, myths, art, and a variety of cultural practices exemplify many of the same figurative schemes found in everyday thought and language.

Many aspects of word meaning are motivated by figurative schemes of thought.

Figurative language does not require special cognitive processes to be produced and understood.

Children's figurative thought motivates their significant ability to use and understand many kinds of figurative speech.

These claims dispute many beliefs about language, thought, and meaning that have dominated the Western intellectual tradition. Some of these claims are not radically new but are descended from a minority view that sees poetic thought as a fundamental characteristic of the human mind. Notable scholars, such as the 18th-century rhetorician Giambattista Vico, the 18th-century philosopher Jean-Jacques Rousseau, the 19th-century philosopher Friedrich Nietzsche, the 20th-century philosophers Ernst Cassirer and Suzanne Langer, and the 20th-century literary theorists Kenneth Burke and Hayden White, have each, in their own way, argued that our construction of reality is based upon a collection of symbolic forms that are inherently figurative. In recent years, cognitive linguists George Lakoff and Eve Sweetser, cognitive rhetorician Mark Turner, philosopher Mark Johnson, and legal theorist Steven Winter, among a growing group of cognitive scientists, have provided detailed work demonstrating that metaphor, and to a lesser extent metonymy, is the main mechanism through which we comprehend abstract concepts and perform abstract reasoning. These contemporary scholars have been especially influential in putting "the body back into the mind" by showing how metaphorical understanding is grounded in nonmetaphorical preconceptual structures that arise from everyday bodily experience. Part of this book is devoted to exploring some of this contemporary work to illustrate how figurative thought structures aspects of our ordinary conceptual understanding of experience.

My unique contribution to the discovery of the poetic mind comes from my experimental work in psycholinguistics questioning the distinction between literal and figurative meaning and my more recent findings that demonstrate how common metaphorical knowledge motivates people's use and understanding of ordinary and literary language. An important element of this work is my insistence on distinguishing between different aspects of understanding when we think about the role of figurative thought in linguistic understanding. For example, consider five possible ways figurative thought may influence ordinary language use and understanding.

1. Figurative thought has nothing to do with either the historical evolution of linguistic meaning or speakers' ordinary understanding of everyday language.

2. Figurative thought plays some role in changing the meanings of words and expressions over time but does not motivate contemporary speakers' use and understanding of language.

3. Figurative thought motivates the linguistic meanings that have currency within linguistic communities or may have some role in hypothetical or *idealized* speakers'/hearers' understanding of language. But figurative thought does not actually play any part in an individual speaker's ability to make sense of or process language.

4. Figurative thought motivates an individual speaker's use and understanding of why various words and expressions mean what they do but does not play any role in people's ordinary on-line production or comprehension of everyday language.

5. Figurative thought functions automatically in people's on-line use and understanding of linguistic meaning.

Figurative language scholars often play fast and loose between these different possibilities when they claim figurative thought either does or does not play a role in language understanding. For example, it may very well be the case that people use their preexisting metaphorical knowledge to make sense of *why* certain linguistic expressions mean what they do. That is, individuals may recognize that expressions such as *He almost exploded with anger* and *She blew her stack when she heard about her husband's affair* just make sense to use in talking about anger because of their tacit understanding that anger is sometimes conceptualized in terms of heated fluid in containers. We can say here that people's metaphorical knowledge partly *motivates* their making sense of why certain linguistic expressions mean what they do. However, it is not necessarily the case that people automatically activate their preexisting metaphorical knowledge that ANGER IS HEATED FLUID IN A CONTAINER each and every time they read or hear the expressions *He almost exploded with anger* and *She blew her stack when she heard about her husband's affair.* People might easily comprehend the conventional meanings of these phrases without any assessment of the metaphorical knowledge that motivates why these expressions mean what they do in the first place.

Distinguishing between these different possibilities for the role of metaphorical knowledge in linguistic understanding can only be done by using rather sophisticated experimental methods from contemporary psycholinguistic research. Our intuitions alone will not suffice, because many of the automatic processes that operate in ordinary language understanding are beyond our immediate awareness. This book considers in some detail the extensive empirical research in cognitive psychology, psycholinguistics, and developmental psychology that has accumulated over the past 20 years to illuminate long-standing controversies about the nature of figurative meaning and figurative language understanding. The discussion of these topics considers not only the voluminous studies conducted on metaphor but also the work done on metonymy, irony, idioms, proverbs, indirect speech acts, nominal tautologies, and oxymora. My main aim is to show that our easy facility with figurative discourse is suggestive of the poetic mind.

The plan for the book is as follows. The next chapter challenges the widely accepted assumption that thought and language are inherently literal. Most accounts of meaning and mind presuppose that ordinary literal language reflects the underlying content of ordinary thinking and knowledge. This chapter offers an overview of the search for literal meaning in the cognitive sciences and concludes that there is no independent stable account of literality for either concepts or language. Although it seems possible at times to identify the apparent context-free meanings of words and sentences, a closer examination reveals the difficulty of defining what is literal about thought and language. However, the search for literal meaning uncovers important characteristics of the poetic mind by showing that much of what we normally see as literal thought or literal language is itself constituted by fundamental processes of figuration.

Chapter 3 discusses the role that literal meaning may play in understanding figurative language. One consequence of the failure to acknowledge the poetic structure of mind is the widespread assumption that understanding figurative language requires special mental processes. Most traditional accounts of figurative language use suggest that nonliteral speech violates widespread communicative norms of speaking truthfully and unambiguously. This pragmatic view of figurative language understanding follows the centuries-old belief that literal language is a veridical reflection of thought and the external world, whereas figurative language distorts reality and only serves special rhetorical purposes. Because in this view figurative thinking is an unusual mode of cognition, the use and interpretation of figurative language is seen as a violation of standard communicative norms.

This theory on the use and interpreting of figurative language is completely wrong. Figurative language is in most respects readily understandable without being perceived as violating communicative norms, because such language is a direct, automatic, and natural reflection of the way people think, reason, and imagine. Chapter 3 and aspects of Chapters 4 through 9 outline the empirical evidence showing how the traditional pragmatic view of figurative language understanding is misleading. Although pragmatic knowledge plays a very important role in the immediate interpretation of figurative language, we must recognize that our understanding of most language, whether it is consciously identified as literal or figurative, is very much constrained by the poetic structure of mind.

Chapter 4 explores the ubiquity of metaphor in thought and

language. Contrary to the accepted notion that metaphor requires a special intellectual talent or is used only in special rhetorical situations, metaphor is found in virtually all aspects of our everyday thinking and speech. I discuss some of the ways metaphor is constitutive of everyday communication and thought as well as of more specialized forms of legal and scientific reasoning, artistic expression, myth, and cultural experience.

Chapter 5 discusses the major theoretical approaches to understanding verbal metaphor. Much of the disagreement that arises in the interdisciplinary study of metaphor stems from theorists' differing interest in some aspects of linguistic understanding to the neglect of others. Philosophers, linguists, and literary theorists focus on metaphor understanding as a rational process and generally study how metaphor is identified, consciously interpreted, and appreciated. From an examination of the various products of metaphor recognition and interpretation, these scholars try to infer something about metaphor comprehension or the early, unconscious mental processes that operate in normal linguistic understanding. On the other hand, psychologists and psycholinguists study metaphor comprehension processes with an eye to explicating something about the later products of metaphor interpretation and recognition. Chapter 5 evaluates the major theories of metaphorical language proposed by linguists, philosophers, and psychologists in light of these claims about the time course of understanding and the constraining influence of conceptual and pragmatic knowledge in the interpretation of metaphorical discourse.

Most scholars assume that idioms and proverbs (e.g., *A rolling stone gathers no moss*) may once have been metaphorical but have lost their metaphoricity over time either through overuse or because we have forgotten their metaphorical origins. Consequently, idioms and proverbs now exist in the mental lexicon as frozen semantic units or as dead metaphors. Although metaphors are perceived as lively, creative, and resistant to paraphrase, idioms and proverbs are seen as dead, hackneyed expressions that are equivalent in meaning to simple literal phrases. However, recent work in cognitive linguistics and psycholinguistics suggests that idioms and proverbs are ubiquitous in discourse and that these phrases are not simple dead metaphors but actually retain a good deal of their metaphoricity. Scholars often treat idioms as dead metaphors because they confuse dead metaphors with conventional ones. This position fails to distinguish between conventional metaphors, which are part of our live conceptual system (e.g., LOVE IS A NUTRIENT, ANGER IS HEATED FLUID IN A CONTAINER), and historical metaphors that are no longer useful or part of how we ordinarily think. The mistake derives from an assumption that things in our cognition that are most alive and most active are those that are conscious. On the contrary, those things that are most alive and most deeply entrenched, efficient, and powerful are so automatic as to be unconscious and effortless. Chapter 6 reviews the experimental work on idiom and proverb understanding to show that everyday metaphorical knowledge motivates our use and understanding of idioms and proverbs.

Metaphor and metonymy are closely related, as described above. The purpose of Chapter 7 is to show how metonymy is distinct from metaphor and independently structures a good deal of everyday reasoning. Metonymy is primarily used for reference, and our understanding of innovative metonymic expressions (as when one waitress says to another *The ham sandwich is getting impatient for his check*), as well as both indirect requests (*Can you lend me five dollars?*) and nominal tautologies (*Boys will be boys*), reflect metonymic modes of thinking, where the mention of a salient part of the whole refers to the whole and where the mere mention of the whole can instantiate a salient part.

Our ability to conceptualize incongruous situations via irony and oxymora (e.g., *sweet sorrow* and *screaming silence*) is the topic in Chapter 8. Irony is difficult to define, because of the variety of ways people conceptualize situations where there is some incongruity noted between what is expected or believed and what actually happens. This chapter explores many of the complexities of irony in thought and language and again suggests that our ability to speak and comprehend ironic discourse is a direct reflection of our ability to see situations ironically. A similar ability motivates our rather frequent use of oxymora, phrases that appear to be contradictory (*screaming silence*) but capture significant aspects of how we think of inchoate experiences.

One of the long-standing beliefs in psychology is that children are incapable of figurative thinking and consequently are unable to use and understand nonliteral speech. Chapter 9 explores this mistaken assumption and reviews various studies which show that even young children demonstrate some ability to produce and understand many kinds of figurative discourse. This work is suggestive of the idea that young children possess significant ability to think in poetic ways.

The final chapter presents summary conclusions and outlines some important directions for the empirical study of the poetic mind.

Chapter 2
Thinking and speaking
literally

What does it mean to say that people can think and speak literally? Understanding what something literally means is complicated by the different ways concepts and words can be used. Consider the concept "working." Now imagine the situation of a Mr. Smith mowing his lawn on a Saturday morning (Rommetveit, 1983). Inside the house, Mrs. Smith receives a telephone call from a friend, who asks *Is your husband still in bed?*, to which Mrs. Smith replies *No, he is already outside, working in the garden.*

Consider now the same situation, except that we also know that Mr. Smith is a firefighter who is often on duty on Saturdays. A friend of his knows this is the case and is wondering whether Mr. Smith on this particular Saturday might be free to go fishing with him. He therefore calls and asks Mrs. Smith *Is your husband working today?*, to which she replies, *No, he is outside mowing the lawn.*

Why is the word *working* appropriate to use in referring to Mr. Smith's activities in one situation but not the other? Neither Mrs. Smith's friend nor her husband's friend is likely to accuse Mrs. Smith of lying or of contradicting herself. Nor would they insinuate that Mrs. Smith has employed indirect or metaphorical speech in her use of the word *working*. On the contrary, each addressee should be convinced that Mrs. Smith told the truth, using ordinary literal language. The word *working* seems entirely appropriate in each situation, yet in one case it describes Mr. Smith's lawn-mowing activities and in the other case it does not. How do we determine the literal meaning of *working* across these different situations?

Defining the meaning of the term *literal* seems particularly important, because most scholarly discussions of figurative language presuppose some distinction between figurative and literal meaning. *Webster's Third International Dictionary* defines the word *literal* as having the following senses: (a) *according to the letter of the scriptures,* (b) *adhering to fact or to the ordinary construction or primary meaning of a term or expression,* (c) *being without exaggeration or embellishment, plain, unadorned, or unimaginative,* (d) *characterized by a concern mainly with facts,* and (e) *represented word by word.* These different but related senses of the word *literal* capture some of the ideals of language and meaning that have been implicitly used in understanding what appears to be special or unique about figurative language and thought.

Ordinary speech shows that the term *literally* has a wide variety of uses. Consider the following expressions containing the adverb *literally*:

Every word of this is literally as the man spoke it.
We had literally one minute to catch the twelve o'clock train.
With his eyes, he literally scoured the corners of the room.
When we got home, I literally died of exhaustion.
During the Super Bowl, our eyes were literally glued to the television.
He literally swept her off her feet with flowers and perfume.
In the 1930s, cures for the depression literally flooded Washington.

These expressions illustrate that the term *literally* is polysemous, capable of expressing several senses. Some of these meanings refer to the idea of exact fidelity of representation, and others convey the idea that the proposition mentioned should be taken in the strongest admissible way (as hyperbole, not literally!). But which of the several senses of *literally* applies when we state the common belief that people usually think and speak literally? What does it even mean to say that any idea or expression has a particular literal content?

The traditional view that the mind has objectively determined concepts and categories leads to the equivalent assumption that the meanings of words and sentences can be objectively defined in terms of "literal" meanings. Most linguistic theories presuppose that the literal meanings of words and sentences can be precisely stated and that literal meaning serves as the foundation for figurative language interpretation, with figurative meanings being parasitic upon literal ones. It is ironic that so much of the vast literature on figurative meaning has had little to say about literal meaning, apart from the attempt to describe the ways in which figurative meaning may differ from it. Part of the reason for this is that literal meaning is traditionally not seen as just one kind of meaning among others. In fact, very few theories of linguistic meaning offer any explicit mention of literal meaning, as it is assumed that a theory of meaning is about literal meaning and nothing else. Literal meaning is viewed as so pervasive, so much part of our thinking, that it is mostly seen as theory-neutral. Scholars look to literal meaning to clarify muddles and confusions of meaning and as the starting point for all considerations of figurative language. Literal meanings are thought to provide the answer to the riddle of how one state of intersubjectivity or shared meaning can be attained by linguistic means between people with different subjective worlds. We assume that there *must* be literal concepts and literal meanings in order for people to communicate successfully, given our different subjective experiences.

Although there are remarkably few attempts to define "literal" meaning explicitly, the long-standing interest in concepts, word meaning, and sentence meaning in linguistics, philosophy, and psychology provides fertile ground for beginning the search for the literal properties of thought and language. This chapter will show that the idealized, mythical view of literal meaning as being well specified and easily identifiable in thought and language is incorrect. It is, in fact, quite difficult to specify the literal definitions of concepts and the words that refer to these concepts.

The consequences of this conclusion about the literal properties of thought and language are significant and wide-ranging for theories of mind and meaning. Most generally, this negative appraisal of the holy grail of literal meaning will point the way to an alternative conception of mind as being fundamentally constituted by various figurative processes that are then linguistically communicated by speakers/listeners and authors/readers in socially shared environments. This alternative view will be elaborated upon in later chapters. For now, my aim is to scrutinize theoretical and empirical attempts to identify the literal properties of thought and language. Much experimental evidence demonstrates that the idea of literalness varies considerably according to culture, individuals, context, and task. I will argue that the theoretical notion of literalness should be replaced by a set of other terms referring to more specific aspects of concepts and meaning.

DEFINING THE LITERAL PROPERTIES OF WORDS AND CONCEPTS

One way to begin seeking the literal meaning of a word or concept is to consult the dictionary. Lexicographers work hard to pin down the meanings of words, and so the dictionary is a good place to begin the search for literal meaning. Suppose that an English-speaker, for some reason, desires to look up the definition of *horse* in a respectable source, such as the *Compact Oxford English Dictionary* (Haiman, 1980). A *horse* is defined here as *a solid-footed perisodactyl quadruped (Equus caballus) having a flowing mane and tail, whose voice is a neigh. It is well known in the domestic state as a beast of draught and burden and especially as used for riding upon.*

Does this definition capture what *horse* literally means? One purpose of a definition is to enable speakers to use a word correctly. But words like *perisodactyl* are not very informative, because most people do not know this word. Some speakers, such as children, may not even know what *quadruped* means but still understand the meaning of *horse* and be capable of using *horse* correctly in conversation. On the other hand, the definition of *horse* above leaves out much information that most speakers of English have about horses. For example, people generally know that horses are relatively large domesticated animals who like to eat carrots and hay. People also do not normally think of horses as food, at least in our culture, unlike cattle. Yet a dictionary definition of a word can't include everything that is known about the concept to which the word refers, for this would make the entry for a word considerably longer than an entire dictionary. Perhaps the proper place for the compendium of everything that is known about a concept should be the encyclopedia. On a practical level, it makes sense to keep the dictionary entry for *horse* rather brief and to put most of the remaining information about horses in an encyclopedia. Linguists often argue that speakers' internal knowledge of their language should include only linguistic information and exclude encyclopedic facts based on general knowledge (J. Katz & Fodor, 1963). Encyclopedic information is not properly part of the human lexicon, and so one's knowledge and beliefs about words should not be represented as part of their literal meanings. Separating encyclopedic and linguistic knowledge is seen as providing a clear demarcation for the study of language in linguistics and philosophy.

But is there any theoretical basis for deciding what goes in the dictionary and what goes in the encyclopedia? Lexicographers make many tacit assumptions when they define the meaning(s) of particular words, yet these assumptions are nearly impossible to state formally and are most likely not consistently applied when defining all words in a language. Defining what words literally mean is difficult not only for the problem of distinguishing between dictionary and encyclopedic information but also because it is extremely difficult to determine what information of any sort really defines a concept.

Nevertheless, our belief in the possibility that words and concepts can be defined stems from the folk idea that words *contain* meaning and that in using words and sentences speakers are able to convey these meanings to other individuals. This "container view of meaning" underlies both formal and informal theories of word meaning and presupposes that meaning can be studied independent of word users. From this general conception, the meanings of words may be specified – as in a dictionary – objectively and definitely. Each word has a set of properties or attributes that is critical for defining the class of objects that satisfies its description in the real world.

We seek criteria for determining the set of properties or attributes that constitutes what a word or concept literally means so that we can differentiate each word or concept from all others (the *principle of contrast*: Bolinger, 1965; E. Clark, 1987). Psychologists attempt to discover exactly which set of properties associated with a word is activated each time the word is read or heard. Consider now the most important attempts to define the literal meanings of words and concepts, beginning with those that reflect the notion that words "contain" meaning.

REFERENTIAL THEORY OF WORD MEANING

The simplest version of the "container" approach is that word meaning specifies the relation between a word and the object(s) in the world to which the word refers. Under this view, known as the *referential theory of meaning*, or *extensionalism*, the problem of defining word meaning is equated with the problem of reference. Just as proper names, such as *George Washington*, refer to individuals, common nouns refer to classes of objects, verbs refer to classes of actions, adjectives to properties of individuals and objects, and so on. For instance, the meaning of *dog* is taken to be the set of all dogs in the real world (or in the set of all possible worlds).

Various refutations have been offered to the referential theory of word meaning, the most notable being Frege's (1892/ 1952). Frege showed that the two expressions *the morning star* and *the evening star* both refer to the same object, the planet Venus, but do not have the same meaning. If they did, the sentence *The morning star is the evening star* would be understood in the same way as *The morning star is the morning star*. But the first sentence is informative, whereas the second is uninformative or tautological. Similarly, the expressions *The first person to run a four-minute mile* and *Roger Bannister* are not synonymous, but they refer to same person. Identity of reference is therefore not a sufficient condition for identify of meaning.

Frege's work led philosophers and linguists to distinguish between sense and reference, or between the meaning of a word and its referents. This distinction is sometimes referred to as the difference between the connotation of a word and its denotation, and most recently by philosophers as the difference between the intension of a term and its extension. For example, the intension of a term is the set of critical properties that determines the applicability of a word. Intensions and/or senses are really contrastive relations with other words and presuppose nothing about the existence of objects and properties outside the vocabulary of the language in question (Lyons, 1968). To know the meaning of a word, under this view, is to know its intension.

The extensionalist view assumes the key presupposition that there is a one-to-one relation that can be uniquely specified between a word and some object or class of objects to which it may be said it refers (i.e., the direct representation view of language). Some words may certainly refer to a number of distinct objects or classes of objects, in which case a number of distinct, specifiable relations may be established. But there is a preponderance of words, such as *round, do, have, hello, very*, and *in*, for which no clear-cut relations with the world can be established. Some words and expressions clearly cannot be thought of as containing meaning without some reference to speakers, listeners, and the context of utterance. Indexical and deictic terms, such as *here, today*, and *now*, and the personal pronouns, such as *I, you, he, she, we*, and *they*, each require information about the context of use in order to specify their exact meanings. The presence of indexicals and words such as *round, do, have*, and *very* suggests that theories of word meaning cannot be established on the putative one-to-one relations between language and the world (T. Moore & Carling, 1982).

Many philosophers and linguists exclude indexicals and deictic terms from their accounts of word meaning by arguing that aspects of meaning having to do with the knowledge, beliefs, and circumstances of language users should remain outside the proper domain of semantic theory (i.e., pragmatics). Such a move may or may not be desirable from a linguistic or philosophical perspective, but it severely limits the utility of such a theory in understanding what ordinary speakers might know about the meanings of words.

Thinking and speaking literally

Since the 1950s, philosophy and linguistics have taken a decisive turn away from behaviorism and have adopted mentalism. Under this view, semantic theory is no longer just an approach to the study of language (or logic) but must be rich enough to characterize speakers' intuitions about semantic properties of sentences, such as inference, presupposition, anomaly, and synonymy of meaning. The task for semanticists is to discover the set of necessary and sufficient conditions that taken together are adequate to encapsulate a word's meaning as understood by speakers. Just as objects in the real world have sets of necessary and sufficient conditions that define them, so too do words have sets of conditions that define their proper – literal – meanings.

Consider the word *bachelor*. According to the checklist theory, there are sets of necessary conditions, such as ADULT, HUMAN, MALE, and UNMARRIED, that together are sufficient for defining the meaning of *bachelor*. People presumably have an internal list of such characteristics, sometimes called "semantic markers" or "features" (J. Katz, 1972), for each word in their mental lexicon, similar to sets of necessary and sufficient conditions that define that word's extension in some possible world. This "checklist" theory (Fillmore, 1975) is appealing because it resembles the way dictionaries work. One might define the literal meaning of a word as simply the collected list of its individually represented senses.

Over the past 30 years, various scholars have attempted to map out the universal set of semantic features, or primitives, that underlies all word meanings. These primitive features represent *certain deep seated, innate properties of the human organism and the perceptual apparatus* (Bierwisch, 1967: 3). Although many theorists postulate the existence of a universal set of semantic primitives, few researchers actually offer concrete lists of primitives. One early attempt proposed that the main semantic components of lexical items are part-of-speech markers (e.g., noun, verb, adjective) and semantic features (J. Katz & Fodor, 1963). The semantic features are binary attributes, such as (+concrete), (+living), (+animate), and (+human). These features are not to be considered real English words but abstract concepts in a metalanguage, which is precisely defined language used in an exact discussion of another language. The word *boy*, for example, has a meaning representation of +concrete, +living, +animate, +human, +male, –adult. Various redundancy rules, such as +adult = +living, +animate, +human, make it possible to shorten the semantic components associated with any word definition and to show how any word is related to other words in the vocabulary.

The general idea behind "checklist," or componential, analyses of meaning is that there should be a much smaller set of atomic components than there are words in the vocabulary. Researchers argue that the main advantage of componential analyses of word meaning is that they can account for meaning relations among words in the lexicon. For instance, synonyms have nearly identical sets of semantic features. Antonyms contrast on only one significant feature. Thus, *man* and *woman, boy* and *girl*, and *dead* and *alive* are all antonyms because each pair differs by only one binary component. Other formal characteristics of word meaning, such as semantic anomaly, converseness, hyponymy, and so on, are thought to be well accounted for by semantic feature theories (J. Katz & Fodor, 1963; J. Katz, 1972).

Numerous criticisms of checklist theories of word meaning point to difficulties in the ontological status of semantic primitives, the inadequacy of semantic primitives to account for certain classes of words, and, most generally, the failure to specify exactly what semantic features are supposed to be (Bolinger, 1965; Kempson, 1977; Pulman, 1983; Quine, 1960, 1966; Sampson, 1980; Shannon, 1988). Nevertheless, semantic primitives were widely used in the 1970s and early 1980s in semantic descriptions of language in artificial intelligence systems (Norman & Rumelhart, 1975; Schank, 1972, 1973; Wilks, 1972, 1978). At the same time, many experimental studies in psycholinguistics considered whether or not people actually analyzed or decomposed words into their more primitive features during normal sentence comprehension (i.e., the lexical decomposition hypothesis).

Some of the early studies examined people's ability to evaluate sentences containing unmarked and marked lexical items (e.g., to compare *present* and *absent* in *The square is present* and *The circle is absent*). Marked words, such as *absent*, should be more difficult to understand because they are semantically more complex (e.g., NOT(PRESENT)) than unmarked words, such as *present*. Various studies indicate that people take longer to verify sentences with marked items (H. Clark, 1969, 1974; Sherman, 1973). These experimental findings were taken as providing initial support for the lexical decomposition hypothesis and gave some plausibility to the idea that literal word meanings are defined in terms of underlying semantic primitives. However, the fact that lexical markings affect the verification of sentences does not necessarily corroborate the lexical decomposition hypothesis (H. Clark & Clark, 1977). Participants in these studies might have performed their evaluation of the test sentences *after* they actually understood what these sentences meant. Later studies looking at people's evaluation of sentences with marked and unmarked terms obtained results against the lexical decomposition hypothesis (J. D. Fodor, Fodor, & Garrett, 1975). Finally, more sensitive on-line experiments (Cutler, 1983) examined lexical analysis as it immediately occurred during sentence comprehension. These studies found no evidence to support the idea that people automatically decompose complex words into their underlying semantic components (cf. J. A. Fodor, Garrett, Walker, and Parkes, 1980; Gentner, 1981; Kintsch, 1974; Thorndyke, 1975).

The weight of the experimental evidence does not support the lexical decomposition hypothesis. It appears that people do not have readily stored literal meanings for individual words that are automatically activated during ordinary sentence comprehension. Some aspects of a word's meaning may, when the task demands it, be processed separately from others. Consider the word *newspaper* for a moment and note which of its features comes to mind. Now consider *newspaper* in the context of building a fire. The feature "flammable" probably didn't come to mind when you considered *newspaper* in isolation, but it probably did when you considered it in the context of building a fire (Barsalou, in press). Similarly, people find it easier to answer a question about a diamond's hardness after reading *The goldsmith cut the glass with the diamond* than a question about a diamond's value (Tabossi & Johnson-Laird, 1980). Many experiments on the semantic flexibility of words generally showed that understanding words did not require that the same set of linguistic information or meaning be retrieved each time a word was heard or read (R. Anderson & Ortony, 1975; R. Anderson et al., 1976; Barclay, Bransford, Franks, McCarrell, & Nitsch, 1974; Barsalou, 1982; Conrad, 1978; Greenspan, 1986; Roth & Shoben, 1983; Whitney, McKay, Kellas, & Emerson, 1985). People incorporate different features of a concept in their memory for a word, depending on the encoding context. Such empirical demonstrations clearly make it difficult to assume that people ordinarily access a word's putative literal meaning during language comprehension.

Most theories of word meaning assume that the lexicon is the repository of all the knowledge needed to specify the meanings of words in sentences. Once a word's meaning, perhaps the literal meaning, is accessed from the lexicon, it is passed to the conceptual system for further nonlinguistic interpretation. But some experimental findings support the idea that a word's lexical representation simply points to a general-purpose conceptual system in which the meanings of words are retrieved and combined using both linguistic and nonlinguistic (e.g., conceptual) information. One series of studies asked people to judge quickly whether a sentence was plausible both when one of its words was replaced with a picture, called a rebus sentence (e.g., a picture of a stool replaced *stool*), and when the sentence contained all its words (Potter, Kroll, Yachzel, Carpenter, & Sherman, 1986). Because a pictorial object is conceptually but not lexically equivalent to the corresponding noun, the ability to understand rebus sentences would support the hypothesis that a noun acts as a conceptual element. The logic of these experiments was to present sentences so rapidly that a delay in encoding the rebus pictures in the needed linguistic form would be highly disruptive. Difficulty with understanding a rebus sentence would support the hypothesis that a noun (e.g., *stool*) taps specific lexical information during the composition of sentence meaning. However, the main result of these studies was that rebus sentences were not more difficult to understand, and later remember, than equivalent all-word sentences. These findings support the idea that a word's lexical representation simply points to a general-purpose conceptual system in which the meanings of words are retrieved and combined.

The possibility that word meanings are retrieved from our general-purpose conceptual system is inconsistent with the idea that understanding word meanings only involves analysis of their individual semantic features. Recent work in the psychology of concepts extends this conclusion to conceptual combinations in which two or more concepts are combined to form a new concept. Many English noun phrases are constructed out of category terms, such as *blue couch, pet fish,* or *typewriter table.* How do we understand these complex concepts? We might analyze the semantic properties of each term and combine these to form the meaning of the noun phrase. However, this doesn't work for many noun–noun concepts (Hampton, 1987; Medin & Shoben, 1988; Murphy, 1988, 1990; Wisniewski & Gentner, 1991). For example, a *typewriter table* does not have a roller or keys, does not type letters, does not accept ribbons, does not use electricity, and so on. Interpreting conceptual combinations requires more than accessing the individual features of each concept. People must access their general knowledge about the domains of the individual concepts and attempt to construct interpretations that satisfy both this knowledge and specific past examples encountered. Having once seen a table with a typewriter on it, we can use very specific information about that experience to construct a general interpretation of the phrase *typewriter table.* This interpretation will also be constrained by our general knowledge about tables, typewriters, and common typing practices (Murphy, 1988). Defining the literal content of conceptual combinations simply cannot be accomplished without extensive use of real-world knowledge that is not usually considered to be part of a word's individual semantic properties.

CAN PEOPLE DEFINE WORDS?

Disillusionment with the checklist view of word meaning led some psychologists to define words in terms of *meaning pos-*

tulates (Kintsch, 1974; J. D. Fodor et al., 1975; J. A. Fodor et al., 1980). Meaning postulate theories assume that comprehension consists in translating utterances into a mental language (called *mentalese*) in which the representation of the sentence is very close to its surface form. Each word in the language is accordingly represented by a corresponding unanalyzed token in the mental language. Meaning postulates are useful devices for capturing relations between the meanings of words. For example, there is some relation between *bachelor* on the one hand and *unmarried* and *male* on the other. This relation would formally be expressed as *for any* x (*if bachelor*(x) *then unmarried*(x) *and male*(x)). The important claim of meaning postulate theorists is that there are no semantic primitives into which the meanings of words can be decomposed, and accordingly there are no mental dictionary entries representing the meanings of words (J. A. Fodor et al., 1980). Under this view, the literal meaning of a word is simply the set of instructions for a word that constitutes its meaning postulate.

One argument often used to support meaning postulates is that most people have difficulty defining words. Just as people are able to ride a bicycle without being able to describe what they are doing, people may know the meanings of words in terms of being able to use them correctly without being able to give their literal definitions. Even though lexicographers are successful in defining words for dictionaries, some psychologists have looked at the dictionary-making enterprise with some skepticism, noting that there are really few good definitions of English words (ibid.).

Consider the verb *paint* (J. A. Fodor, 1983). One plausible characterization of this verb's meaning is "to cover a surface with paint." But this definition seems inadequate. It shouldn't apply in the case of an explosion in a paint factory that causes the walls, floor, and ceiling to become coated with paint. Moreover, the definition of *X paints Y* is not coextensive with "X is an agent and X covers the surface of Y with paint, and X's primary intention in covering the surface of Y with paint is that the surface of Y should be covered with paint as a consequence of X's having acted upon it." For example, a painter's dipping a brush into a bucket full of paint in preparation for work would not normally be viewed as the painter painting that brush. It seems clear that the search for a literal definition of *to paint*, never mind more complex and abstract words, is quite unconstrained.

At best, dictionary definitions mediate meaning by connecting up a new word with other words that the reader presumably knows from experience. Nevertheless, the success of some dictionaries is testimony to the possibility that many words in English can be defined. Longman's *Dictionary of Contemporary English* defines the meanings of 55,000 words using a vocabulary of only 2,000 words (Johnson-Laird, 1983). The definitions provided by dictionaries may not be totally adequate, but the utility of dictionaries suggests that they might serve a useful function for students. But does the success of dictionaries imply anything about the specification of literal meanings for words?

One philosophical position related to this issue maintains that words do have fixed meanings that can be concretely specified but that only a few experts know these meanings (Putnam, 1975). People may know that the words *beech* and *larch* denote different kinds of trees, but they cannot tell a beech from a larch. Ordinary people must consult experts if they are to know the essential nature of something. A botanist, for example, might be able to say what differentiates a beech tree from a larch, and this knowledge captures the "real meaning" of the words *beech* and *larch*. Putnam concluded that the meaning of a word is not something in the mind of an individual speaker. It is conceivable, therefore, that there is a fixed literal meaning for individual words but that ordinary people do not actually possess such knowledge.

The difficulty with this account of meaning is that nonexperts make use of words such as *beech* and *larch* even though they may have only partial knowledge about their meanings (Garnham, 1979). At the same time, experts often disagree as to the definitions of concepts. Even when experts concur on the definition of some concept, people don't necessarily incorporate that view into their own understanding of a word. For example, botanists tell us that an onion is simply a kind of lily (Dupre, 1981), but this information doesn't seem at all necessary for a working knowledge of onions and lilies or of the words used to denote these concepts (Aitchison, 1987).

Another problem in defining words is that some words are in and of themselves vague. Whether or not a certain object is to be called a *cup* or a *vase* or a *bowl* depends on the presence of a number of features. For example, the choice between *cup* and *bowl* is usually determined by the relationship between the diameter and height of the object, but one can change a bowl back to a cup just by adding a handle to it (Labov, 1973). Furthermore, the designation *bowl* may be changed to *cup* just by saying *There is coffee in it* and back to *bowl* again by *There's potatoes in it* (Hormann, 1983). Certain features become effective in defining the appropriateness of the word, even though such features do not usually belong to the list of features characterizing or defining the word's literal meaning. How can we define what words literally mean when certain semantic features (e.g., "has a handle") are sometimes important and sometimes not? This problem provides even more evidence to suggest that understanding a word may no longer be conceptualized as the activation of a list of features corresponding to that word's literal meaning.

Many words are even more difficult to define than *cup, bowl,* and *vase.* Certain words, such as *good, love,* and *a few,* seem especially fuzzy, even though in context the fuzzy area of denotation is often made precise. For example, when people were presented with sentences like *John bends paperclips* and asked afterwards *How many does he bend?*, most people responded *Oh, about three or four,* even though the utterance itself does not contain this information (Kanouse, 1972). Why not six or seven, or a dozen, or twenty? It's unlikely that the lexical entry for *to bend* specifies "if said about paperclips, three or four; if said about iron rods, at most one; if said about pipe cleaners, five to seven"; and so on.

Indefinite quantifiers (e.g., *a few, some, several*) are also very difficult to define, even though these words are used frequently with little difficulty in ordinary discourse. In one study, participants were asked to state how many of the objects in question would actually be meant when *a few* was used in different situations (Hormann, 1983). People on average estimated the following.

a few people standing before a hut	4.55
a few people standing before the house	5.33
a few people	5.72
a few people standing before City Hall	6.37
a few people standing before the building	6.99

The data show the difficulty in defining the literal meanings of many words. It makes no sense to specify the meaning of *a few* in the mental lexicon as being "5.72 if said of people, 4.55 if said of people standing before a hut," and so on. Listeners do not simply look up the particular number associated with *a few* but construct its meaning, given some specific situation. This is also true of a fairly concrete word, such as *red* (H. Clark, 1991). Dictionaries generally define *red* as describing the color of blood when predicated of most objects. But note that *red* is (a) tawny when predicated of a skin type, (b) pinkish red when predicated of potatoes, (c) orange when predicated of hair, (d) purply when predicated of wine, (e) pinkish red when predicated of wood, and so on (ibid.). The exact color that *red* denotes depends on what it is predicated of, and our mental lexicon would presumably have to list each one of these examples.

One factor to consider in attempting to define words literally is that different words may require different kinds of semantic analysis. Some words are nearly impossible to define accurately because they express primitive semantic notions. Highly frequent words in English, ones that are likely to express primitive notions, are indeed harder to define (Jorgensen, 1990). Yet college students are often able to provide quality definitions for many concrete words, especially when a large number of uses of the word are provided (ibid.). Natural-kind terms, such as *gold* and *lemon*, may be particularly difficult to define, in contrast to analytic terms, such as *bachelor*, that may have both necessary and sufficient conditions (Johnson-Laird, 1983). One study showed that difficulty in defining words depended on how close each word was to its underlying semantic primitives (Johnson-Laird & Quinn, 1976). Words that express meanings close to their putative semantic primitives were harder to define than words with more complex meanings. For example, verbs like *move* and *see* were difficult to define because they express primitive semantic notions. People were most accurate defining semantically complex intentional verbs, such as *chase, steal,* and *lend.* These empirical results demonstrate that some words are easy to define because their meanings are at least analyzable. Such findings are contrary to the view of meaning postulate theorists, who assume that few words can be adequately defined and that most are merely translated into corresponding tokens in the mental language. The fact that people are sometimes partially successful in defining words does not necessarily indicate that such words have well-specified literal meanings. Nor does it mean that people ordinarily access these definitions during language comprehension. Rather, people are often able to provide definitions for words that are useful to others in learning how to use words in context.

AMBIGUITY, POLYSEMY, AND LEXICAL INNOVATIONS

Three phenomena that are problematic in the search for literal properties of words and concepts are ambiguity, polysemy, and lexical innovations. Ambiguous words have more than one meaning, usually meanings that are unrelated. For example, the word *bank* can refer either to a financial institution or to the side of a river. There is some historical evidence that these meanings stem from the same source, but the meanings of most ambiguous words are thought to be independent. In most instances of lexical ambiguity it is difficult to extract a core meaning for the word, as with the word *race*, which can refer either to an ethnic group or to speed competition. These two meanings of *race* do not appear to have any higher-order abstract meaning that captures both senses. It is an instance of homonymy. Polysemy, on the other hand, refers to words whose meanings are related. For instance, the meanings of the word *bug* (e.g., insect, spy device, computer error) seem to relate to the more abstract idea of "a small annoying thing that is difficult to get rid of." Most words are to some degree polysemous. One analysis has shown that 98 of the 100 most frequently used words in English are polysemous (Lee, 1990).

Distinguishing between ambiguity and polysemy is in practice difficult to do. In many cases it is unclear whether different uses of a word should be represented as separate lexical entries. One purely linguistic test has been offered for determining whether two meanings of a word are part of the same lexical entry (Kempson, 1977). Consider the sentence *Tom ran the race and Bill did too*. The "to do so too" construction requires identity of meaning of the noun phrases *Tom ran the race* and *Bill ran the race*. But if Tom were an organizer of the race and Bill a participant, then the sentence *Tom ran the race and Bill did too* would be literally unacceptable (or maybe a pun). Thus, these two senses of *run* must correspond to distinct lexical items with distinct semantic representations (i.e., an instance of ambiguity, or the *homonymy view*).

However, many words that fail this linguistic test appear to have meanings that are highly interrelated. Consider the sentences *John worked hard at the problem until he found the answer* and *Mary telephoned Bill, but there was no answer*. The word *answer* seems unacceptable in constructions such as *John got an answer and Mary did so too*, where John is doing algebra and Mary is making a telephone call (Williams, 1992). We would therefore expect *answer* to have different lexical entries for each of its different uses. But empirical evidence shows that people often judge different uses of polysemous words, such as *answer*, to be highly related (Durkin & Manning, 1989). Other experimental evidence from on-line processing studies indicates that people activate many of the different senses of a polysemous word even when these meanings are contextually inappropriate (Williams, 1992). Similar findings have also been obtained for the processing of such ambiguous words as *bank* and *port* (Seidenberg, Tannenhaus, Leiman, & Bienkowski, 1982; Swinney, 1979). But processing polysemous words, unlike ambiguous words, results in the continued activation of inappropriate senses for quite some time after the word has been encountered (Williams, 1992). Most generally, understanding polysemy results in the activation of a large network of senses, a finding that supports the idea that the meanings of polysemous words are highly interconnected.

The interrelatedness of different senses of polysemous words might best be handled by positing one or more central senses, with other senses being peripheral (see Colombo & Flores d'Arcais, 1984, for evidence on the structuring of Dutch prepositions around central senses). Consider the word *dropped* in the following list of sentences (Ross, 1981).

> She dropped a stitch.
> She dropped her hemline.
> She dropped her book.
> She dropped a friend.
> She dropped her courses.

Many of these uses of *dropped* seem literal, although each occurrence of the word is different in meaning. The variety of meanings for *dropped* may arise through analogy with extended senses being derived from one of a few primary meanings. Efforts to locate and differentiate primary, as opposed to derived, meanings have not, however, been successful. Consider the following pairs of sentences in which the two senses are obviously related (Nunberg, 1979).

> The window was broken. (= "window glass")
> The window was boarded up. (= "window opening")
>
> The newspaper weighs five pounds. (= "publication")
> The newspaper fired John. (= "publisher")
>
> We got the news by radio. (= "medium")
> The radio is broken. (= "radio set")
>
> The chair was broken. (= "chair token")
> The chair was common in nineteenth-century parlors. (= "chair type")
>
> France is a Republic. (= "nation")
> France has a varied typography. (= "region")
>
> The game is hard to learn. (= "rule")
> The game lasted an hour. (= "activity")

It is not clear that one sense of these polysemous words can be defined as primary and the others as secondary (ibid.). To take another example, consider the numerous things to which the word *cell* may refer (ibid.). There are cells of the body, battery cells, prison cells, communist cells, photocells, the cells of a matrix, and so on. Each of these uses may possibly be members of a single "fuzzy" or "vague" extension; for example, the uniform constitutive parts of a large structure. But people speak of single-cell organisms. Moreover, speakers use *cell* to refer to political organizations only when they are secret. Prisons and monasteries may have cells, but not libraries, dormitories, or cruise ships (divided into compartments). The problem of polysemy cannot be solved by simply distinguishing between a primary, or literal, and a derived meaning.

What are the principles that relate the meanings of polysemous words? One possibility is that there is an abstract sense for each polysemous word and that its extended senses can be derived through context (Bennet, 1975; Ruhl, 1989). This abstract sense or configuration of senses might best represent the literal meaning of a polysemous word. Consider the word *line* in the sentences *The shortest distance between two points is a straight line* and *They came to different conclusions using the same line of reasoning.* The *abstractionist view* of word meaning assumes that there is a single very general and abstract concept "line" that is neutral between the spatial meaning of *line* and the form-of-reasoning meaning of *line*. Both sentences contain special cases of the same abstract concept. Some experimental findings suggest that the many different uses of *line* all share the common semantic feature EXTENSION (Caramazza & Grober, 1976).

The abstractionist view is the most frequently advocated theory of polysemy in psychology and until recently was the usual view in linguistics. It suggests that the literal meaning of any word can be captured by a small set of abstract senses. Some theorists even argue that the abstract senses of words are *so* abstract as to be semantically unspecifiable (Ruhl, 1989). But such a view is *unfalsifiable*, in that no data can falsify the theory because one can always claim that an abstractionist account can be given for any polysemous word, even though one cannot actually state what that account really looks like.

Moreover, many polysemous words resist being defined under a general core sense. Consider the verb *climb* (Fillmore, 1982). One of its meanings is seen in *The boy climbed the tree,* where *climb* refers to a complex locomotion process of going from a lower to a higher spatial location by means of arduous manipulation of the limbs, a process that can be characterized in terms of the attributes ASCEND and CLAMBER. Now consider *The locomotive climbed the mountainside.* The ascent here proceeds through the turning of wheels, not the manipulation of limbs. Both uses of *climb* thus far refer to motion that is self-propelled.

In *The plane climbed to 30,000 feet,* the verb *climb* no longer retains any sense of clambering but refers to the powerful upward motion of the plane with respect to vertical dimension. Of course, not everything that ascends can be said to climb. Balls thrown in the air don't climb, nor does steam rising from a kettle. Other uses of *climb* show that ascent still appears to be a prominent feature, as in *The temperature climbed into the 90s* and *The stock market climbed 50 points today.* Although the earlier examples referred to the idea of ascending in the spatial sense, the use of *climb* in this latter pair of sentences is made possible through metaphorical extension.

ASCENT might be the common core feature of the different meanings of *climb* just considered. But not all uses of *climb* have to do with ascending: for example, *The boy climbed down the tree* and *We climbed along the wall.* Many activities that include the laborious use of one's limbs can be described as climbing (e.g., climb into a car, under a table, out of bed, out of or into clothing). All these examples illustrate that the different senses of *climb* cannot be unified on the basis of a common semantic denominator.

One view of polysemy advocated by many cognitive linguists is that the meanings of polysemous terms can be characterized by metaphor, metonymy, and cognitive models (G. Lakoff, 1987). Consider again the word *line* in the sentences *The shortest distance between any two points is a straight line* and *They came to different conclusions using the same line of reasoning.* According to the cognitive view, we understand *line* in *We came to different conclusions using the same line of reasoning* because of a preexisting conceptual metaphor in which we partly structure our understanding of thinking in terms of a different domain of experience (a physical journey). When we think about something, we start out at a certain point, travel along some path, occasionally encounter obstacles, and eventually arrive at some destination or conclusion. The path we travel has the spatial characteristics of a line. Given that the concept "line" is part of our understanding of journeys, the meaning of *line* can follow from the meaning it has in the concept "journey." There is no reason, then, to posit an independent definition for the concept "line" in the sentence *We came to different conclusions using the same line of reasoning.* Nor is it reasonable to suppose that a single abstract sense can capture all the different meanings of *line*. Instead, people have complex intuitions about the meanings of polysemous words that are not arbitrary but motivated by people's figurative understanding of various concepts. Under this view, the various meanings of a polysemous word can be related through meaning chains to form a radial category (ibid.). In a particular meaning chain, any two adjacent members may be related in meaning, whereas those not adjacent may well have very little in common.

A good example of a radial category for a polysemous word has been given for the preposition *over* (Brugman, 1981; Brugman & Lakoff, 1988). Consider some senses of the word *over*.

The plane is flying over the hill.
The painting is over the mantel.
The wall fell over.
Sam is walking over the hill.
Sam turned the page over.
Sam turned over.
Sam lives over the hill.
She spread the tablecloth over the table.
The guards were posted all over the hill.
The play is over.
Look over my corrections, and don't overlook any of them.
Do it over, but don't overdo it.
You've made over a hundred errors.

These different senses are not independent and arbitrarily determined but are motivated by a small number of relations that are principled, systematic, and recurrent throughout the lexicon. For example, the two sentences *Sam walked over the hill* and *Sam lives over the hill* exemplify a single relationship between two senses of *over*. The first sentence expresses the shape of a path relative to a reference location and collocates with a motion verb. The second sentence expresses a stative location that is understood to be the endpoint of a path of the same shape as that coded by the motion sense of the preposition. The systematicity of this relationship between the two senses justifies the hypothesis of a single principle relating path focus to end-of-path focus (Brugman & Lakoff, 1988). This same general principle explains the different senses of other prepositions that convey a path, such as *Harry walked through the doorway* and *The office is through a doorway* as well as *The truck sped past the post office* and *The truck is parked past the post office.*

It is not surprising to find that the same principle that relates path focus to end-of-path focus for spatial uses of prepositions can also apply to metaphorical uses. For example, the sentence *He's finally over the most difficult part of the job* exemplifies a metaphorical projection of the end-of-path schema to include two fundamental conceptual metaphors – CONTROL IS UP and LACK OF CONTROL IS DOWN – that map one domain of experience (control) in terms of a different domain (space). The person who has completed the most difficult part of a job is now in control of the task and can metaphorically be thought to be *over* it. Other metaphorical projections motivate other figurative uses of *over*. For instance, the MORE IS UP metaphorical mapping applies to the stative sense of *over* to yield a quantity sense of the word, as in *Our sales were over $20 million last year.*

There are many other senses of *over* in the spatial and metaphorical domains (see Brugman, 1981). The point here is that each of these senses is linked by metaphorical mappings to the sense adjacent to it. By a series of such linking relations, each of the 100 or so senses of *over* may be tied into a network or a radial structure. This lexical network is not a repository of random, idiosyncratic information structured only by principles characterizing lexical redundancies but is structured by general cognitive principles, some of which are figurative. The complexity of the lexical network for most polysemous words casts doubt on the simplistic possibility that every lexical item has a definite set of senses that constitutes its core, or literal, meaning.

Novel uses of words are another problem for theories of literal word meaning (Shannon, 1988). Consider the case of a newspaper agent asking someone *Is the delivery boy porching your newspaper now?* (H. Clark, 1983, 1991). The word *porching* is not in our mental lexicons, nor is it listed in the dictionary. Yet most listeners can create a meaning for this word on the spot. How do we figure out what a novel word like *porching* means? We probably consider relations that newspapers might have to porches, especially in terms of what delivery boys might do with newspapers and porches. In a similar way, when a speaker says *I'm tired of eating at the same old Chinese restaurant – do you want to pizza tonight?*, listeners use their world knowledge of the relations of pizza to eating in order to understand that the speaker is proposing that they eat pizza for dinner (Gerrig, 1986). As was the case for *porching*, there is no ready-made representation of *to pizza* in lexical memory. Mention of *the same old Chinese restaurant* certainly prompts access of our knowledge of restaurants and eating that facilitates our comprehension of *to pizza*. In another situation, we can use *Do you want to pizza tonight?* to refer to a desire to work on a jigsaw puzzle that pictures a pizza (ibid.). These examples also illustrate the difficulty of assuming that all words have well-specified literal meanings.

One model that doesn't assume that words have specific core meanings is the *competition model* (MacWhinney, 1987, 1989). This model, which is similar to various parallel distributed processing models (Rumelhart & McClelland, 1986), suggests that mental processing involves a continuous decision-making process in which many possible candidates (i.e., words or concepts) compete for each category decision within some *semantic ecological niche* (MacWhinney, 1989). For example, the word *on* has a cluster of meanings in the area of "on the table," another cluster in the area of "on call" and "on drugs," and yet another in the area of adverbial uses. It is clear that the extensions of meaning in the second and third areas are governed more by those areas or ecological niches than by any core meanings in the first area. By looking at words as competitors for semantic ecological niches, we come to see meaning as being shaped by the various contrasts in which it participates. To take another example, the meaning of *to pizza* in *Do you want to pizza?* is constrained not by what *to pizza* literally means but by the competition it faces with other words, such as *to eat pizza*, as a contrast having to do with what to have for dinner.

Furthermore, the meanings of words are not fixed by their places in preformed ecological niches, because many words also shape these niches and push other words around in them (MacWhinney, 1989). Prepositions seem to be particularly good at pushing their objects around. When the preposition *in* is combined with a noun that does not have a natural enclosure, that noun is forced into a polysemic reading that allows us to see it as an enclosure. For example, when we say *The soldier is in the field*, we conceptualize the field not as a flat surface but as an extension with certain perimeters within which the soldier is located. But when we say *The soldier parachuted onto the field*, we think of the field as a flat surface upon which the soldier has landed. We understand *The truck is in the road* as referring to a road not as a line connecting two points but as an expanse of asphalt. However, we understand *The truck was on the road to Cincinnati* as referring to the road as a line. Finally, if we say *The trout is under the water*, our focus is on the part of the water between us and the trout. When we say *The trout is in the water*, however, we focus on the entire body of water in which the trout is submerged.

These cases illustrate how prepositions push their arguments into particular polysemic pathways. In each case, the speaker's choice of one competing preposition over another signals that the option that did not win was somehow less appropriate. Because of this, we need to think about characterizing the meanings of these words not in terms of core or literal meanings but in terms of the contrasts or competitions in which they participate (MacWhinney, 1989).

Thinking and speaking literally

The attempts to define the literal meanings of a word in terms of its semantic features that constitute its core meaning or which are part of each sense of a word's meanings, corresponds to the classical belief about the nature and structure of concepts and categories. According to the classical view, a category is that set of instances sharing common properties identified by some similarity detection process (E. Smith & Medin, 1981). To count as a member of a category, a novel instance must possess all of the necessary properties or features that define that category. A property or feature is binary in that it is either involved in the definition of a category or it is not. Categories have clear boundaries. There are no ambiguous cases or entities that belong to a category "to some extent" or "to a certain degree." All instances of a category are equal in that no instances are better or more representative of a category than others.

What might we learn about literality in thought and language from the study of human categorization? Most philosophers, psychologists, and linguists traditionally conceive of literal meaning as mirroring the classical view of categorization. But the classical view of categories has come under attack, and alternative ideas about categorization have arisen in various areas of the cognitive sciences. These new views of categorization have significant implications for the search for literal aspects of language and thought. The starting point for the attack on the classical view comes from Wittgenstein (1953) in his well-known thesis that necessary and sufficient conditions are inadequate for defining the meanings of many words. His example of the concept "game" showed that there are few properties, if any, shared by all games. Instead, one game shares features with another game, and that second game might share features, though not necessarily the same ones, with a third, and so on. Together the different instances of game form a category that is structured as a *family resemblance* (similar to the idea of a radial category).

Later empirical work in cognitive psychology showed that a family resemblance principle offered a better account than did the classical model of how people identify an instance as belonging or not belonging to a category, or how typical an instance is of a category. For example, for Americans sparrows are closer to the prototypical bird than are penguins or ostriches, and this makes it easier for people to verify statements like *A sparrow is a bird* than *A penguin is a bird* (Rosch, 1975; Rosch & Mervis, 1975). Such findings are not simply due to some exemplars being more common than others, because even rare instances of a category may be closer to the prototype than more frequent examples. Thus, people rate rare items of furniture like love seats, davenports, and cedar chests as being better exemplars of the category "furniture" than are frequently encountered objects such as refrigerators (Rosch, 1975). These prototype effects observed for concrete objects have also been found with a variety of other kinds of domains, including action-based concepts (Pulman, 1983), artistic style (Hartly & Homa, 1981), chess (Goldin, 1978), emotion terms (Fehr, 1988; Fehr & Russell, 1984), medical diagnosis (Arkes & Harkness, 1980), and person perception (Cantor & Mischel, 1977). These effects are also observed in the study of linguistic phenomena in phonology, syntax, and semantics (Bates & MacWhinney, 1982; Bybee & Moder, 1983; Jaeger, 1980; G. Lakoff, 1987).

Another view of conceptual structure that differs from the classical view denies that there is a single summary representation for a category, as suggested by the prototype view. This view of categorization, called the exemplar view, proposes that categories are represented by means of individual examples (Medin & Schaffer, 1978; Medin & Smith, 1981; Oden, 1987; E. Smith & Medin, 1981). Some instance may be seen as a member of a category not because it is similar to some prototype but because it is similar to some other instance that is thought to be a member of a category. For example, you might classify one animal as a rodent because it reminds you of a rat (which you know is a rodent) but classify some other animal as a rodent because it seems similar to a rabbit (which you also know is a rodent). Furthermore, your knowledge that large birds, such as penguins and ostriches, are less likely to sing or fly may be derived from retrieving examples of small and large birds (Medin & Ross, 1992).

Might literal meaning for words and sentences best be accounted for in terms of prototypes or exemplars? Prototype and exemplar theories of concepts and categorization have been widely discussed and debated among experimental psychologists, linguists, and philosophers during the past 20 years. Although both theories are generally quite popular in cognitive science and could easily be applied to the search for a theory of literal meaning, various empirical data exist that are problematic for each view. Many experiments have contrasted the predictions of the prototype and exemplar models of categorization (Barsalou & Medin, 1986; Estes, 1986; Homa, 1984; Nosofsky, 1988, 1991). Exemplar models are somewhat better at predicting various kinds of human categorization behavior, particularly because many kinds of learning depend heavily on the use of examples (Medin & Ross, 1992). However, exemplar models are inadequate as theories of categories, because they do not explain how concepts are constructed in the first place. The only explanation for why a new example should be placed in a category is that it is similar to an old example. On the other hand, prototype theories assume that categories are organized around what is, on the average, true. But an average is not enough. For example, people know that small birds are more likely to sing than large birds. But prototypes do not capture this awareness of correlational information (Malt & Smith, 1983).

Prototype theories also assume that concepts are context-independent. Yet typicality judgments often vary as a function of context (Roth & Shoben, 1983). Tea is judged to be a more typical beverage than milk in the context of secretaries taking a break, but the opposite is true in the context of truck drivers taking a break. Birds that are typical from an American point of view, such as robins and eagles, are atypical from the point of view of an average Chinese citizen (Barsalou, in press). Furthermore, the typicality of combined concepts cannot be predicted from the typicality of their several constituents (Medin & Shoben, 1988). Consider the concept "spoon." People rate small spoons as being more typical than large spoons, and metal spoons as being more typical than wooden spoons. If we represent the concept "spoon" as a prototype, then a small metal spoon should be viewed as the most typical spoon, followed by a small wooden and large metal spoons, and large wooden spoons should be seen as the least typical. But people judge large wooden spoons to be more typical spoons than either small wooden spoons or large metal spoons. Such findings are contrary to both the prototype and exemplar views of categorization.

The prototype and exemplar models of concepts both rely on the same similarity principle. That is, category membership is determined by whether or not some candidate is sufficiently similar to the prototype or to a set of already represented examples, where similarity is based on matches and mismatches of independent, equally abstract features. Yet similarity does not explain many kinds of prototype effects. For example, goal-derived categories, such as "foods to eat while on a diet" and "things to take on a camping trip," reveal the same typicality effects as do other categories (Barsalou, 1983, 1985, 1989, 1991). But the basis for these effects is not similarity to some prototype but rather similarity to an ideal. For instance, typicality ratings for the category of things to eat while on a diet are determined by how clearly each example conforms to the ideal of zero calories. In a similar way, "jumping into a swimming pool with no clothes on" is not generally associated with the concept "intoxicated" (Murphy & Medin, 1985). But seeing someone jump into a pool fully clothed might lead one to classify the person as drunk. Thus, real-world knowledge is used to reason about or explain properties, not simply to match them to some prototype. Even though categories like "things to take on a camping trip" have prototypic structure, such a structure does not exist in advance, because the category is ad hoc and not conventional (Barsalou, 1991).

One important consequence of the idea that categories are not necessarily preexisting but arise from the results of various cognitive models is that categories must be viewed as dynamic and context-dependent. Much research points to the flexibility of concepts. One set of studies asked people to provide definitions for such categories as bachelor, bird, and chair (Barsalou, in press). An analysis of the overlap in the features participants provided for a given category revealed that only

47% of the features in one person's definition of a category existed in another individual's definition. A great deal of flexibility also exists in individuals when asked to provide definitions of concepts. When participants in the study above returned two weeks later and defined the same categories again, only 66% of the features noted in the first session were produced in the second session. These results indicated that substantial flexibility exists in how a person conceptualizes the same category on different occasions (ibid.).

The fact that categories appear to be flexible does not necessarily indicate differences in the underlying knowledge of a category that people store in long-term memory (ibid.). Different people appear to have highly similar knowledge of the same category, and this knowledge seems to remain highly stable over time for individuals. Evidence in support of this claim comes from the study above on category definition. All of the features produced for a given category, for example bird, were pooled and then shown to a new group of people. These new participants were asked to specify whether each property listed by the earlier subjects held for their respective categories. People's judgments of feature validity should have varied considerably if people had varying underlying knowledge of a category. Similarly, if a given individual's knowledge of a category changed over time, other people's assessment of feature validity should change as well. However, there was nearly perfect agreement, not only between raters but within raters as well, about which features were valid for a given category.

These findings demonstrate that different people store highly similar information for a category in long-term memory and that this information remains quite stable in individuals over time. The significant flexibility shown by many experiments on defining categories arises not from differences in knowledge but from differences in the retrieval of this knowledge from long-term memory (ibid). On different occasions, different individuals retrieve different subsets of features from their extensive knowledge of a category. In the same way, an individual may retrieve different aspects of his or her knowledge of a category on different occasions. This suggests a view of concepts as temporary constructions in working memory constructed on the spot from generic and episodic information in long-term memory rather than as stable structures stored in long-term memory. Because conceptual information in memory is so richly interconnected, all the information associated with a concept cannot be retrieved every time the concept is used, just as people access different meanings for a word in different contexts. Different information is retrieved under different task conditions, producing instability in observed category structure. Because temporary conceptualizations are doing the traditional work of concepts in controlling categorization behavior, it is important to refer to these as *concepts*, and to use *knowledge* for referring to the body of information in long-term memory for which concepts are constructed (Barsalou, in press).

One reason cognitive scientists mostly assume that both concepts and word meanings are preexisting mental structures is that they commit the "effects = structures" fallacy (G. Lakoff, 1987). This fallacy reflects a working hypothesis of many cognitive psychologists that the goodness-of-example ratings obtained in psychological experiments on human categorization are a direct reflection of degree of category membership. It assumes that categories are explicitly represented in the mind in terms of prototypes and that degree of category membership for examples is determined by degree of similarity to the prototype. But the "effects = structures" interpretation cannot account for many of the types of data reviewed above, especially the problems of complex categorization. In fact, many kinds of prototype effect can be explained by principles that do not assume that the effects obtained in experiments reflect the structure of preexisting knowledge.

For example, ordinary people, unlike mathematicians, do not distinguish between numbers and their names. We understand numbers in terms of our base-10 naming system where single-digit numbers are all generators and multiple-digit numbers are comprehended as sequences of single-digit numbers. The single-digit numbers therefore have a privileged place among all numbers. Double-digit numbers are less privileged; large numbers in general, less privileged still. A model for understanding all numbers in terms of single-digit numbers is a metonymic model whereby a part of something stands for the whole. Single-digit numbers should be viewed as better examples than double-digit numbers, which should be viewed as better examples than larger numbers, just as the data indicate (Armstrong, Gleitman, & Gleitman, 1983). Thus experiment participants judged the number 3 as being the best member of the "odd number" category; the numbers 447 and 91 received the lowest degree of membership. Even numbers showed the same effect, in that 2 and 4 were excellent members of the category, whereas 106 and 806 had the lowest membership. Even though all numbers are equal with respect to the category "number," it is clear that we often think about numbers in metonymic terms, so that certain numbers have privileged status. In this way, the prototype effects observed for numbers can be explained in terms of metonymic reasoning without our having to assume that our categorization of numbers in some task directly reflects the structure of our knowledge of numbers. There need not be any direct correlation between the empirical effects observed in categorization research and the structure of concepts in long-term memory.

The work on categorization and prototype effects in cognitive psychology casts some doubt on the possibility of finding well-specified or literal definitions of mental concepts. Most generally, our description of the contents of a concept or a word will vary according to culture, individual, context, and task. The haphazard nature of conceptual content poses a significant problem for traditional theories that assume that concepts and words can be precisely, or literally, defined as stable structures in long-term memory.

In recent years there has been a profound shift in the cognitive sciences away from traditional theories of concepts and meaning that assume well-defined sets of concepts and categories. Just as some philosophers of science argue that our observations of the world are necessarily theory-based, so too do cognitive scientists now suggest that the organization of concepts is knowledge-based and driven by theories about the world (Carey, 1985; Gelman, 1988; Keil, 1986, 1989; G. Lakoff, 1987; Markman, 1989; Medin, 1989; Murphy & Medin, 1985;

Oden, 1987; Rips, 1989). These new ideas about concepts and categories have significant implications for how we view the literal content of concepts and word meanings.

Theory-based approaches to categorization assert that classification is not simply based on a direct matching of properties of the concept with those in the example but requires that the example have the right "explanatory relationship" to the theory organizing the concept (Murphy & Medin, 1985). To illustrate this idea, consider the category members children, money, photo albums, and pets. Without context the category seems odd, but it makes good sense in the context of the category "things to take out of a house in case of a fire." To take another example, people view white hair and gray hair as being more similar than gray hair and black hair, but the terms *white clouds* and *gray clouds* were judged as being less similar than *gray clouds* and *black clouds* (Medin & Shoben, 1988). The reason for this judgment is that white and gray hair are grouped by a theory (i.e., about aging), whereas white and gray clouds are not theoretically linked.

Cognitive linguistic studies also demonstrate how theories are used in human categorization. For example, the Japanese classifer *hon* is used to classify not only long, thin objects, such as sticks, pencils, candles, trees, and hair, but also martial arts contests, baseball hits, rolls of tape, telephone calls, radio and TV programs, and injections (G. Lakoff, 1987). These diverse objects and events do not all have something in common with long, thin objects. But Japanese-speakers make sense of these different things via various cognitive theories and principles. For instance, martial arts contestants use staffs and swords, which are long and thin. Baseball hits are instances of *hon* because when a baseball is hit solidly it travels in a long, thin path (pop flies and foul balls are not considered *hon*). Injections are another case where the principal functional object (the needle) is long and thin. Because needles can be classified with *hon*, so too, by metonymy, can the injections. *Hon* can also be used to classify telephone calls, since telephone wires fit the "long, thin object" schema. Telephone calls also fit the CONDUIT metaphor, the principal metaphor for communication. Radio and TV programs are forms of communication at a distance, and they too are motivated by the

CONDUIT metaphor. Thus, sticks and TV programs are both in the *hon* category even though they do not have relevant common properties. *Hon* is a wonderful example of a radial category that is partly organized by people's theories about the relationships between objects and events. It is virtually impossible to specify a set of abstract features that is common to all uses of the Japanese classifier *hon*.

Many researchers now argue that even though the things called by a category name may not have any common properties, people may believe in the existence of such properties (Keil, 1989; Malt, 1990; McNamara & Sternberg, 1983; Medin, 1989; Medin & Ortony, 1989). One theory, called *psychological essentialism*, suggests that representations of concepts do encode essences but that these essences lie in rather deep theories, not in surface characteristics (Medin & Ortony, 1989). These theories putatively generate a more superficial set of features (e.g., visual and semantic features) that can be used for identification of instances of a category. However, these features do not provide the defining characteristics for any concept. For example, people in our culture believe that the categories "male" and "female" are genetically determined, but we pick someone out as being male or female based on such characteristics as hair length, body shape, height, and clothing. Even though these characteristics are more unreliable than the genetic evidence, they are far from arbitrary (Medin, 1989).

Psychologists suggest that people adopt an *essentialist heuristic* in their everyday behavior and assume that things that look alike tend to share deeper essences. In the same way, people's intuitive beliefs that some word or linguistic expression has a particular literal meaning correspond to their intuitions that some categories have true underlying essences (even though they don't). That is, people's theories about words and their meanings may somehow motivate the common intuition that words have literal meanings in the same way that people's intuitions that concepts have true essences motivates their use and understanding of many concepts.

One way of explaining people's intuitions of literal meanings for words is to think of such meanings as reflecting different kinds of knowledge or theories called *idealized cognitive models*, or ICMs (G. Lakoff, 1987). An ICM is a prototypical "folk" theory or cultural model that people create to organize their knowledge. ICMs make some sense, given that ICMs are idealized and don't fit actual situations in a one-to-one correspondence but relate many concepts that are inferentially connected to one another in a single conceptual structure that is experientially meaningful as a whole. For example, the concept "bachelor" and the corresponding linguistic label *bachelor* are defined in respect to an ICM in which there is a human society with typically monogamous marriages and a typically marriageable age. This idealized model does not fit the world very precisely, because it oversimplifies various background assumptions. Some segments of society represent the ICM for "bachelor" rather well. But this ICM does not fit the case of the pope or people abandoned in the jungle like Tarzan (G. Lakoff, 1987). So our assumption that words like *bachelor* have literal meanings reflects the ICMs we have for the corresponding concept.

In a similar way, the concept "a lie" and the corresponding lexical item *lie* are defined in respect of two ICMs (Sweetser, 1987). The ICM of *ordinary knowledge* supposes that people have adequate reasons for their beliefs, that adequately justified beliefs are true, and therefore that something that is false is not believed. This ICM reflects the idea that for most people what is meant by "knowledge" is that we have adequate reason to believe that something is true. The second ICM, the ICM of *ordinary conversation*, assumes that in ordinary conversation truthful information is helpful, that the speaker has information that the listener wants or needs, that the speaker intends to help the listener by sharing that information, and that the speaker who intentionally shares false information intends to harm the listener. Although people generally define a *lie* as a false statement, research shows that factual falsity is the least important of three criteria used to identify statements as lies (Coleman & Kay, 1981). Falsity of belief is the most important element in the prototype of "lie," intended deception the next most important element, and factual falsity the least important.

These ICMs of ordinary beliefs and ordinary conversation help yield the conventional definition of *lie* that focuses on factual falsity despite the fact that it is the least important criterion. In the ICM of ordinary knowledge, factual falsity entails falsity of belief. Given the ICM of ordinary conversation, falsity of belief in turn entails intent to deceive. Thus, the conventional definition of a *lie* is a metonymic device for the more complicated ICMs that actually make up the concept of "lie." Conventional definitions are cognitively easier to remember and store than are the more complicated ICMs used to construct the category for any concept to which a word refers.

Analyzing word meanings in terms of idealized cognitive models provides for a more accurate description of our intuitions about the literal meanings of words than is provided by other approaches to linguistic meaning. One way of looking at what lexicographers do in writing dictionary definitions is to describe rough theories or cognitive models for the various meanings of words. Even though some philosophers optimistically suggest that dictionaries are particularly good at providing accurate, informative definitions of words (Putnam, 1975; Quine, 1960), there is some evidence that children (Deese, 1965; G. Miller & Gildea, 1987) and adults (Jorgensen, 1990) do not find dictionary definitions particularly informative. Dictionaries capture only rough aspects of people's theories about what words mean. Given that we understand words in terms of often complex cognitive theories or models (e.g., ICMs), it is unlikely that anyone, even professional lexicographers, will be able conclusively and unambiguously to say that a concept has a putative literal content or that a word has a specific literal meaning. People's intuition that words have literal meanings is not defined by an abstract set of features common to each use of a word (a principle of similarity) but represents a form of psychological essentialism where people act *as if* words have well-defined essences.

ARRIVING AT THE LITERAL MEANINGS OF SENTENCES AND TEXTS

The search for literal aspects of language and thought considers not only the relations between individual words and concepts but also the relations between sentences/texts and propositions. This section describes the notable attempts to specify the literal meanings of sentences and texts. Once again, the journey toward an objectivist description of what sentences and texts mean will lead us to a cognitive view where sentences and texts are seen as reflecting different aspects of people's cognitive models.

THE TRADITIONAL VIEW

The traditional view about the literal meanings of sentences stems from Frege's (1892/1952) principle of compositionality. Frege's position was that a large number of sentences in a natural language can be understood by a competent speaker/ hearer without knowing who said the sentence, where it was said, or when or why. In other words, the interpretation of many sentences is independent of knowledge of extralinguistic context.

This position on the semantics of natural language led to a number of widely held assumptions about the nature of literal meaning (Gibbs, 1982, 1984, 1989). First, all sentences have literal meanings that are entirely determined by the meanings of their component words (or morphemes) and the syntactical rules according to which these elements are combined. Certain sentences may have more than one literal meaning, for example, ambiguous sentences. Moreover, the literal meaning of a sentence may be defective or ill specified, as with nonsense sentences. In addition, the literal meaning of a sentence should be sharply distinguished from what the speaker means by use of the sentence, since the speaker's utterance may depart from the literal sentence in a variety of ways, as in metaphor, irony, indirect speech acts, and other figures (Searle, 1980). Finally, and significantly, the literal meaning of a sentence is its meaning independent of context.

Many semantic theorists working in the framework of generative grammar embrace this idea of literal meaning (J. Katz & Fodor, 1963). Accordingly, semantic competence is what an ideal speaker/hearer would know about the meaning of a sentence without any information about its context, as in the anonymous-letter situation (J. Katz, 1972). In the anonymous-letter situation, an ideal speaker/hearer of a language receives an anonymous letter containing just one sentence of that language, with no clue about the motive, circumstance of delivery, or any other information relevant to its understanding in normal discourse. Imagine walking into your office and finding an envelope on your desk. Inside the envelope is a single piece of paper with the sentence *Whales eat plankton.* Many semanticists claim that a theory of semantic competence should capture the linguistic knowledge used in understanding this sentence where no other information is available concerning its intended meaning (J. Katz & Fodor, 1963). The goal here is to distinguish between semantic and pragmatic interpretation by taking the semantic component to represent only those aspects of the meaning of a sentence that an ideal speaker/hearer of the language would know in such a "context-free" situation. Assuming this goal allows scholars to differentiate between *literal* or *sentence* meaning and *contextual*, implied, or *speaker* meaning, where the former represents a semantic interpretation and the latter a pragmatic interpretation.

The traditional view of literal meaning also assumes that there is an intimate connection, and sometimes a strict equivalence, between literal meaning and truth. This connection between literal meaning and truth has its roots in the writings of Aristotle and the early Stoics and more recently in the 20th-century work of the logical positivists. Literal meaning is identified with "propositional meaning," and "propositional meaning" with "truth conditional meaning" (Ayer, 1936). Under this view, the literal meaning of a sentence is the set of conditions that are both necessary and sufficient to establish the truth of that sentence (cf. Carnap, 1956; Davidson, 1979; Lewis, 1972). In this manner, literal meaning can be distinguished from other meanings, which might be labeled "metaphoric," "emotive," or "poetic," that cannot be explicated in terms of truth conditions. For instance, to know the literal meaning of the string of words making up the sentence *Snow is white* is to know what conditions must hold for *Snow is white* to be true (i.e., *Snow is white* is true if and only if snow is white). To take another example, *John killed Bill* is true if and only if John caused Bill to die. The suggestion that literal meaning can be explained in terms of truth conditions is really at attempt to base a theory of meaning on some "operational" concept that is understandable and open to rigorous empirical examination.

The attempt to link literal meaning with truth is often extended to suggest that an intimate connection exists between literal meaning and notions of exactness and explicitness. Many philosophers and linguists specifically assume an idealized view of linguistic communication whereby anything that can be meant can also be stated in colloquial language (Hjelmslev, 1953; Tarski, 1956). One explicit proposal, the *principle of expressibility* (Searle, 1969: 20), states that "for any meaning X and any speaker S whenever S means (intends to convey, wishes to communicate in an utterance, etc.) X, then it is possible that there is some expression E such that E is an exact expression of or formulation of X." The principle of expressibility claims (a) that what can be meant can be expressed in some way, that a "meaning" is the sort of thing that is capable of expression, (b) that what can be meant can be said or can be expressed in language as opposed to other forms of expression, and (c) that what can be meant can be said exactly.

The principle of expressibility defines the meaning of any utterance as being reducible to a single unequivocal speech act. In other words, any utterance is a more or less monological instantiation of one and only one exact expression. Even when an utterance communicates several types of things at once, it is still possible analytically to isolate the literal meaning of an utterance from the communicative effects that an utterance may produce in discourse (ibid.). One significant consequence of this principle is that "cases where a speaker does not say exactly what he means – the principal cases of which are nonliteralness, vagueness, ambiguity, and incompleteness – are not theoretically essential to linguistic communication" (Searle, 1969: 20).

How does exactness of expression relate to the idea of literalness? Speech act theory proposes that literal speech acts occur when a speaker's utterance meaning and sentence meaning do not "come apart" (Searle, 1975). Literal speech acts are performed whenever sentences having literal meanings are employed by a speaker without any intent of communicating anything other than the sentential literal meaning. To say something exactly or explicitly is to speak literally! Such literal speech acts represent the "simplest cases of meaning" (Searle, 1975: 60).

The suggestion that literal meaning is equivalent to speaking exactly or explicitly really constitutes two different claims about literal meaning (Powell, 1985). First, literal expressions are sentences that contain explicit performative verbs. Under this view, explicit expressions are those with illocutionary force indicators in a sentence that show how a proposition is to be taken. Thus, the sentence *I request that you tell me what time it is* contains the performative verb *request* that explicitly marks this expression as having the illocutionary force of a directive. Speakers may perform any kind of literal act by including explicit performative markers in their utterances.

Second, literal sentences are those that have a direct correspondence between grammatical mood and illocutionary force. Declarative sentences have the semantic function of assertions, interrogative sentences function as questions, and imperatives function as commands. Grammarians have traditionally associated these major syntactic types with these characteristic semantic functions. Each of these syntactic–semantic pairings expresses a literal meaning.

These two kinds of literal expression can be straightforwardly tied to truth conditional meaning, and Searle (1979: 113) explicitly notes this connection in his discussion of metaphor when he asks *What exactly are the principles according to which the utterance of an expression can metaphorically call to mind a different set of truth conditions from the ones determined by literal meaning?*

CRITICISMS OF THE TRADITIONAL VIEW

One reason why a truth conditional account of literal meaning fails is that it is difficult to imagine well-established conditions of truth for nonindicative sentences, such as questions and commands, and for sentences that are used as performatives, such as *I now pronounce you husband and wife* or *I promise to meet you at noon for lunch*. Performative utterances like these do not normally describe anything to which truth conditional meaning can be applied but constitute actions in and of themselves (Austin, 1962). For instance, *I now pronounce you husband and wife* constitutes the act of pronouncing, and *I apologize for kicking you in the shin* constitutes the act of apology. Performative utterances like these resist truth-based analyses of their meaning. We may recognize that a particular performative utterance is stated infelicitously, but this awareness is different from being able to specify a set of conditions under which a sentence is true or false.

Scholars often presume that a theory of literal meaning should provide the foundation for theories of language interpretation, in that people should ordinarily analyze sentences according to their literal meanings as a first step toward understanding what speakers/authors intend by their utterances. Recognition of a sentence's truth conditional meaning should therefore be an immediate and obligatory part of understanding what utterances mean in discourse. But to specify a set of truth conditions for a sentence presupposes that *some* interpretation has *already* been given to that sentence. In other words, one must have some understanding of what sentences like *Snow is white* or *All men are mortal* mean in order to determine the conditions under which they may be true or false. Analysis of a sentence's literal truth conditional meaning cannot be a primary aspect of linguistic comprehension if literal meaning is influenced by other, potentially contextual, factors that operate during immediate sentence interpretation. Although defining what a sentence means in terms of truth conditions may have some appeal to philosophers, logicians, and linguists interested in studying linguistic meaning as an abstract, platonic concept, truth conditional views of literal meaning have little use in psychological views of ordinary language comprehension. This conclusion seems particularly apt, since truth conditional analyses of meaning never consider expressions that are literally defective or utterances that reflect "poetic," "emotive," or "metaphorical" meaning. Yet we clearly wish to be able to specify something about how literal meaning may or may not function in people's understanding of these non–truth conditional aspects of language.

Thinking and speaking literally

The attempt to link literal meaning with the concepts of exactness and explicitness is also quite problematic. Defining exactness of expression, measure, calculation, direction, and so forth can only be done relative to some purpose or goal (Wittgenstein, 1953). For instance, to say that it is *almost ten* is a rather imprecise formulation of the time when talking about the standards set by atomic clocks but works quite well in response to a request for the time issued by a passerby. Even if one first looked at a digital watch, responding that it is *almost ten* seems far more intelligible and contextually appropriate than is the response that it is *nine fifty-eight and thirty-two seconds* (Bogen, 1991). Anyone answering a request for the time with such detailed information might be seen as having a peculiar "exact time" fetish. This single instance is enough to bring into question the idea that literal meaning is somehow intimately tied to some other well-understood notion, such as "exactness." How anyone speaks "exactly" or "explicitly" depends on social context and the speaker's particular communicative goals.

A related problem for speech act accounts of literal meaning arises from the idea that when a speaker does some speech activity, he or she means the literal and exact sentential paraphrase of that activity. According to this idea, when speakers explicitly utter the performative verbs *promise, request, assert,* and so on, they are literally promising, requesting, asserting, and so forth. But speakers rarely include such performative verbs in their utterances to mark their illocutionary intent. Only under special circumstances do people use such "literal" and "exact" expressions. For instance, I might say to my girlfriend *I promise to take you to the ballet next weekend* only if I had said earlier that we would go to the ballet and had not actually done so. In this way, performative verbs function as emphatic assurances rather than to mark expressions as "literal" and "exact." One might even say *I promise* or *I request such-and-such* without necessarily meaning the same thing each time these performative verbs are used. For example, listeners often understand speakers' utterances with *I promise* not to refer literally and exactly to an obligation to do some future action (Gibbs & Delaney, 1987). Most generally there is no one-to-one correspondence between particular lexical items, such as performative verbs, and the illocutionary activities utterances accomplish. Ordinary discourse clearly illustrates the implausibility of maintaining a context-free standard for literal meaning as "exact" or "explicit" expression.

Perhaps the best way to argue against the traditional view of literal meaning is to examine "favorable" cases for the view that literal meaning is context-free and show that literal meaning can only be determined relative to a set of background assumptions (Searle, 1980). Consider the sentence *The cat is on the mat*. Determining the literal meaning of this sentence is difficult unless some further assumptions are made, namely that the cat and mat are not floating free in outer space and that gravitational forces exist. It is only through these kinds of background assumptions that the literal meaning of the sentence can be precisely determined. However, these assumptions are not specifiable as part of the semantic analysis of the sentence, nor are these assumptions fixed in number and content. It appears impossible to know when to stop the process of specifying which assumptions need hold for determining literal meaning. Each assumption tends to imply other assumptions, which themselves must be specified in some way. For these reasons, it is unlikely that the background assumptions needed to specify the literal meanings of even simple sentences, such as *The cat is on the mat*, can be included as part of the semantics of the sentence (Searle, 1980, 1983). Moreover, a single word may have the same semantic content in different sentences but make a distinct contribution to their respective truth conditions. Consider the sentences *Bill cut the grass* and *Sally cut the cake*. The activity of cutting grass is quite different from the activity of cutting cake. These examples suggest that one cannot hold both that the literal meaning of a sentence is the meaning it has in a null context and that the meaning of a sentence determines the truth conditions of that sentence (Searle, 1980).

Viewing literal meaning relative to a set of background assumptions does not necessarily invalidate the distinction between the literal sentence meaning and the speaker's utterance meaning (ibid.). Listeners still presumably process sentences according to their literal meanings before contextual information is used to figure out what speakers intend. Nevertheless, the special role that context plays in utterance interpretation needs to be distinguished from the background knowledge that plays a role in the analysis of literal meaning. Background assumptions are very general shared knowledge, which would be absurd to miss, whereas context includes those assumptions that are involved in interpreting nonliteral or indirect utterances, such as irony, metaphor, and indirect speech acts. Unlike context, background is not part of meaning, since it is nonrepresentational and preintentional (Searle, 1983). But background still plays a crucial role in our understanding of linguistic expressions, since it provides the foundation for determining what sentences literally mean.

The notion of context-based literal meaning represents a compromise between a commitment to formal truth conditional semantics and a proper recognition of the situatedness and inherent perspectivity of human cognition (Rommetveit, 1988). The alleged distinction between background and context is, however, problematic, because there are good reasons to believe that there is not a clear demarcation between intentional mental states and preintentional mental and bodily capacities (M. Johnson, 1987). Even if such a distinction could, in principle, be made, there is still the problem of determining *when* background and context operate during linguistic processing. Simply put, the idea that background knowledge is deeply presupposed and quite unconscious does not entail that such knowledge must be evaluated *before* other knowledge in the foreground (i.e., contextual information) is accessed and evaluated. To assume, though, that literal meaning can be determined only relative to a set of background assumptions leads to the clear prediction that people must go through an extra stage of analysis in comprehending indirect and nonliteral speech. Nevertheless, this hypothesis is not supported by the experimental data. I discuss this conclusion in Chapter 3.

THE TRADITIONAL VIEW REVISITED

The idea that literal meaning is somehow determined only via nonrepresentational and preconceptual background knowledge assumptions is clearly disturbing to scholars who embrace the traditional view of literal meaning as either truth conditional or context-free. Defenders of the traditional view contend that many of the criticisms directed at their position conflate a theory of sentence meaning and a theory of sentence use. There should be, so these scholars argue, at least two distinct theories of linguistic meaning, one dealing with the grammatically determined literal meanings of sentence types and the other dealing with the extragrammatical information speakers use, in combination with their knowledge of the meanings of sentence types, to perform speech acts (J. Katz, 1977, 1981). This view sharply distinguishes between linguistic competence (i.e., meaning) and performance (i.e., use) to purify the study of language of all performance elements.

Advocates of the traditional view of literal meaning challenge the supposition that such sentences as *The cat is on the mat* undermine the thesis that sentences have compositional meaning independent of context (J. Katz, 1981). They argue that the compositional meaning of a sentence need not specify whether an utterance of that sentence is literally true or false. Certain selectional restriction rules specify whether a sentence like *The cat is on the mat* has a literal compositional meaning that can be determined apart from context. Moreover, the semantic content of *cut* (namely, the concept of dividing something) in *Bill cut the grass* and *Sally cut the cake* is identical insofar as what the sentences mean (ibid.). Each instance of *cut* differs in terms of what speakers mean by their literal utterance of sentences including *cut*. The belief in absolutely context-free sentence meaning does not deny that background assumptions shape the meanings of sentence uses in actual speech. But it makes little sense to suppose that such background assumptions are relevant to the meanings of sentences in the language.

Other defenders of the traditional view argue that literal meaning should not determine truth conditions in all contexts (M. Dascal, 1987). Searle incorrectly assumes that the literal uses of a sentence's literal meaning should completely capture the intended meaning of any utterance. But the total significance of an utterance depends on many factors, one of which is the literal meaning of the sentence used. If literal meaning is only one factor in the determination of a speaker's meaning, then there is no need to specify literal meaning in terms of nonrepresentational background assumptions (ibid.).

Some of the difficulty scholars face in distinguishing literal from figurative meanings has led to alternative proposals on literal meaning as something other than compositional meaning. One suggestion, called *moderate literalism*, abandons the attempt to offer a set of necessary and sufficient conditions in order for something to be a literal meaning (ibid.). In its place, several conditions and criteria are semantically relevant to literal meaning, with no single condition or criterion being strictly necessary or sufficient to define the literal meaning of a sentence. Even though compositionality is not sufficient to give a complete determination of literal meaning, it is still one source of information used in constructing the literal meanings of sentences. This less formal description of literal meaning should allow one to include as part of the literal meanings of sentences such aspects of meaning as emotive meanings, context invariance meanings, and criteria of noncancelability (in Grice's sense) and invariance (ibid.). Each of these aspects of meaning converges with compositionality to produce the literal meaning of a sentence. In this way, literal meaning can be determined apart from background knowledge and still play an obligatory role in the process of leading listeners to identify the contextually appropriate meanings of utterances (ibid.).

Although there may not be a set of necessary and sufficient conditions for specifying the literal meaning of a sentence, there should be some defined set of heuristics that is employed in determining the literal meaning of any utterance (Gibbs, 1989). This is especially true if people normally analyze the literal meanings of sentences as part of their comprehension of speakers' utterances. But what sources and criteria are capable of generating literal meanings for sentences in such a way that listeners can use such information in ordinary language understanding? The set of heuristics used for determining literal meaning should operate in such a manner that literal meaning can be automatically computed in real time (i.e., within a few hundred milliseconds).

However, it is not at all clear that any particular set of heuristics can actually specify unique literal meanings for each potential utterance in the language, given the constraints of on-line linguistic information processing (ibid.). If the determination of literal meaning is a *necessary* part of understanding language, then there must be some way of differentiating the criteria used in specifying literal meaning from those criteria, including literal meaning itself, that apply when understanding speaker meaning. But what are these differences? What sources of information are used in constructing the literal meaning of an utterance that are different from those used in comprehension of speaker meaning?

One possible way of determining the literal meaning that is used in recognition of speaker meaning versus that used in specifying the literal meaning of a sentence is to maintain the distinction between background and context (Searle, 1978, 1980). For instance, background knowledge plays a crucial role in our understanding but is not part of meaning, because it is nonrepresentational and preintentional (Searle, 1983). Nevertheless, as pointed out above, this distinction is problematic, because there may be no distinct demarcation between intentional mental states and preintentional mental and bodily capacities (M. Johnson, 1987).

The problem here is that the aspects of meaning and criteria, supposedly used in determining literal meaning, do not converge in any natural way. It appears that some of the sources of information contributing to literal meaning are themselves *products* of interpretive acts. If a listener uses different information as part of the criteria for determining a sentence's literal meaning, which itself requires an interpretive act, why can't that same information be used in the actual interpretation of the speaker's utterance? Part of the reason why some sentences seem so literal is that listeners are influenced by the interpretive context in which such judgments are made. People will judge a sentence as having literal meaning because it is isomorphic with the situation in which the sentence is interpreted (Fish, 1980). Even the determination of conventional meaning is context-driven (cf.

Gibbs, 1981a, 1986a). Speakers might agree that the conventional meaning of the indirect speech act *Can you pass the salt?* is "Pass the salt." But his meaning presupposes a typical context of use where salt is being requested and not where one's ability to pass the salt is questioned. The conventional interpretation of an utterance presupposes some context of use perhaps so widely shared that we think that context has no role in determining that meaning. Literal meaning cannot be *uniquely* determined, since our understanding of situations will always influence our understanding of sentences. To speak of a sentence's literal meaning is already to have read it in light of some purpose, to have engaged in an interpretation. What often appears to be the literal meaning of a sentence is just an occasion-specific meaning where the context is so widely shared that there doesn't seem to be a context at all.

LITERAL MEANING AND TEXTUAL MEANING

Interpreting what texts mean is a great intellectual challenge whether one is a biblical scholar who seeks to understand the truth in the scriptures or a Supreme Court justice who seeks guidance from the Constitution in adjudicating legal disputes. Written texts of all sorts provide a heritage for our cultural and social beliefs. We tend to view written texts as "containing" meaning for us to discover. This idea of autonomous text meaning is widely recognized as an important product of literacy (Ong, 1982), and our belief in the concept of literal meaning is closely tied to our understanding of the development of writing and the impact of literacy on oral language (Rommetveit, 1988). The historical roots of belief in the autonomy of written texts are seen in the work of Martin Luther, who argued for placing meaning in the text of scripture while rejecting the traditional interpretations of the Church. Before Luther, it was assumed that meaning could not be stated explicitly but required interpretation by central authorities. After Luther, there began a new trend toward an increasingly clear, logical, and above all self-explanatory style of writing. The 17th-century British essayists, such as Locke and Bacon, embraced the idea that a pure expository style allowed a sentence to have only one interpretation. Armed with an explicit lexicon and a set of rules governing the use of logical argument, skillful writers could presumably produce unambiguous literal meaning.

Today many theorists argue that understanding written language differs from comprehension of verbal speech because written language tends to be more "decontextualized," with far fewer cues being available to authors' possible communicative intentions (Olson, 1977). Oral language conveys meaning that is largely drawn from extralinguistic sources found in the surrounding context, whereas written language conveys meaning through the linguistic units that make up any text. Listeners must rely on shared prior knowledge to understand spoken discourse, but readers rely on logical reasoning to understand the meanings of texts. This logic applied in well-written texts reduces the need for shared prior knowledge. Textual meaning is thought not to depend on recovery of anything about an author's intentions, because there is no common ground between the author and reader. The conventions that exist in written language make a conversational context superfluous. As a consequence, written texts more precisely convey meaning than do spoken words. Well-written texts are unambiguous, autonomous representations of meaning and better communicate ideas than do spoken, implicit utterances. In recent years, many scholars have argued that there exists a strong causal link between literacy and modernity such that the ability to see word meanings as autonomous and objective gives rise to systematic conceptual distinctions between something that is taken as given, fixed, autonomous, and objective and something that is taken as interpretive, inferential, and subjective.

However, the observation that texts are not surrounded by a conversational context does not inevitably lead to the conclusion that texts are impervious to all contextual factors (Snyder, 1990). Both oral and written forms of communication can vary in their degree of contextualization. Certain kinds of oral language, such as formal speeches, assume little common ground between speakers and addressees. Many forms of written discourse, such as private letters, presume a rich common ground between author and reader. Scholars who make such arguments about the lack of author–reader inter-action misunderstand the extent to which readers of literary texts presuppose information about what authors are trying to do or communicate. Readers may assume a great deal about what even anonymous authors know and what these authors may assume about them as readers. These assumptions range from recognition of the mutual belief that author and reader are reasonably competent speakers of the same language, up to very specific mutual assumptions about particular linguis-tic and conceptual knowledge from which readers can draw inferences about what is meant. Literary critics and ordinary readers of texts are not often aware of the many mutual as-sumptions that hold for authors and readers, assumptions that clearly constrain how the meanings of texts are defined.

The context for understanding texts does differ from the physical social context used in the interpretation of oral lan-guage, because understanding texts involves a shared epis-temological context (Willinsky, 1987). Even so, the suggestion that intentionality is extraneous to textual meaning divorces both readers and writers from what then remains an inert, self-contained artifact. Such a division implies that textual meaning can somehow be created outside human experience. Texts are not static containers of meaning but provide the common ground for writer and reader from which meaning may arise. Reading requires constant reference to prior knowledge from speech-based culture, not just the applica-tion of logical rules. For example, when reading legal texts (e.g., interpreting the First Amendment to the Constitution, protecting the right to free speech), meaning is constructed through consideration of the culture of law and the interpre-tation of human intentions that are brought to bear in the oral forum of the courtroom. This mix of cultural knowledge and speech-based understanding clearly contradicts the belief that any sentence has some sort of autonomous meaning in writ-ten language. It simply is not clear how intentionality and culturally derived knowledge can be suspended during text interpretation. Under this alternative view, texts are not re-positories of unambiguous knowledge in which each sentence has clear literal meaning. Instead, texts provide enduring opportunities for readers to construct meaning within a nonspatial epistomological context of shared knowledge and conventions (Snyder, 1990; Willinsky, 1987). Each reading of a text may lead to a multiplicity of meanings rather than a singularity.

To say that a text has a particular meaning requires that a critic employ various cognitive and linguistic processes to construct that interpretation, in the same way that ordinary readers construct interpretations for utterances in discourse. There is recent experimental evidence demonstrating that people understand written language not through the mere application of logical and linguistic rules but via certain presuppositions about texts' being composed by intentional agents (i.e., people). The mere fact that language is produced by human beings, who are assumed to have communicative intentions, affects the meanings ascribed to texts. In one set of studies, participants were presented with various comparison statements and were told that these were written either by famous 20th-century poets or randomly constructed by a computer program lacking intentional agency (Gibbs, Kushner, & Mills, 1991). The participants' task in one study was to rate the "meaningfulness" of the different comparisons and in another study simply to read and push a button when they had comprehended these statements. Readers found metaphorical expressions, such as *Cigarettes are time bombs*, more meaningful when these statements were supposedly written by famous 20th-century poets, who are intentional agents, than when these same metaphors were seen as random constructions of a computer program. People also took much less time to comprehend these comparisons when they were told the statements were written by the poets. Moreover, they took longer to reject anomalous utterances as "meaningless" when these were supposedly written by the poets. Readers assume that poets have specific communicative intentions in designing their utterances, an assumption that does not hold for unintelligent computer programs. Consequently, people make a good deal more effort to try to understand anomalous phrases, such as *A scalpel is like a horseshoe*, when they are supposedly written by poets. They more quickly rejected as "meaningless" these same anomalous expressions when told that they were written by an unintelligent computer program, because computers are assumed to lack communicative intentions. These data testify to the powerful role of authorial intentions in people's understanding of isolated written expressions. Readers are often unaware of the influence of such pragmatic information when they interpret written texts and incorrectly believe that they can recover the putative unambiguous literal meanings in texts.

LITERAL MEANING AND FIGURATIVE LANGUAGE

People cannot reach a stable, unambiguous literal meaning for texts devoid of context and shared knowledge between authors and readers. Why then is it still desirable to maintain some concept of literal meaning? One reason to search for a stable concept of literal meaning is to distinguish it from various types of nonliteral or figurative meaning. Researchers often claim that figurative meaning differs in significant ways from literal meaning. Much of the research in this book examines notable attempts to distinguish literal and figurative meanings. But there is little consensus as to the very definition of literal meaning in these discussions of figurative language. Within the cognitive sciences there are at least five types of literality that are mostly implicit in discussions of figurative meaning (Gibbs, 1993a; G. Lakoff, 1986):

Conventional literality, in which literal usage is contrasted with poetic usage, exaggeration, embellishment, indirectness, and so on.

Subject-matter literality, in which certain expressions are the usual ones used to talk about a particular topic.

Nonmetaphorical literality, or directly meaningful language, in which one word (concept) is never understood in terms of a second word (or concept).

Truth conditional literality, or language that is capable of "fitting the world" (i.e., of referring to objectively existing objects or of being objectively true or false).

Context-free literality, in which the literal meaning of an expression is its meaning apart from any communicative situation or its meaning in a null context.

Both everyday talk and scholarly discourse suggest that some of these definitions of *literal* are closely equivalent (Gibbs, 1993a; G. Lakoff, 1986). For example, ordinary conventional language is directly meaningful and therefore not figurative. Conventional language is also capable of referring to objective reality and of being objectively true or false. Furthermore, there is only one objectively correct way to understand a subject, and the conventional language used to speak of a subject is capable of being true or false. And finally, truth conditional meaning refers to the meaning of an expression apart from any special discourse context.

These definitions of literal meaning contribute to the cluster of beliefs that researchers often assume without comment when they describe figurative language as a violation of communicative norms (see Chapter 3). For example, it is usually assumed that the term *literal* can be used unproblematically to contrast with the terms *metaphorical* and *figurative*. But only the nonmetaphorical definition of literal meaning specifically contrasts literal meaning with metaphoric meaning. Other senses of the word *literal* are more ambiguous in terms of providing a theoretical basis for any distinction between literal and figurative meaning. The polysemous character of the term *literal* is even more problematic, given that there are many kinds of figurative meaning other than metaphorical meaning (meaning based on, e.g., irony, metonymy, hyperbole, indirect speech acts).

Further debate about the role of literal meaning in figurative language understanding requires greater clarity about the many uses of the term *literal*. Scholars' different uses of the term *literal* in theories of figurative language only add confusion to the debate about literal meaning. Recent research demonstrates that different views of literal meaning can result in different intuitions about the "literality" of figurative utterances (Gibbs, Buchalter, Moise, & Farrar, 1993). Ordinary speakers (e.g., college students) judge the literality of different kinds of figurative language (e.g., literary metaphors, nonliterary metaphors, indirect speech acts, idioms, tautologies, hyperbole, and contextual expressions) in different ways when given varying definitions of literal meaning.

Consider, for example, the literary metaphor *The human face is a sealed furnace*. This metaphor was seen as highly literal when viewed in terms of subject-matter literality, because people might reasonably use such an expression when talking about the facial expression of human emotions. After all, we have many common phrases that are similar in character to this metaphor (*He got red in the face, He blew his stack, He was so angry that smoke was coming out of his ears,* and so on). However, *The human face is a sealed furnace* was seen as being *less* literal under the nonmetaphorical definition of literal meaning, because this expression reflected the metaphorical mapping of a source domain (a sealed furnace) onto a dissimilar target domain (the human face). Indirect speech acts (e.g., *Can you help me paint the garage?*) were seen as more literal, given a nonmetaphorical view of literal meaning as opposed to the subject-matter view, because these utterances were directly meaningful, or did not convey information about one idea in terms of a different idea or concept. In contrast, metonymic phrases, such as *The ham sandwich spilled beer all over himself,* were seen as more literal, given the subject-matter view of literal meaning (language used by waiters in a restaurant) than given the nonmetaphorical definition. This interaction between the different definitions and the different types of figurative language suggests that literal meaning is not determined in the same way for each type of figurative utterance.

In general, people's judgments about the literal meanings of figurative utterances differ, depending on the specific definition of literal meaning they are given to make their literality judgments. Part of the reason for this is that figurative language is encountered in varying social situations that both assume and elicit different pragmatic and conceptual knowledge. Judgments of literality are influenced by these different types of knowledge and extralinguistic information, so that it is virtually impossible to determine independently what some utterance literally means. Just as people's theories of concepts and word meanings determine how they judge what is seen as the literal content of ideas and word meanings, so too do people determine the literalness of figurative expressions via pragmatic information. Because speakers produce and hear different kinds of figurative language in different kinds of discourse situations, there is no single way of describing what is literal about all figurative utterances. There is only a remote chance that any principled distinction can be drawn between figurative and literal language. Metaphors will be distinct from nonmetaphorical language in ways that are different from the way that irony differs from nonironic language, idioms differ from nonidiomatic language, and so forth. Although it is sometimes theoretically important to define what constitutes metaphor, irony, metonymy, and so forth, scholars of figurative language should not look to some idealized notion of literal meaning or literal language as the basis for such definitions.

CONCLUSION

The ability to speak and think literally has been assumed to form the bedrock for most theories of mind, language, and meaning. Yet the search for a theory of what is literal about language and thought has not provided any clear answers to the question of what it means to say that we speak and think literally. Simply put, there exists no comprehensive account of literal meaning. What we think of as literal depends on a variety of factors, including culture, the individual, the context, and the task. People often fail to acknowledge that certain knowledge and assumptions drive their judgments of the literalness of words, sentences, and concepts. Even though we can on occasion assume that a word, sentence, or concept has a particular literal content, such judgments do not directly reflect people's underlying mental representations of concepts or of the language we use to express our ideas.

This conclusion may seem overly pessimistic to scholars who continue to adhere to objectivist accounts of the human mind. To claim, as I do, that concepts are temporary representations constructed from knowledge in long-term memory, or that our understanding of words and sentences is primarily based on idealized cognitive models or theories, may appear to many to embrace a nonfoundationalist view of human cognition. But this is not what I am doing. My urgent plea is that we recognize the different ways that the term *literal* is used and develop better accounts of what is *not* figurative about thought and language. We must not make the mistake of those adhering to the generative wager who a priori define what is literal about the human mind. Instead we should adhere to the cognitive wager and empirically explore how many aspects of human cognition are grounded in everyday bodily and perceptual experiences that form the nonmetaphorical part of thought and language.

Chapter 3

Figurative language understanding: A special process?

The most significant assumption of the traditional view of figurative language is that such language is deviant and requires special cognitive processes to be understood. Whereas literal language can be understood via normal cognitive mechanisms, listeners must recognize the deviant nature of a figurative utterance before determining its nonliteral meaning. For example, when a speaker says *Criticism is a branding iron*, he or she does not literally mean that criticism is a tool to mark livestock. Rather the speaker intends this utterance to have some figurative meaning along the lines that criticism can psychologically hurt the person who receives it, often with long-lasting consequences.

How do listeners comprehend such figurative utterances as *Criticism is a branding iron*? Is it more difficult to understand figurative speech than to process literal language? Even if literal meanings are not well defined (Chapter 2), there might still be some processing advantage for meanings that are less distant from what the words of an utterance mean. This chapter explores whether figurative language understanding is a special psychological event. My discussion of the empirical research on understanding different kinds of figurative language points to the possibility that the poetic structure of mind, how people think via metaphor, metonymy, irony, and so on, facilitates the comprehension of figurative speech.

Figurative language understanding

The most influential ideas about figurative language understanding come from Grice's theory of conversational implicature and Searle's work on speech act theory. Grice (1975, 1978) noted that much of the information that is conveyed in conversation is implied rather than asserted. Consider the following brief conversation.

Harry: Would you like a piece of cake?
Jane: I'm on a diet.

Understanding that Jane meant her statement as a refusal of Harry's offer requires that listeners go through a chain of reasoning regarding the speaker's intentions, because Jane's statement does not follow logically as a response to Harry's question. Grice called the second part of Jane's meaning (the refusal) an *implicature*. Thus, Grice distinguished between saying and implicating as two parts of a speaker's meaning.

How do people understand the implicatures behind speakers' utterances? Grice (1975) proposed that implicatures are a natural outcome of speakers' and listeners' cooperation in conversation. His argument was that all speakers adhere to the *cooperative principle*. This states that speakers must *make your conversational contribution such as is required, at the stage at which it occurs, by the accepted purpose or direction of the talk exchange in which you are engaged* (p. 45). When Jane says that she is on a diet, Harry takes her response as being cooperative and therefore as implicating something beyond what the response literally means.

The cooperative principle carries with it four maxims.

Maxim of Quantity: Make your contribution as informative as is required, but not more so, for the current purposes of the exchange.

Maxim of Quality: Do not say what you believe to be false or for which you lack adequate evidence.

Maxim of Relation: Say only what is relevant for the current purposes of the conversation.

Maxim of Manner: Be brief, but avoid ambiguity and obscurity of expression.

These maxims together constitute what it means for a speaker to be cooperative.

Grice realized that speakers do not always uphold these conversational maxims. As long as speakers generally adhere to the cooperative principle, they can violate or flout any of these maxims to produce certain implicatures. Speakers can deliberately violate maxims and specifically intend their listeners to recognize these violations. Grice offers an example of a letter of recommendation from a professor about a candidate for a philosophy position that went as follows: *Dear Sir: Mr. X's use of English is excellent and his attendance at tutorial has been regular. Yours, etc.* (ibid., p. 52). In this case the writer is not being as informative as is usually required in a letter of recommendation for a faculty position. He is obviously flouting the *maxim of quantity* in order to implicate that Mr. X is not suitable for the job.

The distinction between saying and implicating has obvious ramifications for the study of figurative language comprehension. If speakers are assumed to be cooperative, they may flout any of the conversational maxims as part of their attempt to communicate some meaning via figurative language. Listeners can work out in a series of steps the implicatures behind any utterance where the intended interpretation deviates from its literal meaning (Bach & Harnish, 1979; Gordon & Lakoff, 1975; Grice, 1975; Searle, 1975).

Grice assumes, then, that figurative language requires additional cognitive effort to be understood, because such utterances violate one of the conversational maxims (usually Quantity or Quality or both). Searle (1978) offers a similar rational analysis of figurative language understanding. He proposes various principles that allow listeners to figure out just how sentence and speaker meanings differ in metaphor, irony, indirect speech acts, and so on. Searle believes that Grice's principles of cooperative conversation and the rules for performing speech acts are sufficient to provide the basic principles for figurative language understanding.

The Grice–Searle view reflects many traditional analyses of figurative language in philosophy and linguistics. One version of this general idea, dubbed the *Standard Pragmatic Model*, suggests that understanding figurative language requires greater cognitive effort than does comprehending literal language. Understanding any nonliteral utterance, according to this view, can be accomplished in a series of steps. When a speaker says *Criticism is a branding iron*, listeners must (a) compute the literal meaning of the utterance; (b) decide if the literal meaning is the intended meaning of the utterance and if the literal meaning is inappropriate for the specific context; (c) compute the conveyed or metaphoric meaning via a cooperative principle or by the rules of speech acts.

Consider in a bit more detail how someone might, according to the standard pragmatic model, understand such an utterance as *Have you taken out the garbage?* (meaning "Take out the garbage"). When this sentence is taken literally, its utterance can only be a question uttered to elicit information. But in the context of a mother and son standing in a kitchen in front of a full garbage can, this interpretation would lack any communicative function. The son knows that the question would have to be answered in the negative, and he knows that his mother knows this too. In this situation, the question seems to be absurd and its utterance by the mother irrational. Nonetheless, the son does not take the mother's utterance to be irrational, because both speaker and listener (i.e., mother and son) operate in conversation under the *cooperative principle*. With this general principle, the son will reinterpret the mother's literal sentence to give the utterance a different meaning by relating to the accepted purpose of the conversation. In this way, the son will treat the question as a request that he take out the garbage.

The Standard Pragmatic Model assumes that the analysis of literal meaning is primary and that the figurative interpretation of any utterance can be inferred through some set of rules in relation to a listener's/reader's understanding of context. This model predicts that all instances of figurative language should be more difficult to understand than roughly equiva-lent literal discourse, a belief that, again, reflects the long-standing assumption that figurative meaning is deviant, re-quiring special mental processes.

As was described in Chapter 2, determining the specific lit-eral meaning of any utterance is problematic, much more so than most scholars admit. There are now good reasons to sug-gest that listeners do not simply analyze something called "lit-eral meaning" during linguistic processing, particularly given the difficulty of defining literal meaning as something differ-ent from figurative meaning. What evidence is there that people normally find it more difficult to understand figura-tive language than to understand literal speech?

PSYCHOLINGUISTIC RESEARCH

Psycholinguists employ a variety of experimental tasks to as-sess the sequence of unconscious mental events used in the ordinary processing of figurative language. Most of these tasks involve recording the amount of time it takes readers to inter-pret different kinds of figurative language in comparison with literal utterances. Participants in these reaction-time studies are presented with linguistic stimuli to which they must make a quick response. For example, participants may be asked to push a button as soon as they comprehend what they have just read, or they may be asked to judge the similarity of mean-ing between two sentences. In both cases, the decision made is subjective and is thought to represent something about the "click of comprehension" phenomenally suggested by people's experience of understanding language.

Reaction-time experiments generally show that people take between 1 and 4 sec to read and understand figurative utter-ances. These studies often compare the time needed to read or respond to figurative utterances versus the time needed to process "literal" expressions. Average differences of 200–300 msec in the comprehension times of figurative versus literal sentences may appear to be negligible in terms of everyday communication, but such differences can mark important variations in the sequence of mental processes used in understanding figurative language. The traditional assumption that figurative language is deviant because it violates communicative norms suggests that people should take longer to process figurative utterances than to comprehend literal expressions.

However, this idea may be false for two major reasons. First, the poetic structure of mind suggests that figurative language reflects fundamental aspects of everyday thought. People do not find figurative language any more difficult to process than literal discourse, because both types of language arise from figurative schemes of thought that are a dominant part of our conceptual system. For this reason, figurative language does not violate norms of cooperative communication and can easily be understood. Second, people may find figurative language readily understandable when these utterances are encountered in realistic discourse contexts. The pragmatic information that constitutes social situations can provide a framework for understanding language such that figurative expressions seem perfectly acceptable and appropriate.

The rest of this chapter is devoted to the psycholinguistic research on figurative language understanding. These studies generally focus on the constraining influence of context on people's interpretation of figurative language. Later chapters go into more detail about how the poetic structure of mind facilitates the comprehension of figurative speech.

INDIRECT SPEECH ACTS

Imagine a scenario where Robert and Martha are making dinner together and Robert at one point says *Will you hand me the pepper?* How does Martha recognize that Robert is making a request of her to pass the pepper and not simply asking a literal question? According to the traditional view (Grice, 1975, 1978; Searle, 1975), Robert has performed two acts in stating his utterance. First, he is asking a question regarding Martha's willingness to hand him the pepper. Second, he is requesting that she actually do so. The standard pragmatic model assumes that the secondary request meaning is logically dependent on the performance of the literal question.

The first empirical test of the standard pragmatic model

looked at understanding of indirect speech acts (H. Clark & Lucy, 1975). Participants in this study were presented with sentences that could have either literal meaning (*Color the circle blue*) or indirect meaning (*Can you color the circle blue?*). With each sentence, participants were also shown a picture of a circle. Their task was to read the sentence and decide whether the accompanying picture satisfied the sentence request. The hypothesis tested was this: If people actually compute the literal meaning of a sentence before deriving the indirect meaning, participants should take longer to verify indirect requests than direct ones. This prediction was confirmed, with indirect requests taking around 1 sec longer to verify than direct ones.

Participants in this study were also shown such sentences as (1) *I'll be very happy if you make the circle blue* and (2) *I'll be very sad unless you make the circle blue*. Since previous research had shown that it takes longer to verify negative statements than positive ones (H. Clark & Chase, 1972), if the literal meaning is processed first then people should take longer to comprehend a sentence like (2), which contains the negatives *sad* and *unless*, than (1). Again, this prediction was confirmed, in that participants took around 500 msec longer to comprehend (2) than (1). These results were taken as support for the Standard Pragmatic Model, because readers appeared to analyze the literal meanings of indirect requests before determining their conveyed interpretations (H. Clark & Lucy, 1975).

One difficulty with these findings concerns the situation in which people were asked to understand different indirect speech acts. Most psycholinguistic studies in the 1960s and 1970s examined sentence processing apart from linguistic and social contexts. It seemed likely, however, that people could comprehend a speaker's intended meaning by use of a sentence such as *Can you pass the salt?* without first analyzing its literal interpretation when this utterance was encountered in realistic discourse situations. Listeners use their knowledge of the social situation, the speaker and his or her probable intentions, and the conventional forms of sentences for making requests.

One set of studies tested this alternative hypothesis to the standard pragmatic model (Gibbs, 1979). People read, one line at a time on a computer screen, stories ending in either indirect requests, such as *Must you open the window?* (meaning *Please leave the window closed*); literal uses of the same sentences that were considered to be literal questions in their contexts; or direct requests, such as *Do not open the window*. After each story, participants made a paraphrase judgment for that story's last line. Presented below is an example of the different story contexts ending with their respective target sentences and paraphrases.

Literal Context
Mrs. Smith was watering her garden one afternoon.
She saw that the housepainter was pushing a window open.
She didn't understand why he needed to have it open.
A bit worried she went over and politely asked,
"Must you open the window?"

Paraphrase: "Need you open the window?"

Nonliteral Context
One morning John felt too sick to go to school.
The night before he and his friends got very drunk.
Then they went swimming in a cold lake.
Because of this John caught a bad cold.
He was lying in bed when his mother stormed into the room.
When she started opening the window John groaned,
"Must you open the window?"

Paraphrase: "Do not open the window."

If people actually compute the literal meaning of an indirect request before deriving its nonliteral interpretation, then indirect requests should take longer to process than either literal uses of the same sentences or direct requests. The results of these studies, however, showed that indirect requests took *no* longer to understand than either literal sentences or direct requests when these sentences were read in appropriate contexts. Without any preceding context, participants took *much* longer to read and make paraphrase judgments than they did for literal sentences. These results suggest that people do not necessarily analyze the literal meanings of many indirect speech acts before deriving their indirect interpretations when these expressions are seen in appropriate situational contexts.

A revised version of the standard pragmatic model suggests that understanding nonliteral language involves the simultaneous computation of both the literal and nonliteral meanings of an utterance (H. Clark, 1979; H. Clark & Schunk, 1980; Estill & Kemper, 1982; Swinney & Cutler, 1979). This model proposes that people do not first process the literal interpretations of nonliteral utterances but do so at the same time as they understand their indirect or figurative meanings.

There is some evidence to support this idea. In one series of experiments, ordinary requests for information were made of local merchants on the telephone (H. Clark, 1979; and see A. Munro, 1979). Many of these requests were stated indirectly and included such expressions as *Can you tell me what time you close?* and *Will you tell me what time you close?* Most merchants included *Yes* in their verbal responses to these indirect requests, as in *Yes, we close at six.* People presumably included *Yes* in their response to adequately address the literal question; *we close at six* provided the information that was indirectly requested. It appears that listeners ordinarily analyze the literal meanings of these indirect requests, perhaps in parallel with computing the nonliteral meanings. This strategy seems particularly useful to enable listeners to know when a speaker is being polite and when they should, in turn, respond politely (H. Clark & Schunk, 1980). Most generally, these findings suggest that nonliteral language processing requires some additional process that operates in parallel with normal literal speech comprehension processes.

It is not entirely clear, though, that the presence of the word *Yes* in people's verbal responses to indirect requests necessarily reflects their computation of a sentence's literal meaning. People may simply include *Yes* in their responses because it is conventionally polite to do so in many situations, even though they don't actually analyze the utterances' literal interpretations. One reason to suspect that this might be true is that merchants often responded with *Yes* to requests like *Would you mind telling me what time you close?* (H. Clark, 1979).

People should have responded with *No,* as in *No; we close at six* if they were responding to the literal meaning of this question.

Analyzing the literal interpretations of indirect speech acts might be necessary only in social situations where listeners know that polite verbal response to the speakers' requests are desired. This may be true when responding to requests for information over the telephone (ibid.) or in complying with requests like *Can you tell me the time?* where a verbal response completely satisfies the speaker's need. Nevertheless, not all request situations require that a verbal response be made. Furthermore, requests for time phrased indirectly, as in *Could you . . . ?* might be interpreted as simple requests without any analysis of the sentence's literal interpretation but are still conventionally responded to with an affirmation plus compliance, not simply with compliance (Goffman, 1976; A. Munro, 1979). The results showing that people change their responses according to the politeness of the indirect request (H. Clark, 1979) may be due to people's knowing what is conventionally thought of as being polite rather than to their computing the literal meaning of the sentence at some point during on-line comprehension. People may analyze what a sentence literally says, but they may not necessarily do this automatically when they understand speakers' utterances.

Two experiments were conducted to examine these possibilities (Gibbs, 1983). Participants in these studies read stories that ended with sentences intended either as indirect requests or as literal questions. After reading each story, participants were presented with a word string. Their task was to decide whether the word string constituted a meaningful English sentence. Presented below are two stories followed by four word strings.

Literal Context

Martin was talking with his psychiatrist.
He was having many problems with relationships.
He always seemed hostile to other people.
Martin commented to the psychiatrist,
"Everyone I meet I seem to alienate."

The shrink said,
"Can't you be friendly?"

Literal: "Are you unable to be friendly?"
Indirect: "Please be friendly to other people."
Unrelated: "The weather is quite hot today."
Anomalous: "Have you never car the."

Indirect Request Context

Mrs. Connor was watching her kids play in the backyard.
One of the neighbor's children had come over to play.
But Mrs. Connor's son refused to share his toys.
This made Mrs. Connor upset.
She angrily walked outside and said in a stern voice to her
   son,
"Can't you be friendly?"

Indirect: "Please be friendly to other people."
Literal: "Are you unable to be friendly?"
Unrelated: "The weather is quite hot today."
Anomalous: "Have you never car the."

The indirect meanings of these stories' last lines can be viewed as their conventional interpretations. When understanding the literal, nonconventional uses of these sentences, participants may analyze the conventional request meaning of these expressions before deciding that the nonconventional, literal meanings are appropriate. When reading literal questions, participants' responses to both the literal and conventional targets should be fast relative to the time it takes to respond to unrelated targets. However, participants' response times for literal targets should be slow if they do not ordinarily analyze the literal interpretations of indirect requests. The results of this study showed that when people read indirect requests they were much faster to make the sentence classification responses for indirect targets than for literal ones. Moreover, there was no significant difference in response times for the literal and unrelated targets when participants read indirect requests. These data indicate that there was no residue from the participants' processing of the literal meanings of the indirect requests that subsequently facilitated their responses to the literal targets. This suggests that people do not *neces-*

sarily analyze the literal interpretation of an indirect speech act during their immediate comprehension (Gibbs, 1982, 1983).

It is interesting to note what happened when people read stories ending with literal questions. Participants' response times were significantly faster for the indirect targets than for the literal ones, despite the fact that they had just read a sentence intended to be understood quite literally. These data suggest that participants immediately analyzed the indirect request meanings of these literal sentences. Another study showed that when people read literal questions that could not be viewed easily as having nonliteral meanings (e.g., *Is it possible for you to be friendly?*), they were significantly faster in responding to the literal targets than to the indirect ones (Gibbs, 1983). In general, people are biased toward the conventional interpretations of sentences even when these conventional meanings are nonliteral or figurative. Certain sentence forms, such as *Can you . . . ?* and *May I . . . ?*, conventionally seem to be used as indirect requests. Listeners' familiarity with these sentence forms, along with the context, helps them immediately comprehend the indirect meaning of these indirect requests. People may not automatically compute both the literal and indirect meanings of indirect speech acts.

IDIOMS

Idioms have traditionally been defined as expressions whose meanings are noncompositional or not functions of the meanings of their individual parts (Chomsky, 1980; Fraser, 1970; Heringer, 1976; J. Katz, 1973). For example, the figurative interpretation of *kick the bucket* ("to die") cannot be determined through an analysis of its individual word meanings. Some scholars propose that idioms are dead metaphors, expressions that have lost their essential metaphoricity over time and now exist as frozen semantic units, perhaps in a special phrasal lexicon (cf. Gibbs, 1993b). People supposedly comprehend idioms, such as *kick the bucket*, by first processing a phrase's literal meaning and then directly retrieving the phrase's figurative meaning from the special phrasal lexicon once the literal meaning is found to be defective in some context. This hypothesis implies that people should have more difficulty understanding *kick the bucket* when used as an idiomatic phrase than when used in its literal sense ("to strike one's foot against a pail").

One study tested this hypothesis by presenting participants with either four literal sentences (e.g., *John saw the children, John ran into the house, John observed the Indian dance*) or four idiomatic, and thus grammatically ambiguous, sentences (e.g., *John let the cat out of the bag, John was in hot water*) (Bobrow & Bell, 1973). The participants were then shown an idiomatic test sentence (e.g., *John and Mary buried the hatchet*). Their task was to say which meaning, literal or idiomatic, they perceived first. When people were presented with a list of literal sentences, they most often gave literal interpretations to the test sentences. However, they gave idiomatic interpretations to the test sentences when they saw a list of idiomatic expressions first. These data are consistent with the idea that people normally employ a literal mode of processing and will interpret phrases in an idiomatic manner only when they are put in an idiomatic mode of processing.

This conclusion about idiom comprehension is difficult to accept, given that people's processing of idioms was examined long after they had actually understood each phrase. Theories of figurative language understanding must be sensitive to the temporal moments of linguistic processing. Studies that examine linguistic understanding long after people actually encounter linguistic expressions are generally not informative about the immediate, unconscious processes that operate during on-line processing. For example, other studies on idiom processing measured the time it took participants to judge the meaningfulness of word phrases. These experiments showed that idiomatic expressions (*kick the bucket*) took significantly less time to verify than literal phrases (*lift the bucket*) (Burt, 1992; Gibbs & Gonzales, 1985; Gibbs, Nayak, & Cutting, 1989; Swinney & Cutler, 1979). When people read idiom expressions, such as *John is singing a different tune*, in contexts supporting idiomatic interpretation, they took much less time to process the idiom than when they read the same sentence in a literal context (Gibbs, 1980, 1986d). The extra time needed to understand idioms in literal contexts has been attributed to the bias people have for automatically interpreting these phrases according to their conventional, figurative interpretations before recognizing their intended literal meanings (Gibbs, 1980, 1986a).

Some researchers assume that even though the literal meanings of idioms do not have to be computed before their figurative meanings, both types of meanings may be simultaneously initiated upon occurrence of the first word in the idiom string, much as appears to occur for lexical ambiguities (Estill & Kemper, 1982; Glass, 1983; Swinney & Cutler, 1979). This model, called the *lexical representation hypothesis*, holds that idioms are stored and retrieved from the lexicon in the same manner as any other word and that idioms are unified with respect to access, retrieval, and the representation in the lexicon. Idioms should be faster to comprehend than literal phrases, because the simultaneous processing of an idiom's literal and figurative meanings results in a horse race that facilitates participants' responses to idioms over the time required to process literal phrases, where only one meaning is analyzed.

The lexical representation hypothesis is attractive because it does not require any special processing mode for idiom comprehension and because it captures the intuition that idioms are understood almost as if they were single words. However, the finding that idioms take less time to process than do literal phrases does not necessarily indicate that people analyze the literal meanings of idioms at the same time as their nonliteral interpretations are being processed. People's familiarity with idioms could easily have influenced their immediate recognition of these figurative phrases.

One attempt to provide additional support for the lexical representation hypothesis explicitly controlled for the role of familiarity in idiom processing (Glass, 1983). Participants in these studies had to respond as to whether an idiom (e.g., *take one's medicine*) had the same or a different meaning as a paraphrase of either its literal ("ingest a healing substance") or figurative ("endure just punishment") interpretation. The results indicated that there was no difference in the time it took participants to read an idiom and judge whether a literal or a figurative paraphrase had the same meaning. This contrasts with other results, where people took *less* time to read and make paraphrase judgments for figurative interpretations of idioms than for literal ones (Gibbs, 1980, 1983).

In another study, participants were instructed to respond only on the basis of literal meaning. Under this condition, people found phrase–idiom pairs that shared a figurative interpretation (*to be absolutely invariable–hard and fast*) more difficult to reject as different than pairs that shared no interpretation (*to be absolutely invariable–take a powder*). This result was seen as supportive of the idea that whenever a familiar idiom is comprehended, both its literal and figurative interpretations are computed (Glass, 1983). The fact that the figurative meaning of an idiom interfered with participants' literal judgments about that expression suggests that people cannot ignore the figurative meanings of idioms. This does not mean that people ordinarily compute the literal meanings of idioms when they encounter these phrases in discourse. If anything, these results imply that people automatically comprehend the figurative meanings of idioms and therefore do not necessarily process their literal interpretations.

A very different type of study also attempted to show that people normally analyze both the literal and figurative meanings of idioms (Estill & Kemper, 1982). In this experiment, listeners monitored literal and figurative uses of idioms for specific words that appeared at the ends of these phrases. For example, people heard the phrase *bury the hatchet* at the end of a short story that biased either its figurative or literal meaning. The participants were told to monitor for a particular target word as they listened to the story. These target words either were identical to clue words given to the participants beforehand (e.g., "hatchet"), were in the same semantic category as a clue word (e.g., "a tool"), or rhymed with a clue word (e.g., "ratchet"). People were just as good at detecting the different targets for each type of clue for literal as for figurative uses of idioms. These data were viewed as evidence supporting the idea that people process both the literal and figurative meanings of idioms.

It is possible, however, that people may examine aspects of

the conventional meanings of individual words in idioms without actually combining these meanings to form a literal representation of the phrase (Gibbs, 1985a). Some evidence supports this possibility (Cacciari & Tabossi, 1988). Some parts of an idiom are more relevant than others for determining the phrase's figurative meaning. Consider the expression *After the excellent performance, the tennis player was in seventh heaven*. This sentence might be processed literally until the last word, *heaven*, is encountered. Some data demonstrated that without context people appear to process the individual lexical items in an idiom until the key word has been heard (ibid.). From this point on, an idiomatic phrase is understood according to its conventional, figurative sense. Appropriate contextual information may override the literal analysis of earlier words in idiomatic phrases. In any event, it is unlikely that people carry *all* the possible meanings of the words in an idiom to construct its literal interpretation.

Other evidence casts further doubt on the possibility that people automatically compute all the literal meanings of idiomatic expressions at the same time as their figurative meanings are being understood (Gibbs, 1986a). In these studies, people read stories ending with such sentences as *He kept it under his hat*. In one story context, these final sentences had literal meanings ("It's beneath his cap"), and in another story they had nonliteral, idiomatic interpretations ("He didn't tell anyone"). Participants read these stories one line at a time and afterwards made a judgment as to whether a visually presented string of words constituted a meaningful English sentence. These word strings, or targets, were either literal interpretations of the prime sentences (e.g., *It's beneath his cap*), idiomatic interpretations (e.g., *He didn't tell anyone*), unrelated sentences (e.g., *It happened to Sally*), or strings of words that were not meaningful English sentences.

The results of interest were the response times for making the sentence–nonsense judgments for the different targets, depending on whether participants had previously read idioms or literal sentences. When participants read stories ending with figurative uses of idioms, they were not subsequently faster in responding to the literal targets than they were to make the same judgments for unrelated targets. It seems doubtful that people analyzed the literal meanings of these idiomatic expressions at the same time as they interpreted their figurative meanings. But when people read idioms in strong literal contexts (e.g., *He let the cat out of the bag,* meaning "He released the animal from the sack"), they automatically analyzed these phrases' figurative meanings before arriving at their appropriate literal interpretations. This interferes with participants' responses to literal targets. The figurative meanings of idioms appear to be interpreted automatically, regardless of the context in which these phrases are encountered. Another series of studies employed a different on-line measure to demonstrate that people do not necessarily complete all stages of literal processing when reading idiomatic expressions (Needham, 1992).

More recent research has looked at the role of familiarity in people's immediate comprehension of idioms. Highly familiar idioms are generally understood more rapidly than are less familiar phrases (Schweigert, 1986, 1991; Schweigert & Moates, 1988). Idioms also differ in the extent to which their literal or figurative sense is seen as more familiar (Popiel & McRae, 1988). For example, some idioms, such as *pull your leg,* are predominantly seen in figurative contexts ("to joke or tease"), whereas others, such as *take your medicine,* have literal and figurative uses that are roughly equal in frequency and familiarity. The extent to which an idiom has a dominant literal or figurative meaning can influence the difficulty people have understanding these phrases when used in their nonliteral meanings. Other idioms can be used in contexts that simultaneously support both their literal and figurative meanings (Burt, 1992; Mueller & Gibbs, 1987). Thus, *skating on thin ice* has both a literal and a figurative meaning in a situation where someone is skating on thin ice. People experience significantly greater difficulty understanding these "isomorphic" idioms than when they process idioms in simple figurative contexts (e.g., when *skating on thin ice* is used in a situation where there is no skating or ice). These various findings support the idea that difficulty in idiom processing partly depends on the frequency and familiarity of these phrases.

The experimental research on idiom comprehension leads to two conclusions. First, idioms do not require special processes to be understood. Second, understanding idioms does not appear to require an analysis of these phrases' literal meanings. Chapter 6 discusses the metaphorical nature of many idioms and suggests some alternative ideas about the role of lexical information in the on-line processing of idiomatic phrases.

SLANG

Slang expressions are often associated with idiomatic phrases. Although slang is usually seen as having a shorter life span within a language than idioms have and is used only by certain groups of individuals or specific communities (Spears, 1982), it is sometimes difficult to distinguish slang from idioms. Slang metaphors often convey certain attitudes or feelings of the speaker's that idiomatic expressions do not. For instance, the expression *He's on a trip* (meaning "He's taking drugs") can suggest that the speaker is aware of certain social norms and attitudes about drugs and the drug culture. Knowing what slang is appropriate in a particular situation goes a long way toward showing who's hip and who's not.

The standard pragmatic model proposes that people should experience greater difficulty understanding slang metaphors (e.g., *I need some bread*, meaning "I need some money") than literal uses of the same expressions (meaning, "I need some food") or literal equivalent statements (*I need some money*). Once again, this result should be obtained if people normally analyze the literal meanings of expressions before their figurative interpretations are determined. However, people took no longer, and in many cases less time, to comprehend slang metaphors than to process literal uses of the same sentences (referring to bread as food) or nonslang equivalent sentences (Gibbs & Nagaoka, 1985). An additional, and important, finding from this study indicated that participants were faster at processing the first slang metaphor they encountered in the experiment than the first literal sentence. This result rules out the possibility that participants were quicker at understanding slang because they were in some sort of special "slang mode" of processing, given the relatively large number of these

97

expressions in the experiment. As is the case for idioms, people understand the figurative meanings of slang metaphors without first having to reject their so-called literal meanings as defective or inappropriate.

PROVERBS

Proverbs are pithy sayings that express social norms or moral concerns. Early work on the interpretation of proverbs showed that it is difficult to measure the exact point at which proverbs are comprehended (Bühler, 1908). For instance, unfamiliar proverbs, such as *The most glaring colors in which virtues shine are the inventions of those who lack them*, demand quite a bit of thought to interpret and dramatically extend the comprehension process beyond that normally measured by experimental psychologists. Some proverbs can take up to 10 sec to comprehend when first heard. Such long latencies make the data for some proverb experiments difficult to interpret (Honeck, Voegstle, Dorfmueller, & Hoffman, 1980).

Nonetheless, various researchers have tested the idea that many proverbs are analyzed at a literal level before their figurative interpretations can be derived. One reaction-time study presented participants with a pair of sentences and asked them to decide as quickly as possible whether the pair shared a meaning (Brewer, Harris, & Brewer, 1977). Each pair of sentences had a proverb (e.g., *Many leaks sink a ship*) and a paraphrase of either the proverb's figurative meaning ("A lot of small problems can add up to serious trouble") or its literal meaning ("A lot of small holes can cause a boat to sink"). If people first understood each proverb on a literal level, then presenting the figurative paraphrase before the proverb should require more processing than the condition where the literal paraphrase came first. The result of this study showed this to be true. Participants were faster at making their decisions for the literal paraphrase–proverb pairs than for the figurative paraphrase–proverb pairs. These data support the hypothesis that people analyze the literal meanings of proverbs before determining their nonliteral interpretations. However, it should be noted that this experiment did not assess proverb comprehension in appropriate linguistic contexts.

98

Another reaction-time study investigated comprehension of novel proverbs but did not find any evidence that people use special processes (Kemper, 1981). In this experiment, participants read short story contexts ending with proverbs. For example, a story about a person who swore at a police officer for stopping him after violating a traffic law ended with the expression *If you can't bite, don't show your teeth.* This same sentence was also seen by a different group of participants at the end of a story about an old dog. The participants' task was to read stories like these and decide as quickly as possible whether the final sentence fit the story meaning. Comprehending the proverbs in strictly literal contexts took people longer than reading these proverbs at the ends of figurative stories. This finding adds further confirmation to the idea that with sufficient contextual support, novel figurative language need not require inferences beyond those needed to understand literal language.

METAPHOR

Various research demonstrates that the standard pragmatic model does not explain normal processing strategies when people understand metaphors in appropriate social and linguistic contexts. One study had participants read sentences like *Regardless of the danger, the troops marched on* in either a literal or metaphoric context (Ortony, Schallert, Reynolds, & Antos, 1978). An example of the two contexts for this sentence is presented below.

Literal Context

Approaching the enemy infantry, the men worried about touching off landmines.

They were anxious that their presence would be detected prematurely.

Their fears were compounded by the knowledge that they might be isolated from their reinforcements. The outlook was grim.

Regardless of the danger, the troops marched on.

Metaphorical Context

The children continued to annoy their baby-sitter.

She told the little boys she would not tolerate any more bad
  behavior.
Climbing all over the furniture was not allowed.
She threatened to spank them if they continued to stomp, run,
  and scream around the room. The children knew that her
  spankings hurt.
Regardless of the danger, the troops marched on.

Given sufficient context, people may not need to analyze
the literal interpretation of the metaphorical utterances before
deriving their intended metaphorical meanings. This was
found to be true. When participants read the target sentences
at the ends of long contexts, there were no differences in the
times to read literal and metaphorical target sentences. However, when participants read the target sentences in short contexts, metaphorical targets took significantly longer to read
than literal sentences.

A more recent study included a control condition in which
the contexts preceding the target sentences were unrelated to
either the figurative or literal interpretations of the targets
(Inhoff, Lima, & Carroll, 1984). In addition, instead of mea-
suring the total time it took people to read the different targets, which might tap into contextual integration processes
that are extraneous to metaphor understanding per se (Janus
& Bever, 1985), the participants' eye movements were tracked,
and the amount of time people focused on the targets was
recorded. These reaction-time data, which varied between
1,500 and 2,500 msec, confirmed the findings in that metaphors were comprehended as quickly as literal targets when
preceded by longer story contexts. Furthermore, there were
no differences in reading times for literal and metaphorical
targets preceded by shorter story contexts. This suggests that
either the metaphors may not have been interpreted figuratively or, if they were comprehended as metaphors, the process requires no more effort than understanding literal language. The contextual information, as described in the preceding studies, might very well prime a type of processing
strategy rather than priming a particular figurative meaning
(Inhoff et al., 1984).

Another instance of people's being automatically biased toward the figurative meanings of metaphors was shown using a variant of Stroop's (1935) interference technique (Glucksberg, Gildea, & Bookin, 1982). Participants in these studies were asked to make rapid decisions about the literal truth of such sentences as *Some jobs are jails*. This verification task removes the necessity of seeking a nonliteral interpretation for the sentences, since participants were required only to respond to the literal truth of each sentence. If some sort of triggering condition is needed for understanding the nonliteral meaning of a metaphor, then a sentence like *Some jobs are jails* should simply be treated as a false class inclusion statement. However, if people automatically apprehend the nonliteral meaning of metaphorical statements, then the "false" response should be in conflict with the "true" reaction. When such a conflict exists, participants should take longer to execute the correct "false" response to these literally false but metaphorically true statements.

The results of these studies indicated that people correctly judged sentences like *Some jobs are jails* as literally false. However, the availability of a true, metaphoric interpretation (e.g., "Some people are trapped in their occupations") interfered with making the literal judgments. When metaphoric interpretations of literally false sentences were available, participants took significantly longer to decide that such sentences were false. The metaphor interference effect provides evidence that the metaphorical meanings were comprehended *despite* the absence of any literal-failure-triggering conditions. Moreover, these findings also demonstrated that the nonliteral meanings of metaphorical statements can be determined automatically even in the absence of any special context favoring a figurative interpretation (Glucksberg et al., 1982).

A subsequent set of studies examined comprehension of poor metaphors, such as *Her marriage was an icebox* (Gildea & Glucksberg, 1983). This statement is less apt than, for example, *Some jobs are jails*, because there are no readily apparent properties of the vehicle *icebox* that seem uniquely relevant to the metaphor topic *marriage*. However, different contexts might be effective in disambiguating poor metaphors. Participants in these studies were presented with sentences on a screen, one at a time, and told to respond *True* or *False*. Thus, the statement *Some marriages are iceboxes* was preceded by a context statement, such as either *Some summers are cold* (a literal prime) or *Some people are cold* (a figurative prime). People once again experienced difficulty responding that the sentence was literally false when it was preceded by either type of appropriate context sentence, but not when it was preceded by a neutral prime sentence (ibid.; Shinjo & Myers, 1987).

Readers of metaphor appear unable to ignore the figurative meanings of these phrases even when instructed to focus exclusively on the literal meanings of the sentences. One study showed this point most forcefully (Keysar, 1989). Participants were given brief stories to read, such as the following.

> Bob Jones is an expert at such stunts as sawing a woman in half and pulling rabbits out of hats. He earns his living traveling around the world with an expensive entourage of equipment and assistants. Although Bob tries to budget carefully, it seems to him that money just disappears into thin air. With such huge audiences, why doesn't he ever break even?

The participants then decided, as quickly as possible, whether a target sentence, such as *Bob Jones is a magician*, was true or false. This target sentence is literally true, but metaphorically false. With respect to Bob's financial affairs, he is not a magician at all. If people simply stay with the literal when it makes sense, then the "false" metaphorical meaning should not play a role here at all. Yet the metaphorical meaning does play a role and actually interferes with participants' correct "true" decision to the true literal meaning that Bob Jones is a magician by profession (ibid.). When Bob Jones is described in this same context as making a profit despite huge expenses, then people very quickly agree that he is a magician by profession. The metaphorical meaning can thus reinforce or interfere with the literal meaning even when that literal meaning is not defective.

Even though readers cannot ignore metaphorical meaning, at what point does the figurative interpretation of an expression override literal processing? People may start with a literal analysis of a nonliteral utterance but short-circuit it in favor of some nonliteral comprehension strategy as they read or hear the sentence. Under this view, some aspects of literal meaning must be comprehended and rejected even if metaphors do not take any longer to process than literal utterances (Gerrig & Healey, 1983).

Consider the metaphorical expression *The night sky was filled with drops of molten silver*. This metaphor has an implicit topic, *star*, which is referred to by the explicit topic *The night sky*. Participants in one study read sentences and pushed a button when they understood their meanings (ibid.). These sentences could have their explicit topics presented either first or later on in the sentences, and the sentences could be presented in either the active or passive voice. The four possibilities are:

(Topic first – active voice)
The orchestra filled the concert hall with sunshine.

(Topic second – passive voice)
The concert hall was filled with sunshine by the orchestra.

(Topic first – passive voice)
The old woman's face was marked by the furrows of time.

(Topic second – active voice)
The furrows of time marked the old woman's face.

For the first two examples, the implicit topic is *music*, and the implicit topic is *wrinkles* for the last two examples. When the vehicles appear first, people must process the sentence literally, only to discover when reading the subsequent explicit topic that the sentence has an implicit topic that makes it a metaphor. On the other hand, when the explicit topic is presented early in the sentence, participants can rapidly discover the literal mismatch and interpret the vehicle metaphorically.

The results of reading-time experiment confirmed these expectations. Across the active and passive voice conditions, the participants took less time, about 750 msec, to read the sentences when the topic was presented first rather than later in the sentence. However, this effect was markedly reduced when participants read literal control sentences, such as *The night sky was filled with stars.* It appears that people can sometimes begin processing a metaphor at a literal level when the vehicle is presented first, but not when the explicit topic of the metaphor is presented first. In other words, people can initially process some metaphors in a literal manner but will short-circuit the literal meaning when the explicit topic creates a metaphorical context (ibid.). More recent studies demonstrate that very rapid processing of metaphors is facilitated by readers' previous experiences with these metaphors. Highly familiar metaphors can be processed more easily than are relatively novel metaphors (Blasko & Connine, 1993). Even if a metaphorical expression is less familiar, people can still easily understand its figurative meaning as long as that metaphor is highly apt (ibid.). Some research has shown that individual-difference variables, such as analogic reasoning ability, may also influence people's ability to understand metaphors easily (A. Katz, 1989; Trick & Katz, 1986).

The studies mentioned so far tested the psychological plausibility of the standard pragmatic model by examining comprehension of nonliteral language. These studies generally show that metaphor comprehension shares functional properties with literal language processing. Other studies investigated whether metaphor use is a derived process by looking at the production of figurative language. The interest in this research was to see if the production of figurative language requires more cognitive effort than is needed for literal speech. One study looked at the relative difficulty of initiating paraphrases for both metaphorical and nonmetaphorical utterances (R. Harris, 1976). If people must first compute the literal meanings of literary metaphors, such as *He hates the slime that sticks on filthy deeds*, before going on to determine their metaphoric meanings, then participants should take longer to paraphrase these expressions than to paraphrase nonmetaphorical expressions, such as *He hates the rancor that stays on cruel deeds*. The results of this study showed, however, that there were no differences in the times to initiate paraphrases for these two types of expression. Metaphors do not introduce difficulty in comprehension in comparison with understanding nonmetaphorical equivalents.

Another study recorded the co-occurrence of figurative language and pauses in two spontaneous speech situations involving a college instructor delivering a lecture and a patient and therapist engaging in psychotherapy (H. Pollio, Fabrizi, & Weedle, 1982). Speech pauses have been shown to be an operational index of the complexity of cognitive processing involved in speech at each of the syntactic, semantic, and discourse levels (Beattie, 1979; Butterworth, 1975; Goldman-Eisler, 1968). An examination of the pauses in the two situations revealed that common idioms were typically produced without any hesitations. Moreover, speakers did not pause any longer before making novel figurative utterances than before literal ones. The pauses that did occur in a figurative clause usually followed the key metaphorical word rather than preceding it. In general, novel figurative speech takes no longer to produce than either literal or clichéd figurative output (H. Pollio et al., 1982).

Besides the various experimental evidence on producing and understanding metaphorical expressions, a program has been developed by one computer scientist that interprets metaphoric language by applying specific knowledge about the conventional metaphors in the language (Martin, 1992). This program, called MIDAS (Metaphor Interpretation, Denotation, and Acquisition System), can also dynamically learn new metaphors when they are encountered in discourse. The MIDAS program differs from other computational models of metaphor understanding, which assume that metaphor arises from underlying conceptual similarity or analogy between concepts representing the literal meanings of the words and concepts in utterances (cf. Carbonell, 1981; Gentner, Falkenhainer, & Skorstad, 1988; Indurkhya, 1987). These systems use no knowledge about the metaphors that are a conventional part of how we think and speak and consequently see metaphor understanding as a special-purpose, problem-solving task. In contrast, MIDAS specifically employs hierarchically organized knowledge about conventional metaphors in interpreting and learning the meanings of metaphorical expressions. For example, MIDAS recognizes that the term *kill* in the question *How can I kill a computer process?* has a conventional metaphoric meaning similar to *kill* in *to kill a conversation*. MIDAS thus extends well-known metaphors in a systematic fashion. Unlike most computational models, then, MIDAS uses the same processes to interpret metaphor as it does to understand other aspects of speech. This kind of AI model seems most consistent with the available psychological evidence showing that metaphor understanding does not require special mental processes.

METONYMY

Consider the metonymic sentence *The ham sandwich is getting impatient for his check*. This figurative expression makes little sense apart from some specific context, as when one waiter wants to inform another that his customer, who was served a ham sandwich, wants to receive the check (Nunberg, 1979). Metonymy serves in these instances as a kind of *contextual expression*: words or phrases whose meanings depend on the context in which they are embedded (E. Clark & Clark, 1979; H. Clark, 1983; Gerrig, 1986). Because potential contexts are unlimited, contextual expressions have an unlimited number of potential meanings. For example, listeners must create the meaning "uniformed police officers" for the word *uniforms* in the utterance *There are 20,000 uniforms in the city* (Gerrig, 1989a). The word *uniform* is metonymic (or a synecdoche) because it exhibits a stands-for relationship where a salient part (the uniform) stands for a whole (the person wearing the uniform).

Psycholinguistic research shows that readers can easily determine the appropriate referents for metonymic expressions in discourse (Gibbs, 1990b). Thus, readers can easily recognize that the word *tuxedo* in the statement *John fired the tuxedo because he kept dropping the tray* refers to a waiter, despite the literal incongruity of this sentence. But how do readers arrive at the correct interpretation of this seemingly anomalous utterance, one that violates maxims of truthfulness?

Most theories of sentence processing assume that all the possible senses of each word in an utterance are listed in the mental lexicon and that listeners select among them to understand a word. But understanding contextual expressions involving metonymy requires that a process of *sense creation* must operate to supplement ordinary *sense selection*. For instance, the contextually appropriate meaning of *tuxedo* cannot be selected from a short list of potential meanings in the lexicon because the potential senses are unlimited. Listeners must instead create a new meaning for a word that already has a conventional interpretation. One idea, called the *error recovery* model, assumes that sense creation is initiated only after the conventional meaning has been found to be in error (cf. Gerrig, 1989a). This model posits that listeners recognize the need for a figurative interpretation of such an utterance as *The ham sandwich is getting impatient for his check* after it is seen as violating maxims of truthfulness. After all, it is untruthful to claim that inanimate objects, such as ham sandwiches, exhibit human traits, such as impatience. An alternative view of how metonymic expressions are understood, called the *concurrent processing* model, claims that sense creation and sense selection processes operate simultaneously, perhaps in competition with each other, in the determination of figurative meaning (Gerrig, 1989a).

An experimental test of these hypotheses had participants read short stories that established preempting meanings for old words (ibid.). For example, people read stories ending with *The horse race is the most popular event.* In a conventional context, this final phrase referred to a standard race between horses; in the innovative situation, it referred to a unique situation where snails competed in a race that was the length of King Louis's horse. Readers took roughly the same time to comprehend the statement in both contexts. This overlap in reading times suggests that error recovery cannot be operating. Instead, readers seem to be creating and selecting meanings for the phrase *the horse race* at the same time. These data are similar to those obtained for metaphor comprehension that show that contextual expectations drive the recovery of metaphorical meanings at the same time as their literal meanings are being rejected (Gerrig & Healey, 1983; Inhoff, Lima, & Carroll, 1984; Ortony, Schallert, Reynolds, & Antos, 1978).

IRONY

Like metaphor, irony is often taken as a paradigmatic example of figurative language that should require special processes to be understood. The *Oxford English Dictionary* says that ironic utterances are generally thought to include *the use of words to express something other than and especially the opposite of the literal meaning of a sentence*, whereas sarcasm depends for its effect on *bitter, caustic, and other ironic language that is usually directed against an individual*. Thus, if a speaker says *You're a fine friend* to someone who has injured the speaker in some way, the utterance is sarcastic. But if a speaker says *They tell me you're a slow runner* to someone who has just won a marathon, the utterance is seen as ironic. Even though it is possible to make sarcastic remarks without being ironic, most sarcasm uses irony to get its bitter or caustic effect (see Fowler, 1965).

The traditional view posits that irony is properly understood by assuming the opposite of a sentence's literal meaning. Taking the opposite of what a sentence literally means presumably requires mental effort over that needed to simply understand the literal meaning. But in many cases the opposite of a sentence's literal meaning is unclear or doesn't come close to specifying a speaker's true ironic intent. For example, if you perpetrate a grievous deed toward a good friend and he says to you *Thanks*, the traditional view suggests that taken literally the utterance is grossly inappropriate, violating the maxim of quality, and so listeners are forced to render the utterance appropriate by determining in what way the sentence and speaker meanings differ. But the opposite of your friend's comment *Thanks* would be something like *No thanks* or *It is not the case that I'm thanking you*. These interpretations do not capture the true ironic intention in using this utterance, namely, *You have done something that I do not appreciate*. The ironic meaning of *Thanks* denies one of its felicity, not its truth, conditions, because it is infelicitous to thank someone who deserves ingratitude. In other cases speakers actually do mean what they literally say but are still speaking sarcastically (Sperber & Wilson, 1981). For example, a driver can say to a passenger *I love people who signal* when another car has just cut in front without signaling and mean this sarcastically, even though the statement is literally true. Once again, it is incorrect to assume that irony violates some communicative maxim.

These criticisms of the traditional view of irony have led psycholinguists to examine whether understanding irony really requires some tacit recognition that these utterances violate conversational maxims. Research has shown that readers take no longer to interpret ironic, or specifically sarcastic, remarks, such as *He's a fine friend,* than they do to interpret the same sentences in literal contexts or to read nonsarcastic equivalent sentences, such as *He's a bad friend* (Gibbs, 1986b). Similar findings have been reported for understanding sarcastic indirect requests (e.g., *Why don't you take your time washing the dishes?,* meaning "Hurry up and wash the dishes") (Gibbs, 1986c). The data on understanding sarcastic indirect requests are particularly noteworthy, because these utterances are thought to violate conversational maxims in two ways. First, such utterances are sarcastic. Second, they are indirect requests. A traditional view of figurative language understanding would certainly predict that people should experience great difficulty comprehending sarcastic indirect requests. But this is evidently not the case. Understanding irony and sarcasm need not require any special mental processes.

ARE LITERAL AND FIGURATIVE LANGUAGE PROCESSING IDENTICAL?

There clearly exists a large body of experimental evidence against the idea that figurative language understanding requires special mental processes. People do not appear to experience great difficulty understanding what speakers mean by their use of figurative discourse. This refutation of the standard pragmatic model has prompted psychologists to make two related claims about figurative language comprehension (Gibbs & Gerrig, 1989).

1. Comprehension does not take place in three distinct stages. Figurative language interpretation does not follow after an obligatory literal misanalysis.
2. Identical mental processes drive the comprehension of both literal and figurative utterances.

The poetics of mind

Given the range of data reviewed above, claim (1) seems uncontroversial. The second claim, however, does not necessarily follow from the experimental results and warrants further attention. Equivalence of the time required for someone to process a literal or a metaphorical utterance gives no assurance that the *same mental processes* are involved in understanding each kind of expression. This claim is best illustrated in terms of a broader conception of comprehension (ibid.).

A widely held assumption in contemporary cognitive science is that listeners'/readers' recognition of speakers'/authors' intentions is a crucial aspect of utterance interpretation. Intention has taken on a central role for theories of meaning ever since Grice (1957) introduced his theory of "meaning$_{mn}$" ("non-natural meaning"). According to Grice, if a speaker *A* produces an utterance *x*, *A* meant$_{mn}$ something by *x*, which is equivalent to *A*'s intending the utterance of *x* to produce some effect in an audience by means of recognition of this intention. This view assumes that communication consists of the sender's intending to cause the receiver to think or do something just by getting the receiver to recognize that the sender is trying to cause that thought or action. Thus, *communication is a complex kind of intention that is achieved or satisfied just by being recognized* (Levinson, 1983: 16).

What is extraordinary in the psycholinguistic literature is that the difficulty participants have in recovering speakers' intended meanings – as measured by reading and paraphrase times – is relatively invariant across manipulations of pragmatic complexity. Overall, the weight of evidence suggests this (idealized) working hypothesis (Gibbs & Gerrig, 1989):

> The total time hypothesis: *There is a unique total time associated with the recovery of a speaker's meaning when an utterance is performed in an appropriate context.*

This hypothesis suggests that as long as the contexts are equally explicit the same utterance can be used in any one of a variety of pragmatic roles (e.g., literally, metaphorically, sarcastically, as an indirect request) without significantly affecting the manifest difficulty of processing.

However, there is a significant problem with the total-time hypothesis as it relates to the question of whether figurative language requires special processes to be understood (ibid.). Simple measures of the total time it takes people to comprehend figurative utterances may mask certain, perhaps "special," processes. Even though it seems clear that figurative language is not more difficult to understand than corresponding literal speech, the possibility remains that figurative language still requires special processes to be correctly understood.

Imagine that this is a partial list of the processes that make up ordinary language comprehension:

Recover literal meaning
Recover metaphorical meaning
Recover idiomatic meaning
Recover ironic meaning
Recover indirect meaning

We can, for the moment, suppose that each of these (and the rest of the processes in a complete list) requires a certain amount of time to operate in normal language understanding. Also assume that there is some other comprehension process, call it Process X, that always takes *more* time to complete than any of the other processes listed above. We might assume, somewhat arbitrarily, that Process X refers to any number of cognitive operations ranging from a process that updates the word frequency information in long-term memory to checking the grammaticality of an utterance, noting those that are exceptions to standard syntactic patterns. Finally, let's assume, as is actually maintained by many theorists, that all of the individual processes mentioned thus far, including Process X, run in parallel.

When a listener hears such an utterance as *Sure is nice and warm in here*, used as a sarcastic indirect request for someone to turn up the thermostat, the processing time needed to understand this utterance adheres to the total-time hypothesis. In other words, all processes, including X, *must* be complete before a "comprehension" response takes place. The problem, though, is that Process X could mask the operation of any number of special processes that operate in the recovery of what a speaker meant by his or her use of the utterance *Sure is nice and warm in here*. There is just no way to refute the possibility that some special comprehension process operates, including analysis of a sentence's literal meaning, simply on the basis of equivalent total times to read figurative and literal expressions (ibid.).

This argument demonstrates the logical impossibility of rejecting a special-process account of figurative language comprehension based on the equivalence of processing times for utterances. It is possible, however, to provide a parsimonious account of figurative language comprehension that does not rely on special processes. What is needed is a different "list" of processes that yields correct readings of both literal and figurative utterances.

Imagine a different list of the mental processes that might make up ordinary language comprehension:

Understand with respect to conceptual knowledge
Understand with respect to "common ground"

The immediate difference in this list is that the processes now specified relate to general problems in language understanding rather than to particular types of language, such as metaphor or irony. This also makes a speaker's intentions with respect to these two processes somewhat more opaque. But these processes provide some coherence to the claim that figurative language comprehension requires no special processing.

Proponents of equivalence in figurative language processing have often argued that a principle like "understand with respect to conceptual knowledge" is at work. They argue that conceptual knowledge, as encoded in schemas or other memory structures, is called into action in the comprehension of both literal and metaphorical utterances (Ortony et al., 1978; Rumelhart, 1979). Consider the sentence fragment *soiled wisps of cotton*. Readers readily interpret this fragment to mean "smoke" when it appears following a context phrase that evokes appropriate schemas, such as *The chimney belched forth soiled wisps of cotton* (Gerrig & Healey, 1983). Similarly, people view such idioms as *blow your stack* as more appropriate in contexts that evoke metaphorical schemas whereby anger is metaphorically understood as being like heated fluid in a container (Nayak & Gibbs, (1990). In general, contexts that provide access to appropriate conceptual information facilitate figurative language comprehension. These findings support the idea that a process like "understand with respect to conceptual knowledge," originally articulated for the comprehension of literal sentences, is at work in the comprehension of figurative expressions as well.

Appeals to conceptual knowledge, however, cannot explain all the details of figurative language understanding. More specific information is needed about what speakers and addressees mutually know and believe in particular discourse contexts. Consider a situation where Mary and David are talking about their friend Betty and Mary says *Betty is an elephant* (Gibbs & Gerrig, 1989). What might Mary mean? To the extent that *is an elephant* is a conventional metaphor, David would not consider the literal possibility that Mary believes Betty has become an elephant (Gibbs, 1984; Glucksberg et al., 1982). However, that inference alone provides little help in interpretation, because there are many respects in which Betty could be like an elephant: She might be clumsy on the dance floor; she might have an astonishing memory; she might be pregnant; she might have particularly leatherlike skin; and so on. If Mary is a cooperative conversationalist, she should make this assertion only when it will be clear to David what she has in mind. Nonetheless, these interpretations are still based on facts about elephants that might all be considered elements of world knowledge. Things get more interesting, however, when we consider a background of information – "common ground" (H. Clark & Carlson, 1981) – that Mary and David share about Betty.

Suppose, for example, that David and Mary share the practice of referring to their Democrat friends as donkeys and their Republican friends as elephants. In that case, Mary would be informing David that Betty is a Republican.

In a second scenario, David and Mary may share the piece of Marx Brothers' punning shtick in which *an elephant* is substituted for *irrelevant*. With this shared knowledge, David could say *Betty doesn't want to go* and Mary could respond *Betty is an elephant* to communicate "Betty is irrelevant."

A third possibility could even have David and Mary sharing some incorrect belief about elephants. Suppose they were both told that elephants are capable of consuming twice their body weight in food every day. To David's comment *Betty certainly has a hearty appetite*, Mary could respond, *Betty is an elephant*, implying that Betty is capable of consuming vast amounts of food.

To recover the correct interpretation of *Betty is an elephant* in any situation, David would have to avail himself of the process "Understand with respect to common ground." However, it is equally true that utterances that are nonmetaphorical need such disambiguation based on common-ground information. Consider another situation, where Mary says to David *The sky is blue*. This utterance seems to have a straightforward literal interpretation. Nonetheless, we can easily generate scenarios in which proper comprehension would require specific common-ground information.

Suppose Mary and David have an agreement in which Mary walks the dog on rainy days and David walks the dog on sunny days. By uttering *The sky is blue*, Mary would be communicating "It's your turn to walk the dog."

Suppose David is an avid kite flyer but has a great fear of being struck by lightning in the process. By uttering *The sky is blue*, Mary would be implicating "It's safe to fly your kite."

Suppose that David and Mary have in common the knowledge that their friend Betty plays golf on every sunny day. Mary's answer *The sky is blue* to David's question *Where do you suppose Betty is?* would imply "Betty is at the golf course."

In all three examples, utterance of *The sky is blue* prompts the listener to infer a further message that is recoverable only with reference to common ground. What is immediately evident in figurative language comprehension – the necessity for understanding with respect to common ground – is rampant in literal interpretation as well. This suggests that it is shortsighted to try to assimilate all of figurative language processing in the processes we have identified for literal utterances. Rather, we should try to identify processes that seem special to different types of figurative language and demonstrate that they play important roles for all types of language and therefore are not special after all.

THE PROCESSES AND PRODUCTS OF UNDERSTANDING

One of the prime motivations for maintaining a belief in literal meaning stems from the phenomenological experience that different kinds of meaning are recovered during the interpretation of figurative and of literal language. Speakers may be able to state the set of conditions under which "literal" sentences, such as *Snow is white*, are true or false, but this seems practically impossible to do for figurative expressions, such as *Marriage is like an icebox*, which may possess many potential meanings. It is the indeterminate nature of much figurative language that makes its meaning seem special and, by contrast, literal meanings so ordinary and primary.

Where does the intuition that figurative seems special and different from literal language arise from? One reason why many scholars believe that figurative language violates communicative norms is that they confuse the *processes* and *products* of linguistic understanding (Gibbs, 1990c, 1993a). Although people might on some occasions be able to identify figurative language as being distinct from literal language, this conscious judgment is based on a late *product* of linguistic interpretation and should not be taken as evidence regarding the early, unconscious psychological *processes* by which figurative language is ordinarily comprehended. Many defenders of literal meaning appeal to their phenomenological experience that figurative meaning somehow *feels* different as motivation for the idea that different cognitive mechanisms drive the comprehension of literal and figurative speech. What exactly characterizes the feeling of figurative meaning is still unclear. But this phenomenological awareness of figurative meaning refers to the late products of linguistic understanding, not to early and unconscious understanding processes.

Even a cursory examination of theories of linguistic interpretation reveals a tremendous diversity in the emphases on the different temporal points at which an utterance or text has supposedly been understood (Gibbs, in press-b). All language interpretation takes place in real time ranging from the first milliseconds of processing to long-term reflective analysis. This temporal continuum may roughly be divided into moments corresponding to linguistic comprehension, recognition, interpretation, and appreciation.

Comprehension refers to the immediate moment-by-moment process of creating meanings for utterances. These moment-by-moment processes are mostly unconscious and involve the analysis of various linguistic information (e.g., phonology, lexical access, syntax), which, in combination with context and real-world knowledge, allows listeners/readers to figure out what an utterance means or a speaker/author intends. For example, when reading the metaphor *My marriage is an icebox*, readers may very quickly, without any conscious reflection, come to understand that a speaker or writer means by this expression something like "My marriage lacks affection." This comprehension process is facilitated by contextual information or, more specifically, by the common-ground context that exists between speaker and listener, or author and reader, at any one moment. Contemporary psycholinguistic research suggests that comprehension processes operate within the time span of a few hundred milliseconds up to a few seconds at most.

Recognition refers to the conscious identification of the products of comprehension as types. For example, the meaning understood by a reader of a particular utterance may be consciously recognized as metaphorical. Even though many literary theorists and philosophers assume that recognition (e.g., that some utterance is metaphorical as opposed to literal) is a requirement for understanding what an utterance or text means, it is by no means clear that recognition is an obligatory stage in people's understanding of what utterances mean or of what speakers/authors intend. Listeners probably do not, for instance, have any awareness of conscious recognition that different utterances in conversation are ironic, idiomatic, hyperbolic, literal, and so on. Nor would they normally recognize each utterance as an exemplar of a particular illocutionary act (e.g., an assertive, directive, commissive, verdictive, and so on).

Interpretation refers to analysis of the early products of comprehension as tokens. One can consciously create an understanding of a particular type of text or utterance as having a particular content or meaning. Thus, hearing the phrase *My marriage is an icebox* might at some point result in a listener's understanding a particular set of entailments about the ways that marriages and iceboxes are similar. For example, iceboxes are cold in the same way that some marriages might be understood to be metaphorically cold. Iceboxes are small and confining in just the way that a marriage might metaphorically be seen as being confining to the people who are married. A rich set of entailments can be drawn from any metaphor. Some of these entailments may be specifically intended by the speaker or author of the metaphor. Other meanings might be unauthorized but still understood as being reasonable. Interpretation refers to the various late products of understanding that may or may not be intended by speakers/ authors. Some of these interpretive products may be quite elaborate, requiring lengthy conscious analysis to be determined. Interpretation processes operate later than comprehension processes and usually require conscious reflection about what a text or speaker means.

Finally, *appreciation* refers to some aesthetic judgment given to a product as either a type or a token. This, too, is not an obligatory part of understanding linguistic meaning, because listeners/readers can easily comprehend utterances or texts without automatically making an aesthetic judgment about what has been understood. For instance, a reader might especially appreciate the aptness or aesthetic value of such an expression as *My marriage is an icebox*. When people appreciate some instance of figurative language, they are reflecting on some meaning as a product. Psychological evidence shows that comprehension and appreciation refer to distinct types of mental process (Gerrig & Healey, 1983).

In general, figurative language understanding, like literal language understanding, begins in the first moments with comprehension processes and proceeds in time to the later moments of recognition, interpretation, and appreciation. Much of what takes place when figurative language is normally understood in everyday speech, and even during the understanding of some literary texts, does not demand cognitive effort beyond comprehension. In other words, readers may comprehend the meanings of tropes without recognizing that each utterance is metaphorical, ironic, or idiomatic and so on. Readers may also correctly interpret a literary trope without necessarily attaching any particular aesthetic value (appreciation) to it. Whatever set of mental activities operates during the understanding of a specific literary trope, it is clear that each part of the temporal continuum of figurative language understanding demands a unique theoretical explanation.

Figurative language theorists too often make the mistake of assuming that a theory constructed to explain one temporal moment of figurative language understanding can be generalized to account for *all* aspects of understanding. The time course of linguistic understanding requires different kinds of theory at different moments. A theory of the early *process* of figurative language comprehension does not necessarily lead to a theory of the late *products* of trope interpretation (Gerrig, 1989b; Gibbs, 1990b). The experimental evidence indicates that from the earliest temporal moments of processing, figurative language comprehension does not differ in kind from understanding literal language. From this vantage point, there is no need to postulate any special cognitive mechanism to handle understanding of metaphor, irony, and so forth. Figurative language can be understood effortlessly, without conscious reflection. However, the lack of difference in the moment-by-moment processing of figurative and of literal language should not automatically be taken as evidence against the legitimacy of some figurative meanings, such as those found in poetry, as special *products*.

In the same way, the theoretical focus on the late *products* of trope interpretation does not necessarily prove anything about the fundamental nature of early comprehension *processes*. The conscious recognition of, say, a metaphor, or that a metaphor has multiple readings through the free play of signifiers, occurs at a later point than does immediate comprehension and requires a different kind of theory to account for such a psychological and/or literary judgment. The results of the extensive empirical investigations reviewed in this chapter do *not* support many of the hypotheses suggested by linguists, philosophers, and literary theorists who specifically contend that figurative language is special and always demands extra work to be interpreted. Instead, the psycholinguistic research indicates that people can understand many instances of figurative expression effortlessly, without the explicit recognition that such language is special or reflective of deviant thought.

CONCLUSION

My claim that figurative language understanding does not require special mental processes still leaves many important questions unanswered. Exactly how does common ground (the shared beliefs and knowledge held by speakers and listeners in context) constrain figurative language interpretation? How does people's ordinary conceptual knowledge, including their knowledge of figurative concepts, influence understanding of both figurative and conventional discourse? The chapters that follow describe some of the important empirical work that bears on this latter question. Finally, how do common-ground and conceptual knowledge interact during figurative language interpretation? One of the challenges facing figurative language scholars is to determine how common-ground and figurative thought constrain figurative language understanding while, on some occasions, allowing special (poetic or literary) products to emerge as part of what we have understood when we hear or read figurative discourse.

Chapter 4

Metaphor in language and thought

It would not surprise many people to learn that much of what is said in everyday conversation has metaphorical roots. Ask people about some aspect of their lives, and metaphor will inevitably burst forth, sometimes dominating the narrative. Consider how Harry, a factory worker in a midwestern town, describes his view of life (Norton, 1989: 35–36).

> Couldn't say it was a merry-go-round. 'Cause the ends never meet. I don't know. Life is like a straight line. It never ends. Until you're dead. You know? The ends never meet, obstacles that you're going to find. You got to. 'Cause if you don't, you're gonna be down. I mean you're gonna stop dead. You're gonna die. And you're gonna be nothin'. You just gotta keep goin'. You can't let things bother you. You gotta try and put it out of our mind . . . Well to me, you gotta keep forward. You don't wanna make no turns, 'cause if you make a turn you're gonna be off course. And you're not gonna go any further. So you just stay on a straight line. Sure, you're gonna run into some obstacles. But it's just temporary. There's gonna be some obstacles but you gotta jump back on track.

Harry's narrative is an extended analysis of his understanding of life as a journey that travels in a straight line. He starts out by saying that it is not a merry-go-round, an image with no beginning and end, where the ends meet to form a circle. A straight line seems more serious, something that goes forward encountering difficulties or obstacles that are hard to overcome.

Consider now a different view of life as a journey, this time told by Father Dave, a Catholic priest (ibid., p. 106).

> I would describe life in terms of a journey. But we're walking through it. Sometimes we see clearly, and other times it's dark and hidden. And you can still walk and think through it. And walking through it, in walking through a darkness, you come to a fuller understanding. A sense of it. And sometimes tripping and falling. And yet still "come follow me" is what you have to remember. Get up again and continue on the journey.

Father Dave's life journey is motivated by his wish to follow in Christ's footsteps. He sees his experience as a priest as a continuous journey in which he walks "with Him through life." Father Dave also views his work with his parishioners as being like a gardener tending to his plants (ibid., p 107).

> A gardener has a small plot of land and looks after the different needs of the plants. He tries to provide nourishment all year round. He takes an interest in the growth of the different plants. Also, the gardener realizes it's not up to him. He can't provide the sunshine. So a lot of things are beyond the gardener's work. It's also cooperating.

These examples are not extraordinary and represent only a small sample of the hundreds, perhaps thousands, of ways that people use metaphor in talking about their life experiences. Why do people use metaphor so often in talking about their lives? The mere asking of the question "Why metaphor?" implies to many scholars that figurative speech is unusual, perhaps ornamental, whereas literal language is basic and better suited to talking about our experience and the objective world. The fact that figurative language pervades everyday speech simply reflects its usefulness in conveying ideas and knowledge that are really structured in our conceptual system in literal, propositional terms. This view of metaphoric discourse as deviant, ornamental language suggests that nonliteral expressions should be relatively rare in comparison to more normal, literal language. One might argue, following Aristotle, that metaphor requires a special talent or genius and should be alien to most ordinary speakers.

Despite the pervasiveness of this view of metaphor, there are good reasons to question its validity, given the ubiquity of metaphor in both language and thought. Ever since Aristotle wrote that *the greatest thing by far is to be master of metaphor* (*Poetics*, 1450), scholars have studied the many uses of metaphor, primarily in terms of its distinctive rhetorical functions. In the past few decades, many scholars have argued that metaphor is not simply a form of speech but more fundamental: a form of thought with its own epistemological functions. Metaphors and other tropes not only serve as the foundation for much everyday thinking and reasoning, they also continue scholarly theory and practice in a variety of disciplines, as well as providing much of the foundation for our understanding of culture.

This chapter presents a select overview of the evidence on the role of metaphor in language and thought. My discussion of the ubiquity of metaphor is not intended to suggest that all parts of language and thought are metaphorical. There are clearly many aspects of how we think and use language that are not constrained or motivated by metaphor. Yet the empirical work in cognitive science strongly indicates that many facets of everyday thought and language are indeed metaphorical, enough so that we should recognize metaphor as a primary mode of thought. Most of the discussion that follows centers on metaphor's role in (a) constituting ordinary concepts, (b) motivating semantic change, (c) motivating the meanings that linguistic expressions have in contemporary linguistic communities, and (d) influencing how people make sense of why various words and expressions mean what they do. Later chapters focus on metaphor's role in the on-line use and understanding of linguistic meaning. It is, again, important to distinguish among these different issues, because metaphor might influence certain aspects of everyday thought and language understanding but not others.

METAPHOR IN LANGUAGE

THE UBIQUITY OF METAPHOR

Just how frequently do people use metaphor in everyday speech? Many scholars have commented on the ubiquity of metaphor in literature, poetry, and even scientific writing, but only recently have they attempted to make some rough approximation of the frequency with which speakers and writers employ metaphorical language. One historical analysis of the metaphors used in American English prose from 1675 to 1975 revealed significant metaphoric activity in each of the six 50-year periods considered (M. Smith, Pollio, & Pitts, 1981). The most general area dealt with metaphorically by American authors over the past 300 years concerns issues related to the psychological nature of being human. Many human topics, such as rationality, emotions, and the meaning of life and death, were primarily discussed in metaphorical terms. Although different ideas or concepts were used to make these issues metaphorical in different time periods, it is clear that metaphor has been in widespread use during the past 300 years.

Other empirical studies have assessed the frequency of metaphor in specific contexts. One early study examined the metaphoric language found in transcripts of psychotherapeutic interviews, various essays, and the 1960 Kennedy–Nixon presidential debates (H. Pollio, Barlow, Fine & Pollio, 1977). This analysis counted only phrases that were sufficiently nonliteral to be recognized as such and distinguished between frozen and novel metaphors. Frozen metaphors were those that appeared to be about literal uses of language through continued use (e.g., the *leg* of a table, *face* of a clock); novel metaphors constituted nonliteral expressions that were created spontaneously (e.g., *Daddy has a hole in his hair*).

This simple frequency count revealed that people used 1.80 novel and 4.08 frozen metaphors per minute of discourse. If one assumes that people engage in conversation for as little as 2 hours per day, a person would utter 4.7 million novel and 21.4 million frozen metaphors over a 60-year life span (Glucksberg, 1989). These conservative estimates clearly suggest that metaphoric language is prominent in many kinds of discourse and plays a significant role in an individual speaker's behavior over a lifetime. Another analysis of the metaphors produced in television debates and news commentary programs (e.g., the MacNeil/Lehrer news program) showed that speakers use one unique metaphor for every 25 words (Graesser, Mio, & Millis, 1989). Finally, novel metaphors were used about every 2 to 3 min of discourse by U.S. senators during the debate in January 1991 on the use of military force in the Persian Gulf (Voss, Kennet, Wiley, & Engstler-Schooler, 1992). While admittedly crude, these analyses clearly demonstrate that metaphor is not the special privilege of a few gifted speakers but is ubiquitous in both written and spoken discourse.

These crude empirical attempts to count instances of metaphor vastly underestimate the true metaphorical nature of everyday speech. Such frequency counts do not include analysis of literal speech that is motivated by metaphorical thought. For example, an expression such as *Our marriage is on the rocks* seems to be quite literal, yet it reflects a metaphorical conceptualization of love whereby we partly structure one domain of experience, love, in terms of another, journeys. This metaphorical mapping gives rise to various information that is made manifest in everyday speech in expressions such as *Our marriage is on the rocks* and *Our marriage is at an impasse*. Chapter 2 described some reasons why much of what is ordinarily thought of as literal speech is motivated by conceptual metaphor. So it is fair to claim that metaphor is far more ubiquitous in everyday speech than has been shown in empirical research.

THE COMMUNICATIVE FUNCTIONS OF METAPHOR

Why do people speak metaphorically? Scholars traditionally focus on three grounds for using metaphor (Fainsilber & Ortony, 1989; Ortony, 1975). First, metaphors provide a way of expressing ideas that would be extremely difficult to convey using literal language (the *inexpressibility hypothesis*). Consider the metaphorical expression *The thought slipped my mind like a squirrel behind a tree*. It is difficult in literal terms to predicate of thoughts characteristics such as swiftness, suddenness, or ungraspability. We might try to translate the metaphorical sentence into literal language, but we still end up with language that is essentially metaphorical (e.g., *The thought went away* and *The thought evaded me*). The inexpressibility hypothesis states that metaphors enable people to express ideas that simply cannot be easily or clearly expressed with literal speech.

A second function of metaphor is to provide a particularly compact means of communication (the *compactness hypothesis*). Language can only partition the continuity of our conscious experience into discrete units comprising words and phrases that have a relatively narrow referential range. Thus, for example, *The apple is red* conveys only a single piece of information about a specific apple. Metaphors allow people to communicate complex configurations of information that better capture the rich, continuous nature of experience than does literal discourse alone. For instance, the assertion *My love is like a blossoming bouquet of roses* expresses a large amount of information about love (i.e., that it is sweet, delicate, beautiful, perhaps short in its life span, etc.) using relatively few words. Literal language simply does not enable speakers/ writers to convey a great deal of information succinctly in the same way that metaphor does. One of the greatest challenges to educators lies in selecting metaphors that provide succinct and informative descriptions of a topic (Petrie, 1979).

Finally, metaphors may help capture the vividness of our phenomenological experience (the *vividness hypothesis*). Because metaphors convey complex configurations of information rather than discrete units, speakers can convey richer, more detailed, more vivid images of our subjective experience than can be expressed by literal language. These images seem to embellish what is communicated to listeners, providing them with nuances that may be part of the speaker's subjective experience. Thus, *My love is like a blooming bouquet of roses* is likely to evoke various mental images in the listener that reflect the speaker's vivid communicative intentions about the concept of love and his or her experience of love.

Various empirical evidence from psychology has borne out the claims of the expressibility, compactness, and vividness hypotheses. One domain in which the utility of metaphor has been explicitly examined is the verbal expression of emotion. Researchers have noted the high incidence of figurative language when speakers talked about their emotions (Davitz,

1969; Davitz & Mattis, 1964). One study investigated when people use metaphor to talk about their emotional experiences (Fainsilber & Ortony, 1987). Participants were asked to give verbal descriptions of specific emotional states they had experienced and of activities in which they had engaged as a result of these remembered emotional states (i.e., happiness, pride, gratitude, sadness, fear, and shame). The inexpressibility hypothesis predicted that people would be more likely to use metaphor and metaphorical comparisons in descriptions of how they felt when they were expressing an emotion than when describing what they did when they experienced it. Moreover, the vividness hypothesis suggested that metaphorical language would be more prevalent in descriptions of intense as compared with mild emotional states.

This study showed that people's descriptions of their emotional states contained more metaphorical language than did descriptions of their behavior. For instance, people described their negative emotional states with remarks like *It was like someone had just dropped a bomb on me* and positive emotions with statements like *It was like a very bright light was just shining outward*. Metaphor seemed especially useful to participants in expressing what was normally difficult to talk about using literal language. More intense emotions were described using metaphor much more than in descriptions of milder emotions. However, people did not use metaphor any more often to describe intense emotion than they did milder emotion when simply talking about activities that resulted from experiencing a particular emotional state. These findings supported the vividness hypothesis, in that metaphor seemed to be particularly apt in describing intense emotions. Additional experimental evidence demonstrated that creative writers employ metaphor quite frequently when asked to describe their own feelings and actions (Williams-Whitney, Mio, & Whitney, 1992). Most generally, metaphor is not simply used as a linguistic ornament but serves an indispensable communicative function.

The role that metaphor plays in the verbal description of emotion and other psychological states has been widely debated by psychotherapists and psychoanalysts. Some psychoanalysts are not enthusiastic about figurative language, fearing that the use of metaphor may function to mask unacceptable urges (Schafer, 1976; Sharpe, 1940). According to this view, the metaphoric use of ordinary vocabulary items hides the unacceptable impulse in respectability and thereby allows the indulged motivational source to go undetected and unexamined. By clever use of ordinary language, a patient may keep his or her therapist from the real problem area of psychic disturbance. Only through careful analysis of what is learned from asking the patient why he or she employed such language can a therapist unmask what is being hidden. Metaphors are seen here as "pathological," "archaic," and "regressive" (Aleksandrowicz, 1962). Therapists are warned to resist being captured by the "magic" of metaphor, since such language is "addictive." Psychotherapists also fear that the use of figurative expressions may mislead the speaker or listener by a false analogy. So metaphor may not only mask the difficulty, it can also lead the analyst away from a proper evaluation. Furthermore, many psychoanalysts try not to introduce their own metaphors, since, following Freud's belief, they should not burden the patient with their own associations (Arlow, 1979).

These negative appraisals of metaphor in psychoanalysis and psychotherapy do not override the possibility that such language is frequently used in therapy (McMullen, 1989; Siegelman, 1990). There is some evidence that more successful cases of therapy include verbal elaboration of major therapy themes via bursts of metaphor over time. Communication between client and therapist can be facilitated by giving clients metaphors that parallel or match their psychological condition. Some psychotherapists even advocate asking patients to write poetry using certain metaphorical themes as a way of exploring their emotional experiences (Leedy, 1969). The idea that poetry and all figurative language can function as a teaching/learning heuristic in psychotherapy has also been developed by those who argue that interpretation of the patient's metaphor provides an effective way of dealing with a personally dangerous idea in a playful and somewhat disguised form (Caruth & Ekstein, 1966). This method has been used with borderline schizophrenic patients, where it has been found that if the relations expressed in a metaphor are interpreted by the therapist in the context of the metaphor itself, they are likely to be less threatening to the patient than if interpreted directly, and thereby engender communication (Ekstein, 1966; Reider, 1972). One writer comments that the most effective metaphors introduced by the therapist are those that are used infrequently, so as to have "surprise value"; are calibrated to the degree of directness a patient can tolerate; are synoptic, embracing both impulse and defense; and, finally, are synchronic in bringing together past and present (Siegelman, 1990).

Another program looked at the psychotherapeutic potential of enacting movement metaphors (V. Dascal, 1990, 1992). The movement metaphor technique explores our frequent use of bodily movement as a metaphorical way of describing, and sometimes acting out, sensations, emotional states, cognitive states, motivations, and interpersonal relationships. Verbal metaphors are either elicited from patients (e.g., *I feel I am on a tightrope* or *I threw upon him everything*) or presented to the patient by the therapist. Upon the therapist's request, the patient is asked to perform the movement (e.g., to walk on an imaginary tightrope) or to engage in some activity that reflects the patient's verbal metaphor. For instance, a therapist asked a patient to inflate a rubber balloon in different manners. This bodily exercise elicited a number of observations from patients about themselves and their relationships with others. In one case, a patient later wrote in her diary about the issue of control through a twist of the metaphorical/associative value of the balloon activity that connects it with a different conceptual structure. As the patient remarked:

> I enjoy writing, giving expression as to what fills me and changes in me. Like the balloon – no matter how much air I blow and the air becomes imprisoned in some place – still there will be air for further blowings, and the balloon will fly, and the air will escape from it, and a new balloon with be filled . . . (V. Dascal, 1992: 155)

By focusing on the actual performance of the bodily movement metaphorically underlying one's verbal description of

an experience, one is in fact directly confronted with the experiential basis of that metaphor. Movement metaphors provide a handle for the patient to articulate the beginnings of a
new attitude and awareness that mark significant personal
change. Of course, metaphor, like any kind of language or
any single-minded approach to psychotherapy, has its limitations. Yet the examination of metaphors that reflect emotional
experiences and are constitutive of the way we live our lives
is clearly of great value in psychotherapy.

Regardless of one's views about the utility of metaphors for
expressing psychological states (Rosen, 1977; Schafer, 1976),
metaphoric ways of speaking about psychological states have
grown beyond psychotherapeutic situations to infiltrate everyday speech. Images of game playing and parent–child relationships, for example, have replaced some of Freud's earlier psychological metaphors. People are described as *uptight,
up front, laid back, with it, behind it, out of it,* or *ego tripping.*
Many people use the new language of consciousness, sometimes dubbed *psychobabble,* in their everyday speech. We hear
about things like *freaking out, head trips, being in the right space,
being on a bummer, crashing, being stoned,* and so on (Gerrig &
Gibbs, 1988). Not very long ago it would have been impossible to talk about such things without elaborate circumlocu-
tions (Kukla, 1980). Although these represent different classes
of metaphor, there is an unchanging process of talking about
abstract psychological states in terms of concrete, physical situations. The ubiquity of this talk supports the hypothesis that
metaphor is often used to talk about ideas and experiences
that would otherwise be inexpressible.

The belief that metaphor is not only useful but necessary
for describing various ideas has sparked much debate in educational circles. Some educational theorists adopt the position
that metaphor should be avoided in educational material and
should only be used when an author is unable to be explicit or
precise about the information to be conveyed (R. Miller, 1976).
These scholars argue that metaphors are stylistic devices that
tend to hide the real meaning of a message, an idea that has
its roots in the writings of Aristotle. They claim that even
though literal language is unable to name certain things, this

does not necessarily mean that a metaphor can do so. R. Miller (1976) suggested that it is precisely because metaphor goes further than literal meaning that it becomes vague. If metaphors are used to express the inexpressible, they do so at the expense of clarity.

However, the use of metaphor does not lead to loss of precision and clarity, because many metaphors do not allow for a literal paraphrase. In such cases, there is no loss, for either a metaphor is used or nothing at all is said (Ortony, 1976). In other cases, it is conceivable that when a metaphor is used, the loss is not of clarity and precision but of prolixity and incompleteness (ibid.). Even though metaphors can certainly mislead, this does not mean that figurative language should be replaced by literal language, for literal speech can also be used to convey untruths. *One cannot blame language, literal or figurative, for the misdeeds of those charlatans who abuse it!* (ibid., p. 398).

Educators and psychologists have long been interested in understanding the role of metaphor in learning and remembering textual material. Does the introduction of metaphor make it easier to learn and recall text information than when the same passage is presented without metaphor? One analysis of fourth- and fifth-grade social science texts indicated that these texts contained on average about four metaphors per thousand words of text (Ortony, 1976). This superficial analysis revealed that, at the very least, textbook authors used metaphor to achieve a variety of pedagogical goals (e.g., summary, processing of new information, emphasis, advance organization). Various scholars have suggested that analogies used as advance organizers could enhance the quality and quantity of what is learned and recalled from subsequent material (Mayer, 1980). For example, introducing a text on electrical current by having students read a passage about water flowing through pipes might very well provide a conceptual framework for students to learn basic information about electricity.

Despite the enthusiasm for metaphor on the part of some educators, early research indicated that metaphor may have had only a limited effect on comprehension of prose material. Although the metaphors themselves may have been recalled better than their literal equivalents, comprehension of incidental material in the text seemed to be unaffected (Pearson, Raphael, TePaske, & Hyser, 1981). More recent evidence has shown that metaphors facilitate prose comprehension. In one study, participants read short didactic prose passages that were written using either context-dependent metaphor sentences or literally equivalent paraphrases as concluding statements (Reynolds & Schwartz, 1983). An example of the experimental stimuli is presented below.

> The people of Nazi Germany were swayed by Hitler's rhetoric. Although he had committed his people to a course of war, he found it easy to persuade them of the virtue of his actions. Everyone in Europe at the time was aware of the consequences of war, but the Germans had a blind belief in Hitler.
>
> The sheep followed the leader over the cliff. (*Metaphorical target*)
> The German people blindly accepted Hitler's dangerous ideas.
>   (*Literal target*)

After reading stories like these, ending in either metaphorical or literal targets, the participants were asked to write down all the stories they read. An analysis of the participants' recall protocols indicated that people were superior at remembering passages when the concluding statement was expressed metaphorically rather than in literal language. Not only were the concluding metaphors themselves remembered better than the literal paraphrases, but there was also an increase in recall of the preceding context. Thus, metaphor can enhance learning from prose materials. One can, of course, increase the number of metaphors present in a passage to the point of making the text incomprehensible. However, the presence of some easily interpretable metaphors may facilitate people's learning of text material.

A variety of other studies examined the utility of metaphor in learning computers and computer programming. Some research found that novice programmers learned concepts like input, output, and program more quickly and effectively when they were first introduced with concrete metaphors, such as a ticket window, a pad of paper, and a shopping list (Mayer,

1975, 1978). Other anecdotal evidence suggested that novices found it easier to overcome problems learning to use a text editor by using a variety of metaphors. For instance, the "editor is a secretary" metaphor helped familiarize novices with the basic idea of mixing commands and text, but it also led them to other errors, such as failing to signal the end of a text insertion before issuing a command (Rumelhart & Norman, 1981). The metaphor "the editor is a tape recorder" overcame this difficulty, as it forced people to realize that once you have started recording you must stop before doing anything else. Finally, students found it easier to learn abbreviated commands for a computer command language when given metaphorical instructions than when presented with rule-based instructions (Payne, 1988).

These studies show that verbal metaphors can facilitate people's learning of textual materials. Such data are consistent with the compactness and vividness hypotheses of metaphor. But do people remember verbal metaphors better than they do literal speech? Our intuition that figurative language seems special leads to a related feeling that metaphor is, or should be, especially memorable. Our reading of Shakespeare's line *The wind sits in the shoulder of your sail* suggests that there is something quite distinctive about this expression precisely because of its metaphorical character. Literary scholars often suggest that one reason why metaphorical language is so prominent in literature is that metaphors yield vivid images (Ricoeur, 1978). Both the evocation of vivid images and the extra difficulty thought to be associated with understanding figurative language might make these utterances memorable, particularly when compared with more standard literal language.

The vast experimental research on people's memory for figurative language paints a mixed picture regarding the vividness hypothesis. Early work on memory of isolated metaphors found no difference in individuals' memory of novel metaphors (e.g., *The maple tree branches flirted with the telephone wires*), dead metaphors (*The maple tree branches nudged the telephone wires*), and nonmetaphors (*The maple tree branches touched the telephone wires*) that attempted to express the same abstract idea (R. Harris, 1979a). Later studies showed that archaic literary metaphors (e.g., quotations from Shakespeare, such as *Your bait of falsehood takes this carp of truth*, from *Richard III*) were better recognized on a subsequent recognition test than were semantically similar but nonmetaphorical targets (e.g., *Your offering of falsehood takes this gift of truth*) (R. Harris, 1979b). These findings contradict the naive hypothesis that literary metaphors should be more difficult to understand and remember because they are exotic, esoteric forms of language. At the same time, the results provide some support for the vividness hypothesis.

One reason why metaphors might be memorable is that these expressions furnish conceptually rich, image-evoking conceptualizations. Metaphor vehicles (the second terms in metaphoric comparison statements) should facilitate memory to the extent that they evoke vivid mental images (Paivio, 1979). Consider the metaphor *The wind tickled the wheat*. This expression often conjures up the image of a human-type figure floating in the wind, lightly touching a sprout of wheat. One question that is central to a theory of metaphor interpretation is whether the occurrence of imagery with metaphor is simply epiphenomenal to its comprehension or a key element in understanding its figurative meaning. Most metaphor theorists agree that imagery provides a means by which two previously dissimilar domains can be incorporated into one concept, because the task of comprehending metaphor presumably involves fusing two such domains (Verbrugge, 1977).

Earlier research in cognitive psychology demonstrated a strong positive relationship between imagery and memory (Paivio, 1971). Several experiments that specifically addressed the relationship between metaphor and imagery showed that even though imagery was reported to be used more frequently in encoding metaphorical than nonmetaphorical sentences, imagery may not be very effective as a mnemonic device (R. Harris, Lahey, & Marsalek, 1980). Nor did specific instructions to form mental images for proverbs increase people's memory for these figurative expressions (Reichmann, 1975). More recent research demonstrated that the imagery values of the different terms in metaphorical expressions were an excellent predictor of metaphor recall (Marschark & Hunt, 1985; McCabe, 1988). It is important to note, though, that these studies explicitly instructed participants to form mental images for metaphors. It is not at all clear that people normally form images during metaphor comprehension. Therefore, it is difficult to conclude that imaging is any more relevant to metaphor comprehension than to other mental processes.

The various empirical studies on the communicative function of metaphor suggest a couple of possibilities about the positive influence of metaphor on learning. First, metaphor may provide some mnemonic function, enriching the encoding and thus facilitating subsequent recall of information. Furthermore, metaphor can activate appropriate semantic frameworks from long-term memory, allowing the new knowledge to be assimilated into existing mental schemas. Metaphor can act as a prompt to active hypothesis-driven learning because of the intrinsic incongruity and incompleteness of metaphorical expressions, dissimilarities that stimulate experimentation on the learner's part (Apter, 1982; Petrie, 1979).

My discussion of the communicative functions of metaphor suggests that metaphor is indispensable in both everyday conversation and educational instruction. People do not really have a choice about metaphor, in that such language is necessary to communicate in a vivid, compact manner ideas that might otherwise be inexpressible.

SOCIAL FUNCTIONS OF FIGURATIVE LANGUAGE

Beyond the value of metaphor for communicating information or ideas, speakers use metaphors for specific social purposes. Metaphorical talk often presupposes and reinforces intimacy between speaker and listener (L. Cohen, 1979). Intimacy can be enjoyed by all those who are confident that what they say will be understood. It is the bond between those who share not only a basic linguistic competence but a common stock of experiences, interests, and sensibilities and the ability to call upon that information when interpreting language. Many figurative uses of language are inaccessible to all but those speakers and listeners who share specific information about one another's knowledge, beliefs, and attitudes, or their *common ground* (H. Clark & Carlson, 1981; H. Clark & Marshall, 1981).

Consider the following brief conversational exchange, which was discussed in Chapter 3.

David: Does Gladys have a good memory?
Mary: Gladys is just like an elephant.

Why does Mary respond to David's question with a metaphorical assertion and not a simple literal statement? We assume that Mary wants David to use his encyclopedic knowledge of elephants, including, let's suppose, the piece of folklore that elephants have excellent memories. With this information, David could infer "Gladys has a very good memory." Although Mary expects David to recover the implicature "Gladys has a very good memory" and all the implications from it that Mary might be interested in (i.e., ones regarding Gladys' phenomenal powers of memory), it would be unusual if this implicature is *all* Mary expected David to infer. After all, Mary could have stated explicitly *Gladys has a very good memory* in response to David's question. But Mary may want to cultivate some degree of intimacy between herself and David by her use of a metaphorical description of Gladys' memory. Suppose that Gladys really is quite large and could under other circumstances be described as being as large as an elephant. If this belief were part of David and Mary's common ground, then responding to David's question by saying *Gladys is just like an elephant* would be ironic, in that Mary specifically intends David to infer both "Gladys has a very good memory" and "Gladys is quite large" (but not the unauthorized inference "Gladys has a large nose"). It is not unreasonable to assume that Mary could intend David to draw these inferences. If David failed to recover Mary's intention to achieve mutuality, a sense of intimacy or complicity, then it would be incorrect to assume that David fully understands the meanings of the metaphor.

Figuring out speakers' attitudes and beliefs is a key aspect of metaphor understanding. It is the recovery of these nonpropositional affective and sometimes poetic effects that makes figurative language seem so different from so-called literal speech. Such meanings are perhaps best considered to be social rather than formal and propositional. Yet it is the exploitation of the context of shared beliefs held by speakers and listeners that makes the use of many types of figurative language appear to be a special psychological activity (Gibbs & Gerrig, 1989).

A related social function of metaphoric language is to inform others about one's own attitudes and beliefs in indirect ways. Speakers do not always want to make explicit what they think and so say things in such a way that listeners must infer their true beliefs (P. Brown & Levinson, 1987). Such "off-the-record" speech acts include many instances of metaphor (e.g., *Harry is a real fish*, meaning "Harry is cold-blooded or slimy like a fish"). These metaphors provide speakers with the ability to deny that what their words say literally is meant. Nonetheless, speakers mostly assume that metaphors will be understood by listeners in the way they are intended because of the common ground between themselves and their listeners.

Many instances of metaphor function beyond their conventional content to signal intimacy, formality, or hostility or to indicate membership in a particular subgroup (Nunberg, 1979). Speakers may use *booze* to refer to liquor when they want to signal an informal rapport with listeners, or they can use *spirits* to acknowledge that they are in a formal setting. Slang is one of the most important mechanisms for showing certain kinds of social awareness. Although *grass, pot, tea, weed, dope,* and *herb* all metaphorically refer to marijuana, they are not entirely equivalent. Each has its special features and differs along evaluative and affective dimensions. A college student can use *weed* in an ironic sense to show that he or she does not believe smoking marijuana to be harmful. Similarly, *tea* is regarded as outmoded and is often used to frustrate communication, since it creates the possibility of confusion with the beverage. Listeners will often recognize the interests and attitudes of a speaker from his or her choice of figurative speech.

One of the ways that speakers signal their membership in a particular subgroup is to use proverbs and slang. People resort to proverbs when they wish to avoid personal commitment and refutation (Arewa & Dundes, 1964; Barley, 1972; A. Taylor, 1962). Proverbs are especially useful in double-bind situations, when individuals are called upon for a judgment that might hurt another person's feelings. For example, I once heard someone console a friend of mine, whose teenage children had thrown a party for their friends while the parents were on vacation and a family heirloom was broken, by saying that she should have known *When the cat's away, the mice will play*. By invoking tradition and the community as a whole, the speaker not only diminishes as an individual agent but also imposes the weight of social sanctions (in this case telling my friend that she should have expected her teenage children to do something reckless when left alone).

Slang metaphors provide speakers with an outlet for the release or avoidance of unpleasant emotions. One study of hospital slang offers numerous examples (Gordon, 1983). For example, hospital staff may refer to an obese patient as *a beached whale*, and a totally unresponsive or comatose patient is a *gork*. Unclogging a severely constipated person with the fingers is *apple bobbing*, and a patient with third-degree burns on the buttocks has *Betty Crocker syndrome*. Laypersons often view such terms as illustrating a disturbing attitude of callousness and unconcern for the patient on the part of nurses and doctors. But hospital workers may cope better with the horror of severely injured or diseased patients by creating novel expressions that distance them from their emotional reactions to these patients' troubles.

Most of the slang terms for patients refer not to individuals with legitimate medical problems but to people who claim more attention for their condition than is warranted (ibid.). *Crocks* are malingerers who lie about conditions they do not have, hypochondriacs who believe they have conditions they do not, and complainers (or *screamers*) who make more fuss than is justified by their illnesses. *Gomers*, a term that possibly derives from the Scottish *gomeral*, meaning "fool" or "simpleton," refers to patients who are members of groups already negatively stigmatized by society at large, such as derelicts, alcoholics, the mentally disturbed, and the obese (George & Dundes, 1978). These people suffer from various ailments, in many cases through no fault of their own. But society generally holds such people responsible for their own condition, and this is reflected in the attitudes of medical staff. In general, the principal reason medical workers use this slang is to express frustration and irritation at having to provide care when it is not felt to be needed or useful. Frustration over giving care to patients who do not need it implies concern for other patients, not dehumanization, and a wish to care for the most needy. In this way, slang helps establish rapport through a sense of group solidarity in having to deal with patients who are not all that ill.

Speakers will also create and use metaphor to manipulate their social status within a group. American college students create and employ thousands of unique terms to talk about all aspects of college life. To take a most notable set of examples, consider all of these expressions that college students use to refer to having sexual intercourse (P. Munro, 1989):

> to do the deadly deed
> to lay pipe
> to beat someone with an ugly stick
> to get some trim
> to do the nasty
> to play hide the salami
> to jump someone's bones
> to ride the hobby horse
> to give a hot beef injection
> to throw the dagger
> to do the bone dance
> to do the wild thing
> to bump fuzz

These phrases exhibit various metaphorical comparisons. To know these phrases and when best to use them marks a college student as a member in good standing of the "in" crowd. Only *nerds*, *geeks*, *dweebs*, *newts*, and *doughheads* are ignorant of these colloquial expressions.

Another use of metaphor that marks social status is the system of ritual insults used in the Black English vernacular known as *sounding* or *playing the dozens* (Abrahams, 1962;

Kockman, 1983; Labov, 1972). The ability to use the right insult is a way of demonstrating group membership. The winner in insult contests is the person with the largest store of couplets, the best memory, and perhaps the best delivery. Metaphor or simile is often found in these ritualized insults as a part of complex puns. Two examples from South Philadelphia (from Abrahams, 1962) are:

> At least my mother ain't no railroad track, laid all over the country.

> Your mother's like a police station – dicks going in and out all the time.

A prime motivation for the creation of these ritualized insults is enhancement of the speaker's status. People who can use language in new, often metaphoric, ways raise their social status in a particular language community (Goffman, 1971). By social convention, the insults do not denote attributes that real individuals actually possess. The various rules for sounding have the effect of preserving the ritual status of the game, and the symbolic distance between the participants and the language serves to insulate the exchange from further, possibly negative, consequences (Labov, 1972).

A final example of metaphor's role in the manipulation of social status in a community is seen in the competitive oral verses performed by North Yemeni tribesmen (Caton, 1985, 1990). Part of this tribe's wedding ceremony involves a routine of challenges and responses carried out by competing poets (called the *balah*). Wedding guests are invited to participate in the *balah* and begin to compose verse lines in an improvisational manner. For example, a poet might begin to tease another poet about what happened to him on a previous day of the wedding, a point that requires the poet to create something new because no stock formula was available for such an equation. This is the true test of the poet, for he must compete against other poets in this contest of challenge and retort. And it is through the creation of metaphors that a poet can gain honor.

In one such game, the poets enter the circle, which signals

to everyone that the game has begun. At one point, a poet responds to another's challenge by stating *You called yourself a horned ram. In fact, you're our lamb. We'll play the balah all night long and see that you don't shudder with fright* (Caton, 1985). This poet cleverly suggests that his opponent greatly exaggerated his own abilities (the epithet *horned ram* is used in reference to a brave fighting man) because, rather, his opponent will turn out to be the victim (metaphorically, *our lamb*) in this contest of reputations. Rather than being the winner of the contest, the poet's opponent will experience an embarrassing defeat, enough to make him *shudder with fright all night long*. The humor of this verse by itself demonstrates that the poet has more than established his skill in the performance, which enhances his reputation for honor (Caton, 1985).

Metaphor clearly functions to define important social roles and status in various linguistic communities ranging from the youths of American cities to the tribesmen of the Arabian deserts.

METAPHOR AND POLITICS

Contemporary political discourse is packed full of metaphors, many of which reveal important aspects of the figurative nature of political thought. Many of the metaphors used in politics draw heavily and systematically on the languages of sports and warfare. One study of the metaphors used by politicians in recent election campaigns in the United States demonstrated that politics is typically conceived of either as a sports event or as war (N. Howe, 1988). For example, sports metaphors describe politics as a rule-governed contest between two opponents. These metaphors are particularly apt in the two-party political system in the United States, in which one party attempts to defeat the other during national elections. During the 1984 campaign, Ronald Reagan frequently employed sports metaphors in his speeches, in particular emphasizing "team" aspects of political contests. Reagan intended these metaphors to distinguish the Republican "team" (e.g., *the Government Opportunity Team*) from the Democratic "team" (e.g., *the Washington Tax Increase Team*). Walter Mondale, the Democratic candidate, was labeled *Coach Tax Hike*. Reagan varied the team metaphor by referring to the American *team* as engaged in a football game when he rhetorically asked *And isn't it great to see the American team, instead of punting on third down, scoring touchdowns again?* These examples illustrate how American politicians will use specific metaphors as powerful persuasive devices because they can assume that the American public shares similar metaphorical concepts of politics.

Boxing metaphors are also used, primarily to convey the necessary image of toughness. Before the first televised debate with President Reagan, Mondale was urged by one Democratic congressman to *come out slugging* and *come out fighting*. Observers later talked about that debate as if it had been a championship bout. One commentator noted about Mondale's performance that he failed to *score a knockout*, although a newspaper columnist claimed *Fritz outboxes Reagan – Takes bout on points!* These expressions convey ideas about unpredictable politics in the rule-governed terms of a sports contest (ibid.).

Another central metaphor in political discourse is POLITICS IS WAR. When politicians must be portrayed as ruthless or treacherous, speakers usually resort to military metaphors. A frequently used term of this sort is *pointman*, which in military jargon refers to the advanced member of a patrol who is most likely to encounter the enemy, and thus have the greatest risk of being wounded or killed. When he presented Ronald Reagan's controversial budget to Congress, David Stockman was described by colleagues as the *pointman*, or the person who had to take the initial *flak* from critics of the budget plan. Another military term used was *to hit the ground running*. In military jargon, this phrase refers to exiting a helicopter on the run and being ready for combat. After the 1980 elections, members of Reagan's team vowed *to hit the ground running*, meaning that they planned to fight immediately for tax and budget reform. Other military metaphors in political discourse include *damage control*, such as when Reagan's campaign staff initiated *Operation Damage Control* after Reagan's poor performance during his first debate with Mondale in the 1984 campaign. During the 1992 presidential campaign, one of Ross Perot's campaign advisors commented soon after Perot first dropped out of the race *Ross just didn't understand that politics is war.* Candidates for political office will not be successful unless they recognize this metaphorical understanding of politics.

Sports and war metaphors are not just rhetorical devices for talking about politics, for they exemplify how people ordinarily conceive of politics. Because these conceptual metaphors reflect unconscious schemes of thought, people are often unaware of the metaphorical nature of their speech, which can mislead them about the consequences of these metaphors. For instance, metaphors from sports and war often delude people into believing that negotiation and compromise are forbidden by the rules. These metaphors take on the quality of self-fulfilling prophecies (G. Lakoff & Johnson, 1980). It is as if there are no other ways, no other metaphors, in which people can think of politics. Senator Fulbright expressed his own despair over the danger of these metaphors when he noted about U.S.– Soviet relations *Every contest with the Russians we've got to win. There's no thought that you compromise. We have the football mentality. Win. Win. Win.*

The United States and Iraq recently experienced the tragedy of what happens when political decisions are based on a misunderstanding of metaphorical reasoning. G. Lakoff (1991a) described the metaphorical reasoning used by foreign policy experts and by the public at large in thinking about war with Iraq after Iraq invaded Kuwait in the summer of 1990. Two central metaphors dominated people's conceptualization of the war. The STATE AS PERSON metaphor sees a nation-state as a person, engaging in social interaction within a world community. Its land mass is its home. It lives in a neighborhood with various neighbors, friends, and enemies, some of whom are bullies. The health of a person/state is its wealth. Consequently, a serious threat to economic health is seen as a death threat to a nation. When one nation threatens the balance of power in a neighborhood by violent means to further its self-interest, other members of the community must seek to restore balance to the neighborhood. Because morality is a matter of accounting (i.e., "balancing the books"), a wrongdoer increases debt and must be made to pay. The moral accounting books can be balanced by a return to the situation prior to the wrongdoing or by compensation or by punishment. Thus, it is the moral duty of persons/nations within a community to punish wrongdoers.

Another metaphorical system that played a major part in the U.S. justification for war in the Persian Gulf was the JUST WAR AS FAIRY TALE metaphor. We all know of fairy tales where there is some cast of characters – a villain, a victim, and a hero – and some scenario where a crime is committed by the villain against the innocent victim. The villain is not just a decent person who happens to do something wrong but is inherently evil and impossible to reason with. The hero sees the offense that has been committed against the victim and decides to engage the villain in battle, usually at great personal cost. Once this decision is made, the hero must undergo some difficult journey to meet the villain in battle. The hero then defeats the villain and either rescues or recompenses the victim. In the end, victory is achieved and moral balance is restored.

The STATE AS PERSON and JUST WAR AS FAIRY TALE metaphor system is in large measure constitutive of our basic understanding of war and relationships among nations. It is so central to the way Americans understand international relations that it is hard not to use this system when thinking about issues in international politics. Like most conceptual systems, it is largely unconscious and automatic and is not seen as metaphorical.

Many of the metaphorical conceptions underlying the political arguments in favor of the Gulf War were seen in the U.S. Senate debate in January 1991. The Senate met to consider possible military action against Iraq, and two resolutions were vigorously debated. An analysis of the *Congressional Record* of the three-day debate showed that metaphor was widely used by both sides to bolster their positions (Voss et al., 1992). Both sides of the debate used metaphor with equal frequency. Each side, though, used fairly different kinds of metaphor to support its position. Democrats, who generally advocated the continued use of sanctions to force Iraq's withdrawal, frequently referred, for example, to following a particular path to reach an acceptable conclusion to the dispute between Iraq and the United States by saying that we should *stay the course* of sanctions. Republicans on the other hand, frequently expressed the need to triumph over evil by saying that the United States should *run the bad guys out of town*, thus portraying the United States as the *good guys*. Democrats were three times as likely to portray President Bush in metaphorical terms as were Republicans, and they emphasized negative aspects of Bush's leadership by referring to him as a king (*We still elect our presidents, we do not crown them*), as a gambler (*he upped the stakes from a defensive to an offensive position, rolling the dice; strengthened his hand*), and as a magician (*he plucked January 15th out of thin air* and *none of us has a crystal ball*). Republicans described Bush as a captain (*the captain cannot abandon the ship; President Bush has asked us all to get on board . . . for if we are not all on board at the time of takeoff, how can we expect to be on board for the landing*). Bush was also viewed as a conductor (*Congress forgets that its job is to write the music and not to conduct the orchestra*).

Whereas to the Democrats war was a *nightmare*, an *unpredictable tiger ride, unleashing a mad Middle East genie from its bottle, not the Super Bowl*, and *not an Easter-egg Hunt*, the Republicans referred to war in metaphorical terms far less often and used monetary metaphors, such as *spending American lives* or *paying the price*, and compared war to a chess game, as in *men and women as political pawns in the desert*. Sanctions against Iraq were also described in metaphorical ways far more often by Democrats than by Republicans, with the Democrats focusing on actions and the effects and the sanctions. Democrats referred to the embargo as *airtight* or *hermetically sealed* and described the sanctions as *inflicting pain on, squeezing, pinching*, and *corrosive* to Iraq. The Republicans, on the other hand, emphasized the potential failure of the sanctions as being like a leaky pipe or dam, as in *there are already leaks* and *soon there will be a flood*, and the sanctions were seen as *more like Swiss cheese*.

Finally, Saddam Hussein was often described in metaphorical terms by Republicans but less often by Democrats. All senators used the name Saddam Hussein as a metonymic substitute for Iraq or some attribute of Iraq, such as its government or military. Although both sides in the Senate called Hussein a glutton, one Republican senator went to great lengths to elaborate on this theme.

> Saddam Hussein is like a glutton – a geopolitical glutton. He is sitting down at a big banquet table, overflowing with goodies. And let me tell you – like every glutton, he is going to have them all. Kuwait is just the appetizer – He is gobbling it up – but it is not going to satisfy him. After a noisy belch or two, he is going to reach across the table for the next morsel. What is it going to be? Saudi Arabia? ... He is going to keep grabbing and gobbling ... It is time to let this grisly glutton know the free lunch is over. It is time for him to pay the bill. (*Ibid.*, p. 209)

Although it is not clear how effective any of these metaphors were in persuading other senators, or even whether these metaphors actually evoked specific images, associations, or affect, it is clear that metaphors were used as reasons to support claims and to emphasize, concretize, or personalize particular issues (Voss et al., 1992). Much work has shown that metaphor can indeed significantly change people's attitudes toward various political and social topics (Bosman, 1987; Bowers & Osborn, 1966; J. Johnson & Taylor, 1981; Read, Cesa, Jones, & Collins, 1990; Reinsch, 1971). For example, California residents' attitudes toward compulsory seat belt legislation were significantly changed when they read the metaphor that such a law is like having *Governor Deukmejian sitting in your bathtub telling you to wash behind your ears* (Read et al., 1990). Metaphor by itself doesn't necessarily change people's attitudes, but when used in conjunction with other prose material, it is useful for highlighting arguments that are consistent with its entailments (ibid.).

The Senate discussion provides additional evidence that posing a moral justification for the Gulf War through metaphor was not just a rhetorical strategy but a reflection of the way people and professional politicians confront abstract and complex issues. We may at times criticize the particular metaphors that politicians use in talking about problems. Yet metaphoric thought is neither good nor bad, but inevitable, natural, and a necessary part of how we ordinarily think (G. Lakoff, 1991a).

The poetics of mind

The ubiquity of metaphor in everyday discourse is not due to the sophisticated rhetorical abilities of ordinary speakers; rather, it is motivated by the persuasiveness of metaphor in everyday thought. One can easily claim, for example, that the political discourse over the Gulf War reveals many underlying metaphorical ideas of how people conceive of a complex political situation. Yet this claim about the metaphorical character of everyday thought is controversial to many scholars and even to metaphor theorists, who still adhere to the belief that thought is inherently literal, with metaphor acting as a tool for communicating complex, yet still literal, ideas. But there is now significant work in various disciplines to suggest that metaphor plays an essential role not only in everyday thought, language, and culture but also in many aspects of scientific and legal reasoning.

SYSTEMATICITY OF LITERAL EXPRESSIONS

Consider first the following fairly mundane utterances often used to talk about love and relationships:

> Look how far we've come.
> It's been a long, bumpy road.
> We're at a crossroads.
> We may have to go our separate ways.
> Our marriage is on the rocks.
> We're spinning our wheels.

Why is each of these expressions an acceptable way of talking about, and understanding, love relationships? All of these (and other) conventional expressions cluster together under one basic metaphorical system of understanding: LOVE AS A JOURNEY (G. Lakoff & Johnson, 1980). This conceptual metaphor involves understanding one domain of experience, love, in terms of a very different and more concrete domain of experience, journeys. There is a tight mapping according to which entities in the domain of love (the lovers, their common goals, the love relationship, etc.) correspond systematically to entities in the domain of a journey (the traveler, the vehicle, destinations, etc.). These mappings preserve the image-schematic structure of the source domain (G. Lakoff, 1990). That is, the underlying set of recurring bodily experiences that constitute the image schemas within certain domains, such as SOURCE–PATH–GOAL in the domain of journeys, are invariantly mapped onto the target domain under consideration, such as love. This invariant mapping motivates why there is such a tight correspondence between the cognitive topologies of the source and target domains. Just as the metaphorical mapping in LOVE AS A JOURNEY gives rise to certain correspondences that are commented on in different linguistic expressions, so too do other metaphorical conceptualizations of love give rise to different systematic ontological correspondences. For example, the LOVE AS A NUTRIENT metaphor motivates many conventional expressions, such as *I was given new strength by her love, I thrive on love, He's sustained by love,* and *I'm starved for your affection.*

A large number of representative domains of human experience (e.g., time, causation, spatial orientation, ideas, anger, understanding) indicate the pervasiveness of various metaphorical systems in our everyday thought (M. Johnson, 1987; Kovecses, 1986; G. Lakoff, 1987, 1990; G. Lakoff & Johnson, 1980; G. Lakoff & Turner, 1989; Turner, 1987, 1991). Most theories of linguistic metaphor provide no reason why literal expressions like those presented above cluster in the ways they do. In general, metaphor theorists view these literal expressions as having little to do with metaphor, although they sometimes see such statements as reflecting different dead metaphors. Yet it is not just arbitrary or an accident that we use, for example, *thrive, sustained,* and *starved* when speaking of love. We do so because a great deal of our conceptual understanding of love is metaphorically structured.

Consider other sets of literal expressions about love that systematically relate to particular conceptual metaphors. One set relates to the idea of love as a natural force (i.e., LOVE AS A NATURAL FORCE, such as flood, wind, storm, etc.).

147

She swept me off my feet.
Waves of passion came over him.
It was a whirlwind romance.
We were engulfed by love.
We were riding the waves of passion.
She was deeply immersed in love.

Another set focuses on the mapping of love onto our understanding of magic (i.e., LOVE AS MAGIC).

She cast a spell over me.
She has me hypnotized.
I was entranced by her.
She is bewitching.
I was spellbound.
The magic is gone.

Finally, other examples illustrate how love is metaphorically conceptualized as a unity made up of two complementary parts (i.e., LOVE AS A UNITY).

We were made for each other.
She is my better half.
We are one.
We belong together.
They are inseparable.
Theirs is a perfect match.

These conceptual metaphors about love are just some of the perhaps few dozen metaphorical ways that people think about and consequently talk about their love experiences (Kovecses, 1988). The different metaphorical ways we have for thinking about love suggest that we do not have a single cognitive model for love. Instead, we have various interrelated metaphorical ways of thinking about love. Each of these metaphorical models offers different entailments appropriate for thinking and talking about different aspects of our love experiences. Thus, the unpredictability of love is better conceptualized by LOVE IS A NATURAL FORCE, and the togetherness of our love relationships is better viewed in terms of LOVE AS A UNITY.

It might not surprise many people to learn that our emotion concepts, such as love and anger, are structured in terms of metaphor (e.g., the evidence cited on metaphor in psychotherapy). Many other basic concepts are also understood metaphorically. Recent studies in cognitive linguistics provide many good examples in their analyses of systematic conventional expressions (G. Lakoff, 1990). One domain of experience that is clearly metaphorical is event structure. Various aspects of events, including states, changes, processes, actions, causes, and purposes, are understood metaphorically in terms of space, motion, and force. For example, states are seen as bounded regions in space. We speak of being *in* or *out* of a state, of *going into* or *out of* it, of *entering* or *leaving* it, of getting *to* a state or of emerging *from* it. Some basic correspondences follow from this metaphorical mapping. These include the following:

IMPEDIMENTS TO ACTION ARE IMPEDIMENTS TO MOTION

We hit a roadblock.
We are going upstream.
We are fighting an uphill battle.
We are in rough waters.
I've hit a brick wall.

AIDS TO ACTION ARE AIDS TO MOTION

It is smooth sailing from here on in.
It's all downhill from here.
There's nothing in our way.

GUIDED ACTION IS GUIDED MOTION

She guided him through it.
She walked him through it.
She led him through the rough parts.

INABILITY TO ACT IS INABILITY TO MOVE

I am tied up with work.
He is up to his neck in work.
I am drowning in work.
We are stuck on this problem.

A FORCE THAT LIMITS ACTION IS A FORCE THAT LIMITS MOTION

She held him back.
She is being pushed into a corner.

She has a tight rein on him.
I am being pulled under.
He is tied up at work.
He doesn't give me any slack.
He's up against the wall.

CAREFUL ACTION IS CAREFUL MOTION

I'm walking on eggshells.
He is treading on thin ice.
He is walking a fine line.

SPEED OF ACTION IS SPEED OF MOVEMENT

He flew through his work.
He is running around.
It is going swimmingly.
Things have slowed to a crawl.
She is going by leaps and bounds.

LACK OF PURPOSE IS LACK OF DIRECTION

He is just floating around.
He is drifting aimlessly.
He needs some direction.

These examples demonstrate that the event structure metaphor provides an explanation for how all these expressions involving space, motion, and forces can be used to talk about states, actions, causes, and purposes. Even more metaphorical complexity is seen in other expressions referring to causation (G. Lakoff, 1990). Most generally, causation is metaphorically understood in terms of forces (i.e., CAUSES ARE FORCES) (Talmy, 1988). More specifically, caused actions are understood as forced motion, as seen in the following expressions:

He pushed me into doing it.
They dragged me into doing it.
I am being pulled along by the current.
She leaned on him to do it.

There are two main kinds of forced motion: propulsion (e.g., sending, throwing, propelling) and the continuous application of force to produce motion (e.g., bringing, giving). Each type of forced motion has its own particular entailments. With propulsion, the application of force begins the motion, which continues afterwards. With continuous application, motion continues only as long as the force is applied. These different entailments about force are mapped onto causation in the CAUSES ARE FORCES metaphor, and each case of force motivates different kinds of causative expression. Consider the the statements *The home run brought the crowd to its feet* and *The home run sent the crowd into a frenzy.* At first, the sentences seem similar. However, each involves a different kind of forced motion. In the first example, with *brought*, the effect of the force goes on during the flight of the ball and then ceases. The crowd rises to its feet while the ball is in the air. In the second case, with *send*, the crowd's frenzy begins after the home run. Thus, two special cases of force are mapped onto two special cases of causation by the CAUSES ARE FORCES metaphor.

We see, then, that causation is not a semantically primitive notion independent of metaphor. Many abstract concepts, such as causation, times, states, changes, and purposes, are understood metaphorically. This suggests that conceptual metaphors are not simply the mapping of one complex propositional structure onto another (e.g., ARGUMENTS ARE WAR). Instead, the propositional structures themselves are metaphorical.

Finally, another widespread complex example of the metaphorical structuring of experience can be seen in folk ideas about the nature of human communication. It turns out that the bulk of our understanding and talk about human communication is done via the CONDUIT metaphor, which includes these parts: (1) Ideas or thoughts are objects, (2) words and sentences are containers for these objects, and (3) communication consists of finding the right word/container for your idea/object, sending this filled container along a conduit or through space to the listener, who must then take the idea/object out of the word/container. There are hundreds of expressions in the language that exhibit the influence of the CONDUIT metaphor (Reddy, 1979). Some examples are:

It's very hard to get that idea across in a hostile atmosphere.
Jane gives away all her best ideas.

Your real feelings are finally getting through to me.
Your concepts come across beautifully.
It's a very difficult idea to put into words.
A good poet packs his lines with beautiful feelings.
You cannot simply stuff ideas into sentences in any old way.
The entire chapter is completely void of useful ideas.
To unseal the meaning in Wittgenstein's curious phrases is not
    easy.

The CONDUIT metaphor pervades our common understanding of human communication. Moreover, many scholarly theories of language and meaning rest on aspects of the CONDUIT metaphor. For example, the notion that words have meanings reflects the metaphorical idea that words are containers filled with different essences (e.g., senses). Comprehension is often characterized as unpacking or accessing the meanings of words in sentences. Metaphorical ideas about communication clearly influence theoretical explanations of language, meaning, and understanding.

The evidence presented so far describes various metaphors that motivate our use and understanding of conventional expressions. Metaphorical mappings do not occur in isolation from one another. They are sometimes organized in hierarchical structures where "lower" mappings in the hierarchy inherit the structure of the "higher" mappings (G. Lakoff, 1993). Consider one example of a hierarchy with three levels (ibid.):

Level 1: The event structure metaphor
Level 2: PURPOSEFUL LIFE IS JOURNEY
Level 3: LOVE IS A JOURNEY; A CAREER IS A JOURNEY

The event structure metaphor, again, maps the source domain of space onto the target domain of events. This mapping produces various entailments, such as that states are locations, changes are movements, causes are forces, actions are self-propelled movements, purposes are destinations, means are paths to destinations, difficulties are impediments to motion, long-term purposeful activities are journeys, and so on. Because we assume that life is purposeful, we are expected to have certain goals in life that we wish to achieve. The event structure metaphor provides a way of conceiving of these goals, in that purposes are destinations and purposeful action is self-propelled motion toward a destination. A purposeful life is a long-term activity and hence a journey. Choosing a means to achieve a goal is choosing a path to a destination, difficulties in life are impediments to motion, and so on.

Most generally, the metaphor PURPOSEFUL LIFE IS JOURNEY makes use of all the structure of the event structure metaphor in that events in life are conceptualized as subcases of events in general. In this way, the conceptual metaphor PURPOSEFUL LIFE IS JOURNEY inherits the event structure metaphor. Various expressions illustrate these mappings; for example, *He's without direction in his life, He's at the crossroads in his life, I've gone through a lot in life, I'm where I want to be in life*, and *She got a head start in life.*

Just as significant life events are special cases of events, so events in a love relationship are special cases of life events. Thus, the LOVE IS A JOURNEY metaphor inherits the structure of the LIFE IS A JOURNEY metaphor. There are special aspects of the LOVE IS A JOURNEY metaphor, such as that there are two lovers who are travelers and that the love relationship is a vehicle. But the rest of the mapping is a consequence of inheriting the LIFE IS A JOURNEY metaphor. This results in the entailments that the lovers are in the same vehicle, that they have the same destination, and that problems in the relationship are impediments to travel.

The inheritance hierarchy has the important generalization that lexical items that are central to the highest level (Level 1) can also be used metaphorically in talking about lower levels (Levels 2 and 3). For instance, the central meaning of the word *crossroads* is in the domain of space. But this lexical item can be used in a metaphorical sense to talk of any extended activity, like a life or a love relationship. This kind of hierarchical organization is a very prominent feature of the metaphor system in English. Most generally, metaphors higher up in the hierarchy, such as the event structure metaphor, tend to be more widespread than those mappings at lower levels. One speculation is that the event structure metaphor may even be universal, whereas metaphors for life and love might be more culturally restricted (G. Lakoff, in press).

A second source of evidence for the metaphoric nature of everyday thought is seen in the ways conventional metaphors are elaborated upon in poetry and conversation. For instance, verse about love embellishes the more mundane ways of thinking about love experiences. Consider the following poem titled "To My Dear and Loving Husband," by the 17th-century American poet Anne Bradstreet:

> If ever two were one, then surely we.
> If ever man were loved by wife, then thee;
> If ever wife was happy in a man,
> Compare with me, ye women, if you can.
> I prize thy love more than whole mines of gold
> Or all the riches that the East doth hold.
> My love is such that rivers cannot quench,
> Nor ought but love from thee, give recompense.
> Thy love is such I can no way repay.
> The heavens reward thee manifold, I pray.
> Then while we live, in love let's so persevere
> That when we live no more, we may live ever.

This poem manifests a number of metaphorical concepts about love. The first line, *If ever two were one, then surely we*, illustrates the LOVE IS A UNITY metaphor, a conceptual mapping that also motivates such mundane expressions as *She's my better half.* The two line *I prize thy love more than whole mines of gold* and the following line each reflect some aspect of the LOVE IS A VALUABLE COMMODITY metaphor, as do the the two lines beginning *Thy love is such I can no way repay*, which emphasize how love can almost be bartered in an economic transaction. The idea of LOVE AS A NUTRIENT is seen in *My love is such that rivers cannot quench.*

Another metaphorical illustration of love is seen in the following fragment from Pablo Neruda's poem "Letter on the Road," where love is seen as a particular kind of living organism, in this case a flower:

> Your love also helps me:
> It is a closed flower
> that constantly fills me with its aroma
> and that opens suddenly
> within me like a great star.

Two different metaphorical conceptualizations of love are found in poems by Neruda. The first fragment, from the poem titled "Ode and Burgeonings," comments on love as a journey:

> My wild girl, we have had
> to regain time
> and march backward, in the distance
> of our lives, kiss after kiss,
> gathering from one place what we gave
> without joy, discovering in another
> the secret road
> that gradually brought your feet
> close to mine.

A second fragment comes from the opening lines of the poem titled "Love" and expresses the idea of love as a bond or attachment:

> What's wrong with you, with us,
> what's happening to us?
> Ah love is a harsh cord
> that binds us wounding us
> and if we want to leave our wound,
> to separate,
> it makes a new knot for us and condemns us
> to drain our blood and burn together.

It might not surprise many people to see that conventional metaphors for love can be elaborated upon in poetry. But other basic concepts that are understood metaphorically are also elaborated upon in poetic verse. Consider our metaphorical understanding of time. Time's elusive nature makes it a primary candidate for everyday ontological metaphors. For instance, we can conceptualize time, an intangible, as though it were a person or a physical object (e.g., TIME IS A PERSON and TIME IS A MOVING OBJECT). The personification of time is revealed in many proverbial expressions, such as *Time flies, Time waits for no man,* and *Time brings the truth to light.* Poetic verse draws heavily on these conceptual metaphors about time. In *Troilus and Cressida* (IV. v. 202–3), Shakespeare personifies time at one point where Hector greets Nestor by saying,

> Let me embrace thee, good old chronicle,
> That hast so long walk'd hand in hand with time.

This example illustrates three of the most significant entailments of the TIME IS A PERSON ontological metaphor in this play (Thompson & Thompson, 1987): (1) time is moving, (2) time is facing a specific direction in relation to the person in question, and (3) time is doing something with his hand. All three of these entailments contribute to Hector's (or Shakespeare's) unusually friendly conception of time. Thus, his motion is that of walking, implying a slow pace for his elderly human companion, Nestor; he is facing in the same direction as Nestor; and he is holding his hand in a gesture of friendship.

Time can also be viewed as unfriendly to people, a point made most forcefully in *Troilus and Cressida* (III. iii. 165–9) in Ulysses' speech to Achilles in which he stresses the importance of continuing to perform heroic deeds and the dangers of resting on one's laurels:

> For Time is like a fashionable host
> That slightly shakes his parting guest by th' hand,
> And with his arms outstretch'd, as he would fly,
> Grasps in the comer: welcome ever smiles,
> And farewell goes out sighing.

Time here is not actually in flight but is on the verge of flying toward those who are are arriving but away from those who are leaving. His arms and hands are *outstretch'd* as if to assist his flight but also in a gesture of welcoming embrace to Achilles' rivals, while he presumably turns his back on *farewell,* the *parting guest,* after a slight handshake. Thus, all three entailments – movement, direction, and hand gestures – are in this example hostile (from Achilles' point of view) rather than friendly (Thompson & Thompson, 1987).

The time metaphors discussed here show how Shakespeare elaborated upon everyday conceptual metaphors for time. These poetic elaborations extend the ordinary parts of the everyday conceptual metaphors (e.g., TIME IS A PERSON) or develop the normally unused parts. Such imaginative elaborations are not completely novel but reflect metaphoric thought that is part of our everyday cognition.

POLYSEMY

A third source of evidence for the metaphorical nature of thought comes from recent studies on polysemy, a state in which words have multiple meanings that are systematically related. Polysemous words are pervasive in language (97 of the 100 most frequent words in English are polysemous). Traditional linguistic and psychological theories assume that the meanings of polysemous words can be captured by single abstract senses. But there is much evidence that the meanings of polysemous words are related to one another in terms of family resemblance and that many of a polysemous word's meanings are motivated by the metaphorical projection of knowledge from one domain to another (see Chapter 2).

Consider again the fact that the preposition *over* has more than 100 senses (Brugman & Lakoff, 1988). Some of these senses refer to specific physical schemas, such as the "above" meaning in *The bird flew over the house* and *The painting hangs over the fireplace* or the "cover" meaning in *The board is over the hole* and *The city clouded over.* Other senses of *over* are figurative and exhibit the metaphorical projection of knowledge from a physical domain to a nonphysical, or more abstract, domain. For instance, *She has a strange power over me* extends the "above" sense via the very common conceptual metaphor CONTROL IS UP; LACK OF CONTROL IS DOWN. Two different metaphors apply to *Sam was passed over for promotion.* The first, CONTROL IS UP; LACK OF CONTROL IS DOWN entails that the person who passed over Sam was in control of Sam's status. The second common metaphor that applies here is CHOOSING IS TOUCHING, which entails that since there was no physical contact between the person in control and Sam, Sam was not chosen. Both of these independently existing conceptual metaphors motivate why we can easily use *over* to refer to nonphysical domains of experience.

One might argue that the different meanings of polysemous words are really arbitrarily defined (the "homonymy" position) or just based on metaphors that are no longer part of our everyday thinking. Consider the following simple expressions:

> I see what you mean.
> That's a very clear argument.
> What's your outlook on this project?
> The argument looks different from my point of view.
> Let me point out something to you in her argument.
> Tell me no more, I've got the whole picture.

Literal examples such as these are often seen as classic cases of dead metaphors. But these expressions are representative of metaphorical systems of thought that are very much alive. In particular, we conceptualize and talk about intellectual activities in terms of vision (i.e., UNDERSTANDING IS SEEING), and this partially motivates why we talk about understanding or knowing in terms of seeing things. This metaphorical mapping of our knowledge about human vision onto the domain of understanding or knowing is not temporary, but is very much a part of our conceptual structures in long-term memory.

One of the interesting consequences of the idea that our everyday cognition is, at least partially, metaphorically structured is that it helps explain how the related senses of polysemous words, such as *see, point,* and *look,* come to acquire the meanings they do over time. Chapter 2 provides a good example of this in that certain cases of diachronic semantics can be explained by means of culturally shared metaphors (Sweetser, 1990). One such example in particular is the tendency in Indo-European languages to borrow concepts and vocabulary from the more accessible physical and social world to refer to the less accessible worlds of reasoning, emotion, and conversational structure. With few exceptions, words in Indo-European languages meaning *see* regularly acquire the meaning *know* at widely scattered times and places. Traditional theories of diachronic linguistics provide no reason why the same kinds of meaning changes occur over and over again in Indo-European languages. Yet one can easily explain such changes in terms of conceptual metaphors. In the case of *see* words, there is a widespread and ancient conceptual metaphor UNDERSTANDING IS SEEING, which is part of the more general mind is body metaphor (ibid.). Because this metaphor exists in the conceptual systems of Indo-European-speakers, the conceptual mapping between seeing and knowing (SEEING IS UNDERSTANDING) actually motivates why words meaning *see* eventually extend their meanings to *know*.

Another example of how our physical experiences can be metaphorically mapped to structure our understanding of the nonphysical is seen in the meanings of modal verbs, such as *must, may,* and *can* (Sweetser, 1990). Modal verbs pertain to our experience of actuality, possibility, and necessity. Although the study of such verbs is commonly restricted to the purely philosophical concerns of logical possibility and necessity, the meanings of these verbs are intimately related to our everyday understanding of experience. We often represent our experience of things, events, and relations as being actual, possible, or necessary. For instance, we often feel ourselves able to act in certain ways (*can*), permitted to perform actions of our own choosing (*may*), and compelled by forces beyond our control (*must*).

There is a pervasive, coherently structured system of metaphor that relates different senses of modal verbs in which the physical becomes a metaphor for the nonphysical (the mental, rational, and social) (Sweetser, 1990). This MIND IS THE BODY metaphorical structure both guides the course of semantic change in history (diachronically) and provides connections among some senses of polysemous words within a language.

There are two senses of modal verbs, the *root* and the *epistemic*. Root modals denote ability (*can*), permission (*may*), or obligation (*must*) in our sociocultural world. The epistemic senses of modals find their home in the domain of reasoning, argument, and theorizing. The epistemic senses are intimately connected with their root senses, and the basis for this connection is that we understand the mental in terms of the physical, or the mind in terms of bodily experience. In particular, we understand mental processes of reasoning as involving forces and barriers analogous to physical and social forces and obstacles. Consider the following examples of the root sense of modals:

> Your must move your foot, or the car will crush it.
> *(Physical necessity)*

> Sally can reach the fried eel for you.
> *(She is physically capable of reaching it)*

> Paul must get a job now.
> *(Paul is forced by his wife's threat to get a job, though the compulsion is not physical)*

> You may now kiss the bride.
> *(No social or institutional barrier prevents you from kissing her)*

The meanings of these modal verbs in the physical scenarios are not terribly different from when they are used in talking about rational argument and reasoning. For instance, *may* is understood in its root sense as the absence of external or internal restraint or compulsion. There is no barrier blocking the occurrence or performance of some action. To say that a certain action *may* be done implies that some potential barrier to the action is absent or has been removed. We use *may* only regarding actions or events that could conceivably be blocked or compelled by an external obstacle or force, as in *We may be able to cure his illness*, where an event (the cure) is not blocked by any known state of affairs.

Now consider some epistemic senses of modality:

> Paul must have gotten the job, or else he couldn't be buying that new car.
> *(The available evidence forces me to conclude that Paul got the job)*

> You might be right about her motives, but I'm not convinced.
> *(No evidence blocks your conclusion, but neither does any compel me to accept it)*

In the epistemic sense of *may*, there is also no barrier that blocks the speaker's process of reasoning from the available evidence leading to the conclusion expressed in the sentence qualified by *may*. As with the root sense of *may*, the relevant force schema is that of removal of restraint. So when a speaker says *You may be right*, we read this to mean that there is no evidence barring the speaker from drawing some conclusion based on your premise.

Sweetsers' analysis suggests that the key to finding connections between the root and epistemic senses is metaphorical interpretations of force and barrier. This account of modal verbs differs substantially from the traditional view, which assumes that the root and epistemic senses are not related in any systematic way. The root meanings of *must, may, can*, and other modals are thought to involve notions of force and obligation, whereas epistemic senses are seen as involving only combinations of logical operators. In short, the root and epistemic senses are taken to be homonymous. However, the different senses of modal verbs are closely related through the metaphorical elaboration of underlying schemas about force dynamics (Talmy, 1988). The evidence for this analysis of polysemy seems compelling. It points to the reality and indispensability of image schematic structures that are extended in various figurative ways. Metaphors like THE MIND IS THE BODY are pervasive in our conceptual system and motivate exactly how the multiple meanings of polysemous words are related.

PSYCHOLOGICAL EVIDENCE

There is a growing body of evidence from cognitive psychology and psycholinguistics, some of which has been described, that illustrates the pervasive nature of metaphor in everyday thought. One source of evidence for the idea that our conceptual system is very much metaphorical is studies on analogical reasoning and thinking. Metaphoric images are used extensively in both mundane and scientific reasoning. By projecting one family of images but not another, the metaphor can influence reasoning.

One set of studies showed how metaphor could influence

scientific reasoning (Gentner & Gentner, 1983). Students who had very little prior understanding of electricity or electrical circuits were taught either to think of circuits in terms of a hydraulic system (ELECTRICITY IS A FLOWING STREAM) or to think of electricity in terms of a moving crowd (ELECTRICITY IS A TEEMING CROWD). These analogies emphasized different aspects of electrical circuits. The hydraulic analogy conveyed the idea that linking two batteries in a series increased electric current in the same way that linking two reservoirs could increase water flow. The teeming crowd analogy conveyed the idea that having two narrow resistors in parallel increased the current in the same way that having two gates instead of one could affect the numbers of, say, mice, passing through. Each analogy was also capable of presenting the other's strong concept but did not do so very compellingly (in the hydraulic analogy, a resistor corresponded to a narrow place in the pipe, and in the moving crowd analogy, pressure corresponds to shouting more encouragement to the mice). Participants in the study did better answering questions about parallel resistors in electrical circuits if they had been taught to think in terms of moving crowds, but they also did better answering questions about batteries in series if they had been taught to think in terms of flowing water. The different metaphors differentially enhanced participants' success in reasoning about electricity.

A different source of data on the metaphorical nature of thought comes from experimental work on the psycho-linguistics of idiomaticity. This work demonstrates how independent conceptual metaphors in everyday thought provide the foundation for why idioms make sense in having the figurative meanings they do. Traditional theories presume that idioms, such as *flip your lid* and *blow your stack*, have arbitrary meanings because their figurative interpretations cannot be predicted from an analysis of their individual constituents. However, recent psychological data suggest that the meanings of idioms are not arbitrary but can be explained in part by independent conceptual metaphors. For instance, both *flip your lid* and *blow your stack* are specific instantiations of the conceptual metaphors THE MIND IS A CONTAINER and ANGER IS HEATED

FLUID IN A CONTAINER (Gibbs & O'Brien, 1990, 1991; G. Lakoff, 1987; Nayak & Gibbs, 1990). These conceptual metaphors provide coherence to many idioms with similar figurative meanings as well as to many literal expressions (e.g., *My anger welled up inside me* and *I got a rise out of him*).

One way to assess the possible role of conceptual metaphors in motivating idiomatic meanings is experimentally to examine people's mental images of these phrases. The findings from one series of studies demonstrate that people's mental images of idioms are constrained by different conceptual metaphors (Gibbs & O'Brien, 1990). For example, people's images of the idioms *blow your stack, flip your lid,* and *hit the ceiling* share similar characteristics in that stacks are blown, lids flipped, and ceilings hit because of internal pressure that causes the involuntary release of some substance upward in a violent manner. The consistency of meanings for different idioms with similar figurative interpretations comes from the constraining influence of conceptual metaphors that provide part of the link between an idiom and its figurative meaning. On the other hand, people's mental images of nonidiomatic phrases, such as *blow your tire, flip your hat,* and *hit the wall,* are much more varied, because the phrases are not motivated by preexisting conceptual metaphors.

Metaphorical description of emotion concepts like anger (e.g., ANGER IS ANIMAL BEHAVIOR and ANGER IS HEATED FLUID IN A CONTAINER) in discourse contexts facilitates people's speeded understanding of different idiomatic phrases, such as *bite your head off* and *blow your stack* (Nayak & Gibbs, 1990). For instance, people find *blow your stack* more appropriate to use in a situation where the protagonist's anger is metaphorically described as being like heated fluid in a container. But *bite your head off* is more appropriate in a situation where an individual's anger is viewed as being like animal behavior.

More recent studies have shown how specific entailments of idioms reflected mappings of source to target domain that preserved the cognitive topology of the source domain (Gibbs, 1992c). Participants in these studies were questioned about their understanding of events corresponding to particular source domains in various conceptual metaphors (e.g., the source domain of heated fluid in a container for ANGER IS HEATED FLUID IN A CONTAINER). For example, when presented with the scenario of a sealed container filled with fluid, the participants were asked something about causation (e.g., *What would cause the container to explode?*), intentionality (e.g., *Does the container explode on purpose or does it explode through no volition of its own?*), and manner (e.g., *Does the explosion of the container occur in a gentle or violent manner?*).

Overall, the participants were remarkedly consistent in their responses. To give one example, people responded that the cause of a sealed container exploding its contents out would be the internal pressure caused by the increase in the heat of the fluid inside the container; that this explosion would be unintentional, because containers and fluid have no intentional agency; and that the explosion would occur in a violent manner. More interesting, though, people's intuitions about various source domains mapped onto their conceptualizations of different target domains in very predictable ways. Thus, other studies showed that when people understand anger idioms, such as *blow your stack, flip your lid,* and *hit the ceiling,* they infer that the cause of the anger is internal pressure and that the expression of anger is unintentional and is done in an abrupt, violent manner.

These data show how the metaphorical mappings between source and target domains in long-term memory preserve critical aspects of their source domains (i.e., their cognitive topology) – mappings that directly influence people's understanding of idioms. Therefore, it makes sense that the conceptual metaphors underlying the meanings of, say, certain anger idioms (e.g., THE MIND IS A CONTAINER and ANGER IS HEATED FLUID IN A CONTAINER) entail specific inferences about the causes, intentionality, and manner of how the anger is conveyed.

Some of the nicest evidence that metaphor is not merely a matter of language comes from several empirical analyses of the gestures people use when speaking (McNeil, 1992). Nonverbal gestures exhibit people's metaphorical conceptions of experience. *Metaphorics* are like iconic gestures in that they are pictorial, but the pictorial content presents an abstract idea rather than a concrete image or event. These gestures "present an image of the invisible – an image of an abstraction" (ibid., p. 2). Unlike iconic gestures, which depict some concrete object or event by analogically depicting aspects of the object/event, a metaphoric must depict two things. There is the base, or source, which is the concrete entity of action and is actually presented in the gesture. There is also the referent, or target, which is the concept that the metaphoric gesture is presenting.

Several examples of metaphorics were collected by video-taping people in discussion of some topic (McNeil, 1992). In one instance, a speaker is telling someone that what he has just seen is a cartoon –

It [was a Sylves]ter and Tweety cartoon.
(hands rising to offer an object)

– where the metaphoric gesture of hands rising up to offer the listener an object coincides with the bracketed material. The cartoon event is concrete, but the speaker is referring to the abstract concept of the cartoon genre, not to a particular event. The speaker makes the abstract idea concrete by forming an image of a bounded, spatially localizable object supported in the hands and presents it to the listener. The cartoon genre serves as the target domain, and the presented object is the source domain. This metaphorical mapping is based on the CONDUIT metaphor, in which language, meaning, knowledge, or works of art are presented as a physical container into which a substance is placed and the whole is moved along a conduit. The conduit image of an abstract idea as a physical container is a major source of metaphoric images for speakers in Western cultures.

There are many examples of gestural CONDUIT metaphors. One such metaphor is a person's presenting a cupped hand when saying

I want to ask you a question
(hand forms a cup)

The speaker presents a base (the cup) and a referent (the concept of a question). Metaphorics take this dual structure into account. Another example showing where meaning is a substance metaphor is

> That book is packed with meaning.
> (*one hand pushes against the palm of the other*)

The conduit portion of the CONDUIT metaphor is presented in a gesture such as

> I've got to tell you something.
> (*palm-up hand moves toward hearer*)

Another interesting demonstration of metaphorics in gestures is seen in the gestures used by two mathematicians in conversation (McNeil, 1992). For example, the two mathematicians exhibit gestural images for the concepts of limits, both inverse and direct. Direct limits are illustrated with the hand moving along a straight line in front of the body. For inverse limits, the hand loops downward and back up. These gestures end in a tensed stop, or "end marking": metaphors for the concept "limit." Thus, the directness of the movement that comes to a tensed stop corresponds to the idea of a direct limit, and the looping or inverted movement maps onto an inverse limit. For quotients, mathematicians use gestures where a plane is created and a hand slices through this plane. Mappings are exhibited by gestures in which the hand carries out an upward loop opposite to the inverse movement.

All of these gestures entify abstract, metaphorical ideas. At one point in the mathematics discussion studied by McNeil (1992), there was a speech error: One of the speakers said *inverse* when *direct* was meant (the other speaker caught the mistake and corrected it). Despite this speech error, the speaker actually exhibited the correct synchronized gesture for a direct limit. The speech error evidently took place after the shared computational stage of gesture and speech, one that is fundamentally shaped by metaphor. Another example occurred when a speaker was again recounting a cartoon, describing how Sylvester swallowed this big bowling ball and started to roll down a street into a bowling alley, and she then said the [you have a s]trike

with both hands spread out during the bracketed segment. The spreading open of the hands metaphorically depicts the entire event of the strike. Later on the speaker talked of Sylvester's crawling up a drainpipe dressed like a monkey. She said,

He's [trying to masquer]ade.

At this point, a metaphoric gesture was presented of both hands spread out and forward with a rotation to represent the concept of trying. Rotation of the hands is a frequent gestural metaphor for trying.

These gestures reveal aspects of speakers' figurative conceptions of experience that are not directly articulated in speech.

AN ALTERNATIVE PROPOSAL TO METAPHOR IN THOUGHT AND LANGUAGE

The preceding sections described four types of evidence in support of the hypothesis that metaphor has a significant role in structuring everyday thought. Before proceeding with further discussion of metaphor in science, legal theory, art, myth, and culture, I wish to outline briefly an alternative attempt to explain, without recourse to metaphor, some systematic relationships between language and conceptual structure. This idea, called the *thematic relations hypothesis,* claims that the conceptual structures expressed by natural language are organized in terms of a set of abstract parameters (Jackendoff, 1983, 1990; Jackendoff & Aaron, 1991). The existence of these abstract parameters is best demonstrated in language about space. Compare the following sets of sentences (Jackendoff, 1983):

(*a*) The freight train crept by.
  The tiger is fast approaching.
  The frontier lies ahead of us.

(*b*) Time crept by.
  Christmas is fast approaching.
  Our future lies ahead of us.

The similarities between these two sets of sentences suggests that some abstract relation(s) are common to both space and time. Although the domains of space and time are incongruous to some degree, the thematic relations hypothesis maintains that space is *not* used as the metaphorical basis for understanding time (Jackendoff & Aaron, 1991). Instead, there is a thematic parallelism between space and time that results in a single set of abstract relations between the two domains.

But consider closely the phrases *ahead of* and *behind* (G. Lakoff, 1991b). In the spatial domain, an observer has an inherent front and back. Moving entities that do not have inherent fronts and backs in the spatial domain get fronts assigned to them in the direction of their motion. However, the temporal domain doesn't have inherent fronts and backs. We impose fronts and backs on the temporal domain by a metaphorical mapping that allows us to use *ahead* and *behind*, as well as *precede* and *follow*, to talk about time. The thematic relations hypothesis would claim that time has inherent fronts and backs or has face (e.g., *I can't face the future, Let's look at the face of things to come, Let's meet the future head on*). This clearly isn't the case.

The language of time suggests that there are two interesting special cases of how we metaphorically understand time as space (ibid.). The first special case states that the observer is fixed, times are entities moving with respect to the observer, and times are oriented with fronts as the direction of motion. Special Case 1 accounts for such expressions as *The time will come when . . . , The time is here, I'm looking ahead to Christmas,* and *I can't face the future.* The second special case states that times are fixed locations and the observer is moving with respect to time. Special Case 2 explains expressions such as *There's going to be trouble down the road, He passed the time happily,* and *We're coming up on Christmas.*

These two special cases reflect different kinds of metaphorical understanding of time. The details of each case are different, and the two cases are inconsistent with one another. For instance, the word *come* is different in *Christmas is coming* (Special Case 1) and *We're coming up on Christmas* (Special Case 2). These different readings are due to different entailments that arise from the two metaphorical mappings of space onto time. To claim, as does the thematic relations hypothesis, that the spatial and temporal domains have thematic parallels simply cannot account for the specific meanings of temporal expressions (ibid.).

This discussion does not mean that time is never understood in its own right apart from metaphor. It may be possible to define time in a nonmetaphorical way that is neutral between the two special cases of metaphor described above. But it is not clear that a nonmetaphorical understanding of time can explain the specific meanings of different expressions English speakers use in talking about time.

I have taken this brief detour to consider the thematic relations hypothesis as an alternative proposal to explain the relationship between thought and language because it is one of the few attempts to argue specifically against metaphor's role in everyday thought (see also Ortony, 1988). Cognitive scientists, to the extent that they disagree with the claims about metaphor's pervasive role in human cognition, must provide specific detailed evidence that metaphor does not have a role in motivating many abstract concepts and the language we use to express these thoughts.

METAPHOR IN SCIENCE

It is commonly thought that science and metaphor mix about as well as oil and water. Because reality is thought to have a preferred description, scientific research seeks to uncover this description through objective empirical means and to present these "truths" in a language that best reflects them. Literal language is commonly seen as the language of science precisely because it presumably matches or reflects objective reality.

The standard view of science and language draws a principled and rigid distinction between literal and metaphorical meanings. Literal meanings are proper; metaphorical meanings are distorted and deviant. This distinction has its roots in Aristotle, even though many writers, including many of the ancient Greeks, saw the deviant metaphorical use of language as being of some value, with special power in poetry and rhetoric. The standard view of metaphor in science, in fact, represents a decisive break of philosophy and science from rhetoric. This separation and consequent identification of science with the literal, or the nonmetaphorical, gained much momentum from the theories of language championed by empiricist philosophers in the 17th century, such as Hobbes and Locke.

Metaphor, according to the standard view, contaminates the precise and stable meanings science attempts to discover behind the terms it uses. This metaphoric contamination compromises scientific inquiry and the integrity of the deductive reasoning so often used in scientific theories and explanations. Although metaphor may play a heuristic role in early scientific discovery, mature sciences should avoid metaphor at all costs. When metaphor is found lurking within some theory, it must be eliminated or reduced to some stable literal set of propositions. For instances, as Hobbes noted, when we say *Man is a wolf* we indirectly present some literal meaning, such as "Man is fierce, avid, cruel, and deceitful." Science must work toward eliminating metaphor to identify the literal set of similarities suggested by these tropes. For this reason, metaphor should be used only for rhetorical purposes and is denied any autonomous cognitive content.

Modern positivists do not radically alter the standard view of metaphor in science. The distinction between the cognitive and emotive aspects of language, along with the belief that scientific knowledge can be reduced to a system of literal sentences, implies that metaphor has no cognitive import. For the positivist, the language of science refers. In the case of observational terms, language refers directly, whereas the reference of general and theoretical terms, such as *electron* and *equilibrium*, must be fixed by explicit conventional definition. Because metaphor says one thing and means something else, it can have no literal meaning and cannot refer to anything.

According to the standard view, metaphor is appropriate to the prescientific stage of a field. For example, early economic theory describes the relations among production, circulation, and distribution of goods in terms of relations among human body parts (Bicchieri, 1988). Economic society was seen as a social body from which the division of labor and specialization of the parts naturally followed. The "social body" metaphor mirrors the organization of economic activities, with the separate body parts working together for the benefit of the whole society. In the early stages of a discipline, metaphors like the "social body" trope are thought to provide a new vocabulary and a general model for how a field should proceed. As a discipline develops over time, metaphor should be replaced by a more rigorous, self-contained vocabulary.

However, a closer look at scientific language provides good evidence of metaphor even in mature disciplines. A paradigmatic example has been found in contemporary physics. The mechanical models of 19th-century physics described gases as collections of moving particles obeying Newtonian laws and atoms as miniature solar systems. The conventional wisdom in the philosophy of science held that these metaphoric descriptions would give way to more direct, complete, literal descriptions of the primary system. In fact, many 19th-century models have been replaced in modern physics, but not so their underlying metaphorical processes (Kuhn, 1979). When Bohr's model replaced the solar system model, the new model was not intended to be taken literally: Electrons and nuclei were not seen as being exactly the same as small billiard or Ping-Pong balls.

Models, and the metaphorical processes underlying them, are an integral part of science. They organize the primary system, provide scientists with a new vocabulary, and introduce new predicates in the domain of the primary system, allowing new predictions to be made. Some metaphors may eventually come to be rejected. Yet unsuccessful metaphors fail precisely because they have cognitive content and are not merely rhetorical devices.

Many 20th-century philosophers now contend that metaphors are in many respects constitutive elements of scientific theory rather than mere ornaments or dangerously misleading figures of speech. These revisionist theorists argue that metaphors play a significant role in science, even in highly specialized technical, mature sciences. Metaphor is closely linked to arguments about whether or not language is constitutive of science itself, of what scientists do, and of the theories they construct. Since the early 1960s many theorists have been arguing for the constitutive nature of metaphor in virtually every natural and social science discipline (Arbib & Hesse, 1986; Bono, 1990; Boyd, 1979; R. H. Brown, 1976, 1987; Bruner & Feldman, 1990; Carroll & Mack, 1985; Gentner & Grudin, 1985; Gordon, 1978; Gould, 1977a, 1977b, 1983; Gruber, 1974; Harre, 1970; Hesse, 1966; Hoffman, 1980; Jones, 1982; Kuhn, 1979; Leary, 1990; Letherdale, 1974; MacCormac, 1976, 1985; Rogers, 1978; Sarbin, 1990; Turbayne, 1962). These references represent just a small portion of the work that has begun to study the ways in which metaphorical thinking has helped to constitute, and not merely reflect, scientific theory and practice.

Contemporary philosophers distinguish between "pedagogical" metaphors and "theory constitutive" metaphors in scientific language and reasoning. Pedagogical metaphors are considered to encourage memorability of information to generate a better, more insightful, and more personal understanding. They play a role in the teaching or in the explanation of theories that can already be formulated completely, or almost completely, in a nonmetaphorical way. Theory constitutive metaphors function, on the other hand, as indispensable parts of a scientific theory. They cannot be reformulated in literal terms. Whereas pedagogical metaphors invite the reader to view the new subject matter in light of a known subject matter, theory constitutive metaphors go further by exploring the similarities and analogies between the two subject matters (including aspects of the new subject matter that have not yet been discovered or fully understood).

Metaphorical claims in science function like any other hypotheses. They are articulated, clarified, disambiguated, and extended by diverse members of the scientific community. Such metaphors do not reside in a single work, nor are they the property of a single author. Like literal hypotheses, metaphorical ideas will be incorporated into a scientific theory if they prove fruitful, explanatory, and at least approximately true. Some scholars suggest that scientific metaphors differ from literary metaphors precisely because scientific metaphors become the property of the entire scientific community, whereas literary metaphors are the creation and property of individual authors (Bicchieri, 1988; Boyd, 1979). For this reason, theory constitutive metaphors in science may, and perhaps should, be capable of being fully explicated, because they are not subjective but are the products of the scientific community's collective insight.

Scientific metaphors differ from literary metaphors in how they are used and explicated. If scientific metaphors were only literary devices or embellishments imposed on other basic, literal language, we might be justified in treating them as we often do poetic metaphors. Most literary metaphors grow stale when overused. But scientific metaphors are made to be overused. As they undergo further analysis and examination, more similarities and dissimilarities are noticed between the two domains being contrasted and compared. How do gas particles behave like small elastic spheres? In what ways is the human mind like a computer? Scientific metaphors invite us to publicly, collectively probe their entailments. Successful scientific metaphors become dead when they become a well-established part of our knowledge.

There seem, then, to be few differences in the cognitive roles of literal and metaphorical claims in science. Both are open to intersubjective scrutiny. Both can be contested, confirmed, or disconfirmed by evidence, accepted and incorporated into science, or rejected as false or as trivial, or as lacking in explanatory power. It is difficult to maintain that metaphors do not have cognitive value or are dispensable in light of the ways metaphors function in science.

It is important and interesting to note that not only are scientific theories metaphorical, but so is the concept "theory." A popular conceptualization of "theory" is to see theories as buildings (G. Lakoff & Johnson, 1980). There are various literal expressions that are systematically motivated by the THEORIES ARE BUILDINGS conceptual metaphor. These include:

Is that the foundation for your theory?
The theory needs more support.
The theory is shaky.
We need to buttress the theory with solid arguments.

The theory will stand or fall on the strength of the data.
The theory collapsed.
The new data exploded his latest theory.
I haven't figured out the form of his theory.
We have to put together the framework of the theory.

Other expressions extend regularly used parts of the THEORIES ARE BUILDINGS metaphor. For instance, *These facts are the bricks and mortar of my theory* refers to the outer shell of the building, whereas the conceptual metaphor THEORIES ARE BUILDINGS does not specify the materials used to construct the building (i.e., the theory).

Various other expressions specify mostly unused parts of the conceptual metaphor. For instance, *His theory has thousands of little rooms and long, winding corridors* and *Complex theories usually have problems with the plumbing* specify aspects of how the interior structure of the building is laid out. It should again be clear that what appear at first to be random metaphorical examples are not at all random. Instead, these different expressions used to talk about theories work together in a consistent manner to show the complex way in which we metaphorically conceptualize theories. These metaphors arise from our concrete experiences that we then use to partly structure highly abstract and elaborate concepts, such as those pertaining to theories.

One discipline where constitutive metaphors have been examined closely is experimental psychology. Metaphors abound in experimental psychology in theories about most aspects of human experience (cf. Sternberg, 1990). For instance, the concept of memory is described as a *wax tablet*, a *dictionary*, an *encyclopedia*, a *muscle*, a *telephone switchboard*, a *conveyor belt*, a *storehouse for ideas*, a *computer*, and a *hologram*. Descartes referred to memory as being like a *riverbed* through which sensory impressions *flow*. Freud talked of memory as a *house full of rooms*. Most modern theories of memory are variations of a metaphor theme of mental space with recall as a search through the contents of this space (Hoffman, Cochran, & Nead, 1990; Roediger, 1980). Mental images are viewed as *drawings, working spaces, blackboards, scratch pads,* and *cathode ray tubes* (Roediger, 1980).

Information processing psychology sees the mind as consisting of a set of cognitive *demons*, each of which is responsible for some small bit of knowledge (Lindsay & Norman, 1977; Selfridge, 1966). In visual perception, for example, there are individual demons for particular visual features, such as lines or angles. The demons are said to *look* for inputs that match their patterns and to *loudly shout* if there is some degree of match between the input and the demon. The *decision demon* responds to the loudest demon, labeling the input pattern with the category of that loudest demon. This metaphorical view of mind supposes that homunculi (the individual demons) recognize, compute, decide, and shout. At a theoretical level, the demons' activities correspond to hypothetical neural processes, supposedly making the model more literally real. However, the metaphors in theories of memory, mental images, and information processing, to take just three cases, cannot be discounted as merely illustrative or decorative, for psychologists currently have few ways of marking such distinctions other than through metaphor.

An examination of the metaphors employed in psychological texts shows that the domains from which metaphors are chosen are often related to new technology (Van Besien, 1989). An analysis of a corpus of reports on psychological research shows that the computer metaphor is the most important theory constitutive metaphor in contemporary psychology. The computer metaphor, with its talk of inputs, accessing, retrieval systems, and the like, facilitates communication and verbal reasoning concerning human cognitive processes. The metaphor then organizes the phenomena for investigation and provides a vocabulary with which to carry out that investigation. It is implausible, at best, to claim that a metaphor that plays these roles is not functioning cognitively.

How did psychologists conceive of the mind before the rise of computer technology? One study reviewed the evolution of mental metaphors in a corpus of articles published in *Psychological Review* between 1894 and 1975 (Gentner & Grudin, 1985). During this time period, four main categories of mental metaphors were employed: animate being metaphors, neural metaphors, spatial metaphors, and systems metaphors.

In *animate being metaphors*, ideas or certain aspects of the human mind are compared with animate beings. For example:

> Through lying, the mind grows wary or strong from swimming against the stream. (Dewey, 1984: 110)

> Reaction arcs block each other, varying in tension, until one waxes strong enough. (Dashiell, 1925: 59)

> . . . super discriminating preperceiver who selectively prevents recognition (Minard, 1965: 76)

In *neural metaphors*, the physical system is taken as a domain. For example:

> Wider ideas shortcircuit smaller ideas. (James, 1905: 17)

> Thinking is neural impulses shifting along associative fibers from one area to another. (Dashiell, 1925: 20)

> . . . loudness perhaps proportionate to the number of mental impulses (Zwicker & Scharf, 1965: 24)

Spatial metaphors are derived from the position or movements of an object in space. For example:

> Anything hidden in the background is not mental activity. (James, 1905: 7)

> . . . habitual connections between ideas (Peterson, 1935: 8)

> . . . reservoir model for fixed action patterns (Moltz, 1965: 43)

System metaphors compare certain mental phenomena with a system of lawfully constrained interactions between elements. For example:

> A body moves in empty space by its own momentum as when our thoughts at their own sweet will (James, 1905: 6)

> The nervous system is like a switchboard mechanism. (Gray, 1935: 111)

> . . . serial, iterative operations (Carpenter & Just, 1975: 47)

Besides these four main categories, a large number (71 of a total of 265 metaphors) of *conventional metaphors* were found. These expressions have some kind of metaphorical basis but supposedly have lost their metaphorical associations, as in "mental health," "intellectual growth," "mental state," and so on. Of course, even conventional phrases, such as "intellectual growth," may reflect the strong tendency of psychologists to conceive of the mind in metaphorical terms.

The evolution of mental metaphors in Gentner and Grudin's review discovered two main tendencies: a shift in the number of metaphors and a change in the kinds of metaphor. An analysis of the metaphors used in three bidecades – an early period (1894–1915), a middle period (1925–45), and a recent period (1955–75) – showed a U-shaped distribution, with many metaphors used in the early and recent periods and far fewer in the middle period. In the early period, spatial metaphors and animate being metaphors dominated. The latter category showed a strong drop in use over the years. Use of spatial metaphors also dropped, though less severely. System metaphors, on the other hand, were an unimportant category in the early period but increased in use over the years. System metaphors were responsible for the overall increase of metaphors in the recent period. The decline of metaphors in the middle period was likely due to the influence of behaviorism: Articles in this period (1925–45) were most often straightforward reports of data without any discussion of the internal functionings of the mind. Mental metaphors and all other forms of mentalistic language were rarely employed. Metaphors that did occur in this period were either mathematical metaphors or neural ones.

This empirical analysis of the metaphors used by experimental psychologists demonstrates just how significant metaphor is in psychological theories of mind. Psychologists, like most scientists, often make the mistake of ignoring the metaphorical character of their own theories. One of the worst criticisms a scientist can make of a theory is that it is "just" metaphorical. Such an accusation is tantamount to saying that the theory is false, unscientific, and of no value. It's interesting, though, that theories substituted for offending metaphorical positions are themselves often constituted by metaphor (Hoffman et al., 1990). Many classic examples of this blindness to one's own metaphors can be found in the scientific literature. One examination of scientific discovery in cognitive psychology claims that scientists' tools shape theories of mind (Gigerenzer, 1991). Tools include both analytical and physical methods of evaluating theories. Analytical tools can be either empirical or nonempirical. Analytic methods of the empirical kind are tools for data processing: statistics, for example. Nonempirical tools include normative criteria for the evaluation of hypotheses. Examples of physical tools of justification are measurement instruments, such as clocks and computers.

The history of science reveals many instances where scientists' tools, both analytical and physical, end up as theories of nature (Hackman, 1979; Lenoir, 1988; Wise, 1988). Experimental psychology also employs a tools-to-theories heuristic whereby theories of mind are discovered through the analogy of various tools. To take one notable example, experimental psychologists view descriptive and inferential statistics as being closely tied to scientific method. Descriptive and inferential statistics, in turn, provide a large part of the new concepts for mental processes that became part of the cognitive revolution in the 1950s and 1960s. Theories of cognition are cleansed of terms like "restructuring" and "insight," and the new mind has come to be portrayed as "drawing random samples from nervous fibers," "computing probabilities," "calculating analyses of variance," and "setting decision criteria." With the institutionalization of inferential statistics in particular, a wide range of cognitive processes, conscious and unconscious, elementary and complex, are reinterpreted as involving "intuitive statistics" (Gigerenzer & Murray, 1987). These new theories exemplified the metaphor MIND AS INTUITIVE STATISTICIAN and were suggested not by new data but by new tools of data analysis.

To take just one example of the tools-to-theories heuristic, the hypothesis-testing view of perception, which reconceptualized Helmholtz's idea of "unconscious inference," accounts for the stability of perceptual forms by suggesting that there is something akin to statistical significance that must be exceeded for a stimulus to be detected and discriminated (ibid.). According to this theory of signal detectability (Tanner & Swets, 1954), the mind calculates two sampling distributions of noise and signal-plus-noise and sets a decision criterion after weighing the cost of two possible detection errors (false alarms and misses). Thus, a sensory input is transduced into a form that allows the observer to calculate its likelihood ratio. The observer will say *Yes, there is a signal* or *No, there is no signal*, depending on whether this ratio is greater than or smaller than the set criterion. This new view provides a different perspective of perception than the one assumed for more than 100 years. The analogy between a statistical technique and the human mind shows how the mind's decision criteria can be manipulated and how two kinds of error (false alarms and misses) can be distinguished. Many other areas of cognitive research propose specific quantitative models based on statistical inference for phenomena ranging from psychophysics to pattern recognition, causal reasoning, and memory (Gigerenzer, 1991).

In general, the tools-to-theories heuristic is a metaphorical process that can account for the discovery and acceptance of cognitive theories, all of which share the view that cognitive processes can be modeled by statistical hypothesis testing. The history of science reveals many other instances where scientists' tools, both analytical and physical, ended up as theories of nature (Hackman, 1979; Lenoir, 1988; Wise, 1988).

METAPHOR IN LAW

Some of the most exciting work on metaphorical thinking is seen in recent discussions of the role of metaphor in legal theory. Just as the change in metaphors accompanies paradigm shifts in science, so too do changes in metaphors result in significant legal precedents. One such precedent that beautifully illustrates how legal reasoning operates metaphorically is the landmark case *National Labor Relations Board* v. *Jones & Laughlin Steel Corp.* (301 U.S. 1, 1937) (Winter, 1989). The National Labor Relations Board (NLRB) found that the steel manufacturer had intimidated and discriminated against its employees in an effort to prevent them from organizing a union. The jurisdictional question was whether the federal government could exercise its commerce clause powers to regulate labor relations in manufacturing. The National Labor Relations Act originally addressed this issue by stating that interference with the right to organize and to bargain collectively had

> the necessary effect of burdening or obstructing commerce by (a) impairing the efficiency, safety, or operation of the instrumentalities of commerce; (b) occurring in the current of commerce; (c) materially affecting, restraining, or controlling the flow of raw materials or manufactured or processed goods from or into the channels of commerce . . .; or (d) causing diminution of employment and wages in such volume as substantially to impair or disrupt the market for goods flowing from or into the channels of commerce . . . . It is hereby declared to be the policy of the United States to eliminate the causes of certain substantial obstructions to the free flow of commerce by encouraging the practice and procedure of collective bargaining.

Note the frequent use of fluid metaphors in how the NLRB expressed the relevance to labor relations of Congress's commerce clause power. In its finding on uniform labor practice, the NLRB elaborated on the fluid metaphor by invoking a cardiovascular analogy and suggesting that steel plants

> might be likened to the heart of a self-contained, highly integrated body. They draw in the raw materials from Michigan, Minnesota, West Virginia, Pennsylvania in part through arteries and by means controlled by the respondent; they transform the materials and then pump them out to all parts of the nation through the vast mechanism which the respondent has elaborated.

The solicitor general's argument in defense of the Board's ruling commented that the steel company's *activities constitute a stream or flow of commerce, of which the . . . manufacturing plant is the focal point*. The steel manufacturer, on the other hand, argued that it should not be held to the commerce clause, because it was a manufacturing company and not, strictly speaking, involved in commerce. When the Supreme Court ruled in support of the NLRB's original decision, Chief Justice Hughes rejected the steel manufacturer's argument. Although Hughes recognized that manufacturing may be different from commerce, he was most interested in what motivates the *stream of commerce*, or the fluid metaphor.

The stream of commerce metaphor is motivated by an underlying source–path–goal image schema. Hughes certainly did not put the issue this way, but he elaborated on the metaphoric entailments of the stream of commerce metaphor. Suppose commerce is conceptualized not as a stream but, in the government's metaphor, as a *great movement of iron ore, coal, and limestone along well-defined paths*. If commerce is a movement along a path, it can be personified as a traveler and should not suffer undue burdens or be impeded by obstructions. No harm should come *due to injurious action springing from other sources*.

Hughes's opinion essentially reorganizes the idealized cognitive model (ICM) of commerce power from one based on a stream metaphor to one based on the journey metaphor. These metaphors entail very different conceptions of the federal government's role in regulating commerce. If commerce is viewed as a stream, Congress must regulate its flow and protect it from obstructions. But if commerce is a traveler on a journey, then the potential sources of interference stem from harms of all sorts – *throttling, danger, injurious action springing from other sources*. Chief Justice Hughes's opinion in the Jones & Laughlin case represents a paradigm shift in the ICM of congressional power over commerce. Congress is no longer the floodgate operator who assures regular flow in the channels of commerce but the interstate policeman who protects the traveler (Winter, 1989). This case illustrates how metaphor provides part of the foundation for reasoning about constitutional law.

Another example of how metaphoric thinking influences legal reasoning concerns the first amendment to the Constitution (ibid.). Among other things, the first amendment guarantees the right of free speech (*Congress shall make no law . . . abridging the freedom of speech*). It represents a powerful set of social values and conventions that allows people to use streets and parks for public protest and protects newspapers from censorship (except when they directly jeopardize the government's conduct of a war). Despite the clarity of this prototypical model of the first amendment, it is often difficult to generalize it to account for the various kinds of situations that may be seen as protected by it.

The central meaning of the first amendment is not expressed in terms of a well-defined set of propositional rules or mediating principles that explicitly define, for example, what is meant by "reasonable time," "place and manner" restrictions, the "autonomy principle," or the "public debate principle." Instead the first amendment was defined and is now understood in metaphorical terms. Consider the fundamental rule of the first amendment against prior restraints. The traditional English view of free speech in the 17th century was expressed by John Milton, who defined it in terms of an extended metaphor: *Truth is compar'd in Scripture to a streaming fountain; if her waters flow not in a perpetuall progression, they sick'n into a muddy pool of conformity and tradition* (1644/1967: 265). During the early stages of its development, the first amendment merely insured the free *flow* of ideas by protecting them from prior restraint. The direct experience of unhealthy, stagnant water structured the conception of the evil to be avoided in terms of the halting of intellectual progress toward truth. However, ideas that had already been spoken and found not to contribute to progress were vulnerable to coercive governmental action, as was clearly the case when the Alien and Sedition Acts were adopted in 1798, shortly after the first amendment itself. Later development of the modern first amendment came in Justice Holmes's opinions during World War I. Holmes argued in his dissent in *Abrams* v. *United States* that *the ultimate good desired is better reached by free trade in ideas – that the best test of truth is the power of the thought to get itself accepted in the competition of the market* (see 250 U.S. 616, 630, 1919, Holmes J. dissenting). This passage provided the critical "marketplace of ideas" metaphor for the 20th-century idealized cognitive model of the first amendment.

This metaphor is not novel but highly conventional, and it relates several conventional metaphors for minds and ideas. These include THE MIND IS A MACHINE (*She grinds out those reports; She had a nervous breakdown; After working all morning, I ran out of steam*), IDEAS ARE PRODUCTS (*We need to refine our hypothesis; She is our most productive writer*), and IDEAS ARE COMMODITIES (*Her idea is valuable, but yours is worthless and it just won't sell*). Holmes' "marketplace of ideas" metaphor calls to mind these underlying cultural metaphors for mind and ideas, together with the ICM of a commercial transaction, to structure a new ICM for the first amendment. Among the obvious entailments for this metaphor are that persuasion is like selling, acceptance is like buying, and truth is produced by the test of competition. Our contemporary understanding of the first amendment is very much dependent upon the marketplace metaphor and its various entailments. This metaphor expresses certain normative cultural assumptions about the value of autonomy and "free trade in ideas." Unlike the earlier view of the Constitution's framers that saw "truth" in objective terms, the 20th-century view suggests that there can be many competing "truths." For example, the first amendment traditionally applies to newspapers. Not only is the government forbidden to enjoin publication of an offending story, but it cannot either require that a newspaper publish a retraction or tax the print media differentially. Yet the rule against prior restraint is relaxed substantially for less prototypical newspapers (e.g., student newspapers). By the same token, the nonprint media are subject to quite extensive constraints, such as the fairness doctrine and censorship of obscene language. These decisions are extremely problematic in terms of the doctrinal rules. But they are quite understandable as products of the radial structure of first amendment analysis. Legal reasoning is socially contingent in just this way, with metaphor lighting the path for how laws are to be interpreted.

METAPHOR IN ART

Metaphor has not traditionally been associated with the visual arts because of the assumption that metaphor is a linguistic device. Many literary, film, and art critics argue that most attempts to find metaphor in the visual arts arise from the confusion of metaphor with symbolism, where metaphor is linked to the domain of language and symbolism belongs to the domain of things (Arnheim, 1933; Pryluck, 1975; Stanford, 1936). Yet more and more scholars are beginning to study metaphor in the visual arts and music with an eye explicating how figurative thought is made manifest in artistic creations. My focus in this book is primarily on how natural language reveals figurative thinking, but I wish briefly to touch on how art also reveals metaphoric thought (see Hausman, 1989, and Whittock, 1990, for further discussion of metaphor in art and film).

Consider the depiction of cinematic metaphor. At the most general level, metaphoric thinking plays an important role in how we interpret movies. For example, we understand *Taxi Driver* in metaphorical terms as referring to the loneliness of individuals (i.e., the cabbie played by Robert DeNiro) struggling to make sense of their lives in the vast urban jungle. *Apocalypse Now* presents director Francis Ford Coppola's own interpretation of Joseph Conrad's novella *Heart of Darkness*, in which the protagonist's search deep in the jungle for the evil Kurtz parallels his private journey toward personal redemption.

Many movies have individual images that reflect different metaphorical conceptions of experience. In *The Graduate*, there is one memorable scene where Benjamin, played by Dustin Hoffman, donning flippers and goggles, flees to the bottom of the family swimming pool during a large party, primarily to escape the overbearing camaraderie of his parents and their friends. While the metaphor of diving is reflecting Benjamin's introversion and retreat from the "plastic" suburban world of his parents, the camera is assuming his point of view: The world becomes gloomy, from the motion of the green-blue water. "Benjamin has escaped one reality, only to find himself adrift in a new and turbulent world of ghostly color and shapes" (Scott, 1975: 149).

Another terrific and fairly transparent metaphoric image is seen in Alfred Hitchcock's film *The Birds*. At the beginning of the film, actor Rod Taylor is shown in a bird shop trying to capture a canary. Once he captures the bird, he puts it back in its cage and says to Tippi Hedren, who plays a wealthy playgirl, *I'm putting you back in your gilded cage, Melanie Daniels.* Later on, when the gulls attack the village, Melanie Daniels hides in a glass telephone booth, showing her as a bird in a cage. This time, however, it isn't a gilded cage but a cage of misery. As Hitchcock once said about the scene, *It's a reversal of the age-old conflict between men and birds. Here the human beings are in cages and the birds are on the outside* (Truffaut, 1969: 62). We conceptualize Melanie Daniels's situation when she was attacked by the gulls in terms of our understanding of birds in gilded cages.

Each of these examples shows how very ordinary real-world scenes can convey powerful metaphorical messages. Like verbal metaphors, cinematic metaphors present one idea in terms of another that belongs to a different domain of experience. Unlike prose or speech, film has the special property of being able to present a variety of images concurrently. By the unobtrusive use of metaphoric devices (e.g., *The Graduate* scene described above), the audience can follow the action without distraction while still being almost subliminally or unconsciously affected by cinematic tropes. Many mainstream films employ metaphors that are embedded nonfiguratively in the "text" of the narrative. In this way, metaphorical and literal levels of meaning are made to coexist on film to a greater degree than is thought to be the case with literary works. The figurative meaning is dominant, yet it need not be at odds with the nonfigurative (Whittock, 1990). Dreams may also be understood in terms of their cinematic metaphors, even though they, too, are composed of very literal images (Freud, 1900; Shannon, 1990).

Paintings often convey metaphoric meanings, although by their very nature they tend to do so in a more static manner than film. Consider the example of René Magritte, who playfully manipulated both metaphor and metonymy in his surreal images (Dubnick, 1980). Using only familiar objects and traditional perspectives, he gleefully upsets normal contiguity and arbitrarily juxtaposes disparate objects to reveal hidden similarities. Magritte's contribution to surrealist ideas is that he not only "juxtaposed dissimilar objects in what had become the classic surrealist manner; he now explored the hidden affinities between objects" (Gablik, 1970: 103). Metaphor is at the heart of these subtle "hidden affinities," or associations.

Imagine one of the metaphoric images predominant in many of Magritte's paintings. In *La Durée poignardée* (*Time Transfixed*, 1939), a locomotive is frozen in a fireplace while smoke pours from its smokestack and goes up the chimney. The metaphor here is visual. The fireplace resembles a tunnel in shape and color and also because of the locomotive's position in it, which reconciles the disjunction in scale. This metaphoric image substitutes one object for another. The locomotive replaces the fire that normally produces smoke in a fireplace, and the smoke from its smokestack backs up and rises up the flue. The duration of this substitution is limited to a particular moment. Were the train to continue forward out of the fireplace/tunnel, the engine could no longer take the place of the fire.

Magritte's delight with hybrid objects is also seen in *Hommage à Alphonse Allais* (*Homage to Alphonse Allais*, 1964). This painting presents a cigar and a fish merged into one. Although the two objects merge easily enough from the physical point of view, being similar in shape and proportion, the combination is paradoxical. One object is native to water; the other would be extinguished by it. If the fish is in the water, as it appears to be, how can the cigar be smoking? Perhaps the hidden similarity between a fish and a cigar is based on a pun – both can be smoked! A good deal of the tension produced by this image relies directly on metaphorical similarity and opposition (Dubnick, 1980).

Our ability to see metaphor in painting and artist's ability to make "visible poetry" is not limited to surrealistic art. Some of the best evidence for metaphorical thinking in art is seen in 20th-century painters' and sculptors' fascination with machinery. Francis Picabia, Marcel Duchamp, Man Ray, and others created many works that centered on the machine as a metaphorical image for human fallibility. For instance, when Francis

Picabia in his *Portrait d'une jeune fille américaine dans l'état de nudité* (*Portrait of a Nude American Girl*, 1915) reinvented nubile sexuality in the guise of a sparkplug, he was not making a statement about the ontology of automobile parts. Nearly every one of Marcel Duchamp's mechanical sculptures (e.g., the urinal presented as *Fountain*) is metaphoric or ironic and calls us to understand the objects themselves in terms of something else (Fox, 1982).

In recent years, such sculptors as Vito Acconci, Alice Aycock, and Dennis Oppenheim have at once followed and advanced the metaphorical ideas of their predecessors (Fox, 1982; Kardon, 1981). These artists' creations with familiar objects and structures, such as bicycles, vacuums, conveyor belts, crankshafts, and windmills, are intended less to demonstrate the dehumanizing influence of machines than to celebrate the "morphology of machines," or how the parts of machines systematically interact. In these examples, we must conclude that the bicycles, conveyor belts, crankshafts, and so forth do not describe themselves, they describe something else or express cerebral and spiritual concerns that have little to do with the material world. The titles of these mechanical sculptures (e.g., Aycock's *How to Catch and Manufacture Ghosts*) give direction to some of the possible metaphoric readings of the works. Because of the dominance of metaphor and other tropes in our everyday experience, we make metaphoric sense of much visual art, and artists create their art for just such purposes.

METAPHOR AND MYTH

The English word *myth* comes from the Greek *mythos*, meaning word or story. The stories and patterns called myths have dominated human experience throughout recorded history. Myths are not falsehoods but reflect the power of metaphor to breathe life into the essential human story, the story of the relationship between the known and the unknown both in the external world and in our inner experience – the story of the search for identity in the context of the inward struggle between order and chaos. Myths are known to have helped early societies understand such phenomena as the movement of the sun across the sky and the changing seasons, as well as such events as the creation of the universe and the nature of the gods. Myths also serve as the basis for rituals through which the ways of humanity and those of nature can be psychologically reconciled (Campbell, 1972).

The dominance of myths in all cultures provides another source of evidence for the thesis that human thought is fundamentally constituted by such figurative schemes as metaphor. There are generally four types of myth that serve as organizing principles for human experience (Leeming, 1990). Cosmic myths are concerned with the great facts of existence (e.g., the Creation, the Flood, the Apocalypse). Theistic myths involve cultural hierarchies (e.g., the twelve Olympians, the Egyptian gods). Hero myths are stories dealing with individuals (e.g., Achilles, Odysseus, Jesus, Moses, Rama). Place and object myths concern either mythical places (e.g., Atlantis, the Labyrinth) or objects (e.g., King Arthur's sword, the Golden Fleece).

Mythologies come alive for us most forcefully in stories whose heroes are our personae. Artists often explore the inner myths of life in the context of a particular hero's journey. If the story of Odysseus in the *Odyssey* is humanity's story of loss and rebirth leading to transformation, so is *War and Peace* in a 19th-century Russian context, and so is the *Star Wars* movie trilogy in a 20th-century American one. The usual hero pattern, or (as Joseph Campbell puts it) the "monomyth," involves a process by which the hero leaves the ordinary world of waking consciousness, enters the dark world of the supernatural, overcomes those who would destroy him or her, and returns to the ordinary world possessed of new powers and knowledge to help people. The many versions of the hero's journey seen in the world's cultures must be seen as a universal metaphor for the human search for self-knowledge.

The myth of a hero's journey reveals significant aspects of our fundamental ability to conceptualize our lives via metaphor. A journey is a movement from here to there, from Point A to Point B, and as a metaphor for life the two points are obviously life and death. Metaphorical journeys have the day's journey at their core, the amount of space we can cover under the cycle of the sun. By a very easy extension, we get the day's journey as a further metaphor for the whole of life in regard to the cyclical process of birth, death, and renewed life. Thus, in A. E. Housman's poem "Reveille,"

> Clay lies still, but blood's a rover;
> Breath's a ware that will not keep:
> Up, lad: when the journey's over
> There'll be time enough to sleep.

Here awakening in the morning is a metaphor for continuing a journey of life, a journey clearly ending in death. Many hero journeys have the cyclical movement, called the quest, where the hero goes out to accomplish something: kill a dragon, deliver people from giants, or help destroy a hostile city, for example. A successful quest leads to the return home, which is often a long and arduous journey. The great model for this returning journey is, of course, the *Odyssey*.

Other journeys have different shapes (Frye, 1990). In a Y-shaped journey, a choice must be made between the right way and the wrong way. The story of Hercules in Greek mythology is one great example, wherein Hercules must choose between pleasure and virtue in the form of a forking road. On the other hand the doctrine of original sin, and parallel doctrines in other religions, indicates that everyone is on the wrong path to begin with. Hence the frequency of such themes as the one in Robert Frost's "The Road Not Taken."

> Two roads diverged in a yellow wood,
> And sorry I could not travel both
> And be one traveler, long I stood
> And looked down one as far as I could
> To where it bent in the undergrowth;
> Then took the other, as just as fair,
> And having perhaps the better claim,
> Because it was grassy and wanted wear;
> Though as for that the passing there
> Had worn them really about the same,
> And both that morning equally lay
> In leaves no step had trodden black.

Oh, I kept the first for another day!
Yet knowing how way leads on to way,
I doubted if I should ever come back.
I shall be telling this with a sigh
Somewhere ages and ages hence:
Two roads diverged in a wood, and I –
I took the one less traveled by,
And that has made all the difference.

    This poem shows how every choice excludes every other choice and how every life is full of roads not taken that continue to haunt us with a sense of missed opportunities. Ancient myths elaborate upon this metaphorical theme not only by speaking of journeys over the surface of the earth but also in other spatial relationships above and below the earth (Leeming, 1990). Mircea Eliade tells us of the shamanism centered in Siberia, where a major part of the shaman's arduous spiritual training consists of journeys to heights and depths. The symbol of ascent may be a tree, a mountain, or a ladder. The ladder, or staircase, appears in the Book of Genesis with Jacob's vision, and the same ladder figure recurs in Plato's *Symposium* as the image of the progress of love from fascination with a physically beautiful object to union with the ideal form, Beauty. Very frequently the image of ascent takes the form of a spiral path going around a mountain or tower. Such towers, or ziggurats, were common in the ancient Near East, and the Tower of Babel, which was designed to reach heaven from earth, is the demonic parody of Jacob's vision in Genesis. Herodotus relates that some of these towers had seven turnings, each a different color, to represent the seven planets. The greatest literary development of this image is seen in Dante's *Purgatorio*, in which purgatory is represented as a vast mountain on the other side of the world where at each of the seven turnings one of the seven deadly sins is removed. At the top is the Garden of Eden, where Dante recovers his freedom of will and the innocence that he possessed as a child of Adam before the Fall. In this century, Ezra Pound's *Cantos* are, according to his own statement, "erecting a verbal tower corresponding to those in Herodotus, whose terraces were the colors of stars" (Frye, 1990: 262).

There are many patterns of the metaphorical journeys in myths (Frye, 1990). There is the journey to the sea or the bank of a sacred river like the Ganges or Jordan, where sins are metaphorically washed off. Angels are often invoked to account for one recurring feature of mystical experience, the involuntary journey, where they suddenly transport a visionary to a quite different place. Ezekiel in the Old Testament represents himself as being physically in Babylon with other Jewish captives but transported to Jerusalem to see visions of its present desolation and future glory. Mohammed also had an experience, alluded to in the Koran, of a journey from Mecca to Jerusalem at night. Of course, the central involuntary journey is death, where the metaphor of travel seems inescapable. As Kent says in his dying speech in *King Lear* (v. iii. 322–3),

> I have a journey, sir, shortly to go;
> My master calls me, I must not say no.

Many myths about the journey toward death focus on the practice of giving instructions to people about how they will meet death and how to deal with it. This aspect of journeying forms the theme of the various sacred books written for the guidance of the dying, of which the Egyptian and Tibetan Books of the Dead are the best known. The Egyptian journey is to a world like this one, where anything dangerous or sinister can be warded off by spells or by a proclamation of one's virtue during life. The Tibetan Book of the Dead is set in the Buddhist belief in reincarnation. Here the recently dead soul is informed, by a reading of the book, that it will see a series of benevolent and hostile deities. As these are self-projected hallucinations, the dead soul should not commit itself to any belief in their substantial existence. In virtually all cases, the discarnate soul is assumed to wander in an intermediate world between death and birth until it is finally attracted to a female world and enters it. Here again there is a continuing cycle within which all journeys take place.

Comparative studies clearly show that similar mythic tales are found in almost every culture on earth. Why might this be so? My discussion of journey myths is intended to illustrate how myths are not falsehoods but reflect patterns of imaginative thinking rooted in metaphor. People have always experienced a significant part of their everyday lives from early childhood in terms of source–path–goal image schemas. These recurring bodily experiences are abstracted to form part of the foundation for higher-order reasoning. This abstraction is one reason why journey metaphors are seen so frequently in the way people think about their mundane lives and in the way different cultures reconcile their humanity with the world around them. As Joseph Campbell (1972: 10) once commented about myth,

> When these stories are interpreted, though, not as reports of historic fact, but as merely imagined episodes projected onto history, and when they are recognized, then, as analogous to like projections produced elsewhere, in China, India, and Yucatan, the import becomes obvious; namely, that although false and to be rejected as accounts of physical history, such universally cherished figures of the mythic imagination must represent facts of the mind.

METAPHOR IN CULTURE

Anthropologists have long recognized the significance of metaphor in culture. Sensitivity to local figures of speech, especially metaphor, is of critical importance to ethnographers, because metaphors are primary devices for the representation of experience. Although it is sometimes unclear to what extent the presence of metaphor in a culture can be attributed to the minds of individuals, it is clear that metaphor provides the basis for communities' understanding of some aspects of their collective experience. The ethnographic literature provides many examples of metaphor's role in defining cultural experience (Fernandez, 1986, 1991).

The Nayaka (a tribal group in South India) relate metaphorically to their natural environment (Bird-David, 1990, 1992). For instance, the intrafamily caring relationship, particularly between adults and their children, constitutes the primary metaphor by which the Nayaka think about and relate to their natural environment and also how they conceptualize economic behavior and organization. Many hunting–gathering societies use adult–child caring metaphor in understanding human–nature relatedness (Endicott, 1979).

Much anthropological material shows how everyday language illustrates different metaphorical conceptions of experience. For example, in Chalcatonga Mixtec, an Otomanguean language of western Mexico, spatial locations are understood via the metaphorical projection of body-part terms onto objects (Brugman, 1983, 1984). For instance, if you want to say *The stone is under the table*, you say *yuu wa hiya cii-mesa*, which word-by-word comes out as *Stone the be located belly-table*, where *belly-table* is a possessive construction equivalent to "the table's belly." Similarly, if you want to say *I am sitting on the branch of the tree*, you say the Mixtec equivalent of *I am sitting the tree's arm*, and if you want to say *My son is lying on the mat*, you say the equivalent of *My son is lying on the mat's face*. Mixtec expressions must use aspects of relative location using body projections because the language has no system of prepositions and cases, as do Indo-European languages. This kind of conventional system of projecting body parts metaphorically onto objects in order to conceptualize spatial locations is not rare. Many languages of Mesoamerica and Africa employ similar systems for expressing spatial location via body-part concepts. We can understand the Mixtec system, for example, precisely because we too have the capacity for metaphorical projections of this sort, even though our own conceptual system is not organized in this way (G. Lakoff, 1987).

Political discourse among the Cuna tribe of Panama shows how a Cuna chief resolves various sorts of social problems via metaphor and in doing so adds to his own prestige as a problem solver (J. Howe, 1977). The chief's role is to represent the moderating and conservative influence of Cuna tradition, propriety, and good sense, and it is imperative that he maintain a respectable distance from the squabbles and ambiguities of day-to-day living. His use of metaphors provides him with means for keeping this distance. As a variety of indirect speech, which the chief seldom explicitly interprets himself, the metaphors allow the chief to express his opinion by innuendo and without "naming names."

Trees and their wood play a central role in medicine, ritual, and mythology among the Cuna. Chiefs will metaphorically express their views via analogy to trees. The planting of a tree often describes the installation of a new chief, and the discovery of a valuable tree at a distance in the forest often describes the process of choosing a new chief. Chiefs who last only a few years are trees that become uprooted soon after planting, and the toppling of a tree by an earthquake described one event in which a chief was removed because of scandalous behavior. One chief elaborated on this image in a chant that deals with the Cuna revolution of 1925, the chiefs who were deposed during it, and the process of reestablishing order (ibid.).

> A severe storm has passed over this land of ours and the trees were overturned by it. By reason of the tempest, the animals that had made their abodes in the trees were thus dispersed. Now we shall build up again all that the tempest has torn down. According to my way of thinking, we should plant a tree that will last many years, a tree possessing great resistance, and when we have planted it, we also ought to plant others about every village. I think that when our trees bear fruit, to its branches there will come grouse, parrots, and birds from all directions to eat the fruit of the tree. For this reason the tree should be of a kind that bears much fruit. Then we ought to keep the ground about it very clean so that the vultures (Panamanians, Blacks) may not come and besmirch our tree. We should securely fence in the flowers (women) that we are going to plant about our tree. We should plant cocoa trees . . .
> (Howe, 1977: 149)

The Cuna consider that metaphors do more than merely provide a conventional means of talking about one thing in terms of another. Cuna metaphors suggest ways of conceptualizing Cuna political organization; that is, they teach an official native model of politics, a constitution of sorts in metaphor.

Work on the Fang people of western equatorial Africa provides another example of metaphor's constitutive role in defining cultural practice (Fernandez, 1986). The Fang are a neo-Bantu culture practicing slash-and-burn agriculture in the equatorial forest. The Fang institution of palabra, or council house, is at the center of their daily lives. There is constant activity in the palabra, including various crafts, folklore performances, daily discussion, debates, and moots involving marriages, brideprice, debts, and inheritances. Men are not appointed, nor do they have permanent positions as judges, to hear disputes in the council house. Instead, men are selected to hear disputes by virtue of their reputation for wisdom, persuasion, and eloquence in speech. One does not say of a man that he is wise or eloquent. One says rather that he *breaks* palabra or he *slices* them. This metaphoric description of juridic technique refers to how men do forest work. Fang men must work the forest with great skill to provide for their families adequately. However powerful, if you are so clumsy as to break apart palabra instead of carefully slicing them, you leave jagged edges that are hard to fit back together. If you cut or slice palabra, you can more easily put the pieces back together. Workers must be craftsmen who carefully slice and not break raffia palm wands, lianas, and other fibers and all the various woods of the forest.

The metaphoric linking of the forest worker to techniques of argument and judgment is particularly convincing for the Fang, who are heavily dependent on forest exploitation and forest crafts. When making a decision, judges are said to have made their way skillfully through the forest to the *elik*, the site of a former village deep in the forest. These former village sites metaphorically refer to places where the resentment originally lay that gave rise to the present conflict. A clumsy judge is disruptive, chopping down the forest as he makes his way through it – actions that only lead to further dispute. Being a good judge is not a matter of wisdom or eloquence but of cutting and slicing, pathfinding, and hunting. In general, because of the complexity of most palabra situations, it is difficult to state what makes a good litigant or judge. Metaphor extends that inchoate experience to more concrete domains of Fang experience where comparisons in performance are more easily recognized and understood (ibid.).

Another example of metaphor's significant role in cultural thinking and practice is found in recent work in Polynesia on the associated concepts of *mana* and *tapu* (Shore, 1991). *Mana* refers to power, luck, and efficacy and is often linked to gods, chiefs, and, in certain regions of Polynesia, to men as opposed to women. Physical attributes of *mana* include large size, brightness, and shininess. The related concept *tapu* refers to notions that are sacred, dangerous, set aside, marked, or bound. *Tapu* contrasts with *noa*, which is seen as referring to what is secular, unmarked, free, and unbounded.

Mana and *tapu* are active concepts in Polynesian thought. Both concepts illustrate culturally orchestrated experiential schemas involving intimate connections between bodily experience and abstract political and religious principles (ibid.). *Tapu* and *noa* are alternative conditions of *mana* and are understood in relation to a general cultural schema involving bodily distinctions between inside and outside, stasis and movement, and tight muscular control and muscular relaxation. For example, the imposition of *tapu* on people or objects involves experiences of binding, containment, immobilizing, and centering. The relation of bodily experiences to more abstract concepts begins at an early age in Polynesian culture. Small children are allowed to cry and have tantrums as a way of expressing their needs. But when a young child begins to walk, this indulgence in impulse gratification is replaced by a new emphasis on impulse control. Crying and tantrums are no longer tolerated, and children must wait to receive parental attention. Older children are strongly encouraged to sit in what is called the *fa-tai* position, with legs crossed and arms resting on the thighs. This position reflects control, containment of limbs, and withholding movement. Moreover, this posture also informs a wide range of aesthetic and political practices, such as dance style, postural attributes of different kinds of chiefs, and gender styles.

In Samoa, high rank is symbolically equated with, among other things, absence of movement and centrality (e.g., seating place, house position within a community). The distinction between sitting/resting and moving that is implicit in these cultural beliefs also points to a wide range of abstract associations that in many cases form part of the linguistic conventions in a community. For example, the village *taupou* is a ceremonial virgin who is often referred to as *'o taupou fa 'anofonofo*, or "the sitting maiden." This name for a ceremonial virgin reflects the strong metaphoric link between bodily experience of containment and the more abstract concept of what is sacred, marked, and set aside. Thus, the shared experiences through which Samoans understand power concepts provide the basis for the projection of bodily imagery into social institutions as linguistic and kinetic metaphors.

The grounding of the abstract concepts *mana*, *tapu*, and *noa* in bodily experience illustrates the important role of metaphor, especially synesthesia, in the construction of cultural meaning. Metaphor provides part of the perceptual foundation for more complex and culturally mediated cognition. Under this view, culture serves to provide a great number of "prepackaged" metaphoric, as well as metonymic, associations that can be reconstructed by individuals through their own bodily experiences. Adult perception differs from that of young children because it employs more abstract associations that are mediated by conventional models. Yet metaphoric thought processes are evident not only in primitive symbol formation but in higher-level meaning integration, as is evident in the mapping of Samoan bodily experiences onto their understanding of the abstract concepts *mana*, *tapu*, and *noa*. The Samoan data underscore the often noted conclusion that the human body is treated as an image in many cultural communities (Douglas, 1973). Even more generally, these data illustrate how conventional representations come to have psychological force for everyday speakers through metaphoric reasoning.

This discussion of metaphor in culture has described only a few of the numerous research projects devoted to how metaphor constrains cultural experience. Cultural anthropologists are, by tradition, less interested in whether metaphors or other cultural representations are "in the head" of individuals than in the role metaphors have "in culture." In this way, metaphor might best be conceived of as something that is cultural and not part of the bedrock of cognition.

Recent anthropologists have attempted to reclaim culture from metaphor theorists, particularly those in cognitive linguistics, who appear to place metaphor as somehow above culture or who see metaphor as somehow being constitutive of culture. The most vigorous attack on the cognitive linguistic work argues that cultural understanding underlies metaphor use and that there is more to culture than just metaphor (Quinn, 1991). The empirical work in support of this point about culture and metaphor comes from an analysis of the metaphors Americans use to talk about marriage (Quinn, 1987). This examination of many hours of discourse on the topic of marriage shows that only eight classes of metaphors occur continually when people describe their marriages. Included among these are metaphors of sharedness, such as *I felt like a marriage was just a partnership* or *We're together in this*; metaphors of lastingness, such as *It was stuck together pretty good* or *It's that feeling of confidence we have about each other that's going to keep us going*; metaphors of mutual benefit, such as *That was really something we got out of marriage* or *Our marriage is a very good thing for both of us*; metaphors of compatibility, such as *The best thing about Bill is he fits me so well* or *Both of our weaknesses were such that the other person could fill in*: metaphors of difficulty, such as *That was one of the hard barriers to get over* or *The first year of marriage was really a trial*; metaphors of effort, such as *She works harder at our marriage than I do* or *We had to fight our way back almost to the beginning*; metaphors of success or failure, such as *We knew that it was working* or *The marriage may be doomed*; and, finally, metaphors of risk, such as *There're so many odds against marriage* or *The marriage was in trouble*.

The reducibility of a superficially varied list of metaphors that people use to talk about marriage to eight distinct classes is taken as a demonstration that metaphor is highly constrained by understanding rather than constituting understanding (Quinn, 1991). The eight classes of metaphor presumably reflect the conceptual elements that together define the single model of marriage held by most Americans. For example, Americans expect marriage to be shared, mutually beneficial, and lasting. These expectations arise from the mapping of our cultural conceptions of love onto the societal institution of marriage and the consequent structuring of marital expectations in terms of the motivational structuring of love.

People want to be with the person they love and so expect marriage to be shared; they want to fulfill the loved person's needs and have their own needs fulfilled, so they expect marriage to be beneficial to both people; and they do not want to lose the person they love and wish for that person to go on loving them, so they expect their marriage to be lasting. None of these examples is itself metaphorical, even though Americans often use metaphorical language to talk about their cultural ideas about love and marriage (ibid.).

Other aspects of the cultural model of marriage reflected in the metaphors for compatibility, difficulty, effort, and so on arise from the contradiction that results from the expectations of mutual benefit and of lastingness. We expect to fulfill our spouses' needs, and vice versa, but when such mutual benefits do not occur, either of us is free to leave, just as in any voluntary relationship. Yet the expectation that marriage is supposed to last conflicts with individuals' freedom to leave the marriage when they wish. The further expectation that marriage is shared results in another dilemma. Although couples are supposed to have common goals and interests, too much of an overlap may threaten the ability of each spouse to meet his or her autonomous needs. All these difficulties in marriage pose a threat that American couples must overcome to achieve a lasting, mutually beneficial, successful marriage. It appears, then, that the cultural model for marriage held by most Americans is complex, with potentially contradictory elements, yet this model is not in and of itself constituted by metaphor.

Each element in this reconstructed cultural model of marriage can be and often is instantiated by a wide variety of metaphors. For example, speakers will talk of marital lastingness using a metaphor of a manufactured product that is well made, such as *stuck together pretty good*, with a solid foundation, a sound framework, and good, well-fitting parts. But there are many other metaphors used to convey these expectations of lastingness in marriage, such as a marriage being like an ongoing journey that a married couple takes together (*that's going to keep us going*), the couple as two inseparable objects (*We knew we were going to stay together*), marriage as an unbreakable bond (*That just kind of cements the bond*), and so on. People vary in how frequently they employ these metaphors, but no one metaphor is seen as being more central than others in capturing Americans' understanding of marriage.

The verbal metaphors people use to talk of their experience simply name parts of underlying independent cultural models. Consider the following example from one participant's discussion of marriage (ibid., p. 73):

> Accepting the differences that were there and that were going to – you know, and that I would have to put up with some of the situations that I didn't like and continue to until we had worked it out. But that however long and stony a road it was, we had agreed to set out on it and meet each small situation as it came.

The *long and stony road* metaphor conveys the difficulty of marriage and also its lastingness. Does this metaphor give rise to these inferences about difficulty and lastingness? Quinn argues that speakers employ verbal metaphors to clarify one part of the complex cultural models for marriage, such as the idea that marriage is difficult and lasting. Speakers will even comment in more detail about the point they express metaphorically, as shown in the following excerpt from an interview (ibid., p. 75):

> And then I see marriages where it's just like they are brother and sister, they cross paths occasionally. They don't have anything in common or they don't ever do anything together.

This further commentary on a chosen metaphor is seen as indicating that the speaker adopted the metaphor to make a point already in mind rather than being led to this point by a previously unrecognized entailment of the metaphor (Quinn, 1991). Unlike the participants who were explicitly asked to reason about a phenomenon, such as electricity, that they did not understand very well (Gentner & Gentner, 1983), people who talk about marriage already have much understanding of the target domain and so use metaphor only to comment on that understanding. Metaphor may play a special role in science and in special instances of reasoning, such as that studied by psychologists (Quinn, 1991), but metaphor does not constitute people's grasp of most ordinary domains or situations, such as marriage.

A final argument against the constitutive view of metaphor in cultural understanding comes from an analysis of people's extended reasoning in talking about marriage. The following passage is from an interview with a male participant (ibid., p. 84).

> But it could be that the situation when we got married, that it was such that we had lots of room to adjust. Because we didn't have any idea what we were getting into. That gave us a lot of room to adjust. And by the time we had been through the first year we realized, you know, there would have to be adjustments made. And a few years afterwards, when things really got serious we were – you know, when the marriage was strong, it was very strong because it was made as we went along – it was sort of a do-it-yourself project.

This narrative describes how the initial incompatibilities faced by the speaker and his wife did not result in divorce, because each spouse tried especially hard to be more compatible. Because each had few preconceived expectations about the marriage, the husband and wife were able to make appropriate adjustments to make a stronger marriage. The chain of reasoning underlying the husband's narrative rests on an overlapping entailment of two metaphors – MARRIAGE IS A CONTAINER (*we didn't have any idea what we were getting into*) and MARRIAGE IS A MANUFACTURED PRODUCT (*a do-it-yourself project*). The expression *it was made as we went along* refers to the adjustments that were made that led to greater compatibility between the husband and wife. But the idea that lack of prior expectation leads to compatibility is not an obvious entailment of a do-it-yourself project, nor does a lack of prior expectation necessary entail anything about the outcome of such a project. As is untrue of building projects, lack of preconceived expectations is seen by the husband as facilitating mutual benefit and lastingness. The speaker starts out using one metaphor to make his point (the container metaphor) but finds it inappropriate and therefore switches to another (the manufactured product metaphor) to complete the line of reasoning he wishes to communicate.

The variety of verbal metaphors selected by Americans to talk about marriage implies that there is not one central metaphor for marriage in the way there seems to be for anger (ANGER IS HEATED FLUID IN A CONTAINER). Moreover, the metaphors that are evident in people's discourse on marriage are not reducible to a central schema or to a single stable assemblage of schemas, as seems to be the case for anger. For this reason, it appears to some cultural anthropologists that Americans' cultural model of marriage is independent of metaphor (Quinn, 1991).

Quinn's arguments against the constitutive metaphor view of cultural understanding must be taken seriously because they raise an important issue about trying to infer something about conceptual structure from a systematic analysis of linguistic structure and behavior (Gibbs, in press). Most generally, there are limitations to inferring anything about human concepts and culture from an analysis of what people say. The primary limitation is that shared by most linguistic research; namely, the problem of reaching conclusions about phenomena based on the individual analyst's own intuitions. Cognitive psychologists, for example, are generally skeptical of hypotheses about human conceptual knowledge that are based on a theorist's intuitive speculations, even when such speculations are based on asystematic analysis of linguistic structure and behavior. To many, the idea that conceptual metaphors underlie our everyday experience or motivate our use and understanding of different linguistic expressions cannot be accepted as "psychologically real," because such a theory is based on intuitive explanation. Cognitive anthropologists' criticisms of the metaphor view of culture are worthy of attention, at the very least, because of the difficulty of making claims about conceptual knowledge based on an analysis of systematic patterns in everyday life. Furthermore, criticisms from anthropologists of the metaphor view of culture also help to keep in focus the problem of making claims about culture and human experience based on an analysis of only a single cultural model or a single culture.

Despite Quinn's criticisms of the idea that models of cultural knowledge are constituted by metaphor, there are good reasons to be cautious in accepting her arguments against the metaphor view of everyday experience. Many of her arguments against metaphor's place in cultural understanding rest on mistaken assumptions about metaphor, cognitive and cultural models, and the coherence of everyday discourse. Consider one widely discussed analysis of how Americans construct an idealized cognitive model for the emotion of anger (Kovecses, 1986; G. Lakoff, 1987). This model claims that Americans have a general metaphor in their conceptual systems, such as THE BODY IS A CONTAINER FOR THE EMOTION (*He was filled with anger, She couldn't contain her joy*). This general metaphor is combined with a specific conceptual metaphor, ANGER IS HEAT, to provide the central metaphor for anger, ANGER IS HEATED FLUID IN A CONTAINER (*You make my blood boil, She was seething with rage*). The metaphorical mapping from a source domain, such as heated fluid in a container, onto the target domain of anger yields a variety of metaphorical entailments. For example, when hot fluids begin to boil, the fluid moves upwards, and so when the intensity of anger increases, the fluid rises (*She could feel her gorge rising, His pent-up anger welled up inside him*). Intense heat produces steam and creates pressure on the container, and so intense anger produces steam (*She go all steamed up, I was fuming*) and pressure on the container (*I could barely contain my rage*), and too much anger results in an explosion (*She blew up at me, I blew my stack*).

These metaphorical entailments are seen by cognitive linguists as part of our everyday conceptual system. The domains organized by such metaphoric relations comprise "experiential gestalts" that are the products of our bodily experiences in interaction with the physical environment and other people. Some of these experiences may be universal; others may vary across cultures. Because metaphors organize our experience through their entailments, they help create social realities for us and become guides to action.

The argument that metaphors used to talk about marriage do not cohere into a single stable model for marriage in the way that appears to be the case for anger metaphors misrepresents the complexity of the cognitive model of anger and really confuses metaphor with idealized cognitive models. There may be a variety of conceptualizations of anger to which different metaphorical expressions refer. Both ANGER IS HEATED FLUID and ANGER IS ANIMAL BEHAVIOR, for example, give rise to many similar entailments about the causes and consequences of anger (Gibbs, 1990a). But each conceptual metaphor refers to a different aspect of the ICM for anger. Thus, the conventional expression *I was getting hot under the collar* (from the ANGER IS HEAT metaphor) points to an earlier temporal stage in the anger ICM than does the expression *I bit her head off* (from the ANGER IS ANIMAL BEHAVIOR metaphor) (Nayak & Gibbs, 1990). People appear to conceptualize different aspects of their complex concept of anger in terms of different metaphors.

In a similar way, there may possibly be one general cognitive or cultural model for marriage, just in the way Quinn suggests, that is motivated by a cluster of contiguous conceptual metaphors. The variety of expressions people use to speak of marriage reflect their different conceptual metaphors for different aspects of their experience of marriage. Yet the variety of expressions do not mean that there is not some sort of cultural model of marriage based on a complex configuration of different types of conceptual metaphors. A lasting marriage can be both a well-made product and an ongoing journey as well as a firmly held position, a secure bond, and a permanent location. The fact that speakers often employ a variety of metaphors in talking about marriage, sometimes switching quickly between tropes, does not mean that those expressions only name or refer to aspects of some nonmetaphorical cultural model. As is the case for anger, people use different metaphors, even within the same narrative, because each metaphor reflects a different aspect of their metaphorical understanding of some experience. One's cognitive model of marriage may consist of various metaphors that capture different aspects of our understanding of marriage, such as compatibility, mutual benefit, and lastingness. These metaphors may be contiguously linked, perhaps as a kind of radial structure, yet need not be internally consistent. For example, we may at times see marriage as being a container but at other times as being like a manufactured product.

One difficulty with Quinn's work is that her marriage interviews were with relatively young couples with happy or successful marriages. Recent work by T. Boellstorff at the University of California at Berkeley suggests that looking at different kinds of marriages (e.g., unhappy marriages, broken marriages, couples who have been together for decades) actually reveals that there are several overlapping cognitive models for American marriage. For example, "ideal" marriages reflect people's concept when they first marry and are very much in love and see no conflicts. "Typical" marriages, on the other hand, involve couples who love each other but who fight and often face internal and external obstacles to their marriage. There are also concepts of "good" and "bad" marriages, which people readily conceptualize as different. Overall, there are a variety of cognitive models for American marriage that reflect the diversity of Americans' marriage experiences.

One reason, then, for the variety of metaphors that motivate our talk of marriage is that Americans do not have a single cultural or cognitive model of marriage. Contrary to Quinn's claim that people truly understand marriage in a way that they may not understand more abstract concepts, such as electricity, people's understandings of their marriages are complex and change over time. As our experience of marriage changes, so too might we conceptualize these differing experiences in terms of very different metaphors. Quinn's own narratives of individuals talking about the history of their marriages clearly illustrate this idea.

What is remarkable about Quinn's interviews is not the diversity of metaphors they reveal but the fact that people's verbal metaphors in talking about marriage are so limited. If people really had a completely nonmetaphorical cultural model of marriage and used verbal metaphors only to highlight different parts of this model, we would expect people to use a tremendous variety of verbal metaphors. Yet people don't talk about their marriages in just any manner. For instance, people don't talk about their marriages in terms of mowing the lawn, doing the laundry, reading books, going to the store, or mailing a letter; they talk about their marriages in terms of journeys, being in good locations, and being balanced. The fairly limited range of conventional metaphors that underlie people's talk about marriage reflect the constraints of their metaphorical understandings of their various marriage experiences.

None of this means that people's conceptual understandings of marriages are totally metaphorical. Some of our conceptual understandings of love, marriage, anger and other abstract concepts may be nonmetaphorical, but a great many of these abstract concepts appear to be constituted by metaphor. The challenge for theorists who adhere to the position that metaphor is used primarily for talking about experience and does not constitute our conceptual understanding of experience is to provide explicit evidence that people do not think of these concepts in metaphorical ways. We should not simply focus on whether the mind or culture is inherently metaphorical or nonmetaphorical. Rather we should focus our attention on the explicit, detailed examination of various concepts to determine the ways in which these are constituted by both metaphorical and nonmetaphorical schemes of thought. My claim in response to Quinn is that much of our cultural understanding of marriage is motivated by metaphor. We may be able as analysts to abstract from people's metaphorical understanding of their experience and provide a detailed idealized, even culturally sensitive, model that appears independent of metaphor. Yet we don't know if these idealized cultural models are constitutive of individuals' ordinary experiences: They might be convenient fictions created by scholars to suggest regularities in human experience that are really motivated by figurative schemes of thought. At the very least, determining whether any set of abstract concepts is constituted by metaphor requires the analytical tools of linguists and anthropologists and also the special experimental methodologies created by cognitive psychologists to examine automatic, unconscious mental processes.

CONCLUSION

Metaphor is not merely an instance of language, a special rhetorical device used for communication and persuasion. Instead metaphor is a fundamental mental capacity by which people understand themselves and the world through the conceptual mapping of knowledge from one domain onto another. The overwhelming ubiquity of metaphor in language, thought, science, law, art, myth, and culture illustrates that metaphor is an integral part of human life. My point in this chapter has been to outline some of the evidence in support of this conclusion. But I have tried to show that the issue of what role metaphor plays in language and thought actually involves a series of different questions. Metaphor appears to affect semantic change, how linguistic communities create and make sense of different linguistic expressions, and how individual speakers make sense of the meanings of various kinds of poetic and ordinary language. The next chapter considers in more detail whether metaphorical knowledge influences people's use and understanding of language.

My enthusiasm for metaphor's significant role in thought and language should not be understood to imply that metaphor is constitutive of all aspects of human thought and language understanding. It is clearly the case that much of what we know about ourselves and the world arises from nonmetaphorical bodily experiences and nonmetaphorical patterns of thought. Yet it is, at the very least, appropriate to conclude that by adopting the cognitive wager and specifically looking for metaphor's presence in language and thought we can find that a great deal of human cognition is determined by the natural reflex to think metaphorically. The challenge for both advocates and critics of metaphor's role in cognition and culture is to establish the boundaries of metaphor in shaping everyday thought.

Chapter 5

Understanding metaphorical expressions

The language of poetic imagination is highly figurative, with metaphors serving as the primary trope. Metaphor scholars since Aristotle have sought to understand how people interpret the meanings of metaphorical expressions, particularly those that express some comparison between ideas or objects from dissimilar domains, as in Robert Burns's famous example *My luve's like a red red rose* or in these lines from Keats, who tells us that a summer day is

> . . . like the passage of an angel's tear
> that falls through the clear ether silently.

Much of the symbolism in poetry rests with metaphor, and literary critics have taken great pains to elaborate on how metaphor works to convey symbolic meaning. Consider this poem by the 19th-century poet Christina Georgina Rossetti.

> Does the road wind up-hill all the way?
> Yes, to the very end.
> Will the day's journey take the whole long day?
> From morn to night, my friend.

> But is there for the night a resting place?
> A roof for when the slow, dark hours begin.
> May not the darkness hide it from my face?
> You cannot miss that inn.

> Shall I meet other wayfarers at night?
> Those who have gone before.

Then must I knock or call when just in sight?
They will not keep you standing at that door.

Shall I find comfort, travel-sore and weak?
Of labour you shall find the sum.
Will there be beds for me and all who seek?
Yea, beds for all who come.

Reading these lines, we immediately recognize that Rossetti means to convey something other than a description of a day's journey. Her words are intended to draw deeper comparisons between a day's journey and a person's life whereby the up-hill road represents the course we travel in life and the way-farers' inn the resting place after death.

How do we arrive at an understanding of poetic metaphors? The past 30 years have witnessed an overwhelming boom in the empirical study of metaphor. This chapter considers many of the important theories on metaphor understanding from cognitive science in light of empirical evidence from psycholinguists on how people comprehend the meanings of metaphorical utterances. Chapter 3 reviewed evidence indicating that similar cognitive mechanisms drive people's interpretation of literal and figurative utterances. My aim in the present chapter is to explore in greater detail exactly how people understand verbal metaphors. Particular attention is paid to three general concerns. First, what empirical evidence is there to support some of the widely held views in philosophy, linguistics, and psychology about metaphorical meaning and its interpretation? Second, how can rival theories of metaphor be distinguished, based on the different temporal moments of understanding that each theory highlights? Third, to what extent does understanding metaphorical language depend on preexisting metaphorical knowledge that is part of our everyday conceptual system? In responding to each of these questions I once again emphasize the different possible ways figurative thought interacts with linguistic understanding. The overall goal here is to recognize the particular approaches to the study of metaphor understanding that have the greatest psychological validity in regard to how people make sense of why verbal metaphors mean what they do and to how metaphoric knowledge influences on-line comprehension of verbal metaphors.

Aristotle provided the first scholarly treatment of metaphor in his writing on the art of poetry. The reason for starting with Aristotle is not simply chronological but is that Aristotle's views have been so influential in both traditional and contemporary discussions of metaphor interpretation. Aristotle gave metaphor the following definition: *Metaphor consists in giving the thing a name that belongs to something else; the transference being either from genus to species, or from species to genus, or from species to species, or on the ground of analogy (Poetics, 1457b)*. For example, a transfer from species to genus is *Indeed ten thousand noble things Odysseus did*, in which the phrase *ten thousand*, a species of meaning, is being used instead of the word *many*. Metaphor by analogy is *Old age is to life as evening is to day*, where one calls the evening day's *old age* and old age *the evening of life*. This classification served as the basis for later distinctions among figures of speech, such as synecdoche and metonymy, as well as analogy.

Two important ideas come from Aristotle's definition of metaphor. First, metaphor is a matter of words, because metaphoric transfer takes place at the level of words, not sentences. Second, metaphor is viewed as deviant from literal usage because it involves the transfer of a name to some object to which that name does not properly belong. Aristotle said *Diction becomes distinguished and non-prosaic by the use of unfamiliar terms, i.e., strange words, metaphors, lengthened forms, and everything that deviates from ordinary models of speech (Poetics, 148a)*.

A third characteristic of metaphor for Aristotle is that metaphor is based on similarities between two things. Each metaphoric transfer from genus to species, species to genus, species to species, or by analogy requires that some underlying resemblance or similarity be noted that permits the transfer to be made. As Aristotle noted for poets, *the greatest thing by far is to be a master of metaphor. It is the one thing that cannot be learned from others; and it is also a sign of genius, since a good metaphor implies an intuitive perception of the similarity in dissimilars* (*Poetics*, 1459a). Metaphors are implied analogies or elliptical similes.

Although Aristotle's definition treats analogy as one kind of metaphor, it suggests that metaphorical figures of speech are essentially comparisons. Metaphors are more powerful than similes because they are more condensed (*Rhetoric*, 1406b). Perhaps Aristotle's most widely debated claim concerns whether metaphor involves some similarity between disparate things. Many scholars have interpreted his view as suggesting that metaphor can be reduced to antecedently known likenesses. However, others have suggested that Aristotle regarded metaphor as producing either something new or a discernment of formerly unrecognized relations or properties that might be said to be new (Hausman, 1989).

I. A. RICHARDS'S CONTRIBUTION

Aristotle's views have prompted much discussion among metaphor theorists, particularly in the last 50 or 60 years. In the 1930s, I. A. Richards (1936) revived the study of metaphor by, among other things, offering a terminology that has become widely accepted in talking about metaphor. According to Richards, metaphor consists of two terms and the relationship between them. Consider the expression *The question of federal aid to parochial schools is a bramble patch* (Ortony, Reynolds, & Arter, 1978). The subject term *federal aid to parochial schools* is called the *topic* or *tenor*, and the term being used metaphorically, *bramble patch*, is the *vehicle*. The relationship between the topic and vehicle is the *ground*. Richards also introduced the notion of *tension* to describe the literal incompatibility of the topic and vehicle. For example, the concept federal aid is literally incompatible with the concept bramble patch, and so our understanding of *The question of federal aid to parochial schools is a bramble patch* produces metaphorical tension arising from that literal incompatibility.

Metaphor scholars have focused primarily on explaining

how we arrive at the ground from the comparison or interaction of the topic and vehicle. But it is not always easy to identify precisely the topic, the vehicle, or the nature of the literal incompatibility in metaphorical expressions. Still, Richards's terminology has provided a useful framework for discussing the problem of metaphor.

THE METAPHOR-AS-COMPARISON VIEW

Max Black (1955) elaborated on Aristotle's and Richards's views to present two different theoretical descriptions of metaphor. The *substitution view* holds that in understanding a metaphor, its metaphorical terms are replaced with literal terms that can fit the same context. For instance, a metaphor of the "A is B" form (e.g., *Man is a wolf*) is nothing but an indirect way of presenting some intended literal meaning "A is C" (e.g., *Man is fierce*).

Two things motivate people to replace a straightforward statement with a metaphorical expression the meaning of which must be derived (Black, 1962). First, metaphors are stylistic devices that serve an ornamental function in discourse. Readers should experience some aesthetic delight when they discover the hidden meanings of metaphor. Second, metaphors are useful for coining terms for new concepts, such as the *leg* of a triangle (Ortony, Reynolds, & Arter, 1978). The substitution view assumes that metaphor plays only a minor role in language and is at best an affectation that obscures literal meaning.

The more popular *comparison view* suggests that a metaphor consists of the presentation of some underlying analogy or similarity in the form of a condensed or elliptical simile (Black, 1962; Henle, 1958). Our interpretation of metaphor is accomplished by converting each expression into a complex simile-like form (G. Miller, 1979). Thus, a metaphor of "A is B" form indirectly implies the speaker's intended literal meaning "A is like B in certain respects." For instance, the metaphor *The car beetles along the road* describes the movement of the car as being like the movement of a beetle. Interpreting any metaphor requires that one determine the general nature of the situation being described in its literal sense (the movement of a car along the road) and link this analogically to a more specific situation that we have inferred (the movement of the beetle). A nominal metaphor, such as *John is an octopus*, is interpreted by seeing two properties such that the topic having the first property is like the vehicle having the second. *John is an octopus* can be understood not by simply applying the property "having tentacles" to John but by searching for a type of human behavior that could be considered to bear some resemblance to this property of the octopus (e.g., the ability to influence many things simultaneously). For predicative metaphors, such as *President Bush steamed ahead with his pro-life campaign*, a listener must construct a corresponding complex simile via a rule that reconstructs one predicate as being like some entity in a certain way. Thus, President Bush is doing something that is like steaming ahead; that is, President Bush's progress with his pro-life campaign is like a ship steaming ahead along some path. Sentential metaphors are understood as comparison statements through their irrelevance to the surrounding discourse when literally construed. For example, when a speaker asks *What kind of mood did you find the boss in?* and the addressee replies *The lion roared*, we interpret this metaphorical description by searching for a property of a lion's roaring that is similar to something the boss would do. Thus, the lion's roaring is like the boss displaying anger.

One popular version of the comparison theory, the semantic feature view, proposes that metaphor interpretation requires the cancellation, transfer, combination, or exchange of semantic features associated with the topic and vehicle terms (L. Cohen, 1979; Levin, 1977; Weinreich, 1966). Semantic features are not usually intended here to be confined to those elements that are strictly entailed by a term but can also include features that are typically associated with the terms in a metaphor. Metaphor specifically involves the cancellation or transfer of some of those features, usually from the nonliteral to the literal term. For instance, understanding *Their legislative program is a rocket to the moon* (L. Cohen, 1979) proceeds via canceling of the features of *rocket to the moon* that are incompatible with those of *legislative program* (mature object, air-cleaving, cylindrical, etc.) while retaining features such as fast-moving, far-aiming, and so on that provide some basis of similarity.

However, the idea that metaphors receive their interpretations through the addition or deletion of semantic features cannot account for semantically nondeviant sentences that are still used metaphorically, such as when *The rock has become brittle with age* is uttered in reference to a person (Kittay, 1987). Proponents of this view recognize that not all metaphors are semantically deviant sentences and see "pragmatic deviance" as characterizing a whole class of sentences of this sort (Levin, 1977). But it is not clear how the semantic feature and the pragmatic view operate together to produce metaphorical readings of nondeviant sentences.

Another difficulty with the feature addition or deletion view of metaphor can be found by looking at the opening lines of Yeats's poem "The Crazed Man" (Kittay, 1987).

> Crazed through much child-bearing
> The moon is staggering in the sky

One could interpret this metaphor of a childbearing moon by displacing features of *moon* that violate selection restrictions on what can be childbearing and replacing them with just those features appropriate to things that are childbearing (e.g., things that are [animate], [human], [female]). Readers must presumably disregard the inanimate, nonhuman, sexually neutral features of *moon*. However, this act of feature transfer alone does little to capture the specific metaphorical meaning of Yeats's opening lines. The idea of a childbearing moon is not metaphorical because some of the features of *moon* are deemphasized, but because it is capable of making readers grasp both the actual barrenness of the moon and its procreative cycle of going from a thin sliver to a rounded shape (ibid.). It is the tension that exists between these two not easily reconciled concepts that is responsible for the special metaphorical character of these lines.

Even more problematic for the semantic feature view is that the necessary semantic features to be associated with both the literal and nonliteral terms are not independent of their occurrence in metaphorical expressions (Pulman, 1983). For example, most people would agree that one interpretation of *That girl is a lollipop* is that it suggests that the girl in question is frivolous in some way. It is quite unlikely that "frivolous" is semantically associated with *lollipop* in our mental lexicon, even though it is true that "frivolous" is somehow compatible with *lollipop*. The only way the semantic feature theory offers us a way of getting from *lollipop* to "frivolous" is via preexisting semantic associations. In a general way, it isn't clear that the literal and nonliteral features of a metaphor's terms are interpreted in the same way. Consider again the metaphorical expression *The legislative program was a rocket to the moon.* The feature "fast moving" when applied to *rocket to the moon* is not interpreted in the same way when applied or transferred to *legislative program*. Legislative programs move fast only in a nonliteral sense, so the problem of interpreting metaphorical sentences reappears as the problem of interpreting semantic features metaphorically. Such a move only pushes the problem of metaphorical meaning to a different level of explanation; it does not solve it.

A final difficulty for semantic feature theories is that the trading of features between the literal and nonliteral terms is often more complex than the proposed mechanisms can handle. Consider the following description of a battlefield: *The battlefield was the playground floor of some giant willful child* (ibid.). The interpretation of this metaphor is rather complex, but it includes such meanings as (a) that the battlefield was a scene of great destruction and disarray, (b) that the destruction and disturbance seemed to be the result of some immense force over which the things affected had no control, (c) that some of the things destroyed may have been precious and fragile, and (d) that all of this was for no apparent reason other than obstinacy or stubbornness. It is immediately clear that no simple process of adding or canceling semantic features will account for this complexity. People cannot simply transfer some features of the nonliteral term to the literal term, for in the absence of the literal term we will never know what mappings are correct or most apt.

The semantic feature version of the comparison view of meta-phor has inspired many psychological experiments on meta-phor understanding. Several series of studies showed that judgments of both goodness and comprehension for meta-phors could reliably be predicted from a knowledge of the relationship between the topic and the vehicle (M. G. Johnson & Malgady, 1979, 1980; Malgady & Johnson, 1976, 1980). Good metaphors, ones that were also easily interpretable, were those in which the topic and vehicle terms shared a number of com-mon properties and had a number of salient (high frequency) common properties. These results have been taken to support a perceptual account of metaphor comprehension suggesting that metaphor interpretation involves experiencing an essen-tially perceptual context in which a metaphor makes sense. Properties that people list when asked to do so specify com-mon characteristics of the topic that are essentially character-istics of the context triggered by the metaphor. Metaphors that are easy to interpret generate contexts with a large number of highly salient properties (M. G. Johnson & Malgady, 1980).

However, context can change the quality of figurative lan-guage. Although a high correlation may exist between judged metaphor quality and the degree of similarity of an isolated metaphor's topic and vehicle terms (Malgady & Johnson, 1976; M. G. Johnson & Malgady, 1980), the results of one study show that no such relationship exists for these same metaphors when they are placed in context (McCabe, 1983). Clearly, the resem-blance between the topic and vehicle terms does not deter-mine the quality of metaphor when seen in extended discourse contexts.

Another difficulty with the comparison view is that it is unclear whether the comprehension of metaphor produces the similarity or feature overlap or the other way around. Some studies show that people do not interpret metaphors by infer-ring grounds that consist of familiar features shared by the tenor and vehicle. One study, for example, presented partici-pants with metaphorical sentences, such as *Billboards are warts on the landscape* (Verbrugge & McCarrell, 1977). Later on, par-ticipants attempted to recall the metaphors with the aid of recall cues. Some participants received the topic (*billboards*) as cues, others got the vehicle (*warts*), others got the ground that linked the two terms ("are ugly protrusions on a surface"), and, finally, some people received irrelevant grounds ("tell you where to find businesses in the area"). The results showed that the relevant grounds facilitated recall of the metaphorical sentences about as well as the tenor and vehicle terms themselves. These findings imply that the grounds were good recall cues because participants inferred them when they comprehended the metaphors and then formed an abstract representation in memory for the metaphor based on the topic, vehicle, and ground.

Other work also suggests that metaphor comprehension does not depend on preexisting semantic associations between the topic and vehicle terms. One set of experiments supporting this claim started with the well-established finding that people are faster in responding to pairs of words that are semantically associated (e.g., *doctor, nurse*) than they are in responding to nonassociated word pairs (e.g., *doctor, butter*). If the topic and vehicle from a metaphor are associatively related independent of a metaphorical context, one would expect that the time needed to make a decision about the pairs would be shorter than for unrelated words. But experimental results show this not to be the case (Camac & Glucksberg, 1984). These results suggest that the topic and vehicle terms in novel metaphors do not have to be associatively related prior to being interpreted as components of a metaphor. Furthermore, the idea that feature overlap accounts for metaphorical meaning does not explain why metaphors have directionality. If metaphorical meaning assumes overlap of the topic's and vehicle's semantic features, then one would expect that such expressions as *The surgeon is a butcher* and *The butcher is a surgeon* would have the same meaning. But this is clearly not the case. To say *The surgeon is a butcher* implies something negative about surgeons. The statement *A butcher is a surgeon* implies something positive about butchers.

There are several other major problems with the comparison view of metaphor understanding. First, some metaphors do not seem to be based on similarity. When the phrase *Sally is a block of ice* is converted into simile form, as in *Sally has an emotional makeup similar to the coldness of a block of ice*, the metaphor is still unreduced (Searle, 1978). There is no relation of similarity between Sally and a block of ice, or even between unemotional behavior and coldness as they are literally understood. Moreover, converting a metaphor into a simile does not always produce an intuitively correct paraphrase. For example, the figurative meaning of *The interviewer hammered the senator* is not really illuminated when expressed as "What the interviewer did to the senator was like someone hammering a nail" (Levinson, 1983). These examples suggest that metaphors are not necessarily understood as implicit similes.

Even when metaphorical comparisons are expressed as similarity statements, there are significant differences in the interpretation of *like* or the underlying similarity. Thus, the comparison statement *Encyclopedias are like dictionaries* draws attention to key features shared by both dictionaries and encyclopedias (e.g., both are reference books that are alphabetically organized). However, the metaphorical comparison *Encyclopedias are like gold mines* only suggests that certain abstract attributes are shared by both gold mines and encyclopedias (e.g., both are valuable). Metaphorical statements such as *Encyclopedias are gold mines* are not necessarily well understood simply when converted into similes, because the nature of the similarity can differ in different situations. Almost all comparison view theorists assume that the ground of a metaphor consists of common category membership, or a set of features, shared by tenor or topic (usually the metaphor's first term) and vehicle (usually the metaphor's second term) (Bickerton, 1969; Guenther, 1975; G. Miller, 1979; Tversky, 1977). Given that any two things are similar in some respects (Goodman, 1972), the comparison view doesn't really explain what is interesting and important about metaphor.

THE METAPHORS-WITHOUT-MEANING VIEW

A highly controversial but increasingly popular view of metaphor is that any account of what is special about metaphorical utterances belongs to a theory of language use rather than to semantic theory (Cooper, 1986; Davidson, 1979; Rorty, 1989). Metaphor is a special use of literal language (as are jokes, lies, etc.) that needs to be explained by a theory of language use. In the case of metaphor, at least, there is no special propositional content or meaning associated with such use. Rather *metaphor means what the words mean and nothing more* (Davidson, 1979: 30). Metaphor is a special *use* of this literal meaning to *intimate* or *suggest* some new insight that might otherwise go unnoticed. Thus, a speaker who says *John is a pig* can mean only what that sentence means literally (namely, that John has a four-legged, cloven-hoofed, and bristle-covered body). But the speaker can utter the sentence to intimate (not *mean*) something about John. What listeners notice in this metaphorical seeing-as process is not propositional in character.

The metaphor-without-meaning view is radically different from the theories of metaphor understanding previously discussed. It suggests that theorists are quite mistaken in their attempt to specify the content of the thoughts or insights that a metaphor produces and in reading that content into the meaning of the metaphor. The great difficulty we have in specifying the meanings of metaphors, Davidson suggests, lies precisely in the fact that there is really no limit to what a metaphor calls to our attention. These additional insights should not be confused with the meanings of metaphors. Davidson's account is directed at all those who try to defend the irreducibility of metaphor by reference to a special metaphorical "meaning." It may be impossible in the absence of either a context or knowledge of the speaker to state conclusively what any metaphor means without drawing on all that it *could* mean. Metaphors state a patent falsehood or an absurd belief and thus need no paraphrase, as this is already given in the literal meanings of the words themselves. Davidson's theory reduces the problem of specifying the meanings of metaphor to an account of such utterances' literal meanings along with their usual sets of associated truth conditions. Once that "meaning" has been determined for any statement, the additional nonpropositional effects of metaphor are relegated to the mysterious and remain outside proper theoretical consideration.

The idea that metaphor does not have meaning has been embraced recently by philosophers who believe that the mind is not a mirror of reality (Rorty, 1979, 1989). According to this view, knowledge does not correspond to any objective external reality. Instead, knowledge is a matter of social justification for the beliefs we have about the world. The nature of epistemic justification is determined solely by those whose beliefs are dominant at a given moment. Thus, what counts as knowledge will depend also on who gets to define the vocabulary, or the "language game," of epistemic justification. Metaphors are merely indicative of a move from one vocabulary or language game to another and thereby from one view of epistemic justification to another. The creation of a new metaphor is something that just happens, a result of mere contingencies that end up changing our view of what counts as knowledge. In this view, metaphor is not a part of meaning but is instead a nonsemantic means for breaking away from one vocabulary or language game and supplanting it with another (Rorty, 1989). *Tossing a metaphor into a conversation is like suddenly breaking off the conversation long enough to make a face, or pulling a photograph out of your pocket and displaying it, or pointing at a feature of the surroundings, or slapping your interlocutor's face, or kissing him. Tossing a metaphor into a text is like using italics, or illustrations, or odd punctuation or formats. All these are ways of producing effects on your interlocutor or your reader, but not ways of conveying a message* (ibid., p. 18). Once again, metaphors suggest, intimate, or get us to notice things, but they do not carry meaning.

The primary reason for placing such a restriction on a theory of metaphor lies in the centuries-old belief in the importance of an ideal univocal scientific-type language for every form of discourse. In Quine's terms: *Metaphor, or something like it, governs both the growth of language and our acquisition of it. What comes as a subsequent refinement is rather cognitive discourse itself, at its most dryly literal. The neatly worked out inner stretches of science are an open space in the tropical jungle, created by clearing the tropes away* (1979: 160). Metaphor obviously lies outside the clear areas.

Another impetus for denying metaphor "special meaning" or "cognitive content" is a theory-driven need to restrict the study of meaning to truth conditional sentences. The determination of an ideal literal language is not an interpretive process. We can say little about the determination of literal meaning other than to assume that such meaning exists and can be uniquely specified for each sentence in the language. Yet even at a theoretical level of analysis it is not clear that literal meaning can be specified apart from the set of underlying metaphors and the knowledge that serve as the foundation for all meaning (Gibbs, 1984, 1989). Supporters of the metaphor-without-meaning view have done little to articulate how the literal meanings of any sentence are determined, whether in real time or in an extended theoretical analysis. In contrast, some philosophers are now trying to show how to provide a semantic theory of metaphor precisely by embracing it as a kind of context-dependent expression on the order of demonstratives and indexicals (Leezenberg, 1991; Stern, 1985, 1991).

The temporal point at which the metaphor-without-meaning view suggests that metaphor is understood implies a fairly traditional model of figurative language understanding, assuming that listeners first seek to determine the literal, truth conditional meaning of any sentence. This stage of linguistic understanding occupies the earliest moments of metaphor processing (i.e., comprehension) and is assumed to function for the most part automatically and independent of contextual and world knowledge. As discussed earlier in this chapter, there are good reasons why such an assumption about the earliest time course of understanding is unfounded, particularly with regard to the idea that listeners always derive a literal meaning for each metaphor understood. The Davidsonian view of metaphor nevertheless proposes that it is only after the *meaning* of an utterance has been determined that listeners go on to derive further metaphorical *effects*, which are not, strictly speaking, meaningful or propositional in nature. This theory of metaphor understanding offers no account of how the literal meaning of a sentence is connected to what listeners come to notice when hearing a metaphor.

Furthermore, to be able to say that a given sentence has a set of truth conditions governing its meaning must depend on whether one understands it literally or metaphorically, and whether a sentence is understood literally or metaphorically may alter the truth value of that sentence. Moreover, context must have some bearing on the determination of truth conditions, because it can affect whether an ambiguous sentence is interpreted literally or metaphorically. It requires a special context to give *Men are pigs* a literal interpretation. Without any mention of metaphorical meanings, it appears that the truth conditions appropriate to a sentence's interpretation can be affected by the understanding gained through contextual consideration of whether an utterance is to be interpreted literally or metaphorically (Kittay, 1987). This argument shows that some semanticists' need to tie the meanings of metaphor to Tarski-like literal truth conditions leads them to adopt a vantage point in the time course of understanding far beyond the temporal stage when metaphors are normally understood. Of course, many philosophers argue that the beauty of the metaphor-without-meaning view, despite its problems, lies in its attempt to describe the semantic competence or knowledge that is proper to metaphorical meaning, away from the other contributing factors that together determine full metaphorical understanding (Stern, 1991). Nevertheless, the metaphor-without-meaning view is of little value to cognitive theorists interested in how metaphors are understood.

METAPHOR AS ANOMALY

Many theorists in linguistics and philosophy have attempted to formulate a precise set of rules for the identification of metaphor based on its various deviant features (Beardsley, 1962; Bickerton, 1969; Binkley, 1974; Levin, 1977; Loewenberg, 1975; Matthews, 1971). They suggest that if a metaphor were interpreted literally it would be grammatically deviant, semantically anomalous, conceptually absurd, or simply false. For example, *The stone died* violates certain selection restrictions; that is, rules that govern the different grammatical categories and subcategories in which the terms in permissible word strings may be combined. Many metaphors appear to be statements that result when there is some violation of a selection restriction rule. Thus, inanimate objects, such as stones, are restricted in the possible actions they can take, so that sentences such as *The stone died* would be marked as semantically anomalous. The anomaly view of metaphor proposes that metaphor comprehension proceeds through the recognition that certain rules or norms have been violated. The listener's task is to translate the metaphorical expression into another – nondeviant – expression (i.e., "The stone-like individual died"), which is *presumably* related to the original sentence in a rule-governed way.

A number of difficulties arise with the anomaly view of metaphor (Stern, 1983). Many grammatically deviant sentences are not usually seen as metaphorical. Thus, *The book who you read was a best seller* or *The grass who you cut was bright green* are grammatically deviant sentences that result from the violation of selectional feature rules. Although both expressions are interpretable, neither is metaphorical. Proponents of the grammatical deviance view cannot contend that metaphors violate arbitrary selectional feature restrictions, because in some cases this is not so. In a similar vein, many whole sentences which are in no way grammatically deviant can be used metaphorically (Loewenberg, 1975; Reddy, 1969). Consider *The rock is becoming brittle with age* in the context of either a group of people on a geology expedition or a group of students discussing an emeritus professor. In the first scenario, the sentence takes on a very literal interpretation, but it is easily recognized as metaphorical in the second context despite its lack of grammatical deviance.

Problems with the grammatical deviance version of the anomaly view have led some theorists to propose the related notion that metaphors are identifiable by their literal falsity (Beardsley, 1976; Goodman, 1968; Loewenberg, 1975). Shakespeare's statement *Juliet is the sun*, for example, is literally absurd, and its falsity is thought to trigger the mechanism for detecting metaphor. When understanding such phrases, the listener initially assumes that the utterance is to be interpreted literally. Because the literal interpretation is patently false, and because the listener believes that the speaker is competent with the language, the listener is led to attribute to the speaker an absurdly false belief. To adhere to the assumption that the speaker is rational, the listener re-identifies the utterance as having a metaphorical interpretation.

Of course, any metaphor expressed negatively is literally true, such as *No man is an island* or Mao's statement *A revolution is not a dinner party*. Understood literally, these utterances are trivial but true. But when interpreted metaphorically, they convey a particular set of implications that does not follow for the literal statement alone (Kittay, 1987). Furthermore, to insist on literal falsity as the defining feature of metaphor entails making an unacceptable distinction between metaphors and similes, since the latter are in some sense literally true, as in *Juliet is like the sun* (Stern, 1985).

Despite the venerable tradition to the contrary, there do not seem to be any necessary and sufficient conditions that serve to identify a particular utterance as metaphorical. Part of the difficulty with the metaphor-as-anomaly view is that the grammatical deviance or literal falsity of a sentence does not in any way specify which of the numerous possible metaphorical meanings is correct or intended. It is not even clear what criteria listeners use in seeking an alternative meaning. Various figurative interpretations, some of which are not metaphorical, may be reasonable alternatives, and there must be some way of selecting the *best*, rather than the *only*, possible interpretation for any given metaphor (Gibbs, 1987a, 1987b; Kittay, 1987; Stern, 1983). These problems indicate that the anomaly view can only explain, *at best*, something about metaphor recognition (i.e., that a particular word string is metaphorical). Yet it does not specify anything about metaphor interpretation (i.e., that a metaphor has a specific interpretation) other than to assume that the recognition of metaphor precedes its interpretation.

As a result of their aim of formulating criteria for the recognition of metaphor, theorists espousing the anomaly view draw two inferences about earlier temporal points of metaphor comprehension. First, the anomaly, or semantic, view assumes that people actually compute syntactic representations for sentences *before* assessing semantic or pragmatic knowledge in order to derive appropriate and meaningful interpretations. Similarly, the idea that literal falsity facilitates the recognition of metaphor assumes that the truth conditional structure of a sentence is determined as part of the comprehension process. Both assumptions are questionable, and there is a great deal of philosophical, linguistic, and psycholinguistic debate over these issues (discussed below). For now, it is important to note that the anomaly, or semantic, view suggests that the locus of metaphor understanding is situated at some point *after* a sentence has been recognized as literally false or ungrammatical, a recognition that triggers the search for figurative meaning. The anomaly view suggests no possibility that metaphorical utterances can be understood at an earlier point of linguistic processing, before recognition supposedly occurs. Yet psychological research has shown that people quickly find many anomalous statements to be metaphorically meaningful at a point long before these statements are seen as, strictly speaking, anomalous (McCabe, 1983; Pollio & Burns, 1977). At this point, it is questionable whether the anomaly view theorists' focus on one temporal stage of metaphor understanding (recognition) warrants their theoretical claims about the entire process of metaphor understanding (comprehension). The metaphor-as-anomaly view attempts to demonstrate something about the *products* of metaphor recognition, but does it tell us what goes on during the *process* of metaphor understanding?

METAPHOR AND SPEECH ACTS

The inability to specify simple criteria for the recognition of metaphor has led some theorists to adopt the view that it is only in its total context, and not necessarily at the sentence level, that an utterance can be understood as metaphorical. Speech act theorists formulate the question of how metaphors work in terms of the distinction between *word* or *sentence* meaning (i.e., what the word or sentence means literally) and *speaker* meaning (i.e., what the speaker means by uttering words or sentences with literal meanings). Metaphor in this view arises from the disparity between the words used and the speaker's/ writer's intentions. The central problem of metaphor in speech act theory is how to state the principles relating literal sentence meaning to metaphorical utterance meaning (Searle, 1979). For example, in making a metaphorical statement, such as *Sally is a block of ice*, the speaker intends the utterance to have a different *speaker meaning* than its so-called *literal* or *sentence meaning*. Words always retain their invariant locutionary meaning, but when they are used to request, warn, or make metaphors, the listener notices that there is something odd about them and infers unstated suggestions or meanings (i.e., illocutions). For example, a listener may find odd the literal use of the expression *No man is an island* and seek some alternative, perhaps metaphorical, reading to make sense of the intended meaning of the speaker's assertion (T. Cohen, 1976).

Following this line of reasoning, some proposals suggest that metaphor is a particular type of speech act, similar to a directive or commissive, with its own illocutionary force and accompanying set of felicity conditions (Loewenberg, 1973; Mack, 1975). Much of the argument over this possibility rests on Searle's (1969; and see Chapter 2 under "The Traditional View") *expressibility principle*, which states in part that what can be meant can be stated exactly. If a metaphor has meaning, then it should be possible to explicate its meaning clearly in the same way as that of any literal assertion, commissive, directive, and so on (Binkley, 1979). Although every metaphorical utterance has a specific illocutionary point (e.g., an assertive, directive, commissive) that is expressible, this fact alone does not specify the content of the speech act (i.e., its particular propositional content). Furthermore, literal speech acts lose their speaker meaning in direct discourse (e.g., *Tom told Sally that he was sorry* does not carry the illocutionary force of an apology), but metaphors remain metaphorical when repeated (e.g., *Tom said George was a fire-eater*). Both these observations suggest that a metaphor does not constitute a unique class of illocutionary acts (L. Cohen, 1979).

Nevertheless, speech act theory offers a number of principles that listeners presumably use to derive the figurative meaning of a metaphorical utterance. For any metaphor, the problem, according to Searle (1979), is to characterize the relations between the three sets S, P, and R, together with the principles and other information used by the listener, to specify how it is possible to derive "S is R" from "S is P." In literal utterances, the speaker meaning ("S is R") and sentence meaning ("S is P") should be identical. Understanding literal utterances does not require any extra information beyond a listener's knowledge of the rules of language, his or her awareness of the conditions of the utterance, and a set of background assumptions shared by the speaker and hearer. However, in order to understand that when speakers say "S is P" they metaphorically mean "S is R" requires something more than hearers' knowledge of the rules of language, their awareness of the conditions of the utterance, and the background assumptions they share with speakers. Listeners must also resort to some other set of principles that permits them to derive "S is R" from "S is P." These principles include the following (Searle, 1979):

1. Things that are P are by definition R. So R will be one of the salient defining characteristics of P. Thus, *Sam is a giant* will be taken to mean "Sam is big" because giants are by definition big.

2. Things that are P are contingently R. So the property R should be a well-known property of P-type things such that *Sam is a pig* will be taken to mean "Sam is filthy, sloppy, etc."

3. Things that are P are often said or believed to be R, even though both speaker and hearer may know that R is false of P. Thus, *Richard is a gorilla* can be uttered to mean "Richard is nasty, mean, and prone to violence" even though both speaker and hearer know that in fact gorillas are shy, timid creatures. People's folk mythology about gorillas has set up associations (e.g., King Kong) that enable this metaphorical description of Richard to work.

4. Things that are P are not R, nor are they like R things, nor are they believed to be R. However, people often perceive a connection between P and R such that to utter P is to call to our mind R properties. Thus, *Sally is a block of ice* can be uttered to mean metaphorically "Sally is unemotional."

5. There are cases where P and R are the same or similar in meaning but where one, usually P, is restricted in its application and does not literally apply to S. So *addled* is usually said literally of eggs, but one can state metaphorically *This soup is addled* or *The Congress is addled* or even *His brain was addled.*

These rules do not completely account for the understanding of all metaphorical utterances. The goal is more simply to suggest the kinds of principles necessary to interpret metaphorical meanings (i.e., the appropriate values of R), some of which may be indeterminate. Understanding metaphor starts at the earliest moments of sentence processing, where the literal meaning of a sentence is analyzed, and proceeds to the later moments, when the speaker's meaning is grasped. Metaphor is born at the temporal point at which a speaker's metaphorical meaning is recovered. In most respects, the metaphor-as-speech-act view, through its focus on the speakers' metaphorical meaning, provides a more comprehensive method than the anomaly view for identifying *when* any utterance should be viewed, or recognized, as metaphorical. The speech act view, for instance, accounts for those metaphorical utterances that do *not* violate grammatical or truth conditional rules. But, it also makes assumptions similar to those of the anomaly view about the earlier *processes* of metaphor comprehension and interpretation, based on an analysis of metaphorical *products.*

Are such assumptions about the process of metaphor comprehension warranted? Do listeners actually go through the series of steps suggested by the speech act view to derive speakers' metaphorical meanings? It is difficult to assess the adequacy of metaphorical *processes* solely through an examination of their *products.* Different methodologies are needed to investigate metaphor comprehension than those that are used for interpretation or recognition. Although the speech act view says a good deal about both interpretation and recognition, its claims about comprehension may not be correct.

As described in Chapter 3, the results of many experimental studies in psycholinguistics indicate that it is misleading to suppose that one type of meaning (literal) is automatically and immediately determined prior to another (nonliteral). This position denies any fundamental difference between the psychological mechanisms used to comprehend literal and figurative speech, *at least* insofar as very early cognitive processes are concerned. Understanding figurative language does not require recognition of these utterances as violations of the norms of cooperative communication. There are good reasons, then, to doubt the rational account of metaphor understanding proposed by speech act theory.

Of course, even though the processes of comprehending different meanings (e.g., literal vs. metaphoric) of utterances may not be qualitatively different, this idea should not be viewed as implying that there are no differences among these meanings as *products* (Gibbs & Gerrig, 1989). Psycholinguists may have incorrectly overgeneralized from their findings about earlier temporal moments of metaphor understanding (i.e., processes) to later moments in the time course of such understanding (i.e., products). Although it remains unclear exactly how to distinguish between literal and metaphorical meanings, this does not in principle indicate that metaphor has no unique qualities (i.e., products) when viewed at later and more reflective stages of recognition, interpretation, and appreciation.

Some of the difficulties above in determining how literal and metaphorical meanings deviate have led speech act theorists to adopt a less mechanistic view of the comprehension process (Searle, 1983). Even though it may be possible to state various rules of interpretation for some metaphors, one soon discovers that such rules do not function in an algorithmic fashion to specify exactly *how* an utterance is intended metaphorically. Looking back at Principle 4, there can be an indeterminate relationship between P and R, but we still perceive some connection between them because of our "sensibility." As Searle (1983: 149) comments: *It just seems to be a fact about our mental capacities that we are able to interpret certain sorts of metaphor without the application of any underling "rules" or "principles" other than the sheer ability to make certain associations. I don't know any better way to describe these abilities than to say that they are nonrepresentational mental capacities.* Many metaphors seem not to be grounded in any similarity. For example, the metaphorical utterance meaning of the expression *a lukewarm reception* is not based on any literal similarity between lukewarm things and the character of the reception. There may be principles of similarity on which certain metaphors function, but there are many verbal metaphors that function without any underlying principle of similarity.

THE METAPHOR-AS-LOOSE-TALK VIEW

One alternative to the widely held view that metaphor violates or flouts communication norms is that metaphors – and other forms of indirect and nonliteral speech – are examples of loose talk (Sperber & Wilson, 1985/86). The *metaphor-as-loose-talk* view has been developed within the framework of relevance theory (Sperber & Wilson, 1986). According to the relevance theoretic framework, relevance is fundamental to communication not because speakers obey a maxim of relevance, as Grice supposed, but because relevance is basic to cognition: We pay attention to information that seems relevant to us. Since every act of communication stands out as a request for attention, an expectation is created that what speakers communicate will to some degree be relevant.

Relevance is defined in terms of contextual effects and processing effort. Contextual effects are achieved when a speaker's utterance strengthens, contradicts, or denies an existing assumption or when a speaker's utterance is combined with an existing assumption to yield some new contextual implications. Sperber and Wilson claim that newly presented information is relevant in a context only when it achieves contextual effects in that context, and the greater the contextual effects the greater the relevance. They specifically define a notion of *optimal relevance* that outlines what listeners look for in terms of effect and effort: An utterance, on a given interpretation, is optimally relevant if and only if (a) it achieves enough effect to be worth the hearer's attention and (b) it puts the hearer to no gratuitous effort in achieving these effects (ibid.).

In the relevance theoretic framework, it makes no sense to claim that a relevance maxim, or any other maxim, can be overtly violated to create an implication. Under this view, speakers are not constrained to say what is strictly speaking true. In many situations, speaking loosely is the best way to achieve optimal relevance. For instance, if someone asks you how much you earn as salary each month and you respond *Twenty-five hundred dollars* when in fact you actually make $2,457, listeners will still assume that your utterance is appropriate to the situation at hand. The fact that your response is not a completely accurate representation of the true state of affairs does not matter. As long as listeners follow the *principle of optimal relevance*, they will be able efficiently to infer the appropriate contextual implications of your utterance. In this way, an utterance resembles a thought but does not literally represent it. Some utterances may closely resemble a speaker's thoughts, but in other cases an optimally relevant utterance may only loosely resemble the speaker's idea.

Metaphors and other figures of speech can profitably be looked at as examples of *loose talk* (Sperber & Wilson, 1985/86). Consider the utterance *My neighbor is a dragon* (Blakemore, 1992). Listeners generally have immediate access to stereotypical knowledge about dragons and would normally infer that the speaker of *My neighbor is a dragon* means "My neighbor is fierce and unfriendly." Speaking loosely like this requires that speakers have in mind some further idea or contextual implication beyond the single thought "My neighbor is fierce and unfriendly." For instance, the speaker might wish to convey an image of fierceness or unfriendliness that is beyond most people's experience and will expect the listener to make some effort toward exploring a wide range of contextual implications (e.g., having to do with the nature of the neighbor's unfriendliness, the behavior it manifests, and perhaps the neighbor's appearance). These implications are relatively weak, but they best resemble the speaker's thought about the neighbor. The indirect nature of metaphor calls for extra processing effort on the listener's part, but this is offset, according to the principle of optimal relevance, by extra effects not achievable by saying directly *My neighbor is fierce and unfriendly*.

In general, metaphorical utterances are simply one means of optimizing relevance in verbal communication. The metaphor-as-loose-talk view does not assume that metaphor requires special cognitive processes to be understood. Yet the weak implicatures that speakers intend to communicate require extra processing effort for listeners to recover. Although there may be instances when listeners or readers spend considerable mental effort teasing out the weak contextual implications of a metaphor, the psychological research once again clearly shows that listeners do not ordinarily devote extra processing resources to understanding metaphors compared with more literal utterances. The metaphor-as-loose-talk view, therefore, may not see metaphors as violations of communication norms but still incorrectly assumes that metaphors, and other tropes such as irony, obligatorily demand additional cognitive effort to be understood. Furthermore, the very notion of metaphor as loose talk presupposes that metaphorical language only resembles speaker's thoughts rather than being a direct reflection of ideas or concepts that are actually constituted by metaphor.

THE INTERACTIVE VIEW

Much of the emphasis in theories of metaphor has been on explicating the similarity that exists between two terms in a metaphorical expression. Ever since Aristotle's earliest writing, metaphor interpretation has been assumed to involve a comparison of objects to determine what discrete properties or relations applying to one term can also apply to the other term in the same or a similar sense. Again, metaphor has been mostly viewed as a comparison in which the first term (the *topic*) is said to bear a partial resemblance (the *ground*) to the second term (the *vehicle*). Consider the expression *Your article is garbage*. The noun phrase *Your article* is the topic, and the verb phrase *is garbage* is the vehicle. Presumably the point of the utterance is to draw the listener's attention to some similarity existing between *article* and *garbage*, namely the ground or resemblance that the article is of little worth.

However, it is difficult to see how metaphor records some antecedent similarity, given such examples as T. S. Eliot's simile from the opening lines of *The Love Song of J. Alfred Prufrock.*

> Let us go then, you and I,
> When the evening is spread out against the sky
> Like a patient etherised upon a table.

There is little reason to suspect that some preexisting similarity can be found between the evening sky and a patient lying etherized upon a table. The interaction theory of metaphor suggests that understanding metaphor *creates* similarity and does *not* simply emphasize some preexisting but unnoticed aspects of the meaning or similarity relationship (Black, 1955, 1962, 1979). When interpreting a metaphor, such as *Man is a wolf,* listeners do not compare the topic (*Man*) and vehicle (*wolf*) for existing similarities but view each term in a new way to *create similarity* between them. The topic and vehicle *interact* in the sense that the presence of the topic incites the listener to select some of the vehicle's properties to form a *parallel implication complex* that can fit the topic, which in turn induces parallel changes in the vehicle. For example, Wallace Stevens's remark *Society is a sea* is not about the sea but about a *system of relationships* between society and sea signaled by the word *sea.* New meanings are made possible by the interaction of terms in a metaphor and not as a result of shifting attention to marginal aspects of meaning or of highlighting accidental properties of things. At least some metaphors involve the creation of new frameworks of connotation rather than the actualization of potential but unrealized connotations (Ricoeur, 1977). A simpler comparison theory misses this interactive process of "seeing as" or "conceiving as" by which an emergent meaning complex is generated (M. Johnson, 1987). The presence of the topic stimulates the listener to select some of the vehicle's properties and thus to construct a "parallel implication complex" to fit the topic, which in turn induces parallel changes in the vehicle (Black, 1979). Metaphor cannot be reduced to antecedent literal meanings or to rule-governed extensions or variations of those meanings (ibid.).

The interaction view is perhaps the dominant theory in the multidisciplinary study of metaphor. Part of the reason for its great appeal is the theory's potential to inform many aspects of the time course of metaphor understanding. According to the interaction view, at the earliest moments of comprehension of a metaphorical utterance, listeners project two conceptual domains, linguistically represented by the topic and vehicle terms, onto each other (an early comprehension *process*) to arrive at a metaphorical meaning or meanings that highlight the emergent similarity between the two terms (a later interpretation *product*). The contrast of the two domains to which the topic and vehicle refer results in a "parallel implication complex" that produces emergent meanings not directly limited to speakers' or writers' communicative intentions. These later products of metaphor understanding seem open-ended, extending beyond the immediate first-time understanding of a metaphor. Listeners cannot set firm standards for deciding which interpretations are admissible, because metaphors are inherently ambiguous and suggestive of numerous meanings. In general, interactionism not only accounts for metaphorical meaning as a late *product* of understanding, but it also suggests an algorithm for the early unconscious *process* of a metaphor comprehension.

One proposal from philosophy has argued that Black's idea of an "implication system" can profitably be replaced by the notion of *semantic fields*, wherein a semantic field consists of the dependencies holding between concepts in a particular domain (Kittay, 1987). According to this view, the literal meaning of an utterance can be fixed by the role that the utterance plays in some contextually determined semantic field. Metaphorical meaning (or second-order meaning) arises from the introduction of relations from one domain or semantic field (the domain of the vehicle) into another semantic field (the topic domain). To take a specific example, consider Plato's analogy of Socrates as midwife. The semantic field of child delivery in this model is structured as follows (Kittay, 1987: 33):

Main verb: help
Agent: midwife
Resulting state of affairs: verb: create or deliver
                                         agent: mother
                                         result: child
Instrument: potions and incantations

This structure is then mapped onto the semantic field of philosophical instruction in this manner:

Main verb: help
Agent: Socrates
Resulting state of affairs: verb: create or deliver
                                         agent: student
                                         result: ideas
Instrument: dialectic

This view of metaphorical mappings gives greater specificity to the idea that metaphor understanding involves discovery of a "system of commonplaces" resulting in an "implication complex." The incongruity between dissimilar semantic fields shows how the relations between them cannot be characterized in literal language – one reason why metaphors appear irreducible to literal paraphrase. However, this semantic field view of metaphor also assumes that the second-order meanings peculiar to metaphor arise only when selection restriction rules have been violated or when some pragmatic anomaly is noticed. Yet the empirical evidence from psycholinguistics reviewed in Chapter 3 clearly suggests that people can easily understand metaphorical expressions without having specifically to derive a second-order meaning (the metaphorical meaning) from a first-order meaning (the literal one).

There are a number of controversial issues regarding the interactive view of metaphor that have attracted much debate among metaphor scholars. The first concerns some of the vagueness of several notions, such as the terms *implicative complex, system of commonplaces, interactionism,* and *fit.* Consider again the metaphor *Man is a wolf.* Black's formulation of the interactive theory does not specify any criterion for deciding which features of the implicative complex of the vehicle domain (*wolf*) fit the implicative complex of the topic domain (*Man*). Some process presumably occurs that both evokes and suppresses related commonplaces between these two domains. Metaphor interpretation requires a "projection" of implicated predicates from the secondary subject or vehicle onto the primary subject or topic. In the *Man is wolf* metaphor, Black (1981: 75) suggested that those human trials that became prominent could *without undue strain be talked of in wolf-language* while the rest would be *pushed into the background*. But what are the criteria for determining which implications and predicates of the vehicle, literally applicable to the principal subject, are significant in the interpretation of this metaphor? A reader must know not only the dictionary definition of *wolf* but also, more important, must possess certain "folk" beliefs concerning wolves.

The problem here is that implications of the "wolf system of related commonplaces" must be indefinite and perhaps infinite. Therefore, it is absurd to think that each of these implied assertions gets applied to the principal objects. Even if one is confined to commonplace beliefs concerning the vehicle term, there are many predicates that can be formed, such as "are not ironing boards," believed to be true of wolves that have no import whatsoever in the interpretation of the metaphor *Man is a wolf* (Goodman, 1976; Scheffler, 1979). Indeed, just what characteristics of the vehicle get chosen during metaphor understanding depends on the particular topic. The system associated with *wolf*, for example, used as a metaphorical vehicle for man will differ significantly from that associated with the same term when used as a vehicle for another term. That is, our understanding of *wolf* is quite different for *In the desert land, the wind, a lone wolf, howled in the night* than it is for *Man is a wolf*.

Another difficulty with the interactive position is that the vehicle term is seen as belonging to some implicative complex or system, but the topic is not. If the topic does not belong to a system, then the distinction between the topic and the meaning of the metaphor becomes difficult to maintain. In some metaphors the topic is named in the text; in others it must be inferred. Indeed, the topic is sometimes extracted only with the difficulty equivalent to that of arriving at the very meaning of the metaphor. Some metaphors have no single idea to which the vehicle may be said to apply. Consider T. S. Eliot's lines *Then how should I begin / To spit out all the butt-ends of my days and ways?* Are *the butt-ends of my days and ways* the latter part of each day or the end of Eliot's life or the discarded, unusable parts of his days and actions? Each of these interpretations seems viable. The topic itself seems to be a late *product* of the early process of interaction with the vehicle rather than a component of the interaction.

A different problem in the interactive view is reminiscent of a critical, perhaps fatal, issue for the comparison view of metaphor. According to the interactive view, listeners understand metaphor by projecting predicates from the vehicle domain to the topic domain. Consider the metaphor *Marriage is a zero-sum game* (Black, 1979). This expression gives rise to the following implication complex for marriage: (1) A marriage is a game (2) between two contestants (3) in which the rewards of one contestant are gained only at the expense of the other. Do listeners understand these predicates as metaphorical or literal assertions (Kittay, 1987)? Interaction theory assumes that each assertion is literal, but this is clearly not the case for many metaphors. Marriage, understood as an institution or contractual agreement, is not the sort of thing that can properly be described as a game. Even if we assume that married life can literally be described as a game, this does not imply anything about the contestants. To see the individuals in a marriage as game contestants requires a metaphorical inference in which marriage is *already* conceived of as a game or struggle between two people. Similarly, the idea that the rewards of one contestant are gained only at the expense of the other is literal only if the metaphorical framework of marriage as a zero-sum game is already accepted. Each of the supposed literal predicates in the implication complex of marriage assumes some conceptual framework that is metaphorically structured. As noted in Chapter 4, many concepts, such as marriage, appear to be fundamentally understood in metaphorical terms. It makes little sense, then, to assume, as does the interactive view, that the projected predicates used to understand metaphorical expressions must be literally applied.

Another claim of interaction theory is that the topic and vehicle terms in metaphor cause reciprocal changes in meaning. Some researchers explicitly argue that either of the key terms may function as the lens or filter or as a vehicle of a metaphor (Hausman, 1989). Consider Shakespeare's line *The world is an unweeded garden*. If *the world* (antecedently known) is regarded through a qualifier or filter, that is the *unweeded garden*, then so too will *unweeded garden* be regarded through *the world*. The whole point of interactionism is that *both* terms affect the meaning of the other. The "seeing as" often associated with metaphor is multidirectional. If man is seen as wolf, so too is wolf seen as man in *Man is a wolf* (Black, 1979).

This analysis of metaphor is very misleading at both the conceptual and linguistic levels. Consider the conceptual metaphor LIFE IS A JOURNEY. When we structure our understanding of life in terms of a journey, we map onto the domain of life the inferential structure associated with journeys. But we do not map onto the domain of journeys the inferential structure associated with the domain of life (G. Lakoff & Turner, 1989). For instance, we do not usually view journeys as having waking parts and sleeping parts as we do lives. Nor do we assume that travelers can have only one journey in the way that people can have only one life. The mapping we make is from a source to a target domain and is not the bidirectional mapping interaction theory assumes.

It is still possible for two metaphors to share the same two domains but differ in which is the source and which is the target. For instance, the conceptual metaphor MACHINES ARE PEOPLE allows us to conceive of machines as having some characteristics of people. This allows us to make such statements as *The computer is punishing me by wiping out my buffer* (ibid.). Nevertheless, when we reverse this metaphor to get PEOPLE ARE MACHINES, different inferences are made, because different things get mapped. Thus, for PEOPLE ARE MACHINES there is no sense that people have will and desire; people are thought of as having parts that function in specific ways, such as idling steadily or accelerating, and that may break down, need fixing, and so forth. Metaphors are not bidirectional in the way their domains interact.

Extensive psychological research demonstrates that topics and vehicles play different roles in metaphor comprehension. For example, properties of the vehicle are better cues for recall of metaphors than properties of the topic (Verbrugge & McCarrell, 1977). Metaphors are also rated as more comprehensible when the metaphoric grounds are properties of the vehicle rather than the topic (Malgady & Johnson, 1980). The vehicle's imageability correlates more highly with metaphor aptness and comprehensibility than does imageability of a metaphor's topic (Marschark, Katz, & Paivio, 1983). Finally, people's perceptions of the topics in metaphors change significantly more than their perceptions of the vehicles (Kelly & Keil, 1987).

These findings contrast with the position that metaphor comprehension results in reciprocal changes in the topic and vehicle terms (cf. Hausman, 1989). The topic seems to undergo the more significant changes in meaning. Following the given-new convention governing conversation, people assume that first the topic is given and that the purpose of the vehicle is to say something about the topic; thus the asymmetrical weight given each of these "systems" (Camac & Glucksberg, 1984; Hoffman & Kemper, 1987).

PSYCHOLINGUISTICS AND THE INTERACTION VIEW

Since the early period of work on the interaction view, four major models have been proposed in psycholinguistics to explain more fully the "mechanism" by which a metaphor creates new meanings. These models are: *the salience imbalance* model, *the domains interaction* model, *the structure mapping* model, and *the class inclusion* model. Each of the theories associated with these models places constraints on the nature of the interaction between topics and vehicles in metaphorical statements. Since each model entails particular assumptions about what goes on during the temporal understanding of metaphor, each theory is limited to particular aspects of metaphor understanding.

The salience imbalance theory was developed specifically to account for people's judgments of different kinds of similarity statements (Ortony, 1979a). The model assumes that the number of attributes shared between any two terms in a similarity statement depends only on their salience for the second term (the B term). Literal similarity statements contain two terms denoting concepts that are likely to share many attributes, at least some of which are relatively high salience for both. For example, *Sermons are like lectures* should be judged a literal statement, because both sermons and lectures are oral addresses given to groups of people – attributes that are highly salient for both terms. Similes and metaphors, on the other hand, are similarity statements with terms that share attributes, but these attributes should be highly salient for the B term and of relatively low salience for the A term. For example, in the statement *Sermons are like sleeping pills*, the attribute "inducing drowsiness" is more salient with respect to sleeping pills than to sermons. Thus, the contribution of the salience of the "induce drowsiness" attribute to the salience of the terms' intersection is maximized if it is based on the salience for *sleeping pills* (the vehicle). Finally, such a statement as *Sermons are like grapefruit* is an anomalous similarity statement, because there are no obvious salient attributes of grapefruit that are shared with sermons.

In general, the salience imbalance theory holds that high salience of B attributes is viewed as a necessary condition for meaningful (literal or metaphorical, as opposed to anomalous) similarity statements. Metaphorical similarity should show a much greater asymmetry of similarity and meaningfulness than statements of either literal or anomalous similarity. Furthermore, the salience of the attributes involved in metaphorical similarity statements will be much higher for the vehicle than for the topics, whereas for the other kinds of similarity statements the imbalance between the A and B terms will be much less pronounced.

Various kinds of empirical evidence support these ideas about the nature of similarity in metaphor (A. Katz, 1982; Ortony, Vondruska, Foss, & Jones, 1985). People find that the order in which the terms of similarity statements are presented (e.g., *A is like B* vs. *B is like A*) is more important for metaphorical comparisons (e.g., *Cigarettes are like time bombs*) than it is for either literal comparisons (e.g., *Cigarettes are like cigars*) or anomalous comparisons (e.g., *Cigarettes are like furniture*). In addition, people rate the difference in the salience of the attributes contributed by the A and B terms as being greater for metaphorical comparisons than for literal similarity statements. Both sets of findings support the predictions of the salience imbalance model of metaphor.

Recently a number of researchers have criticized the salience imbalance view of metaphor (Glucksberg & Keysar, 1990; Shen, 1989, 1992), arguing that the symmetry versus asymmetry distinction in comparison statements does not specifically distinguish literal from metaphorical comparisons, because both types of comparison exhibit symmetric and asymmetric relations. Some literal comparisons are as asymmetric as some metaphorical comparisons, and some metaphorical comparisons are as symmetrical as many literal comparisons. For example, there is a greater perceived similarity in *Poland is like Russia* than in *Russia is like Poland*, despite the fact that both statements are based on literal similarity (Tversky, 1977). Metaphorical comparisons can also be as symmetrical as some literal statements. *Night is like coal* and *Coal is like night* appear to share the same ground of "blackness," and people appear to have no difficulty understanding either example (Shen, 1989). Similarly, *Snow is like flour* is metaphoric and is symmetrical in that both of its orders (e.g., *Snow is like flour* and *Flour is like snow*) are reasonable (i.e., the similarity between snow and flour equals the similarity between flour and snow). It seems, then, that the distinction between symmetric and asymmetric comparisons cannot be correlated with the distinction between metaphorical and nonmetaphorical comparisons, contrary to the assumption of the salience imbalance hypothesis (A. Katz, 1992; Shen, 1989, 1992).

The domains interaction theory of metaphor proposes that understanding and appreciating metaphorical comparisons requires the assessment of similarity both within and between domains (Tourangeau & Sternberg, 1981, 1982). Within-domains similarity measures the extent to which the features of the vehicle (or source) domain are structurally analogous to the features of the topic (or target) domain. Between-domains similarity assesses the extent to which the vehicle and topic resemble each other, as measured by the overlap in their vocabularies. This model suggests that metaphorical aptness increases when the between-domains distance is high and the within-domains distance is low.

The results of various experiments on how much people liked individual metaphors have indicated a negative relationship between incongruence and liking but a positive relationship between agreement and liking. Participants generally preferred metaphors whose subjects were drawn from distant domains (e.g., *Brezhnev is a hawk*, which maps from the source domain of birds to the target domain of political leaders) and metaphors that confirmed their picture of the primary subject. Thus, metaphors are perceived as more apt to the extent that their terms occupy similar positions within their respective dissimilar domains.

The domains interaction view of metaphor has focused primarily on metaphor appreciation (or "aptness"). Metaphor understanding is presumed to operate on the basis of information similar to that used in judging metaphor aptness. Thus, people understand metaphors in several stages, where the terms of a metaphor are encoded, the relevant domains are inferred, the structures to be seen as parallel are found, the correspondences between these structures are mapped, and finally the terms of the metaphor are compared. One immediately apparent problem with this view is its assumption that the different domains from which the topic and vehicle are drawn must be scaled on common dimensions. For example, *hawk* and *shark* in the metaphor *The hawk is the shark among birds* come from the respective domains of birds and fish, both of which can be scaled on the dimension of aggressiveness. Although the domains are dissimilar in that they occupy different locations in "conceptual space," they are ultimately similar in that they can be scaled on similar dimensions. The requirement that both topic and vehicle terms have common dimensional scales imposes severe limitations on the kinds of metaphor that can be modeled (cf. Gentner & Clements, 1988).

Some metaphors, such as Virginia Woolf's *She allowed life to waste like a tap left running*, have topic and vehicle terms that do not share any common dimensions.

Beyond this significant problem, the domains interaction view of metaphor assumes, as many theories do, that the processes of understanding and appreciating are similar, if not identical. People's judgments that some metaphorical expressions are aesthetically better than others are often used as criteria in formulating theories of metaphor understanding, especially in poetics and literary criticism. But some psycholinguistic evidence demonstrates that comprehension and appreciation are quite different processes. Although people clearly consider some metaphors to be conceptually "good" or "apt" (*The night sky was filled with molten silver*) and other metaphors to be conceptually "bad" (*The night sky was filled with molten resin*), there is no difference in the time it takes to comprehend these two types of metaphor (Gerrig & Healey, 1983). Such findings indicate that listeners/readers may comprehend aesthetically "good" and "bad" metaphors with equal ease but that judgment of metaphor aptness entails a different kind of psychological act, one that demands more conscious reflection. Comprehension and appreciation of metaphor involve different points on the temporal continuum of linguistic understanding, and so what is unique to metaphor, or to some instances of metaphor, at one point (i.e., appreciation) may have little effect on the understanding of metaphorical expressions at an earlier moment (i.e., comprehension). Again, the question of when metaphor becomes unique and special (i.e., a question about late products) limits theoretical analysis of the fast, unconscious processes by which metaphor is actually understood (i.e., a question about early process). For this reason, it is an open question whether the domains interaction view accounts for aspects of both metaphor comprehension and interpretation.

The structure mapping theory attempts to distinguish among analogy, metaphor, and literal similarity (Gentner, 1983; Gentner & Clements, 1988). The basic idea behind this view is that an analogy is a mapping of knowledge from one domain (the base) onto another (the target) that conveys a similar system of relations among the objects in both the base and target domains. Structure mapping postulates two specific informational constraints on the interpretation of an analogy from its constituent terms. First, common relations between the terms are most important, not common object descriptions. In other words, the corresponding objects in the base and target don't have to resemble each other. A second constraint is that the choice of which relations are mapped is guided by a principle of systemacity. This postulate holds that people prefer to map systems of predicates governed by higher-order constraining relations rather than simply to map isolated predicates. For instance, in Ernest Rutherford's famous analogy between the solar system and the hydrogen atom, the intended interpretation consists of a set of common relations rather than a common set of object descriptions. The choice of which common relational structure to map is determined by the fact that the central-force system of both the atom and the solar system is the maximal system structure to be found in both domains.

Different types of similarity can be distinguished in this framework according to whether the match between the terms is based on relational structure, object descriptions, or both. *Analogies* discard object descriptions and preserve relational structure; *mere appearance matches* preserve object attributes and discard relational structure; *literal similarity matches* preserve both relational structure and object descriptions; and *metaphor* can be divided into three partially overlapping categories. Attributional metaphors are mere appearance matches because they convey common object attributes (*Her arms were like twin swans*). The attributes "long," "thin," and "graceful" can be mapped from the base domain *swans* to the target domain *her arms*. Relational metaphors can be analyzed as analogies, because they convey a relational structure common to the target. In Shakespeare's *Look, he's winding up the watch of his wit; by and by it will strike*, the intended commonalities have nothing to do with the object attributes of a watch (a glass face, metal cogs, and so on). Instead, the metaphor conveys the common relational structure of a person setting a mechanism that will later produce seemingly spontaneous external effects. Finally, double metaphors are mixtures of pure relational and attributional matches. For example, *Plant stems are drinking straws for thirsty trees* conveys both the common attributes "long, thin, tubular" and the common relational structure "sucks fluids up from a lower to a higher place in order to nourish some life form."

Experimental research demonstrates that adults prefer relational metaphors to attributional ones (Gentner & Clements, 1988). In addition, people consider metaphors more apt when they can discern relational interpretations (e.g., *A cloud is like a sponge*). Attributional commonalities do not contribute to people's judgments of metaphor aptness. Finally, even metaphors designed to suggest either an attributional or a relational interpretation (the double metaphors) are interpreted relationally. These various findings highlight the idea that people demonstrate a relational focus both in interpreting metaphors and in judging their aesthetic value.

The structure mapping view of metaphor does not necessarily compete with other psychological models. Although this view does describe the informational constraints on which metaphor understanding is based, it does not tell us exactly *how* metaphor comprehension occurs. One possibility is that structure mapping is performed in conjunction with some salience evaluation process such that structure mapping informs the reader of what to look for in a comparison statement, whereas salience assessment tells people where to look first (ibid.). Thus, the salience imbalance model might best be described as a communicative norm in which a rule of conversational cooperativeness is applied to the interpretation of comparison statements. For example, when a speaker uses a simile like *A is like B*, the listener has a pragmatic understanding of what is likely to be conveyed such that the given entity or topic of the comparison is the A term and the new information that is being communicated about the given entity is contained in the B term (Glucksberg & Keysar, 1990; Ortony et al., 1985). Listeners presumably select those attributes of the B term that provide the greatest amount of information about the A term, but they attempt to do so according to relational terms that maximize the systematicity found in both domains.

Significant questions remain to be answered about each of the psychological theories discussed thus far. How can attributes and relational information reliably be distinguished? How can attributes be matched when they are similar but not identical (Ortony, 1979b)? Even more generally, it is questionable whether the mapping of high-salience attributes in B terms onto low-salience attributes of A terms is part of early on-line comprehension processes for metaphorical expressions. The experimental studies that have investigated the plausibility of both the salience imbalance and the domains interaction views asked participants to rate the salience of attributes for the A and B terms in similarity statements *after* reading and interpreting them. People's interpretations of metaphors might easily have influenced their object descriptions, because placing terms in a similarity statement or metaphor can increase the subjective salience of their common attributes (Gentner & Clements, 1988). Thus, people's intuitions about the salience of the attributes for the topic and vehicle terms of metaphors might not reflect the actual salience of these terms when metaphors are first understood. Asking people to rate the attributes of different terms in a metaphorical statement taps into the later product of what has already been interpreted and does not necessarily reflect the information that is processed early on when people first comprehend metaphors. It seems clear that none of the theories discussed thus far is especially informative about metaphor understanding as an early on-line *process*, because they primarily focus on explaining the results, or late *products*, of that understanding.

One recent model that attempts to overcome some of the difficulties associated with other psychological theories of metaphor is the class inclusion model (Glucksberg & Keysar, 1990). This theory differs from previous proposals in its suggestion that all metaphors are class inclusion statements. Consider the metaphorical statement *My job is a jail*. Glucksberg and Keysar argue that metaphors are not understood by converting them into similes (e.g., *My job is like a jail*). Instead metaphors are exactly what they appear to be: class inclusion statements in which the topic of the metaphor (*my job*) is assigned to a diagnostic category (entities that confine one against one's will, are unpleasant, are difficult to escape from). In these statements, the metaphor's vehicle (*jail*) refers to that newly created diagnostic category and at the same time is a prototypical example of that category. This new category may not have a conventional name, but it is possible to use the name of a prototypical category member as the name of the category itself, as in the statements *My job is a jail* and *Cigarettes are time bombs*. The newly created categories to which metaphorical comparisons refer are structurally similar to ordinary taxonomic categories that have conventional names at the superordinate level, such as "food" and "furniture" (Rosch, 1978), as well as to ad hoc categories, such as "food to be eaten on a weight loss diet" (Barsalou, 1983). Most generally, the class inclusion view suggests that when metaphors are expressed as comparisons, they are interpreted as implicit category statements rather than as implicit similes that require recognition of some underlying similarity to be understood. The groupings that are created by metaphors induce similarity relations, so the groupings are formed prior to the recognition of similarity.

The class inclusion model is appealing because it explicitly links categorizing processes to metaphor understanding. Its suggestion that metaphor understanding creates new ad hoc categories, ones with systematic entailments, also provides a concrete model of the "parallel implication complex" to which Black referred in his most recent work on the interaction view (1979). However, the class inclusion view, like the other psychological models, assumes that understanding each metaphorical utterance depends on some unique, novel act of mapping information from a source onto a target domain. That is, the class inclusion view suggests that the process of metaphor understanding *begins* immediately with the creation of a class inclusion relationship that contains both the topic and vehicle. Various metaphorical entailments emerge from this novel grouping. Still, it might very well be the case that such metaphorical groupings already exist as part of our everyday conceptual structures. The vast majority of metaphors primarily reflect underlying conceptualizations of experience that are already structured by metaphorical schemes (e.g., *My mar-*

riage is a long dusty road refers to the LOVE IS A JOURNEY conceptual metaphor). Most metaphorical expressions instantiate,
sometimes in spectacular ways, preexisting metaphorical
mappings whereby knowledge from a target domain is partly
understood in terms of a dissimilar source domain. These conceptual metaphors motivate the meanings assigned to many
verbal metaphors and provide coherence to linguistic expressions that are traditionally viewed in the various interaction
models as idiosyncratic references to novel categories (see
Chapter 4). For this reason, the interpretation of metaphorical
statements does not necessarily require some earlier temporal contrast between, or grouping of, diverse knowledge domains, because such metaphorical mappings may already exist in long-term memory. The next section explores this idea
and its consequences for a theory of metaphor understanding.

METAPHOR AS CONCEPTUAL STRUCTURE

A widely held assumption about metaphor is that people produce and understand verbal metaphors through the juxtaposition of disparate conceptual categories that are themselves
fixed by their objectively defined properties. Recent research
has questioned many long-standing assumptions like this one
by suggesting that metaphor is pervasive in everyday life, not
just in language but also in our structuring of experience. *Our
ordinary conceptual system, in terms of which we both think and
act, is fundamentally metaphorical in nature* (G. Lakoff & Johnson,
1980, p. 3; see also M. Johnson, 1987; G. Lakoff, 1987; G. Lakoff
& Turner, 1989). As discussed in Chapter 4, the way we think,
what we experience, and what we do every day are very much
a matter of metaphor.

The idea that metaphor is conceptually based and structures
much of our worldly experience offers powerful new insights
into the phenomenology of metaphor understanding. Like the
interaction theory of metaphor, the metaphor-as-conceptual-
structure view applies to many points on the temporal continuum of understanding. However, the theory of metaphor

as conceptually based structure makes the more specific claim that our understanding of metaphor is inherently constrained by our conceptualization of experience. Actions, events, and objects are understood in terms of "experiential gestalts" (i.e., structurally meaningful wholes within experience). Meaning emerges at the level of experiential gestalts that give coherence and structure to our experience. In metaphor comprehension we understand one kind of thing or experience in terms of something else of a different kind.

For example, the ARGUMENT IS WAR metaphor structures not only the way we talk about arguments (e.g., *He attacked the weak point of my argument, To defend a position, Her criticisms were right on target, He shot down my best arguments*) but also the very way we conceive of and carry on arguments in our culture (G. Lakoff & Johnson, 1980). The metaphorical meaning is based upon the projections of one common gestalt structure (WAR) onto another (ARGUMENTS). Various concepts, such as arguments, are partially structured by different kinds of metaphorical mappings. Thus, the concept of an argument can be seen in the conventional metaphor ARGUMENT IS WAR and also in the conventional metaphor ARGUMENTS ARE BUILDINGS (e.g., *He constructed a solid argument, He laid the foundation for his argument, His argument collapsed*) and ARGUMENTS ARE CONTAINERS (e.g., *This idea is the solid core of his argument, He expressed two new ideas in his argument*). Each of the conceptual mappings results in slightly different entailments in our understanding of arguments. Such examples demonstrate a tight link between our own metaphorical understanding of experience and the language we use to describe that experience. Linguistic metaphors are not arbitrarily generated through the random contrast of any two conceptual domains but reflect a constrained set of conceptual mappings, itself metaphorical, that structures our thinking, reasoning, and understanding. Various conventional conceptual metaphors, such as ARGUMENT IS WAR and ARGUMENTS ARE CONTAINERS, provide coherence to the many collocations that otherwise would have to be explained individually as exceptions, extensions, and highly marked uses of various lexical items.

The conceptual view of metaphor also explains why people

find such great beauty and power in poetry and literary prose. Verse embellishes the more mundane ways of thinking about our worldly experiences. Consider the following lines from a poem titled "Messenger," by David Smith, where Smith elaborates on the familiar theme of death as the end of life's journey.

> Knowing ourselves
> wingless and bestial, we wait
> for the sun to blow out,
> for the return of that first
> morning of pink blossoms
> when we saw the dark stains
> of our feet printing
> what we were on that
> dew-bed of the world.
> The tree, too, waits
> in its old unraveling
> toward a naked silence,
> its language wild and shocked.

These lines expand upon two central metaphors in our conceptualization of life – A LIFETIME IS A YEAR and A LIFETIME IS A DAY. Each conceptual metaphor suggests a tight mapping according to whichever entities in the domain of life correspond systematically to entities in the domains of a year and a day. With the metaphor A LIFETIME IS A DAY, for example, we would understand *dark stains of our feet printing what we were on that dew-bed of the world* to refer to the morning that metaphorically stands for birth, and *we wait for the sun to blow out* refers to evening and night, when we confront death. These same metaphorical schemes give rise to many different poetic instantiations and partly explain why we personally and aesthetically respond to poetry in the ways we often do. For example, A LIFETIME IS A DAY is nicely reflected in these lines about death from Catullus (see G. Lakoff & Turner, 1989):

> Suns can set and return again,
> but when our brief light goes out,
> there's one perpetual night to be slept through.

The view of metaphor as conceptual structure is particularly valuable as a linguistic theory of metaphor because it suggests a difference between having a metaphorical mapping of two disparate domains already existing as a unit in one's conceptual system and the mental act of putting together the same metaphor for the first time. Unlike many theories of metaphor, particularly the anomaly and speech act views, the conceptual structure view of metaphor provides an explanation for why so many metaphors are understood effortlessly, without conscious reflection. Very rarely do people experience metaphor as an abuse of language. Most metaphorical expressions are direct linguistic instantiations of preexisting conceptual mappings between conceptual domains and may thus be understood quite easily during the earliest moments of processing. Metaphor understanding is generally not problematic or different from comprehension of literal language, precisely because our conceptual system is structured via metaphorical mappings (M. Johnson, 1987; G. Lakoff, 1987). This idea is consistent with the experimental data on the *processes* of metaphor comprehension because it explains *why* listeners so often understand the meanings of metaphors without any conscious recognition (or appreciation) that the utterance understood is metaphorical (contrary to the metaphor-as-anomaly view).

Of course, many linguistic metaphors specify new twists on some conventional conceptual metaphor and may require additional inferential processing to be properly understood. This additional inferential processing often operates on the *products* of earlier comprehension *processes* (i.e., is part of metaphor interpretation rather than comprehension per se). In some cases, interpretation of novel metaphor results in the explicit conscious recognition that a new metaphor is being understood, one that demands greater imaginative powers to be fully understood and appreciated. This kind of understanding process may be lengthy and is most often associated with the scholarly practice of literary interpretation. Still, what makes many uses of metaphor so creative is their novel way of articulating some underlying mapping between concepts that already structures part of our experience in the world. What makes particular metaphors noticeable and memorable – for example, particularly apt scientific and literary metaphors – is the special, nonautomatic use to which ordinary, automatic modes of thought are put. Many linguists, literary theorists, and psychologists miss this important point because they fail to acknowledge the systematic conceptual underpinnings of the vast number of linguistic expressions that are metaphorical and creative. What is frequently seen as a creative metaphorical expression of some idea is often only a spectacular instantiation of specific metaphorical entailments that arise from a small set of conceptual metaphors shared by many individuals within a culture.

A number of important empirical issues regarding the conceptual structure view of metaphor understanding still remain to be addressed. Even though various conceptual metaphors appear to explain why people produce the linguistic metaphors they do, as well as many conventional expressions that seem quite literal, we need to establish that readers actually instantiate or activate some preexisting conceptual mapping when understanding various metaphorical and conventional utterances. Empirical studies in psycholinguistics have begun to provide exactly this kind of evidence. People's common metaphorical knowledge plays an important role in how they interpret literary metaphors in the same way as such knowledge motivates their understanding of conventional, idiomatic, and nonliterary metaphorical expressions.

One series of studies showed how preexisting conceptual metaphors constrain people's interpretations of literary metaphors in love poetry (Gibbs & Nascimento, 1993). A first study simply assessed college students' folk notions about the concept of love, in addition to how they metaphorically conceptualize their own love experiences. Participants in this study wrote their own definitions of love and then described the feelings they experienced when they first fell in love. Presented below is one example protocol from a woman, the first segment describing her definition of love and the second her description of her first love experience.

The overall concern for another person. Sharing of yourself but not giving yourself away. Feeling like you are both one, willing to compromise, knowing the other person well with excitement and electrical sparks to keep you going.

It kicked me in the head when I first realized it. My body was filled with a current of energy. Sparks filled through my pores when I thought of him or things we'd done together. Though I could not keep a grin off my face, I was scared of what this really meant. I was afraid of giving myself to someone else. I got that feeling in my stomach that you get the first time you make eye contact with someone you like. I enjoyed being with him, never got tired of him. I felt really overwhelmed, excited, comfortable, and anxious. I felt warm when I heard his voice, the movements of his body, his smell. When we were together, we fit like a puzzle, sharing, doing things for each other, knowing each other, feeling each other breathe.

There is nothing especially poetic about this woman's definition of love or her own first love experience. But the language she uses to convey her ideas and experience provides good examples of conventional expressions that reflect enduring metaphorical conceptions of love. Among the most frequent conceptual metaphors in participants' descriptions of love and their love experiences were LOVE IS A UNITY, A NATURAL FORCE, PHYSICAL CLOSENESS, A VALUABLE RESOURCE, A JOURNEY, and INSANITY. Some of these conceptual metaphors, such as LOVE IS A UNITY, LOVE IS A NATURAL FORCE, and LOVE IS PHYSICAL CLOSENESS, were employed in conventional expressions by more than half the participants in the experiment. The presence of this fairly limited number of conceptual metaphors in participants' discourse at the very least illustrates the dominance of metaphor in how people talk about love and their love experiences.

A second experiment went on to investigate whether people could generally recognize the presence of conceptual metaphors in various instances of love poetry. Participants read 10 fragments of love poetry, each of which was followed by a list of five conceptual metaphors (e.g., LOVE IS A NATURAL FORCE). The participants' task was to read each fragment and select the conceptual metaphor that best reflected the underlying theme of love in the poem. Overall, participants were very accurate in choosing conceptual metaphors that motivated the poetic fragments they had just read. A third experiment had a different group of participants read the same poetic fragment and then pick from a list of five the conventional expression (e.g., *We were sick with love*) that best reflected the concept of love described in the poem. Once again, participants were quite good at picking the conventional expressions that were motivated by the conceptual metaphors underlying the poems. These data are consistent with the hypothesis that readers partly understand poetry by recovering the conceptual metaphor(s) that motivate what authors express in their poems.

A fourth study employed a talking-out-loud task to see whether the inferences readers drew about the meanings of poems reflected their metaphorical understanding of the poets' own conceptions about love. Consider these lines from the poem titled "Ode and Burgeoning," by Pablo Neruda:

> My wild girl, we have had
> to regain time
> and march backward, in the distance
> of our lives, kiss after kiss,
> gathering from one place what we gave
> without joy, discovering in another
> the secret road
> that gradually brought your feet
> close to mine.

An analysis of the participants' statements made while reading the poems line by line provided good evidence that conceptual metaphor structured their understanding of the poems. Across all the poems and the participants, 78% of all statements in the talking-out-loud protocols referred to the entailments of the underlying conceptual metaphors that partially motivated the meanings of the poems participants had read. For example, when participants read the fragment from Neruda's poem, they referred to entailments of the love as a journey metaphor, such as the path (e.g., *They learned a better path to happiness, They had to retrace their steps to find true love, They found a special road that they could travel together on in the same direction*), the goals (e.g., *The future of their love lay ahead of them, They had to catch up*), and the impediments to travel (e.g., *They managed to get over the rough places, rediscovering what was missed*).

Most generally, it seemed clear that readers were partly making sense of what the poems meant through their every-day metaphorical understanding of love. Although there is some debate as to whether the talking-out-loud procedure accurately reflects normal on-line mental processes, the present data at the very least suggest that people's conscious reflec-tive interpretations of poetry are strongly constrained by their ordinary metaphorical knowledge.

One should note that people do not necessarily *create* novel metaphorical mappings to understand novel poetic language. The vast majority of novel metaphors in poetry and literature reflect fixed patterns of metaphorical mappings between dis-similar source and target domains. Although poets may present novel instantiations for these preexisting metaphori-cal mappings, people do not necessarily have to draw novel mappings in any algorithmic sense in order to understand poetic instantiations of conventional metaphors. Poets do on occasion create entirely novel metaphors that demand new mappings from source to target domains, but these are rela-tively rare.

The evidence on conceptual metaphor in understanding love poetry is consistent with other findings that conceptual meta-phors appear to constrain people's mental images for many metaphorical expressions, such as *Some marriages are iceboxes* (Gibbs, 1992a). Moreover, conceptual metaphor motivates why people make sense of idioms as having the meanings they do (Gibbs & O'Brien, 1990). Finally, people's metaphorical con-cepts influence the immediate processing of idiomatic phrases in context (Nayak & Gibbs, 1990). Chapter 6 reviews in greater detail the evidence on idiomaticity. Although there is not a great deal of evidence showing that conceptual metaphor in-fluences people's on-line understanding of metaphorical ut-terances, some findings are consistent with this hypothesis.

For example, people are faster at reading a verbal metaphor like *The eager suitor assaulted her defenses* than the literal statement *The eager suitor wanted her affection* when they were first presented with the statement LOVE IS WAR (Kemper, 1989). Moreover, participants were faster at deciding that two metaphorical expressions, such as *He laid siege to her heart* and *The eager suitor assaulted her defenses*, were related when these were motivated by the same conceptual metaphor (LOVE IS WAR). Participants also took significantly longer to understand verbal metaphors derived from conflicting conceptual metaphors, such as *He laid siege to her heart* (LOVE IS WAR) and *He swept her off her feet* (LOVE IS A PHYSICAL FORCE) (ibid.). These findings can be interpreted as showing that reading linguistic instantiations of conceptual metaphors facilitates readers' understanding of verbal metaphors that are motivated by these conceptual metaphors.

More recent studies have demonstrated that verbal metaphors are easier to comprehend when read in contexts that instantiate relevant conceptual metaphors (Allbritton, 1992). Consider the following story illustrating the conceptual mapping of LOVE IS A PHYSICAL FORCE.

> John and Martha met at a party about a month ago.
> Since then they have hardly ever been seen apart from one another.
> The attraction between John and Martha was overwhelming.
> Sparks flew the moment they first saw one another.
> It was a classic case of love at first sight.

Participants in one of a series of studies read stories like this, each one instantiating a particular conceptual metaphor. Afterwards, the participants were presented with one of two prime sentences, one of which was relevant to the primary conceptual metaphor in an earlier story (e.g., *The attraction between John and Martha was overwhelming*) and the other was neutral (e.g., *John and Martha met at a party about a month ago.*) Immediately after seeing the prime sentence, the participants were shown a test sentence, such as *Sparks flew the moment they first saw one another*. The participants' task was to decide as quickly as possible whether they had read the test sentence earlier. A series of studies showed that people were significantly faster at making these recognition judgments when primed by sentences that were relevant to the underlying conceptual metaphor in the story. This result supported the hypothesis that metaphor-based schemas could function to relate instances of schema-related information to one another during text processing.

Further studies in this series showed that people automatically instantiated metaphorical schemes (i.e., conceptual metaphors) as they read texts (Allbritton, 1992). Consider the following passage instantiating the metaphor ANGER IS HEAT:

> Edward was boiling with anger.
> The sales clerk had completely screwed up his order.
> The manager saw there might be trouble and rushed over.
> Hoping to prevent a scene, she tried to lower his thermostat.
>
> (*Novel schema-instantiating priming sentence*)
>
> Hoping to prevent a scene, she tried to cool him off.
>
> (*Conventional schema-instantiating priming sentence*)
>
> Hoping to prevent a scene, she tried to fix the problem.
>
> (*Neutral priming sentence*)

Participants read a passage and immediately afterwards were presented with a test word (e.g., *boiling*) that related to the metaphorical schema in the story. These test words were related to the dominant metaphorical schema in the story (*boiling* for ANGER IS HEAT). Participants were faster at recognizing the test words after having just read conventional schema-instantiating priming sentences than after neutral sentences. This result suggested that people actually instantiated an underlying conceptual metaphor, such as ANGER IS HEAT, when reading such conventional expressions as *Hoping to prevent a scene, she tried to cool him off*. Interestingly, the participants were not faster at recognizing the test words after reading the novel schema-instantiating priming sentences. It appears that novel metaphorical expressions (*Hoping to prevent a scene, she tried to lower his thermostat*) were not immediately seen as being related to the general metaphorical schema for the story (ANGER IS HEAT), at least as measured by this word recognition task.

These experimental studies provide some initial evidence that the conceptual structure view of metaphor characterizes aspects of metaphor comprehension as well as metaphor recognition and interpretation. Readers use their metaphorical understanding of texts in their immediate processing of *some* kinds of verbal metaphors presented in these texts. Clearly, more empirical work needs to be done to determine the extent to which people automatically instantiate preexisting conceptual metaphors when they read or hear both conventional and novel metaphorical statements.

The idea that our understanding of metaphorical language is partly motivated by preexisting metaphorical schemes of thought does not account for all aspects of how linguistic metaphors are understood. One frequently encountered metaphor in literary texts is the *image metaphor*. Image metaphors reflect the mapping not of concepts but of mental images from one source of knowledge onto the mental images from another. Poets often write for the express purpose of creating disturbing new images, ones that result from the mappings of image structures from widely disparate knowledge domains. Consider the opening lines from the surrealist poet André Breton's *Free Union* (G. Lakoff & Turner, 1989).

> My wife whose hair is brush fire
> Whose thoughts are summer lightning
> Whose waist is an hourglass
> Whose waist is the waist of an otter caught in the
> teeth of a tiger
> Whose mouth is a bright cockade with the fragrance
> of a star of the first magnitude
> Whose teeth leave prints like the tracks of white mice
> over snow
> Whose tongue is made out of amber and polished
> glass
> Whose tongue is a stabbed wafer
> The tongue of a doll with eyes that open and shut
> Whose tongue is incredible stone

My wife whose eyelashes are strokes in the handwriting
of a child
Whose eyebrows are nests of swallows

These novel image mappings about hair, thoughts, mouths, and teeth open up new possibilities for further exploration of the mappings between different knowledge domains. The power of poetic metaphor comes from the poet's ability to create many such novel, one-shot kinds of mapping between mental images.

Metaphoric image mappings work in the same way as other metaphoric mappings by mapping the structure of one domain onto the structure of another. But in image metaphors the domains are mental images. Consider the mappings that arise from *My wife . . . whose waist is an hourglass*. This example describes a superimposition of the image of an hourglass onto the image of a woman's waist by virtue of their common shape. As with conventional metaphors, the metaphoricity is not in the words themselves but in some conceptual mapping. However, the mapping here is from the middle of an hourglass onto the woman's waist; only that part of the hourglass corresponds to the woman's waist. In most image-mapping metaphors, there is a mapping of the part/whole structure of one image onto aspects of the part/whole structure of another (G. Lakoff & Turner, 1989).

Image metaphors are not involved in everyday reasoning and thus differ from the conventional metaphors that reflect the organizing of experience in terms of mappings between concepts. The highly specific detail found in image metaphors contrasts with robust conceptual mappings, such as LIFE IS A JOURNEY, where rich knowledge and rich inferential structure are mapped from one domain onto another. For this reason, image metaphors are referred to as one-shot metaphors, since they do not ordinarily appear in people's conceptualizations of their experience (ibid.).

No experimental work has been done to look at people's understanding of image metaphors. Yet it is clear that these kinds of verbal metaphor make up a good proportion of the metaphors found in poetry and literature. Because image metaphors reflect temporary mappings of mental images from different domains, unique kinds of psychological mechanisms must be invoked to explain how these image mappings are created and understood.

METAPHOR AND LITERATURE

One of the disappointing aspects of the psychological research on metaphor understanding is that few studies have been devoted to literary metaphor. With only the few exceptions noted in this chapter, the experimental work has examined isolated metaphorical expressions or metaphors in experimenter-created story contexts. Most of the metaphors studied have clearly defined topic and vehicle terms, one reason why metaphor theorists have traditionally been enamored of the question of how the topic and vehicle terms are combined or interact during metaphor comprehension.

However, the phenomenology of metaphor in literature is much richer and more complex than what is seen in psychological studies (Shannon, 1992). Distinguishing between literary and nonliterary metaphors is not easy to do. Literary metaphors are typically rich in meaning; scientific metaphors are typically clear (Gentner, 1982). In this way, metaphor may have two diverse communicative functions in discourse: scientific metaphors are valuable for their explanatory potential, whereas literary metaphors have a predominantly expressive or evocative function (ibid.; Steen, 1993). Recent studies suggest that readers find literary metaphors to be more original, less clear, and less communicatively conventional; to have higher positive value; and to be less committed to moral positions than they do metaphors from nonliterary sources (Steen, 1993). Metaphors are often perceived as being related to literariness. One set of studies examined this issue by having readers underline those parts of a text that they thought were typical of literary passages (ibid.). Participants underlined metaphorical statements significantly more often when reading literary texts (e.g., a selection from Norman Mailer's *Miami and the Siege of Chicago*) than when reading a set of control passages. Many participants later commented when queried that they were quite aware of underlining metaphors because "metaphors are literary." Readers appeared to view metaphoric language as being intentionally employed by authors in an attempt to create literary texts.

Metaphors in literature often appear to be closer to the "anomalous" expressions studied by psychologists. For example, Shannon (1992) presents a wonderful example of a metaphor from literature that makes sense even though we do not know the features of the vehicle. This example comes from Gabriel García Márquez's novel *Love in the Time of Cholera* (1988: 221–22):

> Once he tasted some chamomile tea and sent it back, saying only: "This stuff tastes of window." Both she and the servants were surprised because they had never heard of anyone who had drunk boiled window, but when they tried the tea in an effort to understand, they understood: it did taste of window.

The metaphor of the tea tasting like window is meaningful for us despite the fact that, as Márquez notes, we have never tasted boiled window. Literary metaphors like this create a different perspective on reality than most metaphors seen in science and in mundane speech. One of the challenges for psychologists and others interested in the empirical study of metaphor is to find ways of examining how it is that readers make sense of novel metaphorical texts. Doing so requires that we go beyond the isolated metaphor to envision better how metaphors are recognized as intentionally created by authors to make new the world we live in. Gibbs, Kushner, and Mills (1991) and Boswell (1986) present evidence showing that people immediately seek authorial intentions when reading metaphorical expressions.

CONCLUSION

Much of the disagreement among contemporary theories of metaphor understanding centers on two primary issues. First, to what extent does understanding verbal metaphor depend on preexisting mappings between dissimilar knowledge domains? Second, what psychological mechanisms best account for how people metaphorically map information from a source onto a target domain (or from the vehicle to the topic) when linguistic metaphors are understood? I suggest that the answers to these questions are intertwined, in that the particular mechanism proposed to explain how metaphorical expressions are understood will depend on whether a verbal metaphor instantiates preexisting metaphorical knowledge or actually creates some novel mapping between different conceptual domains. Verbal metaphors based on preexisting metaphorical knowledge are not necessarily mundane or conventional, for many novel metaphors also reflect metaphorical concepts that form a significant part of our everyday cognition.

Our explanation of metaphor understanding must also depend on the specific conception of what it means to understand a metaphorical expression. No single theory provides a comprehensive account of how people understand all kinds of metaphorical language, given all the temporal moments of understanding that are discussed by metaphor scholars (comprehension, recognition, interpretation, and appreciation). Some theories best explain aspects of metaphor recognition (the anomaly and speech act views); others best account for metaphor interpretation (the domains interaction, salience imbalance, structure mapping, and class inclusion models). Psycholinguistic theories evolving out of the interaction view all share the important characteristics of attempting to explain how conceptual structure constrains metaphor use and different aspects of metaphor understanding. In turn, each of these theories differs significantly from the metaphor-as-conceptual-structure view, which explicitly argues that common metaphorical knowledge that structures a good deal of our experience plays a major role in the production and comprehension of metaphorical language. The psycholinguistic theories do not necessarily disagree with the notion that much of our everyday thought is constituted by metaphor, but neither do they explicitly claim a significant role for conceptual metaphor in the ordinary production and understanding of linguistic metaphor.

The position I favor, the conceptual structure view, is best able to explain many different aspects of metaphor understanding, including some parts of comprehension, interpretation, and appreciation. One advantage of the conceptual metaphor position is that it explains how people make sense of a wide range of linguistic phenomena, not simply metaphorical expressions. For example, systematic patterns of conventional expression are shown to be motivated by similar preexisting metaphorical knowledge that gives rise to novel metaphorical language. Thus, the conceptual metaphor LOVE IS A JOURNEY partly motivates why literal expressions such as *Our love is on the rocks, We are at a crossroads in the relationship,* and *We have found a new path to love* make sense in talking about love and love relationships. Because some aspects of our concept of love may be likened to some aspects of journeys, we can have systematic correspondences between entities in the domains of journeys and love. Do such correspondences play an active role in our ordinary understanding of conventional phrases (e.g., *Our marriage is on the rocks*) and novel metaphors (e.g., *Our marriage is a bumpy roller-coaster ride*)? The answer to this question is not yet settled, but there exists a fair amount of data to at least suggest that the answer may be yes. Then again, conceptual metaphors may only motivate why various linguistic expressions make sense to us, even though such knowledge may not automatically operate in the immediate on-line production and comprehension of metaphorical language (Gibbs, 1992a; Glucksberg, Brown, & McGlone, 1993).

At present, only some data suggest that conceptual metaphors might immediately influence some aspects of metaphor comprehension. Readers might automatically instantiate conceptual metaphors when understanding fairly conventional utterances, such as common literal and idiomatic phrases clearly motivated by metaphorical knowledge. But many novel metaphors may be understood without the influence of preexisting conceptual metaphors. Only upon reflection might novel metaphors be recognized as reflecting common metaphorical concepts in long-term memory. Much more work clearly needs to be done before this critical issue is settled. Furthermore, the conceptual view suggests how one-shot metaphors arise from the temporary mapping of mental images from one domain of knowledge onto another. Empirical work must also consider how these image mappings are constructed and how comprehension of image metaphors, such as *My wife . . . whose waist is an hourglass*, differs from understanding of verbal metaphor motivated by preexisting metaphorical structures in long-term memory.

The most important conclusion of this chapter is that there is a growing recognition in the empirical study of metaphor that everyday metaphorical knowledge plays various roles in people's understanding of metaphorical language. Theories of metaphor understanding at all levels of understanding (comprehension, recognition, interpretation, and appreciation) must consider not only how metaphor understanding creates new modes of conceptual understanding but also how it exploits preexisting metaphorical ways of understanding experience that are a fundamental part of the poetic mind.

Chapter 6

Idiomaticity

California is one of the best living laboratories for studying the idioms, cliches, and colloquialisms that make up the poetry of everyday speech. Consider the following brief example from Cyra McFadden's popular novel *The Serial* about the life of an affluent couple living in the suburbs of San Francisco in the late 1970s.

> It sent Kate into the pits when she learned from her "friend" Martha, who seemed to get off on laying bad trips on people, that Harvey was getting it on with Carol.

Most of us, even those people who do not live in California, would probably not experience much difficulty understanding this sentence. *Into the pits* means "to be depressed," *lay on* means "to inflict," *trip* means "an experience," and *get it on* refers to having sexual relations. *Get off on* is a doubly metaphorical expression mostly referring to the achievement of sexual climax but sometimes used, as in this example, to denote nonsexual gratification. The quotation marks around *friend* suggest that this term is being used ironically to mean "my supposed friend." We might roughly paraphrase the example "Kate became depressed when she learned from her supposed friend, Martha, who seemed to enjoy telling people bad news, that Harvey was having an affair with Carol."

Slang, clichéd, idiomatic expressions like those discussed here are the archenemies of many well-intended English teachers. Each of these formulaic kinds of figurative language is mostly seen as lacking in metaphoric creativity. *Slang is the sluggard's way of avoiding the search for the exact, meaningful, word* (Hodges, 1967: 197). Slang acts as *a cheap substitute for good diction* that demonstrates *laziness in thought and poverty of vocabulary* (Foerster & Steadman, 1941: 290). One late-19th-century authority proclaimed that *slang is to a people's language what an epidemic disease is to their bodily constitution; just as catching and just as inevitable in its run. . . . Like a disease too, it is severest where the sanitary conditions are most neglected* (Genung, 1893: 32). Oliver Wendell Holmes even suggested that *the use of slang is at once a sign and a cause of mental atrophy* (Partridge, 1935: 295).

A small number of scholars and writers, however, have called slang *the poetry of everyday life* and said that it *vividly expresses people's feelings about life and about things they encounter in life* (Hayakawa, 1941: 194–95). Walt Whitman (1892/1964: 573) went even further in his praise over a century ago when he said *Slang, or indirection, is an attempt of common humanity to escape from bald literalism, and express itself illimitably, which in highest walks produces poets and poems.*

Everyday language contains many thousands of idiomatic, slang, and proverbial phrases whose figurative interpretations diverge in various ways from their literal meanings. Metaphor clearly plays a significant part in the development of idiomatic vocabulary. Many American teenagers and college students, for instance, have idiomatic words for the adjective *drunk* that are derived from standard words meaning "destroyed" or "torn," such as *blasted, blitzed, bombed, ripped, shredded, slaughtered,* and *tattered*. Each of these terms is motivated by the metaphorical mapping whereby people conceptualize their drunken experiences partly in terms of being bombed, blasted, shredded, ripped, and so on. Slang vocabulary is exceptionally vivid simply because it often makes use of novel metaphors (Partridge, 1935). For instance, *blow chunks* initially seems like a disturbing, colorful way to say "to vomit," yet the literal meaning of this expression is almost the same as the colloquial phrase *throw up*, the difference being that *throw up* is so common that it has lost its power to shock.

Consider now these other examples of idiomatic language from *The Serial*, noting in particular their metaphorical roots.

Idiomaticity

Martha's last wedding had just blown Kate away, so she was look-ing forward to this one too. The phrase *blown away* is meant to be read as "to surprise or astonish."

Leonard, I'm sorry to dump on you like this, but I'm on a real heavy trip right now. The phrase *dump on* is read as "to inflict one's worries upon someone else"; *on a real heavy trip* refers to being "in some serious situation or personal crisis."

Weddings were much less conformist now that people were getting behind marriage again. The phrase *getting behind* means "sup-porting or identifying with."

Now listen, Harvey, his secretary comments when he is suffer-ing from jealousy, *you gotta stay loose, ya know? Hang in there; go with it.* The phrase *stay loose* means "to stay relaxed" or not to be *uptight; hang in there* means "not to lose control"; and *go with it* refers to "not fighting against" the event that provoked Harvey's jealousy.

She had decided to play the whole scene off the wall, to just go with the flow (in a scene where one character was about to confront her husband's girlfriend for the first time). *Off the wall* refers not to its common usage of something bizarre or crazy but to the idea of dealing with something spontaneously in the way that someone deals with a ball bouncing off the wall in sports like baseball or raquetball. *Go with the flow* means "to let events proceed as they will without trying to dictate what happens."

These examples of "California-speak" illustrate the meta-phorical nature of many contemporary idiomatic expressions. Even though many instances of contemporary speech have obvious figurative roots, most scholars assume that idiomatic language may once have been metaphorical but has lost its metaphoricity over time and now exists in the mental lexicon as a set of stock formulas or as dead metaphors. Just as speak-ers no longer view *leg of a table* as metaphoric, few people rec-ognize phrases such as *spill the beans, blow your stack, off the wall, in the pits,* or *a rolling stone gathers no moss* as being par-ticularly creative or metaphoric. After all, metaphors are lively, creative, and resistant to paraphrase, whereas idioms, cliches, and proverbs are hackneyed expressions that are equivalent in meaning to simple literal phrases. To classify some utterance or phrase as "idiomatic," "slang," or "proverbial" is tantamount to a theoretical explanation in itself, given the widely held view that such phrases are dead metaphors that belong in the wastebasket of formulas and phrases that are separate from the generative component of the grammar.

This chapter attempts to expose the myth that most instances of slang, cliches, idioms, and proverbs are simple dead metaphors. The figurative meanings of these formulaic idiomatic expressions cannot be reduced to simple literal paraphrases. People make sense of idiomatic speech precisely because of their ordinary metaphorical knowledge which provides part of the link between these phrases and their figurative interpretations. There is now much evidence from cognitive linguistics and experimental psychology to support the idea that idiomatic language retains much of its metaphoricity. Examination of these phrases reveals several important features of the poetics of everyday thought.

My discussion of slang, idioms, and proverbs does not attempt to define strictly and formally what constitutes each of these types of conventional language. Lexicographers and scholars working in the linguistic tradition of phraseology have long realized that single words are not necessarily the appropriate unit for lexical description. Still, these same scholars have struggled to establish the boundaries between different types of linguistic phrase. Many scholars suggest that slang is simply *not accepted as good formal usage* or consists just of whatever is not in a standard dictionary, even though these expressions are frequently used by a large proportion of the general public (Wentworth & Flexner, 1960: vi). In fact, by this definition, most language is slang except for formal usage and words and expressions that are used in very limited circumstances. Some authorities define slang as *that portion of the vocabulary which changes most frequently* (Gleason, 1961: 6). But even this view overlooks the fact that novelty in an expression is often more apparent than real. For instance, *out of sight*, meaning "excellent," is usually thought to have arisen in the 1960s but is actually first recorded in Stephen Crane's *Maggie* in 1893. In fact, the word *excellent* is now common slang among teenagers and college students, given its prominence in popular movies like *Bill and Ted's Excellent Adventure* and *Wayne's World.*

The *OED* defines slang as *language of a highly colloquial type, considered as below the level of standard educated speech, and consisting either of new words or of current words employed in some special sense.* Idioms are defined by the *OED* as *a form of speech peculiar or proper to a people or country.* These definitions are also not very helpful unless there is some better understanding of what is *highly colloquial, standard speech,* or speech that is only *proper to a people or country.* Perhaps the most sincere statement about idiomatic language in general is *Webster's Third International Dictionary'*s comment about slang *there is no completely satisfactory objective test for slang, especially in application to a word out of context.*

Although there is wide disagreement on the exact definition of what is idiomatic, slang, proverbial, and so on (see Strassler, 1982), one can take a liberal view and accept any of the following expressions as idiomatic to some degree.

Sayings

take the bull by the horns
let the cat out of the bag

Proverbs

A bird in the hand is worth two in the bush
A stitch in time saves nine

Phrasal verbs

to give in
to take off
to get up
to look up

Tournure idioms

to kick the bucket
to fly off the handle
to crack the whip

Binomials

spick and span
hammer and tongs

The poetics of mind

Frozen similes
as white as snow
as cool as a cucumber

Phrasal compounds
red herring
deadline

Incorporating verb idioms
to babysit
to sightsee

Formulaic expressions
at first sight
how do you do?

I hope to show, though, that linguistic items of this general class are not simply frozen, formulaic phrases but are excellent indicators of how people think metaphorically in their everyday lives.

TRADITIONAL VIEWS OF IDIOMATICITY

One enduring belief about idioms is that these expressions are noncompositional because their figurative meanings are not functions of the meanings of their individual parts (see Aitchison, 1987; Bobrow & Bell, 1973; Brooke-Rose, 1958; Chomsky, 1965, 1980; Cooper, 1986; Cruse, 1986; Fraser, 1970; Jackendoff, 1975; J. Katz, 1973; Long & Summers, 1979; Makkai, 1972; Strassler, 1982; Weinreich, 1969). For instance, the figurative interpretation of *shoot the breeze* ("to talk without significant purpose") cannot be determined through an analysis of the meanings of its individual words. Similarly, the individual word meanings of the classic phrase *kick the bucket* seemingly contribute little information to its figurative meaning ("to die").

The noncompositional view of idioms holds that their figurative meanings are directly stipulated in the mental lexicon in the same way the meanings of individual words are listed in a dictionary. Unlike comprehension of literal language, idioms are presumably understood (a) through the retrieval of their stipulated meanings from the lexicon after their literal meanings have been rejected as inappropriate (Bobrow & Bell, 1973; Weinreich, 1969); (b) in parallel to processing of their literal meanings (Estill & Kemper, 1982; Swinney & Cutler, 1979); (c) directly, without any analysis of their literal meanings (Gibbs, 1980, 1985a, 1986d); or (d) when input causes a configuration to be recognized as an idiom (Cacciari & Tabossi, 1988). Many models of natural language processing in artificial intelligence include a special "phrasal" lexicon containing formulaic and idiomatic phrases that are noncompositional, but that can be accessed quickly during linguistic parsing (Becker, 1975; Gasser & Dyer, 1986; Wilensky & Arens, 1980). According to the traditional view, learning the meanings of idioms requires that speakers form arbitrary links between idioms and their nonliteral meanings to recognize that *spill the beans* = "to reveal a secret," *button your lip* = "to keep a secret," *lose your marbles* = "to go crazy," and so on (cf. Ackerman, 1982; Prinz, 1983).

The noncompositional view of idioms also supposedly explains why many idioms tend to be syntactically unproductive, or frozen. For example, one cannot syntactically transform the phrase *John kicked the bucket* into a passive construction (**The bucket was kicked by John*) without disrupting its nonliteral meaning. Linguists have proposed a variety of formal devices to predict the syntactic behavior of idioms (Bresnan & Kaplan, 1982; Chafe, 1968, 1970; Dong, 1971; Fraser, 1970; Gazdar, Pullum, Klein, & Sag, 1985; J. Katz, 1973; Newmeyer, 1972; Weinreich, 1969). One proposal suggests that the base component of idiomatic phrases like *kick the bucket* be marked with a simple feature [−Passive] (Weinreich, 1969). Other researchers argue that idioms can be organized into a "frozenness hierarchy" ranging from expressions that undergo nearly all grammatical transformations without losing their figurative meanings (e.g., *lay down the law*) to idioms that cannot undergo even the simplest transformation without losing their idiomatic interpretation (e.g., *face the music*) (Fraser, 1970). According to this analysis, idioms can be marked with a single feature that assigns them to a class of idioms that behave similarly in the operation of their syntactic rules. Another proposal suggests that some of the constituents of unproductive idioms be marked with syntactic features that block the application of transformations to strings that contain the constituent (J. Katz, 1973). Thus, the idiomatic phrase *breathe down your neck* can be lexically marked as [–Particle Movement, –Passive, –Action Nominalization] to prevent the generation of unacceptable strings such as **I breathed your neck down the other day*. Still other proposals suggest that lexical rules (e.g., subcategorization) operate to limit the acceptable syntactic constructions in which idioms can appear (Bresnan & Kaplan, 1982).

Syntactic devices like those described above can account within a formal theory of grammar for some of the transformational deficiencies of idioms. But the traditional view of idiomaticity provides no explanation of how people come to acquire the rules for knowing which transformations apply or don't apply to which idioms. Speakers are not explicitly taught which idioms are syntactically productive and which are not. Yet people somehow learn about the syntactic behavior of most idioms, including relatively rare and novel phrases. So how do speakers determine, for instance, that the *bucket* of the syntactically frozen phrase *kick the bucket* is understood with the feature [+Idiom] to block application of the passive transformation (we never hear **The bucket was kicked by John* as an idiom), whereas the *law* of the syntactically productive idiom *lay down the law* is not marked with such a feature? Certainly we have never heard *The bucket was kicked by John* as an idiom, but we do not need to hear *The piper was paid by John* in order to produce *John paid the piper* or to recognize the expression as idiomatic (Gibbs & Nayak, 1989; Nunberg, 1978).

The syntactic distinction between idioms like *kick the bucket* and *pay the piper* might be related in some way to the meanings of these phrases (Newmeyer, 1972, 1974). Idioms like *kick the bucket, shoot the bull*, and *make the scene* might not be rendered in the passive because their nonidiomatic paraphrases, *die, talk*, and *arrive*, are intransitive. However, other idioms like *give up the ghost, throw in the towel*, and *pop the question* can be turned into passive constructions even though their nonidiomatic equivalents *die, resign*, and *propose* are intransitive (Nunberg, 1978). It seems clear, then, that the syntactic behavior of idioms cannot be predicted solely on the basis of their grammatical form or figurative meaning alone but must be due in part to some *relation* between their figurative meanings and their individual components (cf. Gazdar et al., 1985; Nunberg, 1978). This conclusion is inconsistent with the traditional idea that the internal semantics of idioms play little role in determining the meanings of these phrases.

Another problem for the traditional view of idioms is that determining the link between an idiom and its figurative meaning is complicated by the vast number of idioms that mean roughly the same thing. Idioms don't have unique figurative interpretations, but, as is true for individual words, many idioms can refer to a single concept or idea. For example, American speakers can convey the idea of revealing or exposing a secret by saying *spill the beans, let the cat out of the bag, blow the lid off*, or *blow the whistle on*. According to the traditional view of idioms, there should be no particular reason why each of these different phrases means "to reveal a secret." Again, the link between an idiom and its figurative meaning is arbitrary and cannot be predicted from the meanings of its individual words.

DEAD AND CONVENTIONAL METAPHORS

Scholars often treat idioms as dead metaphors because they confuse dead metaphors with conventional ones. For example, suppose we encounter a word like *gone* in an expression like *He's almost gone* in reference to a dying person. The traditional dead-metaphor theory would claim that *gone* isn't really metaphoric now, though it once may have been. *Gone* has simply come to have "dead" as one of its literal meanings. In a similar manner, the phrases *spill the beans* and *kick the bucket* are not viewed as metaphorical, though they may at one time have been highly figurative. *Spill the beans* has simply come to mean "reveal the secret," whereas *kick the bucket* now simply means "to die." Each of these idiomatic meanings is presumably listed as one of these phrase's literal meanings alongside the literal meanings that are based on compositional analyses, such as "tip over the beans" and "strike your foot against the pail" (Green, 1989).

Because contemporary speakers have little understanding of the original metaphorical roots of phrases like *spill the beans* and *kick the bucket*, people are thought to comprehend idioms in the same way as they know the meanings of individual words: as a matter of convention (cf. Lewis, 1969). For example, it is just an arbitrary fact of the language or a convention that we use the term *chair* to refer to chairs; we could as easily have used any other word, such as *table* or *dog*. This same arbitrariness of meaning is seen with idioms. Thus, it is conventional in our culture to greet someone by inquiring after the other person's health (e.g., *How are you?* or *How have you been?*), whereas in some other cultures it is conventional to greet someone by asking about the other person's gastronomic welfare (e.g., *Have you eaten?*) (Morgan, 1978). It is somewhat arbitrary, then, whether a particular culture uses one form of greeting as opposed to another. All that matters for individual speakers is that they recognize which phrases to use in particular discourse situations.

The meanings of idioms might be determined by such arbitrary conventions of usage. Thus, the expression *break a leg* to wish a performer good luck before a performance originated with the old superstition that it was bad luck to wish someone good luck. Consequently, people started wishing their fellow actors good luck by wishing them bad luck (i.e., a broken leg). Over time the choice of *break a leg* has become rigidly fixed as a convention, and that is one reason why similar phrases will not serve the same purpose (e.g., *fracture a tibia, I hope you break your leg*). Contemporary speakers may now understand that *break a leg* means "to wish someone luck" simply as a matter of convention, without any awareness of why this phrase means what it does.

Conventions of usage may also determine the appropriateness of idioms in different social situations. Thus, even though *spill the beans, let the cat out of the bag, blow the lid off*, and *blow the whistle on* all mean roughly "to reveal a secret," some convention might exist such that *spill the beans* is judged as appropriate to use in situations where a person is revealing some personal information about someone else, whereas *blow the lid off* might be most appropriate to use when talking about the revelation of a public matter, such as governmental corruption. Although it is not clear what motivates the development of these conventions of usage, it is still possible that speakers learn to use some idioms in particular social contexts and not in others simply by forming arbitrary links between an idiom, its figurative meaning, and a specific social situation.

Idioms are thought to have once been metaphorical because we can often trace a phrase back to its fully metaphorical use in an earlier stage of the language. Consider, for example, the phrase *fork in the road*. The word *fork* in this phrase has an established meaning, just as it does in the phrase *knife and fork*. But we can well imagine that at a time when the word was regularly applied only to the eating and cooking implement, people would use it metaphorically in speaking of a place where a road divided into two, much as the base of an eating fork divides into two or more separate tines. People today do not necessarily make use of this earlier metaphorical mapping between an eating implement and divided paths when understanding *fork in the road* – again suggesting that we normally interpret idioms as dead metaphors (Alston, 1964).

This analysis of *fork in the road*, and many of our intuitions about the historical development of idioms, is wrong (Kronfeld, 1980). As it turns out, the original meaning of *fork* (from the Old English *forca* and Latin *furca*) is not the eating or cooking implement. This is a later sense, first recorded in the 15th century. The original sense seems to be the agricultural implement (pitchfork), and this developed in Middle English into a more general sense: anything that forks, bifurcates, or divides into branches. Thus, *fork in the road* is not really dead metaphor, because it did not develop as a metaphoric extension of *eating fork*, or of *pitchfork*, for that matter. Rather both *fork in the road* and *kitchen fork* are specific tokens of the general sense of "anything that forks," which is a concept that is very much alive in our conceptual system.

This misinterpretation of the development of idiomatic meaning illustrates how difficult it is for speakers using language in ordinary circumstances or even professionally reflecting upon it to gain valid intuitions about metaphoricity in diachronic processes. The more we feel that a particular metaphor is dead, the harder it is to reconstruct the process through which the original metaphor was understood. Our intuitions may not always be sufficient to determine that some idioms were once metaphorically alive but now exist in a petrified state.

Even words that appear to be classic examples of dead metaphors often have vital metaphorical roots. Chapters 2 and 4, for instance, described how in Indo-European languages words meaning "see" regularly acquired the meaning "know" because of the widespread and ancient conceptual metaphor KNOWING IS SEEING (Sweetser, 1990). Because the metaphor exists in the conceptual systems of Indo-European speakers, the conceptual mapping between seeing and knowing provides a motivated reason for semantic change, so that as new words for seeing develop they eventually extend their meaning to knowing. It is incorrect, then, to suppose that *see* has the meanings it does because of a dead metaphor, one that is no longer part of a speaker's everyday knowledge. Instead, the KNOWING IS SEEING metaphor, which is part of the more general MIND AS BODY metaphor, is very much part of contemporary speakers' understanding of the world. In a similar fashion, people understand the word *grasp* to mean "understand" because of the live conceptual metaphor UNDERSTANDING IS GRASPING, a metaphor that motivates such expressions as *I can't catch on to his new idea* (G. Lakoff & Turner, 1989).

Many idioms in American English seem quite dead, and people can only guess why these phrases mean what they do. People generally think that *kick the bucket* comes from the situation of a condemned man with a rope around his neck who suddenly has the bucket he is standing on kicked out from beneath him. However, the phrase *kick the bucket* probably comes from a method of slaughtering hogs where the animal was strung up on a heavy wooden framework and its throat cut. *Bucket* is thought to be an English corruption of *buquet*, a

French word for the wooden framework that the hog kicked in its death struggles. *Buquet* is not a word found in modern French dictionaries, but *boucher* (meaning "butcher") is common and is cognate with the source of the English word *butcher* (Urdang, 1988). Like *kick the bucket*, many idioms in American English have opaque origins, and it is not clear that people possess specific conceptual knowledge that motivates their use and interpretation of these phrases. Of course, even when we don't know exactly where a phrase originated, speakers still have some intuition as to how the internal semantics of a phrase relate to its idiomatic meaning. Some American speakers view *kick the bucket*, for example, as conveying the idea of someone's dying rather abruptly as opposed to dying in a protracted manner.

So it is not always easy to classify an idiom as a dead metaphor. Deciding whether an idiom is dead or just unconsciously conventional requires, among other things, a search for its systematic manifestation in the language as a whole and in our everyday reasoning patterns. There are plenty of basic conventional metaphors that are alive, certainly enough of them to show that what is conventional and fixed need not be dead (G. Lakoff & Turner, 1989). Part of the problem with the traditional view of idioms stems from its inability to reflect contemporary speakers' metaphorical schemes of thought. For this reason, the traditional view simply can't explain why so many idioms make sense to speakers in having the figurative meanings they do.

Fortunately, many of the long-standing assumptions about idioms that have given rise to the traditional view are now being questioned by cognitive linguists and psycholinguists interested in the conceptual foundations of everyday language use (Fillmore, Kay, & O'Connor, 1988; Geeraerts, 1989; Gibbs & Nayak, 1989; Gibbs & O'Brien, 1990; G. Lakoff, 1987; Langacker, 1986). Recent research in psycholinguistics shows that the meanings of many idioms are motivated by people's conceptual knowledge, which includes metaphorical and metonymic schemes of thought. In this way, the study of idioms reveals significant aspects of how people ordinarily think. The first step in this research program has been to demonstrate that idioms are partially analyzable, contrary to the traditional or noncompositional view. The analyzability of idioms has significant implications for explaining the syntactic and lexical properties of these phrases, in addition to how idioms might be processed.

ANALYZABILITY OF IDIOMS

Contrary to the traditional view that idioms are noncompositional, many idiomatic phrases appear to be decomposable or analyzable, with the meanings of their parts contributing independently to their overall figurative meanings (Gibbs & Nayak, 1989; Gibbs, Nayak, Bolton, & Keppel, 1989; Nunberg, 1978). For instance, in the phrase *pop the question* it is easy to discern that the noun *question* refers to a marriage proposal when the verb *pop* is used to refer to the act of uttering it. Similarly, the *law* of *lay down the law* refers to the rules of conduct in certain situations when the verb phrase *laying down* is used to refer to the act of invoking the law. Idioms like *pop the question, spill the beans,* and *lay down the law* are "decomposable," because each component obviously contributes to the overall figurative interpretation. Idioms whose individual parts do not contribute to the figurative meaning of the idiom are semantically "nondecomposable" (e.g., *kick the bucket, shoot the breeze*), because people experience difficulty in breaking these phrases into their component parts (Gibbs & Nayak, 1989; Nunberg, 1978). The analyzability of an idiom does not depend on that word string's being literally well formed (Gibbs & Nayak, 1989). For instance, *pop the question* is literally anomalous but semantically decomposable. All that matters for an idiom to be viewed as decomposable is for its parts to have meanings, either literal or figurative, that contribute independently to the phrase's overall figurative interpretation.

The analyzability of an idiom is really a matter of degree and depends on the salience of its individual parts. Many idiomatic expressions exhibit intermediate degrees of analyzability. For instance, many speakers view the phrase *fall off the wagon* as being less decomposable than *pop the question* because the meaning that *fall* contributes to *fall off the wagon* is not as salient as the meaning that *pop* contributes to *pop the question*. When speakers judge that the idiom *let off steam* is analyzable, or decomposable, they are essentially finding some relationship between the components *let off* and *steam* with their figurative referents "release" and "anger." It is not surprising that speakers find some relationship between the noun *steam* and the concept of anger, because anger is metaphorically understood in terms of heat and internal pressure (G. Lakoff, 1987; G. Lakoff & Johnson, 1980).

A series of experiments revealed that there is reasonable consistency in people's intuitions of the analyzability of idioms (Gibbs & Nayak, 1989). Participants in these studies were simply asked to rate the degree to which the individual words in idioms contribute independently to these phrases' overall figurative interpretations. The findings indicated that American speakers generally see some idiomatic phrases, such as *pop the question, miss the boat,* and *button your lip,* as highly analyzable, or decomposable, and judge other phrases, such as *kick the bucket* and *shoot the breeze,* as semantically nondecomposable. A third group of idioms was identified as being decomposable but abnormally so because their individual components have a different relationship to their idiomatic referents than do "normally" decomposable idioms. For example, we can identify the figurative referent in the idiom *carry a torch* only by virtue of our knowledge of torches as conventional metaphors for descriptions of warm feelings. Similarly, we understand the hitting of certain buttons in *hit the panic button* as a conventional metaphor for how we act in extreme circumstances. Each of these abnormally decomposable idioms differs from normally decomposable idioms, such as *button your lip,* whose components have a more direct relation to their figurative referents.

Proponents of the traditional view might argue that speakers can assign meanings to the parts of idioms *after* they have learned the figurative meaning of each expression. For instance, speakers might recognize that *pop the question* is analyzable only after they have learned that this phrase means "to propose marriage." In this way, people's understanding of the internal parts of many idioms does not motivate their understanding of what idioms mean. There may indeed be cases where speakers recognize that the particular words in an idiom actually provide independent information about the idiom's overall meaning. But people's sudden awareness of the connection between the words in idioms and these phrases' figurative meanings does not deny the possibility that speakers possess tacit knowledge of these connections. Furthermore, if people can use their understanding of what idioms mean to establish links between the words in some phrases and their overall figurative meanings, then why can't speakers assign meanings to the parts of nondecomposable idioms, such as *shoot the breeze*, once they have understood these expressions' figurative interpretations? Simply knowing the figurative meaning of an idiom is clearly not sufficient for it to be seen as analyzable. People appear to have strong intuitions that the words in idioms relate to what these phrases figuratively mean.

SYNTACTIC BEHAVIOR OF IDIOMS

The data showing that people can differentiate between idioms based on their semantic analyzability have important implications for motivating the syntactic behavior of idioms. Some idioms, such as *John laid down the law* (meaning "John enforced the rules"), are "syntactically productive" or "syntactically flexible," since they can be seen in a variety of syntactic formats without losing their figurative interpretations (Gibbs & Gonzales, 1985; Gibbs & Nayak, 1989; Nunberg, 1978; Reagan, 1987; Wasow, Sag, & Nunberg, 1982). Thus, *John laid down the law* can be turned into a passive construction like *The law was laid down by John* without any change in its nonliteral meaning. Other idioms, such as *John kicked the bucket* (meaning "John died") are "syntactically frozen," because they cannot be syntactically altered without disrupting their figurative interpretations (e.g., *The bucket was kicked by John*).

It is still unclear what determines the syntactic productivity of idioms. Most linguistic discussion of the syntactic deficiencies of idioms provides little motivation as to why some idioms are productive and others are not. The hypothesis examined in several studies was that people's intuitions about the syntactic versatility of idioms are affected by the analyzability or decomposability of these figurative phrases (Gibbs & Nayak, 1989).

In these studies, participants were presented with idiomatic phrases in different syntactic constructions (e.g., passive, present participle, adjective insertion, gerund nominalization) along with paraphrases of their figurative meanings (e.g., a passive construction such as *The bucket was kicked by John* – "John died"). The participants' task was to judge the similarity of meaning between the two sentences, with the higher ratings of similarity indicating that people view a particular idiom as being acceptable with a particular syntactic alteration, and low ratings suggesting that an idiom is syntactically frozen. The participants' ratings were averaged across the syntactic constructions to yield a mean syntactic frozenness rating for each idiom. Idioms previously judged as semantically analyzable were expected to be viewed as more syntactically productive than semantically nondecomposable idioms.

The results of these studies supported this prediction. Normally decomposable idioms (e.g., *pop the question*) were found to be much more syntactically productive than semantically nondecomposable (e.g., *chew the fat*) idioms. Abnormally decomposable idioms were not found to be syntactically productive, because each part does not *by itself* refer to some component of the idiomatic referent but only to some metaphorical relation between the individual part and the referent. Thus, readers rarely accept that a passivized construction such as *A torch for Sally was carried by Jim* has a recognizable idiomatic meaning.

These findings suggest that the syntactic versatility of idioms is not an arbitrary phenomenon perhaps due to unknown historical reasons (Cutler, 1982) but can at least partially be explained in terms of an idiom's semantic analyzability. It is interesting to note that the syntactic versatility of other linguistic constructions, including verb particle constructions

(Bolinger, 1971; Lindner, 1983) and binomial expressions (Lambrecht, 1984) can also be explained by appeal to the internal semantics of these phrases. For example, if the particle in verb particle constructions, such as *make up* and *put out*, has little meaning on its own, then it is difficult to move that particle to a position of semantic focus (Bolinger, 1971). Thus, whereas it is permissible to say *Fifty states make up the United States*, it is not reasonable to say **Fifty states make the United States up*, because the postposed particle *up* carries little meaning by itself and cannot be used in the sentence's final position.

LEXICAL FLEXIBILITY OF IDIOMS

The semantic analyzability of idioms also influences people's intuitions about their lexical flexibility. Some idioms appear to be lexically flexible in that their individual lexical items can be changed without serious disruption of these phrases' figurative meanings. For instance, some idioms, such as *button your lip*, can be changed (to, e.g., *fasten your lips*) without loss of meaning, but other idioms, such as *kick the bucket*, cannot (e.g., *punt the bucket*).

A series of studies examined the role of semantic analyzability in the lexical flexibility of idioms (Gibbs, Nayak, Bolton, & Keppel, 1989). Participants were presented with a series of phrases that were left unchanged (e.g., *pop the question*), had their verbs replaced with relatively synonymous words (e.g., *burst the question*), had their nouns replaced with synonymous words (e.g., *pop the request*), or had both their verbs and nouns changed (e.g., *burst the request*). Accompanying each phrase was a figurative definition of the unchanged idiom (e.g., "propose marriage"). The participants' task was simply to read each phrase and judge its similarity to the paraphrase.

Changing the verbs and nouns of both semantically decomposable and nondecomposable idioms was disruptive to their figurative meanings. However, changing the lexical items in semantically nondecomposable idioms was far more disruptive to these phrases' figurative interpretations than was the case for decomposable idioms. For instance, both noun and verb changes were rated as significantly less acceptable for nondecomposable idioms (e.g., *punt the pail* for *kick the bucket*) than for decomposable phrases (e.g., *burst the request* for *pop the question*). These findings suggest that the semantic analyzability of idioms provides important constraints for the lexical flexibility of idioms. Speakers will tend to be significantly more creative in their use of semantically analyzable idioms in terms of both their syntactic productivity and their lexical flexibility.

SEMANTIC PRODUCTIVITY OF IDIOMS

The lexical flexibility of idioms shows that words in analyzable idioms can be changed without significantly altering the meanings of these phrases. More dramatically, the individual words in many idioms can be changed to create new idiomatic meanings that are based on both the original idiom's meaning and the new words. For example, the idiom *break the ice* can be altered to form *shatter the ice*, which now has the meaning of something like "to break down an uncomfortable and stiff social situation flamboyantly in one fell swoop!" (McGlone, Glucksberg, & Cacciari, in press). *Shatter the ice* is an example not of lexical flexibility but of semantic productivity (ibid.). Examples of semantically productive idiom variants appear frequently in conversation, the media, and literature. To take one notable example, the author Donald Barthelme titled an essay on contemporary literature "Convicted Minimalist Spills Bean," a title that nicely fits Barthelme's reputation as a minimalist writer (Glucksberg, 1991). People can understand semantically productive idiom variants (e.g., *Sam didn't spill a single bean*) quite readily, and the more familiar the original idiom, the more comprehensible the variant (McGlone et al., in press). Variant idioms can also be understood as quickly as their literal paraphrases (e.g., *Sam didn't spill a single bean* vs. *Sam didn't say a single word*) (ibid.).

Our ability easily to understand semantically productive

idiom variants is partly due to the analyzability of idiom phrases. In general, when the parts of an idiom have some functional relationship to the idiom's overall meaning, then various lexical operations, such as quantification or negation, will be productive, provided that a plausible communicative intent can be inferred (Cacciari & Glucksberg, 1991). For example, the change from plural to singular in Barthelme's essay title "Convicted Minimalist Spills Bean" is acceptable because of our understanding of the relations between the singular form of the noun *bean* and the concept of minimalism (McGlone et al., in press). In contrast, the phrase *popped the questions* would be difficult to interpret, because a marriage proposal is usually made to only one person at a time. Thus, our general world knowledge combines with our understanding of analyzability of idioms to determine what we think of as acceptable idiom variants. These observations and empirical findings on semantically productive idioms provide further evidence of the importance of analyzability in the creation and comprehension of idioms.

ANALYZABILITY AND IDIOM COMPREHENSION

The analyzability of idioms also plays an important role in their immediate, on-line interpretation. Because the individual components in decomposable idioms contribute systematically to the figurative meanings of these phrases, people may process idioms in a compositional manner where the semantic representation of each component is accessed and combined according to the syntactical rules of the language. For example, the phrases *lay down* and *the law* serve as cues for the retrieval of the figurative meaning of *lay down the law*, since each of the components has independent meaning contributing to the whole idiom's nonliteral interpretation. On the other hand, a strict compositional analysis of semantically nondecomposable idioms (e.g., *kick the bucket, chew the fat, go for broke*) provides little information about the figurative meanings of these expressions. Consequently, readers or listeners might experience greater difficulty understanding the meanings of nondecomposable idioms than they do analyzable phrases.

A series of reading-time studies showed that people took significantly less time to process the decomposable idioms than to read the nondecomposable expressions (Gibbs, Nayak, & Cutting, 1989). Both normally and abnormally decomposable phrases took less time to process than their respective literal control phrases, but nondecomposable idioms actually took longer to process than their respective literal controls. These data suggest that people attempt to do some compositional analysis when understanding idiomatic phrases. When an idiom is decomposable, readers can assign independent meanings to its individual parts and will quickly recognize how these meaningful parts combine to form the overall figurative interpretation of the phrase.

For example, when people hear or read *lay down the law*, they recognize that each component is independently meaningful such that *lay down* refers to the act of invoking and *laws* refers to a set of rules governing conduct. For decomposable idioms, such an analysis more directly facilitates recognition of an idiom's nonliteral interpretations. The compositional analysis of nondecomposable idioms, however, is by itself inadequate to specify their figurative meanings, and so people must recover their directly stipulated meanings from the mental lexicon. Thus, doing a compositional analysis on nondecomposable idioms, such as *cook his goose* or *kick the bucket*, provides inadequate information as to each word's contribution to the overall figurative meanings of these expressions. This processing difference in the comprehension of decomposable and nondecomposable idioms does not imply that readers have no directly stipulated figurative meanings for decomposable idioms. Instead, it appears that the analyzability of decomposable idioms provides a very useful source of information that facilitates people's recognition that an idiomatic word string is meant to have a figurative interpretation.

What role do the words in idioms play in these phrases' interpretations? People probably do *not* combine the context-free literal meanings of words during idiom understanding, because many idioms are literally ill formed or opaque, for example, *by and large, in the know, crack a joke* and *promise the moon*. Literally ill-formed idioms violate selectional restriction rules. For instance, the idiom *swallow his pride* is literally ill formed, or anomalous, because it violates the selection restriction that the verb *swallow* occurs only in sentences with noun phrases referring to some physical object. Most linguistic analyses assume that expressions that do not possess well-defined literal meanings must receive their interpretations by stipulation in the lexicon (Dowty, Wall, & Peters, 1981).

Interestingly, many ill-formed idioms are normally decomposable (e.g., *pop the question, perish the thought*), whereas many semantically nondecomposable idioms are literally well formed (e.g., *chew the fat, hit the sauce, give the sack*). If people perform a compositional analysis on an idiom based on its literal meaning, then people should process literally well-formed idioms faster than they do ill-formed expressions. However, this is not the case (Gibbs, Nayak, & Cutting, 1989). Participants in these studies actually took *less* time to understand ill-formed idioms than they did literally well-formed expressions. It appears that understanding idioms requires only that people assign figurative meanings to their parts; there is no need to automatically analyze each expression according to its entire literal interpretation.

The question remains, though, as to the actual contribution of an idiom's putative literal meaning to its overall figurative interpretation. As described in Chapter 3, there is a vast amount of data showing that people can understand idiomatic meaning more rapidly than the same meaning expressed literally. In fact, idioms are generally understood much more quickly when used figuratively than when used to express nonidiomatic meaning. The direct-access or figurative-first models of idiom processing postulate that the figurative meanings of idioms are immediately accessed or understood when these expressions are read in appropriate discourse contexts (Gibbs, 1980, 1985a, 1986d). However, the direct-access model does not specify exactly what people do on line when processing idioms. The various studies on the analyzability of idioms clearly suggest that idioms are processed in a compositional manner, in which the meanings of the individual parts are, at least initially, examined to see what contributions these parts make to the figurative meaning of the idiom as a whole. As has been carefully noted above, the individual meanings of an idiom's parts are not necessarily their putative literal ones (in whatever way we define "literal"). So at what point during idiom processing does the figurative meaning of an idiom begin to emerge?

My contention in Chapter 2 that questions the very existence of a stable concept of literal meanings for either words or sentences makes the question above difficult, if not impossible, to answer. In this regard, a theory of idiom processing must await a better idea of what is meant when it is claimed that idioms, or any linguistic construction, can be processed or analyzed literally. However, despite the lack of a theory of literalness, some studies have explicitly looked at the role of literal meaning in on-line idiom processing.

One study presented participants with tape-recorded sentences, such as *After the excellent performance, the tennis player was . . .* that could end with either a literal expression, such as *in seventh position,* or an idiomatic phrase, such as *in seventh heaven* (Cacciari & Tabossi, 1988). The idiomatic phrases were either highly familiar and predictable (e.g., people could predict that the word following *in seventh* was *heaven*) or less predictable. After hearing the last word in each sentence, the participants made a lexical decision about a visually presented target (i.e., they decided whether the letter string presented was or was not a word). These target words could be related to the last word in the sentence just heard in three possible ways: related to the literal meaning of the last word (e.g., *saint*), related to the idiomatic sense of the entire sentence (e.g., *happy*), or unrelated (e.g., *table*).

An analysis of the timed lexical decisions indicated that when participants heard predictable idioms they responded faster to the idiomatic targets than to the literal targets. But when idioms were less predictable, responses to the idiom targets were facilitated only after a 300 msec delay, suggesting that the idiomatic meanings took some time to be activated. Responses to literal targets were facilitated both immediately after hearing the last word of the sentence and also 300 msec later. These data imply that the literal meanings of words remain active during idiom processing even if they are not relevant to the figurative interpretation of the idiom phrase as a whole.

One model, called the configuration model (ibid.), that might explain these results states that idiom processing depends on people's recognizing a key part of the idiom and accessing the figurative meaning of the expression at that point in comprehension. If the key part of the idiom occurs early in the phrase or sentence, the figurative meaning may be processed before the literal meaning is fully composed. If the key part occurs late in the phrase, the literal meaning of the expression may be processed before the figurative meaning.

The idea that certain words in an idiomatic expression are more important or key in determining the figurative meanings of these expressions seems very plausible. What constitutes the key word in an idiom is an empirical issue. In any event, the configuration model still generally assumes that language is processed in a literal manner *until* some special or key word triggers some kind of figurative processing. The major difficulty with this hypothesis is that it is not yet clear that there are completely distinct modes of literal and idiomatic processing. Evidence obtained in support of the configuration model actually compares timed responses to targets reflecting the meanings of individual words (i.e., literal targets) with responses to targets reflecting the figurative meaning of an entire idiomatic phrase (the idiom targets). But these targets reflect different types of meaning (i.e., word versus phrase), and so it remains unclear whether or not there are really distinct modes of literal and idiomatic processing that are not confabulated with word and sentence processing mechanisms. Again, without a better idea of what actually constitutes literal meaning at either the word or sentence level, it is unlikely that we will be in a position soon to establish firmly exactly when idioms are understood as having figurative meanings. At the very least, all of the evidence points to the idea that people are not simply comprehending idioms without some kind of analysis of these phrases' individual parts.

LEARNING IDIOMATIC PHRASES

Developmental research demonstrates that children's comprehension of idioms depends on their intuitions about the internal semantics of these figurative phrases (Gibbs, 1987c, 1991; Nippold & Rudzinski, in press). Children's learning of idioms is generally thought to depend on their associating a given sequence of words with arbitrary figurative meanings (e.g., *kick the bucket* means "to die"). Adults may explicitly teach children the nonliteral meanings of idioms, or children may eventually recognize the incongruity between contextual information and the literal analysis of idiomatic phrases. Traditional accounts do not suggest that children learn the figurative meanings of idioms through some sort of compositional analysis.

However, the evidence shows that children attempt to do some compositional analysis when understanding idiomatic expressions (Gibbs, 1991). Younger children (kindergartners and first graders) understood decomposable idioms much better than they did nondecomposable phrases. Older children (third and fourth graders) understood both kinds of idioms equally well in supporting contexts, but were better at interpreting decomposable idioms than they were at understanding nondecomposable idioms without contextual information. Children did not understand idioms with well-formed literal meanings any better than they did ill-formed idioms. Consequently, it is unlikely that young children find analyzable, or decomposable, idioms easier to comprehend simply because these phrases possess well-formed literal meanings. Instead, the younger children found it easier to assign figurative meanings to the parts of decomposable idioms and did not simply analyze each expression according to its literal interpretation.

When an idiom is analyzable, children can assign independent meanings to its individual parts and will learn relatively quickly how these meaningful parts combine to form the overall nonliteral interpretation of the phrase. For example, when children encounter *lay down the law*, they recognize that each component is independently meaningful such that *lay down* refers to the act of invoking and *law* refers to a set of rules governing conduct. Learning the meanings of semantically nondecomposable idioms is more difficult, precisely because the overall figurative interpretations of idioms cannot be determined through analyses of their individual parts.

THE METAPHORICAL MOTIVATION FOR IDIOMATIC MEANING

The analyzability of idioms explains much of what is known about speakers' intuitions about the syntactic and lexical behavior of idioms as well as about idiom learning and comprehension. Beyond these important empirical demonstrations, the idea of analyzability opens up the possibility that the internal semantics of idioms might be correlated in systematic ways with the concepts to which idioms refer. The figurative meanings of idioms may very well be motivated by people's conceptual knowledge, which itself is constituted by metaphor. Although the analyzability of idioms suggests that there are many similarities in the on-line cognitive processing of idiomatic and literal language, there are also significant differences between literal and idiomatic expressions. People's subjective familiarity with idioms certainly facilitates their understanding of these expressions over literal phrases. Moreover, different kinds of meanings are recovered when interpreting idioms like *John spilled the beans* than when comprehending literal statements like *John revealed the secret*. After all, speakers use conventional idiomatic expressions, such as *let off steam, play with fire,* or *steal one's thunder,* because they evoke different meanings than literal phrases do.

Some of the different meanings recovered when understanding literal and idiomatic expressions may be due to the metaphorical nature of idioms. Even though it is often assumed that idioms are dead metaphors, it may very well be that people make sense of many idioms because they tacitly recognize the metaphorical mapping of information from two domains that gives rise to idioms in the first place. People's assumptions about how the individual components of idioms refer to the metaphorical concepts underlying their figurative referents result in different information being activated than when literal language is used. This should be particularly true for idioms that are more analyzable, or decomposable, because it is easier for people to map their individual components onto different kinds of metaphorical concepts for these particular expressions. For example, the idiom *John spilled the beans* maps our knowledge of someone's tipping over a container of beans onto a person's revealing some secret. English speakers understand *spill the beans* to mean "reveal the secret" because there are underlying conceptual metaphors, such as THE MIND IS A CONTAINER and IDEAS ARE PHYSICAL ENTITIES, that structure their conceptions of minds, secrets, and disclosure (G. Lakoff & Johnson, 1980).

Although the existence of these conceptual metaphors does not predict that certain idioms or conventional expressions must appear in the language, the presence of these independent conceptual metaphors by which we make sense of experience provides a partial motivation for why specific phrases (*spill the beans*) are used to refer to particular events (the revealing of secrets).

Linguistic analyses of idioms provide some evidence for believing that idioms do not exist as separate semantic units within the lexicon but actually reflect coherent systems of metaphorical concepts. For example, the idiomatic phrases *blow your stack, flip your lid, hit the ceiling, get hot under the collar, lose your cool,* and *get steamed up* appear to be motivated by the conceptual metaphor ANGER IS HEATED FLUID IN A CONTAINER, which is one of the small set of conceptual mappings between different source and target domains that form part of our conceptualization of anger. But is there any evidence that metaphors like ANGER IS HEATED FLUID IN A CONTAINER are really conceptual and not, more simply, generalizations of linguistic meaning? Various studies have explored the possibility that idioms make sense in the ways they do precisely because they are motivated by conceptual knowledge that is metaphorical. Thus, idioms like *blow your stack* and *flip your lid* make sense to us as referring to the idea of getting very angry in a way that phrases like *run to the store* or *mow the lawn* would not.

The dead-metaphor view suggests no reason why some idioms seem so rightly to have the meanings they do. After all, if the meaning of a phrase is truly dead, then people should not believe that any particular way of talking about something such as anger, like *hit the ceiling* or *blow your stack*, seems reasonable in a way that phrases like *mow your lawn* and *run to the store* do not.

A good deal of empirical work in psycholinguistics has investigated the metaphoric motivation for idiomatic meaning. One way to uncover speakers' tacit knowledge of the metaphorical basis for idioms is through a detailed examination of speakers' mental images of idioms (Gibbs & O'Brien, 1990; G. Lakoff, 1987). Consider the idiom *spill the beans*. Try to form a mental image of this phrase, describe the image to yourself, and then ask yourself the following questions. Where are the beans before they are spilled? How big is the container? Are the beans cooked or uncooked? Is the spilling accidental or intentional? Where are the beans once they've been spilled? Are the beans in a nice neat pile? Where are the beans supposed to be? After the beans are spilled, are they easy to retrieve?

Most people have definite responses to these questions about their mental images of idioms. They generally say that the beans were in some pot that is about the size of a person's head, the beans are uncooked, the spilling of the beans is accidental, and the spilled beans are all over a floor and are difficult to retrieve. This consistency in people's intuitions about their mental images is quite puzzling if one assumes that the meanings of idioms are arbitrarily determined. People's descriptions of their mental images of idioms reveal some of the metaphorical knowledge that motivates the meanings of idiomatic phrases.

One study examined people's mental images of groups of idioms with similar figurative meanings about revelation (e.g., *spill the beans, let the cat out of the bag, blow the lid off*), anger (*blow your stack, hit the ceiling, flip your lid*), insanity (*go off your rocker, lose your marbles, bounce off the walls*), secretiveness (*keep it under your hat, button your lip, keep in the dark*), and exerting control (*crack the whip, lay down the law, call the shots*) (Gibbs & O'Brien, 1990). Participants were asked to describe their mental images of these idioms and to answer questions about the causes, intentionality, and manner of action in their mental images.

Participants' descriptions of their mental images for randomly presented idioms with similar meanings should be consistent because of the constraints conceptual metaphors (e.g., THE MIND IS A CONTAINER, IDEAS ARE PHYSICAL ENTITIES, and ANGER IS HEAT) impose on the links between idiomatic phrases and their nonliteral meanings. If people's tacit knowledge of idioms is not structured by different conceptual metaphors, there should be little consistency in participants' responses to questions about the causes and consequences of actions in their mental images of idioms with similar nonliteral interpretations.

People had little difficulty with the mental imagery task. Most of the reports participants gave for their mental images of idioms contained rich details. For instance, one individual reported that her mental image for *call the shots* was as follows: *An army sergeant standing in front of a line of soldiers, all of whom are faced in the same direction and when the sergeant shouts very loudly the soldiers all commence firing their rifles.* Overall, participants' descriptions of their mental images were remarkably consistent for different idioms with similar figurative meanings. The general schemas underlying people's images were not simply representative of the idioms' figurative meanings but captured more specific aspects of the kinesthetic events with the images. For example, the anger idioms, such as *flip your lid* and *hit the ceiling*, all refer to the concept getting angry, but participants specifically imagined for these phrases some force causing a container to release pressure in a violent manner. There is nothing in the surface forms of these different idioms to tightly constrain the images participants have. After all, lids can be flipped and ceilings can be hit in a wide variety of ways caused by many different circumstances. But the participants' protocols in this study revealed little variation in the general events that took place in their images of idioms with similar meanings.

Participants' responses to the questions about the causes and consequences of the actions described in their images were also highly consistent. Consider the most frequent responses to the probe questions for the anger idioms (*blow your stack, flip your lid, hit the ceiling*). When imagining anger idioms, people reported that pressure (i.e., stress or frustration) caused the action, that one had little control over the pressure once it was building, that its violent release was done unintentionally (e.g., the blowing of the stack), and that once the release had taken place (once the ceiling had been hit, the lid flipped, the stack blown) it was difficult to reverse the action.

Why are people so consistent in their intuitions about the causes, manner, and consequences of the actions described in their mental images of idioms? We argued that people are limited in the kinds of images they create for idioms because of very specific conceptual knowledge that is mostly metaphorical. For example, people's images of the anger idioms are based on folk conceptions of certain physical events. For anger, people use their knowledge about the behavior of heated fluid or vapor building up and escaping from containers (ones that our participants most frequently reported to be the size of a person's head). Thus, people's metaphorical mapping of knowledge from a source domain (e.g., heated fluid in a container) onto a target domain (e.g., the anger emotion) helps them conceptualize in concrete terms what is understood about the target domain of anger. Various specific entailments result from these general metaphorical mappings, ones that provide specific insight into the causes, intentionality, manner, and consequences of the activities described by stacks blowing, lids flipping, and ceilings being hit. The metaphorical ways in which we partially conceptualize experiences like anger actually provide part of the motivation for why people have consistent mental images, and specific knowledge about these images, for idioms with similar figurative meanings.

Of course, any consistency in people's mental images for idioms with similar figurative meanings may be due not to the constraining influence of conceptual metaphors but, more simply, to the very fact that these phrases have nearly identical meanings. Thus, people are constrained in their mental images of *blow your stack, flip your lid, hit the ceiling,* and so on because they all mean "to get very angry," not because they are motivated by similar conceptual metaphors. However, the figurative meaning "to get angry" by itself does not convey much information about the causes and consequences of the actions described in people's mental images, so we did not feel that this alternative hypothesis carried much weight. A set of follow-up studies showed that knowing the figurative meaning of an idiom (e.g., "getting angry") does not by itself account for why people have such systematic knowledge of their images of idioms (e.g., *blow your stack* or *flip your lid*). Asking people to imagine "to get very angry" produced, not surprisingly, a wide variety of mental images. Most important, though, our participants showed very little consistency in their responses to the questions regarding causation, intentionality, manner, and consequences about the actions in their mental images of paraphrases of the idioms. Furthermore, people were much less consistent in their mental images of literal phrases (e.g., *blow your tire*) than of idioms (e.g., *blow your stack*), because they do not possess the same degree of conceptual knowledge about their images of literal phrases as they do of idiomatic expressions.

These mental imagery studies support the idea that the figurative meanings of idioms are motivated by various conceptual metaphors that exist independently as part of our conceptual system. The empirical evidence in support of this conclusion does not in any way suggest that people actually form mental images of idioms as a normal part of their on-line understanding of idioms. The data simply, and significantly, demonstrate how people's common metaphorical knowledge provides part of the motivation for why idioms have the figurative meanings they do. Traditional theories of idiomaticity have no way of accounting for these imagery findings, because they assume that the meanings of idioms arise from metaphors that are now dead and no longer a prominent part of our everyday conceptual system.

CONCEPTS AND THE CONTEXT-SENSITIVE INTERPRETATION OF IDIOMS

The evidence demonstrating the metaphorical motivation for idiomatic meaning has a direct application to how people use and interpret idioms in different social contexts. Consider the following scenario (Nayak & Gibbs, 1990):

When his sister came back with a huge dent in his new Alfa Romeo, it really got on Jeff's nerves. He promptly blew his top. Eventually he cooled down and forgave her.

The idioms *got on his nerves, blew his top,* and *cooled down* refer to the concept of anger and, according to traditional theories of idioms, may be semantically equivalent. But a closer understanding of these idioms suggests that each phrase corresponds to a particular part of the concept anger. The idiom *got on his nerves* refers to the earliest stage, where a person's anger is provoked by some event. This provocation is followed by the next stage, where angry behavior is displayed, which can be expressed linguistically in the phrase *blew his top*. The final stage, returning to equanimity, is exemplified in the idiom *cooled down*. Most people have no difficulty making sense of the story above because it describes a coherent temporal sequence of events that is typical of anger. Readers' sensitivity to the appropriateness of idioms in different discourse contexts might be based on their knowledge of the temporal structure of a concept. Thus, you don't get *red in the face* unless something has *got under your skin,* and if you have *flipped your lid* you have also *blown your top*.

One series of studies examined whether the temporal structure of concepts played a role in readers' interpretations of idioms (ibid.; Gibbs & Nayak, 1991). Much evidence in cognitive psychology and linguistics indicates that our conceptual knowledge is organized around "best examples," or prototypes (cf. Geeraerts, 1989; G. Lakoff, 1987; Rosch, 1975, 1978). These prototype-based conceptual structures, or schemas, often encompass temporal information such that events are organized in a sequence (cf. Abbott, Black, & Smith, 1985; Bower, Black, & Turner, 1979; Schank & Abelson, 1977). People have temporally organized information for mundane concepts, such as "going to a restaurant," as well as for such abstract concepts as those having to do with emotions (Fehr & Russell, 1984; Reiser, Black, & Lehnert, 1985; Shaver, Schwartz, Kirson, & O'Connor, 1987).

For instance, an emotion concept like anger is prototypically understood to be composed of a sequence of events beginning with a set of "antecedent conditions," a set of "behavioral responses," and a set of "self-control procedures" (Shaver et al., 1987). The temporal organization of a conceptual structure like anger is reflected in the language used to refer to that concept (G. Lakoff, 1987). Thus, English has different idioms fitting each of the three stages of our concept of anger. The antecedent conditions (Stage 1) for anger concern a sudden loss of power, status, or respect – ideas exemplified by such idioms as *eat humble pie, kick in the teeth*, and *swallow one's pride*. The behavioral conditions (Stage 2) for anger concern people's behavioral responses to the emotion, an idea best reflected in such idioms as *getting red in the face, getting hot under the collar*, and *blowing your stack*. The self-control procedures (Stage 3) concern an individual's efforts to maintain composure, an idea that is best reflected in such idiomatic phrases as *keep your cool* and *hold your temper*.

Idioms that refer to the same temporal stage of a conceptual prototype appear to be highly similar in meaning. For example, *do a slow burn* and *blow your stack* both mean "to get angry." It is likely that similarities in the figurative meanings of idioms arise from their referring to the same temporal stage of a conceptual prototype (e.g., Stage 2). This possibility implies, contrary to the view of traditional theories, that idioms are linked in the mental lexicon on the basis of the temporal stage of the concept to which each idiom refers. Thus, idioms referring to the same temporal stage (e.g., *blow your stack* and *do a slow burn)* may be more closely linked (with all the phrases sharing the same semantic space or field) than are idioms that express different temporal aspects (e.g., *do a slow burn* and *hold your temper*).

People's sensitivity to similarity in the meanings of idioms may be based in part on whether these phrases express the same temporal aspect of the prototype to which they refer (e.g., *blow your top* and *flip your lid*).

Most pragmatic theories of idiom would suggest that there should be no evidence that some pairs of idioms are more closely related in meaning than others, because all pairs have essentially the same figurative interpretation (e.g., "to be in a frightening or fearful situation"). One study showed, however, that people's judgments of similarity in the figurative meanings of two idioms were influenced by the temporal properties of conceptual prototypes (Nayak & Gibbs, 1990). Idioms referring to the same stage of a conceptual prototype (e.g., *play with fire* and *go out on a limb*) were judged to be more similar in meaning than idioms (e.g., *play with fire* and *shake in your shoes*) referring to different temporal stages.

A second study explored whether the temporal sequencing of idioms in a sentence was related to the sentence's overall meaning. Consider the sentence *John's bad manners got on Sally's nerves, but she didn't flip her lid*, where the two idioms in the sentence are separated by the conjunction *but* plus a negative marker (ibid.). The meaningfulness of such sentences should depend on the temporal ordering of the different idioms. If two idioms in a sentence reflect different stages in the prototype for an emotion concept, such as anger, then combining the two idioms should be acceptable only when the temporal sequence is in keeping with the prototypical scenario, as in *It got on his nerves, but he didn't blow his top*. The idiom *got on his nerves* belongs to Stage 1 (Provocation) of the Anger prototype, whereas the idiom *blow his top* belongs to Stage 2 (Angry Behavior). Any sentence in which the two idioms are in correct temporal order as defined by the conceptual prototype should be judged as relatively meaningful; unacceptable or less meaningful sentences are those that violate the prototypical sequence. For instance, the sentence *He blew his top, but he didn't flip his lid* is an unacceptable contradiction, because the two idioms both refer to Stage 2 (Angry Behavior) of the prototype. Another unacceptable *[Idiom 1] but not [Idiom 2]* sentence arises when two stages of a prototype are reversed, as in *He flipped his lid, but it didn't get on his nerves*. One would expect that the person passes through the stage of something *getting on his nerves* (Stage 1: Provocation) before he *flips his lid* (Stage 2: Angry Behavior), because angry behavior is prototypically preceded by some provocation.

Participants were asked to judge the acceptability of such sentences. Overall, people rated sentences that violated the temporal sequence inherent in the emotion concept as being significantly less meaningful than were sentences containing idioms referring to a correct temporal sequence of the underlying concept. These data demonstrate that idioms are not only categorizable on the basis of the temporal stage of a prototype, but these categories are also systematically related to one another in a strict temporal sequence. Idioms with similar meanings may be clustered around the conceptual prototype to which they refer, with individual idioms being temporally linked, much like our temporal knowledge of the events of such mundane concepts as going to a restaurant (cf. Abbott et al., 1985; Bower et al., 1979; Schank & Abelson, 1977). Such a representation scheme is more parsimonious than the traditional view of idioms, which requires a separately stipulated meaning for each idiom (e.g., *let off steam* = to get angry, *flip your lid* = to get angry, and so on).

The third experiment in this study specifically examined whether or not readers use their understanding of the temporal sequences inherent in emotion concepts when interpreting the appropriateness of idioms in varying discourse situations (Nayak & Gibbs, 1990). Our hypothesis here was that people can reliably distinguish between semantically related idioms because of their conceptual knowledge of the domains to which idioms refer. We explored this idea by looking at people's interpretations of idioms referring to emotion concepts, such as anger, fear, success, and joy. Consider the following example:

When Billy told his father that he had totaled his new Porsche, his father flipped his lid.

When Billy told his father that he had totaled his new Porsche, his father got hot under the collar.

The idiom *flipped his lid* appears to be more appropriate in this context than does the idiom *got hot under the collar*, even though both phrases figuratively mean "to be angry." Such judgments should be made on the basis of how the linguistic context encodes information about a particular stage of the conceptual prototype. Contexts designed to reflect a particular aspect of a temporal stage are distinguishable from contexts that reflect a different part of a prototype. For example, consider the following context.

> When Billy told his father that he had to stay late for detention, his father got hot under the collar.

The idiom *got hot under the collar* fits this situation better than it does the one where Billy totaled his father's new car, even though both contexts describe situations arousing angry behavior. These intuitions may be ascribed to people's knowledge that Billy's staying late for detention evokes less anger than does his totaling his father's new Porsche. *Got hot under the collar* is more appropriate to use in the detention context because of people's expectations that the story character should experience a particular degree of anger given the event described. The idioms that follow the earlier Porsche context are both somewhat compatible with these expectations, but *got hot under the collar* is less compatible with this expectation, as readers expect a greater degree of anger than that reflected in the meaning of this idiom. In general, the conceptual compatibility between an idiom and its context should be the basis on which people judge the contextual appropriateness of idiomatic phrases.

Participants in this study read each story and judged the appropriateness of each final phrase, given the context. Idioms with similar meanings (corresponding to the same stage of a conceptual prototype) were judged as being differentially appropriate, depending upon the specific conceptual content of the discourse in which the idioms were read. Thus, participants rated idioms embedded in conceptually congruent contexts higher than idioms read in conceptually incongruent stories. A second experiment demonstrated that idioms embedded in conceptually congruent contexts were easier to process than were idioms embedded in conceptually less congruent contexts.

People differentiate between idioms with similar meanings on the basis of the specific conceptual information depicted in the contexts in which the idioms occur. There are some idioms, however, that are similar in terms of the broad temporal stages of a concept to which they refer yet differ in terms of the conceptual metaphors that motivate their meanings. For instance, the idioms *blow your stack* and *jump down your throat* both express extreme degrees of anger, and both phrases belong to Stage 2 of the Angry Behavior prototype. Yet each idiom reflects a separate conceptual metaphor. Thus, the figurative meaning of *jumped down his throat* "makes sense" because readers can link the lexical items in this phrase to the conceptual metaphor angry behavior is animal behavior. An animal's jumping down a victim's throat is similar to someone's shouting angrily. But people understand *blew his top* through the conceptual metaphor ANGER IS HEATED FLUID IN A CONTAINER, where a person's shouting angrily has the same explosive effect as does the top of a container's blowing open under pressure.

Do readers use the metaphoric information in the lexical makeup of idioms when determining their applicability to different discourse contexts? Consider the following example of a particular emotion concept that is constructed to prime one of the metaphorical mappings inherent in its prototypical structure (Nayak & Gibbs, 1990):

> Mary was very tense about this evening's dinner party. The fact that Bob had not come home to help was making her fume. She was getting hotter with every passing minute. Dinner would not be ready before the guests arrived. As it got closer to five o'clock the pressure was really building up. Mary's tolerance was reaching its limits. When Bob strolled in at ten minutes to five whistling and smiling, Mary
>
> > blew her top
> > bit his head off

This story depicts Mary's increasing anger in terms of increasing pressure and heat (i.e., ANGER IS HEATED FLUID IN A CONTAINER). The use of phrases like *very tense, making her fume, getting hotter, the pressure was really building up,* and *reaching its limits* are specific references to this mapping. If people access the metaphoric mapping reflected in an idiom's lexical structure, they should interpret *blew her top* as being more appropriate than *bit his head off*, even though both phrases are grammatically and conceptually (at the same stage of the prototype) appropriate for the given scenario.

Consider now a slightly different version of the story about Mary's anger.

> Mary was getting very grouchy about this evening's dinner party. She prowled around the house waiting for Bob to come home to help. She was growling under her breath about Bob's lateness. Her mood was becoming more savage with every passing minute. As it got closer to five o'clock Mary was ferociously angry with Bob. When Bob strolled in at 4:30 whistling and smiling, Mary
>
> > bit his head off
> > blew her top

In this case, *bit his head off* appears to be more appropriate than in the earlier context because Mary's anger is understood according to the metaphor ANGRY BEHAVIOR IS ANIMAL BEHAVIOR.

The participants' task in all cases was to read each story and rate the appropriateness of each idiom for that particular context. Readers' judgments about the appropriateness of an idiom were definitely influenced by coherence between the metaphorical information depicted in a discourse context and the conceptual metaphor reflected in the lexical makeup of an idiom. Coherent idiom–context pairs were rated significantly higher than incongruent idiom–context pairs. For example, participants gave high appropriateness ratings to *flip your lid* in a story that described Mary's anger as being like heat in a pressurized container, whereas *bit his head off* was seen as more appropriate in a story that described Mary's anger in terms of a ferocious animal. Similar findings have been obtained in a study on people's ratings in context of different euphemistic phrases (e.g., *playing mattress hockey*) that are motivated by various metaphorical mappings (e.g., SEX IS A GAME) (Pfaff, Gibbs, & Johnson, 1993).

Most generally, it is clear that the pragmatic conditions of use for idioms are not arbitrary or strictly a matter of convention, but can be directly motivated by people's understanding of the conceptual structures underlying idioms and by people's conceptualizations of the events and concepts in different discourse situations. Although conceptual metaphors may not be instantiated every time readers understand idioms, they provide an additional source of information that people often use to make sense of idioms and to judge when it is appropriate to use an idiom in a particular discourse context (see also Kreuz & Graesser, 1991).

Another important consequence of the conceptual view of idiomaticity is that idioms should not be identical in meaning to their literal paraphrases. Contrary to the dead-metaphor view, which assumes that the meanings of idioms are arbitrary for speakers and can mostly be represented in short phrases or even single words (Palmer, 1981), idioms have rather complex interpretations. For example, phrases like *spill the beans* cannot simply be paraphrased as "to reveal a secret" in the way most idiom dictionaries give definitions (cf. Boatner, Gates, & Makkai, 1975; Long & Summers, 1979). The mapping of source domains, such as containers, onto target domains, such as minds, results in very specific entailments about the act of revealing a secret. Thus, the act of revealing a secret is usually seen as being caused by some internal pressure within the mind of the revealer, the action is thought to be done unintentionally, and the action is judged as being performed in a forceful manner (Gibbs & O'Brien, 1990). One interesting possibility is that people actually draw on these inferences about the act of revealing a secret each time they comprehend the idiom *spill the beans*. If this is the case, people might be less likely to draw such inferences about causation, intentionality, and manner when comprehending literal paraphrases of idioms. Literal phrases, such as *reveal the secret*, are not motivated by the same set of conceptual metaphors as are specific idioms, such as *spill the beans*. For this reason, people do not view the meanings of *spill the beans* and *reveal the secret* as equivalent, despite their apparent similarity.

This hypothesis about the nonequivalence of idioms and their literal paraphrases has been tested in a series of experiments (Gibbs, 1992c). Participants read stories that described different human events: revealing secrets, getting angry, losing control of themselves, and so on. These stories contained information about the causes of the event, the intentionality of the action performed by each story's protagonist, and the manner in which the action was performed. Some stories depicted this information in a manner that was consistent with the entailments of particular conceptual metaphors (the no-violation contexts). Presented below is an example of a no-violation story.

> John heard some interesting gossip about Paul and Mary. Even though Paul and Mary were married to other people, they had recently started having a passionate affair. John was very surprised when he found out about the affair. So John called up another friend who knew Paul and Mary and quickly blurted out what he knew. The friend commented to John that he had really
>
> > spilled the beans
> > (or)
> > revealed the secret

Note that each of the entailments of the cause, intentionality, and manner in which a secret is revealed is stated explicitly and correctly in this story. All of these entailments arise from the conceptual metaphors THE MIND IS A CONTAINER and IDEAS ARE PHYSICAL ENTITIES (Gibbs & O'Brien, 1990).

Now consider a story from one of the violation conditions, in which one of the original entailments (intentionality) has been altered.

> John heard some interesting gossip about Paul and Mary. Even though Paul and Mary were married to other people, they had recently starting having a passionate affair. John was very surprised when he found out about the affair. John fully intended never to say a word to anyone. One day he was talking to someone who knew Paul and Mary, when John accidentally said something about what he knew. The friend commented to John that he had really

spilled the beans
(or)
revealed the secret

The empirical question was whether people would understand idioms and their literal paraphrases in different ways, depending on whether a story context was consistent or inconsistent with the specific entailments of the conceptual metaphors that motivate the meanings of those idioms. In the first study, participants simply rated the appropriateness of each final phrase, given the preceding story. A second experiment measured the speed with which idioms and their paraphrases were processed in different contexts.

The results showed that the participants rated the idioms (e.g., *spill the beans*) and their literal paraphrases (*reveal the secret*) as being equally appropriate in the no-violation story contexts. However, the participants judged idioms as being less appropriate in the different violation conditions than literal paraphrases in these same contexts. Literal paraphrases are not constrained by conceptual metaphors in the way idioms are limited. Consequently, phrases such as *reveal the secret* were seen as appropriate in most story contexts regardless of the cause of the revelation, the intentionality of the act, or the manner in which it is done. This was not the case for *spill the beans*. Data from the reading-time experiment showed that idioms took longer to process when they were read at the end of a violation context than in the no-violation stories, whereas the literal paraphrases were roughly as easy to process in the violation stories as in the no-violation conditions.

These findings demonstrate that idioms are not equivalent in meaning to their simple literal paraphrases. Idiomatic phrases have very specific figurative meanings that result from the entailments of the underlying conceptual metaphors that motivate their figurative interpretations. Literal phrases, such as *reveal the secret*, are not motivated by the same conceptual metaphors and consequently are less specific in meaning. In general, these data provide further evidence against the idea that idioms are dead metaphors and equivalent in meaning to their putative literal paraphrases.

METAPHORICAL KNOWLEDGE AND IMMEDIATE
IDIOM PROCESSING

The experimental evidence on the conceptual basis for interpreting idioms is not representative of research in contemporary psycholinguistics. Psycholinguists traditionally attempt to formulate theories of linguistic understanding to account for the moment-by-moment processes used when people ordinarily process language. Only experimental methodologies that tap into what people actually, and unconsciously, do on line are thought to be appropriate in studying comprehension of normal utterances. Even though my work is quite suggestive of the possibility that people make use of various kinds of conceptual knowledge when understanding idioms, it is inappropriate to conclude from my data that people normally and automatically instantiate conceptual metaphors when understanding language. It might very well be the case that people tacitly recognize that idioms have meanings that are motivated by different kinds of conceptual knowledge. But this does not mean that people always tap into this conceptual knowledge each and every time they hear certain idioms. It might even be true that people rarely make use of this conceptual knowledge during ordinary language understanding.

I have recently begun a series of studies to examine whether people actually *access* metaphorical knowledge during the immediate, on-line processing of idioms. Although the earlier research points to the possibility that such knowledge influences people's ability to make sense of what idioms mean, it has not yet been established that people automatically access metaphorical knowledge each and every time they encounter an idiomatic expression. The conceptual view of idiomaticity does *not* suggest that all idioms are motivated by conceptual metaphor. But there are enough idioms that appear to be motivated by underlying metaphorical modes of thinking to warrant an in-depth examination of whether conceptual metaphor has an immediate constraining influence on people's on-line idiom comprehension.

Participants in the first study read simple stories one line at a time on a computer screen, with each story ending in one of three different phrases. The following is an example of one story, along with each of its different final phrases:

John lent his new car to a friend, Sally.
When Sally later returned the car, the front end was badly damaged.
When Sally showed John the car,

He blew his stack. (*appropriate idiom*)

He got very angry. (*literal paraphrase*)

He saw many dents. (*control phrase*)

After reading the final phrase and pushing the comprehension button, the participants were immediately presented with a letter string on the computer screen. Their task was to decide as quickly as possible whether or not the letter string constituted an English word (i.e., a lexicial decision task). These letter strings, or targets, were either words that represented a conceptual metaphor motivating the appropriate idiom (e.g., *heat*, which represents ANGER IS HEATED FLUID IN A CONTAINER) or a nonword letter string (e.g., *saet*).

If people actually access specific conceptual metaphors (e.g., ANGER IS HEATED FLUID IN A CONTAINER) during understanding of certain idiom phrases (*He blew his stack*), then this activated metaphorical knowledge should facilitate or prime participants' responses to the metaphor targets (e.g., *heat*) in comparison to the time it takes them to respond to these same targets after reading either the literal paraphrases or the control phrases. In fact, participants were significantly faster at responding to the metaphoric targets when they had just read the idioms than to either the literal phrases or the control expressions. Of course, people may respond faster to *heat* having read *blew his stack* simply because of some preexisting semantic association between the literal words in the expression. Yet a follow-up study showed that people were still faster in responding to *heat* when, this time, they read *hit the ceiling*, an idiom motivated by the same conceptual metaphor as *blew his stack* but one that does not have the same preexisting semantic association with the target word *heat*.

These findings provide evidence that people instantiate the underlying conceptual metaphors for idioms when they process these phrases normally. Follow-up experiments will investigate other aspects of the hypothesis that people automatically access metaphorical knowledge during their immediate, on-line processing of idioms.

The conceptual view of idioms presented here offers a reasonable alternative to the traditional dead-metaphor view of idiomaticity. It is important to realize, however, that the dead-metaphor and conceptual views of idiomaticity should not be seen as competing theories. Many idiomatic phrases could very well be dead or have meanings that are arbitrarily determined as matters of convention. At the same time, there exists a wide range of idioms that are extragrammatical, such as *by and large*, *all of a sudden*, and *take advantage of*, and resist a conceptual analysis. Many idioms are motivated by figurative schemes of thought like metonymy (e.g., *it's on the tip of my tongue*) and hyperbole (e.g., *It's raining cats and dogs*). Little empirical research has been directed toward these aspects of idioms, although there are perhaps hundreds of idioms that are created by such figurative thinking (see Goossens, 1990). Yet there are perhaps thousands of idioms that can profitably be understood as being partially motivated by figurative schemes of thought, ones that are very much alive and part of our everyday thinking and reasoning. As we learn more about the complexity of idiomatic phrases, it seems increasingly likely that no single theory or model can account for all kinds of idioms and all kinds of discourse situations (both conversational and literary). Idiomatic phrases do not form a homogeneous class of linguistic items that differ from literal language, differ from metaphor, and resist standard grammatical analysis. Each phrase demands its own analysis in terms of its syntactic, semantic, pragmatic, and conceptual properties. Theories of idiom processing must be flexible enough to explain the tremendous diversity among idioms. This idea suggests, for example, that listeners may not always instantiate specific conceptual metaphors that motivate an idiom's meaning when understanding some phrase in conversation. Similarly, people may not always analyze the literal word meanings of idioms during comprehension. There will be occasions when people do tap into an idiom's conceptual foundation. Readers may also process the individual word meanings when they attempt to comprehend certain kinds of idioms. But it is a mistake to assume that some types of analysis will occur *each and every* time someone encounters an idiomatic expression.

UNDERSTANDING PROVERBS

Proverbs are familiar sayings in common use that express well-known truths (Abrahams, 1968; Burke, 1969). Like idiomatic phrases, proverbs give significant insights into the poetics of mind because they reflect how our metaphorical conceptualization of experience bears on particular social situations. Proverbs appear as special cases of the more general process of metaphorical understanding. Most proverbs assert their veracity about social and moral matters by linking features of social situations to other, more mundane, domains with widely known and clearly identified conceptual entailments. Consider the following proverbs:

> Every cloud has a silver lining.
> The grass is always greener on the other side of the fence.
> There's no use crying over spilt milk.
> Where there's a will, there's a way.
> Necessity is the mother of invention.
> Don't make a mountain out of a molehill.
> A rolling stone gathers no moss.
> It's better to let sleeping dogs lie.

Most of these proverbs are overtly metaphorical. Common objects and events, such as clouds, green grass, and spilt milk, are used to characterize problem situations in terms of more immediate physical images. Each proverb presupposes a discrepancy between some state of the world (green grass, spilt milk) and the state of the person (one's intentions, desires, actions, and so on). For instance, *The grass is always greener on the other side of the fence* uses the notion of visual perception as a metaphor for thought. By asserting that the person has misconceived a problem or goal (has the illusion that grass is greener than it really is), this proverb suggests that a person's judgment or thinking about the problem is in some way flawed. Thus, the metaphor here structures a potentially complex and ambiguous process (such as faulty reasoning) in terms of events that are more closely delineated and accessible to public demonstration (such as determining what things look like). People's paraphrases of proverbs such as those listed above reveal a great sensitivity to the relations between an individual and the problem situation that approximated the proposition asserted in any proverb (G. White, 1987).

Most proverbs specify a fairly rich, memorable, concrete image of a source domain (e.g., stones rolling, dogs sleeping), but they do not explicitly mention target domains in the way linguistic metaphors do. So the mapping between the rolling stone or sleeping dog and human behavior or events does not depend on the explicit mention of people or events. There are many occasions, of course, when a proverb is used in a specific context that makes the target domain somewhat explicit. Consider a case where a student threatens to expose widespread cheating on a class exam and is warned by a classmate *It is better to let sleeping dogs lie*. This phrase specifically maps the source domain of not disturbing sleeping dogs and the target domain of letting the cheating scandal go unreported. Contextual information, such as knowing about the cheating scandal, helps us make sense of proverbs by providing specific target domain information.

On the other hand, people are generally quite good at understanding proverbs outside of context, as when one simply reads a list of proverbial expressions. For example, we know that the statement *A rolling stone gathers no moss* is not merely a description of the physical behavior of rolling stones. Similarly, people recognize that the phrase *There's no use crying over spilt milk* isn't just about the loss of some milk. Our understanding that these phrases have the meanings they do is not simply due to our familiarity with particular proverbs. Indeed, people generally see human concerns as the target domains to which isolated proverbs refer (ibid.). Consider the following set of Asian proverbs, which should be unfamiliar to most English-speakers (Merwin, 1973).

Enough mosquitoes sound like thunder.
Don't judge a man till his coffin's closed.
If you know a song, sing it.
Can't use your belly for your back.
Trying to put out a fire brings on the wind.
Man has twelve arts but can't cook his supper.
Even honey tastes like medicine when it's medicine.
Where money goes flattery follows.
Even from fools the wise learn.

We see these expressions as proverbial and can even make sense of them, despite their unfamiliarity. The ability to make sense of novel proverbs is one reason why proverbs are seen in practically all aspects of moral and legal argumentation (Messenger, 1959; Salamone, 1976).

How do people understand proverbs as having the meanings they do? How do we arrive at a mapping between dogs sleeping, stones rolling, and so on and the domain of human affairs? Most psycholinguistic work on proverb comprehension acknowledges that proverbs tap into conceptual knowledge about abstract ideas and events, knowledge that often reflects significant cultural knowledge. One model, called the *conceptual base hypothesis*, postulates four phases in proverb understanding (Hoffman & Honeck, 1987; Honeck, Kibler, & Firment, 1987). During the problem recognition phase, the listener recognizes the discrepancy between the proverb as literal statement and its context. During the literal transformation phase, the literal proverb information is elaborated and reorganized. These elaborative processes typically result in two or more contrasting ideas. For example, in the proverb *A peacock shouldn't look at its legs*, the contrast between the beauty of a peacock and the ugliness of its legs is recognized as potentially referring to some contrast in the communicative situation. The basis for creating an analogical relationship between the contrasting set of ideas is done in the third, the figurative, phase. This solution usually creates a conceptual base that is necessarily abstract and general because the contrasting ideas cannot be reconciled on a literal basis. That is, there may be nothing in common between peacocks and their legs and features of the discourse context. The conceptual base formed is generally nonverbal, nonimagistic, and generative (i.e., capable of generating new instances). Finally, in the instantiation phase, the conceptual base is extended to new events. For example, people who understand *A peacock shouldn't look at its legs* should recognize the similarity of meaning between this proverb and linguistic expressions such as *The dandy-looking man wasn't aware that he had some annoying habits.* The similarity between instances of the conceptual base is not due to inherent or directly given properties of the instances themselves. Rather similarity is derived, since it is dependent upon the mediating mechanism of a conceptual base. The instantiation phase is used especially when people try to paraphrase the figurative meanings of proverbs.

Various evidence appears to support aspects of the conceptual base hypothesis. Most of this evidence focuses on the abstract meanings that are created when proverbs are understood. Early research shows that a statement of the abstract ground of a novel proverb would work as a cue for recall of that proverb (Honeck, Reichmann, & Hoffman, 1975). For example, the phrase *There is great force hidden in a sweet command* is easily recalled, given a statement reflecting its abstract ground like *A little kindness often persuades better than a rough command.* Furthermore, people can agree on the degree of semantic relatedness of proverbs and their interpretation. That is, people generally view such proverbs as *Industry is fortune's right hand and stinginess her left* and *It takes many shovelfuls of earth to bury the truth* as being closely related in meaning to such statements as *You must work hard and spend money carefully to get wealthy* and *It is hard to conceal what is right,* respectively. Since these proverbs and their interpretations (the grounds) differ in words, phrase structure, and propositional structure, the semantic base created when people understand proverbs appears to be abstract, nonlinguistic, and nonimagistic (ibid.).

Other experiments demonstrate that memory for novel proverbs can be cued by brief statements of events to which the proverbs could apply. For instance, the proverb *In due time the fox is brought to the furrier* can be cued by a very short story about a successful jewel thief who was eventually caught by a detective. Though comprehension of proverbs may be improved if one is given scenarios from widely different domains (Honeck et al., 1985), the interpretations (statement of the abstract ground) are better recall cues than the instantiations (Dorfmueller & Honeck, 1981; Voegstle, 1983).

The idea that proverbs are understood in terms of a conceptual base is appealing because proverbs convey rather abstract meanings. However, the conceptual base hypothesis does not specify the exact form of the conceptual base other than to suggest that it is abstract, nonimagistic, and nonverbal. A more concrete and better motivated proposal on proverb understanding hypothesizes that various generic-level metaphors help motivate why proverbs mean what they do (G. Lakoff & Turner, 1989). There is a single generic-level metaphor, GENERIC IS SPECIFIC, that maps knowledge from specific domains to very general events. The mapping of SPECIFIC to GENERIC information is not defined by a fixed list of elements but by the constraint that the mapping preserves the generic structure of the source domain. These metaphors provide a general mechanism for understanding the general in terms of the specific, one of the key features of proverbs.

For example, consider again the situation where a student is warned not to expose the cheating scandal in her class by the expression *It's better to let sleeping dogs lie*. The "specific-level metaphor" specifies that the knowledge structures used in comprehending the case of the cheating scandal share certain things with the knowledge structures used in comprehending the literal interpretation of *let sleeping dogs lie*. To start, the generic-level schema for the source domain of *It's better to let sleeping dogs lie* has the following characteristics:

There is an animal that is not active.
Animals can sometimes act fierce if provoked.
Therefore it is better to let the animal remain as is rather

than risk disturbing it and having to deal with its potential ferocity.

There are a variety of ways in which such a generic-level schema can be instantiated. For instance, consider the following:

There is an unpleasant situation that is dormant.

Such situations can prove difficult to handle if brought to people's attention.

Therefore it is better to let the situation remain dormant than to risk having to deal with the negative consequences of revealing it.

This leads to the following specific-level metaphoric understanding of the situation:

The dormant animal corresponds to the unpleasant situation.

Disturbing the dog corresponds to bringing the cheating scandal to people's attention.

Therefore it is better to leave the cheating scandal left unnoticed, just as sometimes it is better to let sleeping dogs remain sleeping.

This account shows why proverbs like *It's better to let sleeping dogs lie* do not mean just anything. All proverb understanding appears to involve a conceptual mapping of one specific-level schema from a source domain (i.e., the proverb) onto a generic-level schema from a target domain. Specific-level schemas are concrete, easily imaginable, memorable, and connected to our everyday experiences (G. Lakoff & Turner, 1989). Generic-level schemas have the power of generality that can be applied to a variety of cases. The specific-to-generic schema mapping allows proverbs to express general characterizations that are nonetheless grounded in the richness of the special case (ibid.).

A series of experiments on people's mental imagery of proverbs investigated whether the figurative meanings of these phrases are motivated by metaphorical mappings from generic-level to specific-level schemas (Gibbs, Strom, & Spivey,

1993). The following proverbial expressions are from the first study:

Don't count your chickens before they hatch.
Look before you leap.
The bigger they are, the harder they fall.
You can lead a horse to water, but you can't make him drink.
A rolling stone gathers no moss.
Don't throw the baby out with the bathwater.
The early bird catches the worm.
Too many cooks spoil the broth.
Don't put all your eggs in one basket.
We'll cross that bridge when we come to it.

The participants were asked to write down their mental images of these phrases and then to respond to a series of specific questions regarding the causation, intentionality, reversibility, and manner of the actions depicted in their mental images.

Our findings showed that people's mental images of proverbs were very consistent and detailed. Participants' responses to the questions about their understanding of their mental images were also highly consistent. Take the proverb *A rolling stone gathers no moss*. Our experience of the world shows that stones can roll down hillsides or gather moss in a variety of ways. But participants in this study didn't report a wide variety of mental images of *A rolling stone gather no moss* (or any other proverb). Instead people generally reported that the stone was round and smooth, that the stone rolled down a grassy hillside, and that the stone had a bumpy ride down the slope. Traditional theories of proverb comprehension provide no explanation for this regularity in people's mental images. But the consistency in people's mental images of proverbs can be explained by the constraining influence of conceptual metaphors that provide part of the link between a proverb and its figurative meaning.

Because the individual words of proverbs are not believed to contribute to the figurative meanings of these phrases (just as is assumed for idioms), traditional theories assume that people should have few intuitions about the relationship between a proverb and its figurative meaning. But people demonstrated that there is a motivated link between proverbs and their meanings. The proverb *Don't put all your eggs in one basket*, for instance, is specifically motivated by the conceptual metaphors LIFE IS A CONTAINER and BELIEFS ARE POSSESSIONS. People mapped their knowledge of containers and possessions onto their knowledge of life and beliefs, respectively. People described only one basket in their mental images, suggesting only one opportunity to "gather eggs": one chance in life to accomplish a specific goal. The action of putting all the eggs in one basket was described by people as *placing all their hopes and dreams into something* or *putting all your hopes in one place*, alluding to the idea that beliefs are represented by *eggs* in this proverb. By using the actual word of the proverb as a source domain, the conceptual metaphor linked this literal level of understanding of reality to a target domain, an understanding of the more general abstract, figurative meaning of the proverb. Although people are generally unaware of the motivation that links proverbs with their respective figurative meanings, people nonetheless utilize these conceptual mappings to understand proverbs' meanings.

As was also the case for idioms, the link between a proverb's literal and figurative meanings is not simply a correlation between word meanings. The link is formed by the conceptual mapping of a source onto a target domain. The literal meanings of the words *eggs* and *basket*, for example, may combine well with the idea of "beliefs" and of "life," but this excludes the fact that people generally saw the action in the proverb *Don't put all your eggs in one basket* as intentional and stoppable, that people indicated the presence of only one basket and often referred to the eggs in this proverb as *hopes*. None of these data can be explained by a direct word correlation between literal and figurative meanings. Instead, the relationship between the literal and figurative meanings of proverbs should be seen as the interaction between two conceptual domains, where one domain (e.g., investing human resources in a single objective) is structured in terms of the other (putting all one's eggs in a single basket). Furthermore, this mapping process from a source domain onto a target domain is unidirectional. Thus, life is conceptualized as a container and beliefs are conceptualized as possessions, and not the reverse. As a result of this unidirectional mapping process, people's mental images are highly constrained.

Two other experiments investigated the possibility that the consistency in people's mental images of proverbs had little to do with conceptual metaphors. One study looked at people's mental images of figurative definitions of these proverbs (e.g., "The person who begins a task first is most likely to succeed" in place of *The early bird catches the worm*). The data showed that people were not nearly so consistent in either their mental images or in answering the different probe questions about these figurative definitions as they were about the proverbs themselves. Another study also showed a great deal of variability in people's mental images of matching literal phrases like *A decaying fish pollutes the entire tank* (instead of the proverb *One rotten apple spoils the barrel*). These two experiments provide additional evidence in favor of the idea that the consistency in people's mental images of proverbs is due to the conceptual metaphors that provide part of the link between proverbs and their figurative interpretations.

This research on people's mental images of proverbs does not imply that these sayings are entirely understood as a result of conceptual metaphors. Not all proverbs are well motivated by conceptual metaphors (e.g., *Absence makes the heart grow fonder*, *If you can't beat 'em, join 'em*). Some proverbs do not lend themselves to good mental images (e.g., *All's well that ends well*). But many proverbs do have motivated figurative meanings. People seem to analyze the surface meanings of the words used in proverbs by using conceptual metaphors to make sense of these figurative expressions. As was argued for idioms, it is not entirely clear that people ordinarily activate preexisting metaphorical knowledge each and every time they encounter some familiar proverbial saying. But it seems clear that people at least make sense of what proverbs mean precisely because of conceptual metaphors that form a significant part of our everyday conceptual system.

CONCLUSION

The empirical study of idioms and proverbs in cognitive linguistics and psycholinguistics provides considerable evidence against the idea that all idioms are dead metaphors. People's preexisting metaphorical understanding of many basic concepts provides part of the motivation for why people see idioms and proverbs as having the figurative meanings they do. This metaphorical knowledge influences the linguistic behavior of idioms and also motivates people's use and understanding of many other nonidiomatic expressions and novel verbal metaphors. Many colloquial expressions do not therefore belong to a separate category of linguistic entity (the wastebasket!) apart from both literal and other types of figurative language but reflect various linguistic and conceptual knowledge that is used repeatedly when people speak about their everyday experiences. The complexity of idioms and proverbs and the fact that these phrases differ in terms of their syntactic, lexical, conceptual, and pragmatic properties suggest that it is unlikely that a single theory will account for all aspects of idiomaticity. Yet it seems certain now that the study of clichéd idiomatic expressions can provide significant evidence on how people think metaphorically in everyday life.

Chapter 7

Metonymy

Consider this simple poem by William Carlos Williams, titled "This Is Just to Say."

> I have eaten
> the plums
> that were in
> the icebox
> and which
> you were probably
> saving
> for breakfast
> Forgive me
> they were delicious
> so sweet
> and so cold

This poem appears to resist the poetic foundation of language, in that it has neither meter nor rhyme. We might interpret it as a written message that the author left on the kitchen table for his wife to read. Yet our understanding of this poem depends on our inferring the highly specific context of a kitchen, a certain time frame, and a typical husband–wife relationship (Hedley, 1988). The poem has meaning for us precisely because of the larger situation to which it refers. Our understanding of this poem thus depends on our ability to think metonymically at the mention of parts of some event and infer something about an entire situation.

Metonymy is a fundamental part of our conceptual system:

People take one well-understood or easily perceived aspect of something to represent or stand for the thing as a whole. It is similar to metaphor in that the conceptual basis of metonymy is easily seen in the similarity between various metonymic expressions. Consider again some of the following statements, first mentioned in the opening chapter:

> Washington has started negotiating with Moscow.
> The White House isn't saying anything.
> Wall Street is in a panic.
> The Kremlin agreed to support the boycott.
> Hollywood is putting out terrible movies.
> Paris has dropped hemlines this year.

These examples are not arbitrary single expressions but reflect the general cognitive principle of metonymy, where people use one well-understood aspect of something to stand for the thing as a whole or for some other aspect of it (G. Lakoff & Johnson, 1980). All of the expressions above relate to the general principle by which a place may stand for an institution located at that place. Thus, a place like Hollywood stands for an institution located at that place, namely the major motion picture studios.

This chapter explores the role of metonymy in thought and language. Speakers and writers often use metonymy to refer to people, objects, and events. Many of these metonymies have become conventionalized, as when a television journalist states *The White House isn't saying anything about the scandal* with reference to the president or to representatives of the president's administration. Listeners find conventional metonymies like this one quite easy to comprehend. Novel metonymic expressions can be more difficult. For instance, the metonymic sentence *The ham sandwich is getting impatient for his check* makes little sense apart from a specific context, as when one waiter wants to inform another that a customer who was served a ham sandwich wants to receive the check (Nunberg, 1979). Speakers' frequent use of metonymic expressions and listeners' understanding of these utterances are motivated by metonymic models that form a significant part of our everyday conceptual system. Our ability to make sense of Williams's simple poem partly reflects our ordinary ability to think in metonymic terms.

In this chapter I discuss empirical evidence that reveals that metonymy is not simply a figure of language requiring special processes to be understood. Instead, metonymy constitutes one of the primary ways people refer to people, events, and situations and thus reflects a particular mode of thought. Metonymic thought underlies many kinds of reasoning and allows people to draw inferences about what speakers and writers mean in discourse. My discussion of metonymy extends to studies on colloquial tautologies and indirect speech acts, because these nonliteral utterances also reflect various aspects of metonymic reasoning.

DISTINGUISHING METONYMY FROM METAPHOR

Rhetoricians, linguists, and literary theorists from Aristotle to the present day have achieved little consensus in distinguishing metonymy from metaphor. At first glance, these two tropes appear to be similar, for each describes a connection between two things where one term is substituted for another. Some theorists suggest that metonymy is a type or subclass of metaphor (Genette, 1980; Levin, 1977; Searle, 1979). Other theorists argue that metaphor and metonymy are opposed, because they are generated according to opposing principles (Bredin, 1984; Jakobson, 1971). Metaphor belongs to the selection axis of language, because it is based on similarity. Metonymy belongs to the connection axis, where simple contiguous relations between objects are explored: part–whole, cause–effect, and so on. In contemporary literary studies, the metaphor–metonymy opposition has gradually become a commonplace of practical criticism (Hedley, 1988; D. Lodge, 1977).

Metaphor and metonymy can best be distinguished in making different connections between things (G. Lakoff & Turner, 1989). In metaphor, there are two conceptual domains, and one is understood in terms of another. For instance, when a boxer is likened to a creampuff, as in *The creampuff was knocked out in the first round of the fight*, two separate conceptual domains are contrasted (i.e., athletes and food), and the fighter is viewed as similar to a pastry in being soft and easy to devour. An essential feature of a metaphor is that there must be a certain distance between topic (*boxer*) and vehicle (*creampuff*). The similarity between the topic and vehicle must be accompanied by a feeling of disparity that arises because they belong to different conceptual domains (Ullmann, 1964).

Metonymy involves only one conceptual domain, in that the mapping or connection between two things is within the same domain. Thus, referring to a baseball player as a glove, as in *We need a new glove to play third base*, maps a salient characteristic of one domain (the glove part of the baseball player) as representing the entire domain (the player). When the two things being compared form a part–whole relationship (i.e., when the glove is part of the whole baseball player), the metonymic expression is often referred to as *synecdoche* (Lanham, 1969). Other metonymic statements express "stands-for" relationships between two things; for example, container–contained (*The kettle boiled over*), inventor–invented (*She was reading Proust*), and place–institution (*Wall Street is in a panic*).

There are key differences, then, between metaphor and metonymy, although both express mappings. A convenient way of distinguishing the two kinds of figurative tropes is to apply the "is like" test. Figurative statements of the *X is like Y* form are most meaningful when X and Y represent terms from different conceptual domains. If a nonliteral comparison between two things is meaningful when seen in an *X is like Y* statement, then it is metaphorical; otherwise it is metonymic. It makes sense to say *The boxer is like a creampuff* (metaphor) but not *The third baseman is like a glove* (metonymy).

Metonymy is closely related to the notion of synecdoche. In fact, metonymy and synecdoche are not always clearly distinguishable, since both figures exploit the relationship of larger entities and lesser ones. Synecdoche substitutes the part for the whole, and its terms of reference are concrete. For example, people often substitute *hand* for *worker*, *head* for *person*, and *door* for *house*. These commonplace instances occur in such usages as *They're taking on hands down at the factory, We had to pay ten dollars a head just to get into the concert,* and *Mary Sue lives four doors down the street.* Synecdoche is quite common in colloquial usage and slang, such as when *skirt* is used to signify *woman* in *John is talking to the skirt over at the bar.*

Metonymy, a more subtle and productive trope than synecdoche, substitutes the token for the type, or a particular instance, property, or characteristic for the general principle or function. Its terms of reference often bridge the abstract and the concrete. For instance, people often substitute *pen* for *author, the bench* for *the law, the flag* for *command, the ballot box* for *democracy, the crown* for the *royal government,* and *the bullet* for *terrorism.* These metonymic cliches are found in *the powers of the crown, the dignity of the bench, The pen is mightier than the sword,* and *They prefer the bullet to the ballot box.*

Although the distinction between metonymy and synecdoche seems clear, there are many cases that overlap. In some instances a phrase may be regarded as synecdoche from one perspective and as metonymy from another. When we read *General Schwartzkopf had 400,000 fatigues at his command,* we may suppose *fatigues* to be synecdochic (part for whole) reference to *soldiers,* or we could equally take *fatigues* as a metonymy (token-for-type) signifying "warlike power."

A more troublesome difficulty arises with instances that do not quite meet the part-for-whole requirement of synecdoche or the token-for-type definition of metonymy but that still bear some resemblance to these figures. Consider the following two-sentence narrative: *They were told to expect the prime minister at twelve the next day. Punctually at noon the car drew up in front of the State Department.* There is a sense in which *car* should be read as a reference to the prime minister, or as a token of a type. Although this is not widely recognized as metonymy by literary theorists, the inference that *the car* refers to the prime minister is indeed motivated by metonymic reasoning. Just as listeners must recognize part–whole relationships when comprehending *The ham sandwich is impatient for his check,* people metonymically infer that *the car* is in a certain stands-for relationship with the prime minister in the example above. Many conversational inferences about what speakers mean by what they say require metonymic reasoning. Metonymy serves in many such instances as an important cohesive device in text and discourse understanding.

Certain scholars have argued that metonymy is the figure that tends to predominate in discourse that privileges the contiguity relation (Jakobson, 1960; H. White, 1973). For example, 19th-century realism is seen as a metonymic mode of writing. Jakobson points out that in *War and Peace* Tolstoy uses metonymy for shorthand reference to minor characters in terms of *hair on upper lip* and *bare knuckles* after each character is first described in detail. Metonymy also dominates the ideology of much 19th-century historical writing (H. White, 1973). For instance, many 19th-century historians, such as Tocqueville in his work on the French Revolution, aimed for organicist systems of explanation by understanding particular historical phenomena as a microcosm of a macrocosm. The idea that metonymy serves as a mode of theory in authors' discussive practices is quite suggestive of the claim that metonymy is a fundamental part of everyday thought.

METONYMY AND THOUGHT

There is a growing body of literature in cognitive linguistics and experimental psychology that points to the metonymic character of thinking and reasoning. One important source of evidence is the systematic analysis of conventional expressions. Consider some of the following examples that illustrate various metonymic models in our conceptual system: OBJECT USED FOR USER (*The sax has the flu today, We need a better glove at third base*), CONTROLLER FOR CONTROLLED (*Nixon bombed Hanoi, Ozawa gave a terrible concert last night*), and THE PLACE FOR THE EVENT (*Watergate changed our politics, Let's not let Iraq become another Vietnam*). Many of these models depend on conventional cultural associations, which reflect the general principle a thing may stand for what it is conventionally associated with (Turner, 1987). This principle limits the use of metonymy to certain relationships between entities. For example, we can use the name of any well-known creative artist to refer to the creations of that artist, as in *Does he own any Hemingway?* or *I saw a Jasper Johns yesterday*. Metonymy functions primarily in this way for reference.

There are limits, however, to the use of metonymy in acts of reference. Not any product can be referred to by the name of the person who created the product. I could hardly say *Mary was tasty*, using *Mary* to refer to the cheesecake she made, in spite of the analogy between Mary's mixing and processing of ingredients to produce her cake and Jasper Johns's mixing and application of colors to produce his paintings. Any given instance of a referring function needs to be sanctioned by a body of beliefs encapsulated in an appropriate frame (Nunberg, 1979; J. Taylor, 1989). Thus, one widespread belief in our culture is that the distinctive value of a work of art is due uniquely to the genius of the individual who created it. But we do not normally believe that such a relationship always holds between a cake and the person who baked it.

Some of the best evidence in support of metonymic models of thinking comes from experimental studies of prototype effects in cognitive psychology (G. Lakoff, 1987). Extensive research demonstrates that participants judge certain members of categories as being more representative of those categories than other members. For instance, robins are judged to be more representative of the category "bird" than are chickens, penguins, and ostriches. Desk chairs are judged to be more representative of the category "chair" than are rocking chairs, beanbag chairs, barber chairs, or electric chairs (Rosch, 1978). The most representative members of any category are termed prototypical members.

As was discussed in Chapter 2, prototype effects have been obtained in a number of domains, using a variety of experimental tasks. These findings are clearly inconsistent with the classical theory of concepts and categorization. Yet prototype effects do not themselves imply any specific theory of mental representation (G. Lakoff, 1987; Rosch, 1978). Many psychologists suggest that prototype effects directly mirror category structure in such a way that prototypes constitute specific representations of categories, but prototype effects are simply experimental findings for people's intuitions of category membership. Such findings (e.g., people's ratings) may have many sources.

One source of prototype effects is metonymy. People use metonymic models in reasoning about typical and nontypical members of categories. For example, consider some prototype effects for the "mother" category (G. Lakoff, 1987). People in our culture view housewife mothers as better examples of mothers than nonhousewife mothers. This effect is due to metonymic reasoning, where a salient subcategory (e.g., housewife mother) has the recognized status of standing for the whole category. Other subcategories of "mother" are defined in contrast to this salient stereotypical case. A "working mother," for example, is a woman who raises her children and provides essential nurturance for them yet also works at a job outside the home. We do not consider an "unwed mother" who gives up her child for adoption and then gets a job to be a working mother, since only mothers for whom nurturance is a concern can properly be categorized as mothers. Various other subcategories of mother, such as "stepmother," "birth mother," "adoptive mother," "foster mother," and "surrogate mother," deviate from the central case of the prototypical housewife mother stereotype. The housewife mother metonymically stands for the entire category of mothers in defining how people reason about mothers and motherly behavior. We consequently refer to individuals as *mothers* because we metonymically conceptualize complex categories, such as "mother."

Reasoning about most nontypical cases, such as "surrogate mother," on the basis of typical cases is a significant part of human thought (ibid.). We constantly draw inferences on the basis of typical cases and do so without conscious effort or awareness. Experiments support this conclusion. For instance, participants will infer that if the robins (a typical "bird") on a certain island get a disease, then the ducks (a nontypical "bird") will as well, but not the converse (Rips, 1975). People may also use salient examples of categories in making probability judgments about certain events. For example, California earthquakes are salient examples of the category "natural disasters" (particularly to residents of California!), and people use just such examples in making probability judgments about natural disasters. Participants in one experiment were asked to rate the probability of one of the following statements (Tversky & Kahneman, 1983):

> A massive flood somewhere in North America in 1983, in which more than 1,000 people drown.

> An earthquake somewhere in California in 1983, causing a flood in which more than 1,000 people drown.

The probability given to the second statement was much higher than that given to the first, a finding that violates the law of conjunction, because the probability of the two events' happening cannot be higher than the probability of any one event's happening alone.

These experimental findings show how people reason using metonymic models, where a salient instance of part of a category may represent or stand for the whole category (G. Lakoff, 1987). Such evidence is consistent with the claim that metonymy is a fundamental aspect of ordinary conceptual thought.

Everyday dialogue provides additional evidence for the conceptual basis of metonymy. Consider the following example:

> A: How did you get to the airport?
> B: I waved down a taxi.

Speaker B means to inform the listener A "I got to the airport by hailing a taxi, having it stop and pick me up, and then having it take me to the airport." Successful interpretation of B's remark demands that the listener make this inference about what the speaker meant. Grice called this kind of inference a *conversational implicature*, and we say that B implicates the proposition just mentioned by virtue of what is said along with various background knowledge and beliefs shared with A.

But what kind of knowledge is used by listeners in drawing conversational inferences or implicatures? How does a listener infer that B actually found a taxi to take him to the airport? Traveling from one place to another involves a series of actions, where people find some vehicle to take them to the desired location, get into the vehicle, ride in it to the destination, arrive, and get out. An idealized cognitive model of this series of events includes the following (G. Lakoff, 1987):

Precondition: You have (or have access to) the vehicle.
Embarkation: You get into the vehicle and start it up.
Center: You drive (row, fly, etc.) to your destination.
Finish: You park and get out.
End point: You are at your destination.

It is conventional to use one part of this idealized model to evoke the entire model. Thus, people can simply mention the Precondition, Embarkation, or Center to stand for the entire series of events that make up the travel scenario. In the brief exchange above, Speaker B mentions a Precondition (getting access to a taxi by hailing one) to represent the entire travel scenario. Other possible responses that might work equally well specify other parts of the idealized model, as in:

I drove my car. (*Center*)
I called my friend Bob. (*Precondition*)
I hopped on a bus. (*Embarkation*)
I stuck out my thumb. (*Embarkation*)

People metonymically mention subparts of the travel scenario to stand for the whole scenario. Listeners readily recognize that speakers intend them to understand the entire scenario when one subpart of it is stated, because they share a cognitive model.

Psychological research unknowingly provides good evidence that people reason metonymically when understanding language. Consider the following pairs of utterances (Gernsbacher, 1991):

(1*a*) I need to call the garage (where my car was being serviced).
(1*b*) They said they'd have it ready by five o'clock.

(2*a*) I think I'll order a frozen margarita.
(2*b*) I just love them.

In each of these examples, a plural pronoun occurs in the second sentence. But only singular noun phrases occur in the first sentence. Strictly speaking, these pronouns are illegal because of the prescription that a pronoun must agree with its antecedent in person, number, and case. However, a series of experimental studies demonstrate that people rate as more natural and read more quickly sentences with "conceptual anaphors" (e.g., sentences with *They* and *them* in the above examples) than they do sentences with appropriate singular pronouns (the same sentences with the grammatically correct pronoun *It*) (ibid.). Understanding conceptual anaphors requires our recognition that the singular entities mentioned (e.g., *the garage*) metonymically stand for some conceptual set (the people who work at the garage). Illegal plural pronouns are natural and easily understood precisely because of our pervasive ability to think metonymically about various people, places, events, and objects.

Psychological research also provides good evidence that people immediately infer entire sequences of actions from having heard or read only some salient subpart. In fact, when an inference must be generated to understand some verbal message, people do construct the missing information and often misremember it as having been part of what was originally said. Consider the following simple tale:

> John was hungry and went into a restaurant.
> He ordered lobster from the waiter.
> It took a long time to prepare.
> Because of this he only put down a small tip when he left.

When people hear this brief episode, they presumably activate their knowledge of the activities normally associated with eating in a restaurant and use this information to fill in the gaps to make the story coherent. This type of knowledge, called *scripts* (Schank & Abelson, 1977), consists of well-learned scenarios describing structured situations in everyday life. To comprehend a message like the passage above, listeners must first decide what script is relevant and then how it is to be modified to fit the situation at hand.

A number of experiments show that people automatically infer appropriate script-related actions when these are not explicitly stated. For example, when listening to the story above, people infer *John ate the lobster,* and this inference becomes indistinguishable in their memories from the linguistic material they originally heard (Abbott et al., 1985; Bower et al., 1979; Gibbs & Tenney, 1980; Graesser, Woll, Kowalski, & Smith, 1980). Speakers (and writers) can assume that listeners will supply the necessary scriptlike inference needed to understand what is being said and so typically will leave implicit any information that listeners can supply themselves.

Other experimental studies indicate that reading times for sentences are facilitated if they are preceded by relevant knowledge-based materials (Bower et al., 1979; Garrod & Sanford, 1985; Sanford & Garrod, 1981; Seifert, Robertson, & Black, 1985; Sharkey & Sharkey, 1987). These studies suggest that prior activation of script-based knowledge provides readers with a highly available set of causal connections that can facilitate sentence-by-sentence integration. Whenever information about a goal or plan must be inferred, the story is more difficult to understand. Consider the following tale:

He wanted to be king.
He was tired of waiting.
He thought arsenic would work well.

Understanding this brief passage requires that readers make pragmatic inferences about the connections between the events described in the story. Making these inferences takes cognitive effort. For example, the last statement in this story, *He thought arsenic would work well,* took longer to read in the version above than when the plan was explicitly stated (e.g., *He decided to poison the king*) by being inserted as the next-to-last line (Seifert et al., 1985). When people read the story without the plan's being explicitly stated, they had to infer it, which increased the time needed to understand the story.

All the work on script-based language processing in psychology and artificial intelligence illustrates the importance of metonymic models in everyday thought. People's knowledge in long-term memory of coherent, mundane series of events can be metonymically referred to by the mere mention of one salient subpart of these events. We see that the mention of the subpart metonymically stands for the whole event. This inference facilitates our being able to assume unstated propositions about what speakers and writers mean. For this reason, the extensive work on inferencing in conversational implicature and knowledge-based parsing constitutes part of the evidence about the figurative nature of everyday thought and understanding.

Another demonstration of metonymic thought is people's use of gestures. Many iconic gestures appear to be based on metonymy. One study had a speaker describe to a listener a Sylvester and Tweety cartoon (McNeil, 1992). As the speaker recounted the cartoon, she mentioned how Tweety dropped a large bowling ball down a drainpipe that Sylvester was crawling up. She said:

he's coming up and the bowling ball's coming down and he [swallows it].

At *swallows it*, the speaker presented an iconic gesture: the left hand moving straight down into center while the right hand was moving straight up into center and forming a space around the left hand to show the bowling ball passing into Sylvester's mouth. This iconic gesture presents the right hand as Sylvester's open mouth, standing for the entire event of the bowling ball's going into Sylvester's mouth and his swallowing it. Thus, the right hand metonymically stands for an entire event. The speaker selects a salient part of the swallowing event for presentation.

Another metonymic gesture was seen as part of a speaker's effort to recall a word and/or find an appropriate sentence structure. In the following example, the speaker was describing his recent summer vacation when at one point he stated:

And then we went off to go [. . .] fishing.

During the bracketed phrase, the speaker remained silent for 4 sec and started to flick his wrist back and forth in front of him as if he were fly casting. The selection of the wrist movement used in fly casting metonymically stands for the entire event of going fishing. In general, as was the case with metaphorics (see Chapter 4), speakers use gestures metonymically to refer to certain events. These gestures illustrate people's metonymic understanding of certain actions, events, and situations.

Metonymic thought is not just seen in language and gestures. Many aspects of film and theater illustrate people's common metonymic understanding of situations. Because the very processes of filming (selecting camera angles, focusing, framing) and staging entail selections and rejections, film and theater are inextricably tied to various kinds of metonymies. Film conveys drama by replacing an image of a person with an image of what an audience knows belongs to the person, such as a voice, a shadow, a cap, a ring, or a footstep. The items selected should evoke a whole web of connected ideas and happenings. Consider these examples of metonymy from some classic films (Whittock, 1990).

In Godard's *Vivre sa vie (My Life to Live)*, the sexual transactions with clients are indicated by showing Nana (Anna Karina) reaching for a metal coat hanger. Although its link with prostitution is clear – a prostitute has to undress to some degree, and might well hang up some clothes – this item is selected for repeated emphasis, and it is not one of the more obvious actions one would associate with the practice of prostitution. The novelty of its selection is what makes this metonymy striking and an appropriate figurative correlation for dehumanized and unerotic sex (ibid.).

Synecdoche, where a part stands for the whole, can also be seen in the same film. Nana is negotiating with a photographer late at night in a bistro. She is trying to get him to let her have some money. To bed her, he is using the bait of offering to take publicity pictures of her, which will help her get film roles. As they negotiate, the camera pans from one to the other, but at the limit of each swing, the frame on that side bisects the figure. Such repeated exclusions of part of the figures serve to suggest that neither character exists fully as a person for the other but is only a means to a personal end.

Other films have specific objects that become associated with a particular character or with some event or situation pertaining to that character. Extensive use of props or small objects is evidence of this metonymic implication. Consider the five teacups seen by Mrs. Brenner (Jessica Tandy) in Hitchcock's *The Birds* when she finds the dead farmer. These cups function as a metonymy because they imply the damage done by the birds that have attacked the house, and they hint at some further unspeakable destruction. They also metaphorically represent Mrs. Brenner's tense fragility, glimpsed in the desperation of her endeavors to preserve a domestic and unchanging home life.

Much of the evidence about the metonymic character of everyday thought comes from indirect sources that have not explicitly sought to uncover metonymy in thinking and language. Yet the various evidence from research on categorization, decision making, language processing, and gestures and from an analysis of art and film work provides overwhelming support for the ubiquity of metonymy in everyday thought.

UNDERSTANDING METONYMIC EXPRESSIONS

We clearly have an easy time processing such conventional expressions as *The White House announced a tax hike* and *The buses are on strike today*. These metonymies are directly motivated by long-standing metonymic models in our conceptual system (THE PLACE STANDS FOR THE INSTITUTION and OBJECTS STAND FOR THEIR USERS). Yet no empirical studies have specifically examined people's understanding of these kinds of conventional metonymy. One reason for the neglect is that most language scholars fail to recognize the metonymic character of expressions like *The White House announced a tax hike*, preferring to see such utterances as plain literal language.

It's very easy to find wonderful, creative examples of metonymy in everyday speech and writing. One of the best I know of comes from the satirist Erma Bombeck, who wrote in one of her newspaper columns about her daughter's difficulties finding a suitable roommate (H. Clark, 1983). Consider what Bombeck says as she quotes her daughter:

We thought we were onto a steam iron yesterday, but we were too late. Steam irons never have any trouble finding roommates. She could pick her own pad and not even have to share a bathroom. Stereos are a dime a dozen. Everyone's got their own systems. We've just had a streak of bad luck. First, our Mr. Coffee flunked out of school and went back home. When we replaced her, our electric typewriter got married and split, and we got stuck with a girl who said she was getting a leather coat, but she just said that to get the room.

This passage contains many phrases that are instances of *nonce sense* (i.e., senses "for the nonce," or for the specific occasion) or *contextual expressions* (i.e., expressions with shifting senses that depend almost entirely on context for their interpretation) (ibid.). It seems odd to talk about steam irons' having trouble finding roommates or electric typewriters' getting married. Traditional theories of parsing will fail to handle many of these phrases, even though for the most part we can easily understand what Bombeck's daughter is saying. For example, consider the sentence *Steam irons never have any trouble finding roommates.* Most parsers will search their lexicons for the sense of *steam irons* that is intended, namely "a person who owns a steam iron," and will fail to find anything like this meaning. As would be the case with each of the contextual expressions in this passage, most parsers are unable to create novel, or nonce sense, interpretations for common words and phrases, precisely because they do not have the capacity to make the appropriate inferences about what speakers/authors truly mean. The difficulty parsers, and we as readers/listeners, face is that the meanings of contextual expressions appear to be nondenumerable and depend crucially on the time, place, and circumstance in which these utterances are made.

One scheme proposed to account for how people use and understand contextual expressions is the *innovative denominal verb convention* (ibid.; E. Clark & Clark, 1979). This account, originally offered to explain our understanding of innovative denominal verbs, such as *porched* as in *John porched the newspaper*, states that in using an innovative denominal verb the speaker means to denote:

a. the kind of situation
b. in which there is good reason to believe
c. that on this occasion the listener can readily compute
d. uniquely
e. on the basis of their mutual knowledge
f. in such a way that the parent noun denotes one role in the situation, and the remaining surface arguments of the denominal verb denote other roles in the situation

In understanding such contextual expressions as *John porched the newspaper*, listeners ordinarily infer a hierarchy of goals they believe the speaker is trying to attain. For example, the speaker might have the following goals in making that utterance:

1. For the listener to recognize that the use of *porched* denotes the action John's throwing the newspaper onto the porch.

2. For the listener to recognize that the assertion of what John did with the newspaper is the kind of action that there is good reason to believe that on this occasion the listener can readily compute uniquely on the basis of common ground with the speaker in such a way that porching something plays one role in the act with John as the agent and the newspaper as the patient.

3. For the listener to recognize that the use of *porched* denotes porches.

By inferring the lowest subgoal, (3), from the fact that the speaker is using the noun *porch*, we are to infer the next subgoal up, (2), from the fact that it is being used as a verb too. Finally, we can infer the highest subgoal, (1), from our understanding of (2). Key in this list of goals is the assumption that the listener/reader will interpret the speaker's current utterance in light of what the speaker and listener at that moment both know (called their *common ground*). Because the intended meaning of *porched* in *John porched the newspaper* (namely, "John threw the newspaper onto the porch") is not stored as a conventional sense of the noun *porched*, subgoal (2) is an essential part of the comprehension process in which listeners compute the novel meaning on the spot. Similarly, understanding the contextual expressions in Bombeck's story also requires recovery of the speaker's goal hierarchy, including significant common-ground information. For example, understanding *Our electric typewriter got married and split* has the following goal hierarchy:

1. Bombeck wants readers to recognize that she is using *electric typewriter* to denote the individual (one of her daughter's roommates) who owns an electric typewriter.

2. Bombeck wants readers to recognize that her assertion about getting married is the kind of thing that she has good reason to believe that on this occasion we can readily compute uniquely on the basis of our common ground such that this kind of thing has something to do with electric typewriters.

3. Bombeck wants readers to recognize that she is using *electric typewriter* to denote an object used for typing.

Only by considering our common ground with Bombeck can we recognize when *electric typewriter* is to be construed as having a stands-for relationship in which certain people, places, events, and things may stand for other people, places, events, and things. Many of the inferences required to understand what is meant in this passage are fundamentally metonymic, in that each of these contextual expressions requires readers to understand that the objects mentioned (e.g., *steam irons, stereos, Mr. Coffee,* and *electric typewriter*) stand for the people who own these items (i.e., THEIR POSSESSIONS FOR PEOPLE). Many contextual expressions, but not all, will be readily understood when interpreted in light of such conventional metonymic mappings as OBJECTS USED FOR THEIR USERS, THEIR POSSESSIONS FOR PEOPLE, THE PLACE FOR THE INSTITUTION, or THE PRODUCER FOR THE PRODUCT. These stands-for relationships reflect preexisting patterns of metonymic thought that in many cases substantially constrain the kinds of inference listeners are likely to draw to make sense of what speakers say.

Some psycholinguistic research has looked at how people understand novel metonymic expressions, such as *The electric typewriter got married and split town.* One set of studies shows that readers can determine without great difficulty the appropriate referents for metonymic expressions in discourse (Gibbs, 1990b). Consider how a reader might understand the word *tuxedo* in the statement *John fired the tuxedo because he kept dropping the tray* as referring to a butler. Despite the literal incongruity of this statement, most readers find this sentence to be quite interpretable. How do readers arrive at the correct interpretation of this seemingly anomalous utterance, one that is classically seen as a violation of the Gricean maxim of Quality? Most theories of sentence processing assume that all the possible senses for each word in an utterance are listed in the mental lexicon and that listeners select from among them to understand a word. But understanding contextual expressions involving metonymy requires that a process of *sense creation* must operate to supplement ordinary *sense selection*. The contextually appropriate meaning of *tuxedo* cannot be selected from a short list of potential meanings in the lexicon, because these potential senses are unlimited. After all, *tuxedo* can refer to many kinds of people, not solely butlers. Listeners must instead create a new meaning for the word *tuxedo* beyond its conventional interpretation.

There are two general ways in which people might create new senses during the processing of metonymic expressions. One idea, called the error recovery model, assumes that sense creation is initiated only after the conventional meaning has been found to be in error. This model posits that listeners recognize the need for a figurative interpretation of such utterances as *The ham sandwich is getting impatient for his check* after they are seen to be violations of the maxims of Truthfulness. After all, it is untruthful to claim that inanimate objects, such as ham sandwiches, exhibit human traits, such as impatience. An alternative view of how metonymic expressions are understood, called the concurrent processing model, claims that sense creation and sense selection processes operate simultaneously, perhaps in competition with each other, in the determination of tropological meaning.

An experimental test of these hypotheses had participants read short stories that established preempting meanings for old words (Gerrig, 1989a). For example, people read stories ending with *The horse race is the most popular event*. In a conventional context, this final phrase referred to a standard race between horses; in the innovative situation, the final phrase referred to a unique situation where snails competed in a race that was the length of King Louis's horse. Readers took roughly the same time to comprehend this statement in both contexts. This overlap in reading times suggests that error recovery cannot be operating. Instead, readers seem to be creating and selecting meanings for the phrase *the horse race* at the same time. These data are similar to those obtained for metaphor comprehension that show that contextual expectations drive the recovery of metaphorical meanings at the same time as their literal meanings are being rejected (Gerrig & Healey, 1983; Inhoff, Lima, & Carroll, 1984; Ortony, Schallert, Reynolds, & Antos, 1978). The results of this study provide initial support for the concurrent processing model of metonymy comprehension (see Chapter 3).

What evidence is there to suggest that people create new meanings when they comprehend metonymic expressions? They may simply recognize that statements like *The ham sandwich is getting impatient for his check* or *The scalpel was sued for malpractice* refer to previously mentioned referents without actually determining that there are any figurative connections between these utterances and their referents. This idea implies that people can comprehend metonymic statements without having to create any new senses or meanings for those descriptions. All that is required to understand *The scalpel was sued for malpractice* is that readers establish a temporary arbitrary link or symbol between the figurative term (*the scalpel*) and its referent (*the surgeon*).

One study assessed whether readers actually formed metonymic connections between these figurative statements and their referents (Gibbs, 1990b). Participants in this study read stories ending with such statements as *The scalpel was sued for malpractice* and described what each final expression meant in its context. The participants invariably understood that the final sentence referred to some earlier stated individual in the story context (e.g., that *scalpel* referred to *the surgeon*). More important, people were also asked to describe *why* the initial noun phrase in each final statement referred to its earlier stated referent (i.e., why the surgeon was called a *scalpel*). Participants also correctly described a metonymic relationship between metonymic statements and their earlier stated referents (e.g., "the surgeon was called a *scalpel* because surgeons often use scalpels" or "the athlete was called a *glove* because gloves are an important part of a baseball player") 88% of the time. This finding suggests that readers determine the figurative connections between the final metonymic statements and their previously stated referents. It appears, then, that people may create novel senses for metonymic referential terms during the on-line processing of these innovative expressions. Readers' comprehension of figurative referential descriptions involves both sense selection and sense creation processes.

Other evidence demonstrates that listeners make immediate use of common-ground information – the beliefs, knowledge, and attitudes that are shared by speakers and listeners – in creating new senses for old words (H. Clark, 1983; H. Clark & Gerrig, 1983). Consider the sentences *While I was taking his picture, Steve did a Napoleon for the camera* and *After Joe listened to the tape of the interview, he did a Nixon to a portion of it.* These utterances contain eponymous verbs (i.e., verbs associated with a proper name) that are metonymic because each action stands for some specific act conventionally associated with an individual. Traditional linguistic parsers have significant difficulty understanding contextual verb phrases such as *did a Napoleon for the camera* and *did a Nixon to a portion of (the tape)* (H. Clark, 1983). In contrast, experimental research shows that people usually experience little problem interpreting these phrases, especially when they have specific knowledge of the person referred to by the eponymous verb phrase (e.g., the famous painting of Napoleon) (H. Clark & Gerrig, 1983). Understanding eponyms is guided by a hierarchy of constraints regarding the speakers' and listeners' *common ground* (ibid.).

1. *Identity of the eponym.* The identity of the eponym is assumed to be part of the speaker's and listener's common ground. A speaker wouldn't sincerely say *Please do a Napoleon for the camera* if she did not assume that both she and the lis-

tener recognized that the identity of Napoleon was in the common ground.

2. *Acts of the eponym.* Certain acts associated with the eponym are assumed to be part of the common ground. A speaker may know that Napoleon did many things: ruled France, crowned himself, laid siege to Moscow, was exiled to Elba, etc. A speaker assumes that some of these are part of the common ground shared with listeners.

3. *Relevant acts of the eponym.* Certain acts specified in (2) are part of the common ground and are relevant in the sentence the speaker uttered. For instance, the speaker assumes that from the set of acts associated with Napoleon the listener could choose at least one that a person could do for the camera, such as frown, crown oneself, pose hand-in-jacket, and so on.

4. *The type of act referred to.* It is because of common ground that the speaker assumed the listener could readily and uniquely identify the type of act the speaker intended from the type of act in (3). In this case, out of all the acts Napoleon could have done for the camera, the speaker believes that the hand-in-jacket pose was in the common ground with the listener and that the listener could infer that this was meant.

Listeners presumably interpret an eponym starting at Level 1 and narrow down the possible interpretations by adding constraints at Levels 2, 3, and 4. An experimental test of this hypothesis presented participants with sentence frames containing either known or unknown eponyms (ibid.). These sentence frames either contained restricting context or were unrestricted. Presented below is an example of a known eponym in both a restricted and unrestricted context:

Restricted Context

If during a conversation with a friend, he were to say the following sentence: *After Joe listened to the tape of the interview, he did a Nixon to a portion of it.*

Unrestricted Context

If during a conversation with a friend, he were to say the following sentence: *After Joe listened to the tape of the interview, he did a Nixon.*

Participants then wrote down what the speaker either (a) almost certainly meant, (b) probably meant, or (c) might have meant or simply stated that they (d) couldn't really tell what the speaker meant. The results gave clear evidence of an eponym-centered process. Verb phrases like *did a Nixon to a portion of the tape* were more interpretable when the eponym was known, allowing the reader to get down to Levels 2, 3, and 4, than when the eponyms were unknown (e.g., *did a John Jacobs to a portion of the tape*). The verb phrases with known eponyms were more interpretable when the surrounding context was more restrictive, allowing the participants to reach Level 4, than when it was unrestricted, which allowed readers to get, at best, to Levels 2 or 3.

The influence context has on the interpretation of an eponym depends partly on the type of eponym. Understanding *do a Nixon to the tape* or *do a Napoleon for the camera* may be readily understood without any other contextual information, because each specific act noted by the eponym is especially salient. A speaker wouldn't say *I was in bed doing a Napoleon to a mystery story* and expect the listener to understand this to mean simply "I was in bed reading a mystery story." The type of act intended to be recognized must be peculiar to Napoleon. In this way, understanding eponyms requires metonymic reasoning, since listeners must recognize certain part–whole relationships between the eponym (the whole) and salient acts associated with it (the parts). Understanding *do a Napoleon* requires that listeners recover not just a collection of acts associated with Napoleon but a particular type of act. The more coherent the collection of acts associated with an eponym, the easier it will be to find an acceptable interpretation of a phrase like *do a Napoleon*.

Another study demonstrated that people expect the intended target act to be coherent and salient among the acts associated with an eponym (H. Clark & Gerrig, 1983). Participants read a series of vignettes, each ending with a sentence containing an eponymous verb phrase. Each vignette described three acts associated with an individual. In the first form, two of the eponym's acts were mundane and the other was highly unusual. In the second form of each vignette, all three acts were highly unusual, so that no single act was more salient than the others. Each vignette also ended in different types of completion. In one case, the eponym was unrestricting, containing the bare eponymous verb phrase (e.g., *do an Elvis Edmunds*); in the second case, the eponym was restricted, containing an additional qualifying phrase intended to narrow down the interpretation (e.g., *do an Elvis Edmunds to some apples I bought*). The third kind of eponym was an extending completion, containing a qualifying phrase intended to pick out the same acts as the restricting completion but extended to another domain (e.g., *do an Elvis Edmunds to a piece of driftwood*). Presented below are examples of these two types of vignettes and their different completions:

One Salient Act

Imagine that a friend of yours told you about his neighbor, Elvis Edmunds. Elvis loves to entertain his children in the evening with several card games he knows. He often plays canasta with them. During the day, Elvis is employed as an insurance salesman. He likes to work best on days when there is not a cloud in the sky. To supplement his income, Elvis carves fruit into exotic shapes for the delicatessen down the road. Later your friend says, "I have often thought about

doing an Elvis Edmunds." (unrestricting)
doing an Elvis Edmunds to some apples I bought." (restricting)
doing an Elvis Edmunds to a piece of driftwood." (extending)

Three Salient Acts

Imagine that a friend of yours told you about his neighbor, Elvis Edmunds. Elvis loves to entertain his children in the evenings with several magic tricks that he knows. He often surprises them by pulling dollar bills out of his ear. During the day Elvis is employed as a professional skywriter. He likes to work best on days when there is not a cloud in the sky. To supplement his income, Elvis carves exotic shapes for the delicatessen down the road.
Later your friend says, "I have often thought about

doing an Elvis Edmunds." (unrestricting)
doing an Elvis Edmunds to some apples I bought." (restricting)
doing an Elvis Edmunds to a piece of driftwood." (extending)

The participants' task was to interpret each vignette, rating their confidence in their interpretations. Restricting completions were more interpretable than either unrestricting or extending completions. Thus, people found it easier to interpret *do an Elvis Edmunds to some apples I bought* (meaning "to carve the apples into exotic shapes") than to understand either *do an Elvis Edmunds* or *do an Elvis Edmunds to a piece of driftwood*. These same effects were found regardless of whether there were one or three salient acts or whether the acts were coherent or incoherent.

These data on the interpretation of eponymous verb phrases demonstrate that people use hierarchical information associated with eponyms to create sensible meanings of these novel phrases. The farther listeners get down the hierarchy, the more confident they will be that their interpretation is the correct one. These experimental findings provide further evidence that understanding contextual expressions involving metonymy requires quick access to common-ground information to create novel interpretations for these nonliteral utterances. The difficulty sometimes associated with making sense of metonymic phrases is not in the extra time it takes to resolve the apparent violation of Truthfulness maxims but in the effort needed to access particular information that supposedly constitutes part of the common ground between speakers and listeners in any discourse situation.

Exactly how the sense selection and sense creation processes work together when people interpret metonymic phrases is unclear. For most words and phrases, listeners don't simply adopt one process (as for conventional meaning) or the other (as for novel senses). Readers of metonymy and related contextual expressions must do more than simply search through their mental lexicons to retrieve the appropriate meanings of these terms for the context at hand. After all, the possible meanings of metaphoric referential descriptions, such as *The ham sandwich is really upset with me*, are nondenumerable and not listed as part of their ordinary senses (H. Clark, 1983). One could assume that listeners exhaustively evaluate all the conventional meanings in the lexicon before trying to create the intended senses of a word around one of these conventional senses. This *strict serial process* would be similar to the *Standard Pragmatic Model* discussed in Chapter 3. Another possibility assumes that listeners begin creating senses in parallel to accessing conventional senses from the lexicon. Whatever model is chosen, it must be capable of showing how people can easily create meanings in real-time discourse situations.

The speed with which people determine the correct referent for different metonymies may also be influenced by the conventionality of these figurative terms. There may be certain cases where there is less need for listeners to create new senses for metonymies because the appropriate sense is already represented as part of the meaning of a word or phrase. For instance, athletes are sometimes referred to as *jocks* (a metonymic description). Many slang expressions are metonymically motivated. Someone who says *I need some bread to pay my rent*, meaning "I need some money to pay my rent," has used *bread* metonymically to stand for money, a convention that has evolved in American English, given that a primary use of money is to purchase such basic food items as bread. Slang dictionaries are testimony to the development of specific meanings for metonymic phrases (cf. Spears, 1982). Some figurative descriptions of people might be comprehended through selection of one of their preestablished senses. These conventional slang descriptions of people might actually be understood as fast as, if not more quickly than, literal descriptions. Other research has shown that slang metaphors, such as *I need some bread*, were interpreted more quickly than nonslang equivalent sentences (Gibbs & Nagaoka, 1985).

Finally, it is, again, important to note that understanding metonymic expressions may depend on recovering some underlying metonymic model. For example, the metonymic expressions *The White House isn't saying anything*, *Wall Street is in a panic*, and *Hollywood is putting out trashy movies* don't just occur one by one but are instances of more general metonymic principles, in this instance THE PLACE STANDS FOR THE INSTITUTION. People may comprehend the correct referent of such novel phrases as *Havana is getting divorced from Moscow* through recognition of THE PLACE STANDS FOR THE INSTITUTION conceptual metonymy. Similarly, metonymic referential descriptions of people, such as *The sax has the flu today, The scalpel was sued for malpractice,* and *The glove at third base has to be replaced,* all represent part of the metonymic mapping where THE OBJECT STANDS FOR THE USER. Part of our ability to understand figurative descriptions of institutions and people might be attributed to our recognition that any metaphoric or metonymic utterance is an instantiation of some conceptual mapping (i.e., THE OBJECT STANDS FOR THE USER). The ubiquity of these conceptual models in many aspects of our thinking and reasoning provides part of the motivation for why speakers frequently use metaphor and metonymy and why listeners so readily understand the meanings of such anomalous sentences as *The ham sandwich just spilled beer all over himself.*

COLLOQUIAL TAUTOLOGIES

Referring to a part by mention of the whole is a common aspect of such metonymic expressions as *The government stopped me for speeding last night* and *The* New York Times *is late for the senator's press conference.* Listeners usually experience little difficulty comprehending these kinds of metonymy. Another version of metonymy that has become quite colloquial for speakers is to refer to aspects of people, objects, and events through tautological statements. Consider the following brief exchange between two parents (Gibbs & McCarrell, 1990). A mother asks her husband *Did the children ever clean up their rooms?* The father shakes his head and responds *Well, boys will be boys.* At first glance, the father's response to his wife's question seems nonsensical. The phrase *Boys will be boys* is true by virtue of its logical form alone (as a nominal tautology) and, superficially, contributes no new information to the conversation. But the utterance *Boys will be boys* is readily interpretable, and most listeners would agree that the father intended to convey a particular meaning, something like "Boys will be unruly, and it is often difficult to get them to do what you want." Nominal tautologies are found with surprising frequency in everyday speech, literature (e.g., Gertrude Stein's famous line *A rose is a rose is a rose*), and advertising (e.g., *Motor oil is motor oil*). These expressions are metonymic because the speaker names a general category (e.g., boys) to refer to specific salient parts or attributes of that category (e.g., unruly behavior).

Most discussions of linguistic tautologies, following Grice, have explicitly assumed that the interpretation of utterances like *Boys will be boys* and *A promise is a promise* changes from one situation to another (P. Brown & Levinson, 1978; Fraser, 1988; Levinson, 1983). *Boys will be boys* may convey the idea that boys are unruly in one context but in another can express the notion that little boys are cute and adorable. We cannot strictly derive "boys are unruly" from *Boys will be boys* apart from the specific context at hand and any background knowledge shared by speakers and listeners. The Gricean proposal, the *pragmatic view*, suggests, then, that the interpretation of nominal tautologies is context-dependent, with different meanings attached to the same tautology, depending on the conversational context and the shared beliefs of the participants (Levinson, 1983). For the conversation described above, the father's remark *Boys will be boys* flouts the maxim of Quantity, because the assertion of a tautology is not informative when taken literally. Yet it is clear that despite the apparent failure of cooperation, most listeners normally assume that the speaker is cooperative at some deeper level. We do this normally by inferring that the speaker is trying to remind us of some belief or attitude about boys, namely that boys are often unruly (ibid.).

Critics of the pragmatic view have argued that there is a good deal of regularity in the interpretation of colloquial tautologies because these phrases are to some extent language-specific (Wierzbicka, 1987). This *semantic* account suggests that the meanings of colloquial tautologies must be explicated in appropriate semantic representations for different phrases in different languages. For example, nominal tautologies like *Boys will be boys* are simply not used in French, German, or Russian. Thus, the French sentence *Les garçons seront les (des?) garçons* (i.e., "The boys will be the boys") would simply be incomprehensible. If the variety of interpretations for sentences like *Boys will be boys* and *A husband is a husband* were simply due to pragmatic process of conversational implicature, then the acceptability of such phrases should be identical in different languages. But the extreme variation in the interpretation of nominal tautologies in different languages suggests that these phrases are partly conventional and language-specific. Each tautology has a specific meaning that cannot be predicted in terms of universal pragmatic maxims (ibid.).

The semantic view proposes that English nominal tautologies can be distinguished in terms of their different syntactic patterns and their different nominal classifications (ibid.). For example, tautologies of the syntactic form "N (abstract – singular) is N (abstract – singular)" (e.g., *War is war*, *Politics is politics*, and *Business is business*) convey a sober, mostly negative, attitude toward complex human activities that must be understood and tolerated. Tautologies of the form "N (plural) will be N (plural)" refer to some negative aspects of the topic but also convey an indulgent attitude toward this relatively unchangeable negative aspect (e.g., *Boys will be boys*). Phrases like *Rapists will be rapists* or *Murderers will be murderers* seem less acceptable, because it is unlikely that the speaker would wish to convey an attitude of indulgence toward the topic. In general, contrary to the pragmatic view, a semantic approach to nominal tautologies proposes that the specific syntactic form and lexical content of different phrases contribute significant information to their interpretation and acceptability.

A third approach to colloquial tautologies is a hybrid theory that captures aspects of the previously described views. Within this framework, the systematic and conventional meaning associated with tautological constructions varies with the speaker's/listener's conceptual knowledge of the objects that nouns in the tautology refer to. An English nominal tautology signals that the speaker intends that the listener recognize (a) that the speaker holds some view or attitude toward all people, activities, or objects referred to by the noun phrase, (b) that the speaker believes that the listener can recognize this particular view, and (c) that this view is relevant to the conversation (Fraser, 1988; Gibbs & McCarrell, 1990). The very form of nominal tautologies signals that the speaker intends to convey the belief that the participants share a view about some aspect of the noun mentioned in the tautology and wishes to bring this belief to the listener's attention. The particular beliefs about a noun that a speaker wishes to convey will depend partly on context. For instance, in different circumstances a speaker may state *Business is business* to convey either that business is competitive (a negative attribution) or that business is financially rewarding (a positive attribution).

However, context alone is insufficient to explain the exact interpretations listeners/readers give to colloquial tautologies. Speakers and listeners share information about the social situation at hand, but they also mutually assume specific stereotypical understandings of people, activities, and objects (cf. Putnam, 1975). This stereotypical knowledge is directly used in interpreting exactly what speakers mean when they refer to different people, activities, and objects in nominal tautologies. Listeners should often interpret *Boys will be boys* to mean that boys are unruly not just because of the specific conversational context but because of the assumption that the speaker shares as part of the common ground a similar stereotype about boys. But when speakers refer to objects such as hats and beds or to food such as carrots in tautological phrases, they seem less likely to evoke specific attitudes about these objects, because people generally don't have strong stereotypes for them. People may certainly have strong prototypical representations of particular objects and events (Rosch & Mervis, 1975), but they do not have as detailed stereotypical attitudes toward concrete objects like hats, beds, and carrots (Dahlgren, 1985). Phrases like *A hat is a hat* and *Carrots will be carrots* seem less acceptable as meaningful tautologies than do phrases, such as *Business is business* and *Boys will be boys*, that mention people or activities for which speakers/listeners have strong stereotypes. These observations suggest that people's stereotypical attitudes toward the people, activities, or objects referred to by the noun phrases in nominal tautologies play an important role in the use and acceptability of these colloquial expressions.

One series of studies investigated the relevance of these hypotheses for explaining people's acceptance of different nominal tautologies (Gibbs & McCarrell, 1990). Participants in these experiments were asked to rate the acceptability and affective quality of systematically generated tautological phrases both without any contextual information and in different contexts. A first study showed that people could readily understand the meanings of many nominal tautologies without supporting contextual information. However, there were specific differences in the acceptability of different types of nominal tautologies. People found it easier to assign meanings to tautologies containing human role nouns (e.g., *Salesmen are salesmen, A teenager is a teenager*) and abstract nouns (e.g., *War is war, Promises are promises*) than they did to statements containing concrete nouns (e.g., *Flowers will be flowers, A hat is a hat*). Moreover, participants found modal tautologies with human role nouns (e.g., *Boys will be boys*) the easiest to interpret and modal phases with concrete nouns (e.g., *Carrots will be carrots*) the most difficult to interpret.

Modal tautologies can be used to convey new information about the future. They can not only remind a listener of a pre-existing stereotype but predicate its continued existence. This predication is informative only if a change in the stereotypic behavior is possible. The possibility of change is enhanced by the idea of volition, to which the modal verb *will* also refers. It is difficult to ascribe volitional behavior to concrete objects. For instance, a teacher is more capable of change than is a carrot. Since it is much less likely that concrete nouns will change, the modal tautology predicating their continued existence is much less informative. Modal tautological phrases with concrete nouns do not make as much sense and are judged less acceptable than tautologies with human role nouns. Although there is little difference in participants' acceptability ratings for singular tautologies (e.g., *An X is an X*) with human role, abstract, or concrete nouns, plural syntactic forms (e.g., *X's are X's*) with human role and abstract nouns are more comprehensible than are plural forms with concrete nouns. These findings support the predictions of the semantic view of nominal tautologies (Wierzbicka, 1987), in that both syntactic and lexical information operates to make some tautological phrases more understandable than others.

A second study once again found that tautologies with human role nouns were more acceptable than were phrases with concrete nouns. But the presence of positive and negative contextual information in this study clearly influenced people's interpretations of tautological sentences. People generally found tautologies in negative contexts more comprehensible than in positive contexts. Thus, people found phrases like *Boys will be boys* easier to understand when seen in a context supporting a negative view of boys (e.g., boys will be unruly) than in situations highlighting positive aspects of boys (e.g., boys are cute and adorable). Some tautologies, such as *Telephones are telephones*, were equally comprehensible when seen in either a negative (telephones are annoying and always ringing) or positive (telephones are invaluable for convenient communication) context. Colloquial tautologies containing concrete objects were overall more contextually flexible than tautologies with either human role or abstract nouns. Finally, there were important syntactic constraints on the acceptability of various forms for tautologies that also influence their usage. It seems perfectly appropriate to state the modal construction *Boys will be boys*, but it is less sensible to say *A boy is a boy*. Stereotypes are general impressions of people and things that are most easily evoked in plural and modal syntactic forms that focus on classes of things rather than on individual instances of a concept.

The findings from both studies suggest principled differences in people's interpretations of various types of tautological sentence. Tautologies with human role nouns are the most interpretable and generally convey negative, sober attitudes. This was not the case for tautologies containing nouns referring to concrete objects. Such findings reflect people's stereotypical attitudes toward various people and human activities. People in a linguistic community share certain beliefs, knowledge, and attitudes – their common ground – and use this information in deciding what to say as well as in understanding what is meant from what is said (H. Clark & Carlson, 1982; Gibbs, 1987b; Gibbs, Mueller, & Cox, 1988). Part of the common ground that forms the context for comprehension is the set of stereotypical attitudes people have about other individuals (and types of individuals) and various human activities. Speakers can easily remind listeners about their shared beliefs about certain people and human activities by uttering simple redundant phrases, such as *Business is business* or *Mothers will be mothers.* Colloquial tautologies are convenient devices for evoking the shared stereotypical presuppositions among conversants without having to spell out those beliefs. We understand *Boys will be boys* as expressing a very different meaning from *Girls will be girls* because of our different stereotypical attitudes about boys and girls. Interpreting colloquial tautologies requires metonymic reasoning, in that listeners must recognize how the mention of a whole refers to some salient part (e.g., how mention of boys refers to their unruly behavior). To the extent that speakers wish to remind listeners that they share a negative stereotype about people, activities, or things, we can metonymically refer to the whole of these people or activities and let listeners infer which aspects are intended to be recognized.

INDIRECT SPEECH ACTS

Metonymic reasoning, where people infer wholes from parts and parts from wholes, is also important in other acts of reference where speakers make requests of listeners. Making a request requires that speakers specify enough information to enable someone to recognize which information or action is desired. Yet most situations in which requests are made appear inequitable. Whenever a speaker requests something from someone, it costs the addressee some effort to supply what is desired. This could, and does in many situations, threaten the addressee's face value (P. Brown & Levinson, 1978; Goffman, 1967). Face is defined as consisting of the freedom to act unimpeded (negative face) and the satisfaction of having one's values approved of (positive face) (P. Brown & Levinson, 1978). People usually act to maintain or gain face and to avoid losing face. A speaker's request often imposes on addressees and can potentially threaten the hearer's face. People are polite to the extent that they enhance or lessen the threat to another's face (ibid.; H. Clark & Schunk, 1980). To eliminate any threat to the addressee's face caused by a request, speakers usually formulate their requests indirectly, as in *Could you lend me ten dollars?* Making indirect speech acts provides addressees with options that enable them either to comply with requests or give some good reason why they can or will not respectfully do so without losing face (R. Lakoff, 1973). Speakers who formulate their requests indirectly assume, though, that listeners can recognize that an entire series of actions is being described from the specific mention of one salient part. For example, understanding *Can you lend me ten dollars?* as a request requires that listeners see the question about their ability as referring to a series of actions that ends with a transaction of goods. In this way, speaking and understanding indirect speech acts involves a kind of metonymic reasoning, where people infer wholes (a series of actions) from a part.

There are a number of ways in which indirect speech acts can be made (Gibbs, 1981a, 1981b, 1986d; Gibbs & Mueller, 1988). Each form specifies some part of the transaction of goods between speaker and listener, in which the listener's task is to infer the entire sequence of actions that the speaker wishes the listener to engage in to comply with the request. Requesting that someone shut the door, for example, can be done by questioning the ability of the listener to perform the action (*Can you shut the door?*), questioning the listener's willingness to shut the door (*Will you shut the door?*), uttering a sentence concerning the speaker's wish or need (*I would like the door shut*), questioning whether the act of shutting the door would impose on the listener (*Would you mind shutting the door?*), making a statement about some relevant fact in the world (*It's cold in here*), or simply asking what the listener thinks about shutting the door (*How about shutting the door?*).

Most investigators view these different sentences as *conventional* ways of performing indirect directives, each of which is especially polite (Bach & Harnish, 1979; Ervin-Tripp, 1976; Gordon & Lakoff, 1971; Morgan, 1978; Searle, 1975). That is, for arbitrary reasons people use some sentence forms to make indirect speech acts and not others but tacitly agree to use only those particular forms as a matter of *convention* (see Lewis,

1969). Different kinds of indirect speech acts, however, may not be equally appropriate for a given social situation. Ordering a Big Mac at McDonald's by saying *I'll have a Big Mac* appears to be more appropriate than is the request *Do you have a Big Mac?* Traditional theories of indirect speech acts are unable to specify why speakers view some indirect requests as appropriate in some situations and not in others. Most theories simply stipulate that the decision to use one kind of indirect request as opposed to another is an arbitrary phenomenon.

Formulating the right request in a situation depends on designing a transaction that takes into account a good deal of information (Gibbs, 1985b). A transaction requires the exchange of "goods," such as tangible objects, commitments, or obligations, between people. This process has several parts. First, the speaker decides what goods or entities he or she lacks and so begins to formulate a plan for finding these goods or entities by determining a likely source, such as a book, a look at an object, or information from another person. If the speaker decides to get the goods from another person, he or she selects the person by judging, among other things, who is most likely to have the information, who is most available, and whom it is possible to make a request of. At this point, the speaker plans a social transaction in which the speaker exchanges something with the appointed addressee for the desired information. The speaker must then find a way of inserting this plan for the addressee's contribution (i.e., a response to the request in the form of providing the information) into what the addressee is doing or planning to do at the moment. In some situations, like service encounters (see Merritt, 1976), the addressee's primary activity may be to be a filler of requests – perhaps as a drugstore clerk. The expected transactions that arise in such situations are most easily planned for by a speaker. There are also detour transactions, where the speaker interrupts the addressee's activities or projected plans to impose his or her own goals. These situations are more difficult to plan for, but in each case the speaker finally designs his or her request as a turn in the transaction. To do this, the speaker must first assess what reasons there may be for the addressee not to give the desired information. *The speaker will then formulate an utterance to deal with the greatest potential obstacle.* By doing so, the speaker thereby implicates that the addressee will divulge what the speaker wants to know.

The possibility that speakers formulate their requests to deal with the main obstacles to compliance is called the *obstacle hypothesis* (Francik & Clark, 1985; Gibbs, 1986d). This idea is interesting because it suggests that the apparent conventionality of an indirect request depends largely on the extent to which an utterance specifies an addressee's projected obstacles in complying with the speaker's request (Gibbs, 1986d). Thus, *Do you have the time?* may be conventional to use in requesting the time of a passerby on the street, because the greatest obstacle to the listener in providing the information may be that he or she simply doesn't know it and has no access to a timepiece. Since the speaker cannot rule out this most limiting case, he or she must design the request around it. However, saying *Do you know what time you close?* as a request to a store owner in order to find out what time the store closes is inappropriate, because the owner is presumed to know what time his or her business closes. The most likely obstacle in this situation is the store owner's willingness to provide the desired information. In general, the obstacle hypothesis reflects the way speakers reason metonymically in getting addressees to comply with their desires. By stating some part of the projected transaction of goods, speakers assume that listeners will infer what is desired and adopt as their own plan the intention to complete other actions within this transaction.

A good deal of experimental evidence supports the obstacle hypothesis. One set of studies had participants read various scenarios depicting a protagonist about to make a request (Gibbs, 1986d). In some situations, the obstacles were general or even unknown. An example of this kind of scenario is presented below.

Tracy and Sara were tired of eating dinner at their college's dining hall. So they went downtown to find something exciting to eat. They decided to go to Tampico's. Sara wanted an enchilada, so when the waitress came to take their order Sara said to her . . .

In other situations, the potential obstacle for the addressee in fulfilling the request was specific, as shown in the following scene.

Tracy and Sara were tired of eating dinner at their college's dining hall. So they went downtown to find something exciting to eat. They decided to go to Tampico's. Sara wanted an enchilada, but was unsure whether the restaurant had them or not. The waitress came up to take their order and Sara said to her . . .

The main obstacle in this situation for the addressee (the waitress) in complying with Sara's request was whether the restaurant actually served enchiladas.

The participants' task in a first experiment was to read each scenario and simply write down what they would say in such a situation. Across all the different scenarios, the participants employed a variety of surface forms in making their requests (e.g., *May I . . .? I would like . . . Can you . . .? Would you mind . . .? Do you have . . .?*). Although these forms of indirect request were used most often, all request forms were not equally appropriate in a particular situation. This was seen in how different types of requests were generated in different obstacle contexts. For instance, the participants generated Possession utterances, like *Do you have . . .?* 68% of the time when they read stories where the main obstacle concerned the addressee's possession of the object desired by the speaker. People produced Possession requests only 8% of the time in contexts where the obstacle concerned the addressee's Ability to fulfill the request, and participants never generated Possession utterances in situations with State-of-World obstacles. Similarly, people made requests using Permission sentences, like *May I see . . .?* 51% of the time in Permission contexts but only 10% of the time in Possession scenarios. Speakers clearly seem sensitive to the obstacles present in many situations and choose their requests accordingly.

A second study provided a better assessment of how speakers make requests in more realistic situations. Participants were brought to six locations on a university campus, each of which was carefully designed to highlight a different potential obstacle. For example, an experimenter and a participant went inside the university library and walked over to a table where a student was busily working on a paper assignment. The participant was told to imagine sitting near the student and also working on a paper and having his or her pen suddenly run out of ink. Participants were then asked to state what they would say to the nearby student in order to get that addressee to lend them a pen. Overall, participants produced appropriate requests 74% of the time. Thus, when people were asked to make requests in situations that closely approximated the real world, they had an even stronger tendency to produce utterances that specified the obstacles present for the addressees.

Specifying the potential obstacles for addressees in making indirect requests makes it easier for listeners to comprehend these speech acts. Consider the following story and two possible indirect requests:

> Barbara and her roommate were getting dressed to go out.
> Barbara wanted something to wear with her same old blue pants.
> She wanted to wear her roommates' baby-blue cashmere sweater.
> Her roommate usually lets her borrow it,
> but she may have taken it to the dry cleaners that day.
> So Barbara is not sure that her roommate is able to let her have it.
> So Barbara says to her. . .

> Can you possibly lend me your blue sweater?

> Would you mind lending me your blue sweater?

The obstacles alluded to in this story concerned the ability of the addressee to lend the blue sweater to the speaker. For this reason, *Can you possibly lend me your blue sweater?* is better suited to making a request here than is *Would you mind lending me your blue sweater?*

Although the *Would you mind . . .?* utterance is by no means entirely inappropriate, the results of a reading-time experiment indicated that people process indirect requests that adequately specify the reasons for an addressee's not complying with a request faster than they understand indirect requests that do not specify such obstacles (Gibbs, 1986d). People learn to associate specific obstacles for hearers with different social situations and know when sentence forms best fit these circumstances. A control study showed that, without context, participants found both types of indirect requests equally difficult to process, suggesting that the conventionality of an indirect speech act is not a property of an utterance itself but is due to some relationship between an utterance and a particular social context.

Although scholars have claimed that many indirect requests are understood via some sort of short-circuited process (Bach & Harnish, 1979; H. Clark, 1979; H. Clark & Schunk, 1980; Gibbs, 1979, 1981a; Morgan, 1978; A. Munro, 1979; Searle, 1975), no one has specified what it is about some requests that makes them different. The results of this particular reading-time study establish that people take less time to process indirect requests that specify the addressee's projected obstacles. Seeing indirect speech acts specified in this way makes it easier for listeners to determine speakers' intended meanings. What makes some indirect speech acts apparently "conventional" is the appropriateness of the sentence forms in matching the obstacles present for addressees in a social context.

These studies emphasize the importance of metonymic reasoning in people's use and understanding of indirect speech acts. Speakers plan their requests as part of a transaction of goods in conversation. Consequently, people prefer to highlight potential obstacles to listeners' completing the transaction of goods. By picking out salient obstacles, even ones that are more apparent than real, speakers assume that listeners can metonymically infer the entire sequence of actions that must occur for the transaction of goods to be completed. Once again, we see an instance of people inferring the intended meanings of speakers' indirect or figurative statements partly through an understanding of conceptual metonymy.

CONCLUSION

Metonymy is a widely used figure of thought whereby we take one well-understood or easily perceived aspect of something to represent or stand for the thing as a whole. Although metonymy has traditionally been viewed as a special rhetorical device in poetry and literature, it is a ubiquitous part of how we think of people, places, events, and things. Our conceptual ability to use one well-understood aspect of some domain to stand for the domain as a whole, or to use the mention of a whole domain to refer to one salient subpart, motivates our speaking so frequently in metonymic terms. Listeners are readily able to understand conventional and novel metonymic expressions precisely because the inferences needed to interpret such language are a common mental operation in our everyday conceptual system.

Much of the work in cognitive psychology on the inferences drawn during text understanding illustrate the prominence of metonymic thought. Psychologists have not recognized that many inferences in discourse processing, as well as in everyday reasoning, reflect common patterns of figurative thought. Yet it is clear that our ability to think metonymically constrains what speakers/authors explicitly state and what they leave unstated. In a similar way, metonymy constrains how listeners/readers understand the communicative intentions underlying messages or texts. An interesting challenge for psychologists is to explore the ways that different textual inferences arise from metonymic thinking. At the same time, the constraints that metonymy places on the production and understanding of certain conventional expressions, tautological phrases, and indirect speech acts point to essential, motivated links between linguistic pragmatics and everyday cognition. Linguists, philosophers, and psychologists would do well to adhere to the cognitive wager by investigating these important connections between language and mind.

Chapter 8

Irony

The late comedian/actor Andy Kaufman used to perform a routine where he would challenge any woman from the audience to come up on stage and engage him in a wrestling match. Kaufman's challenge was that no woman could beat him in a wrestling match because of women's "inferiority" to men. On each occasion, one or more volunteers would come forth and wrestle Kaufman, often with tremendous intensity, as the two contestants tried to slam each other onto the mat.

What made this routine so interesting was that you did not really know whether Kaufman really believed in what he was saying or doing. A friend once commented to me as we watched Kaufman's performance on television's *Saturday Night Live* that Andy was *just pulling our chains*. We debated this point, wondering whether Kaufman was indeed serious about his "inferiority" claim or was, in a perverse manner, trying ironically to show the absurdity of using physical strength to try to demonstrate the inferiority of women.

Kaufman's act, if you consider it that, illustrates how we often wrestle with the question of irony in everyday life. We see Kaufman's act as at least potentially ironic because we conceptualize the wrestling match as somehow quite disparate from our concept of comedy. Irony is traditionally seen as a situation that contrasts what is expected with what occurs or as a statement that contradicts the actual attitude of the speaker. In his classic work titled *The Concept of Irony* (first published in the late 19th century), Kierkegaard (1965: 378) wrote *As philosophers claim that no true philosophy is possible without doubt, by the same token, one may claim that no authentic human life is possible without irony.* This chapter advances the claim that people speak and act ironically because they actually conceptualize many of their everyday experiences in terms of irony. The fact that we think ironically motivates our use and understanding of irony and sarcasm as well as the related tropes of hyperbole, understatement, and oxymoron.

Irony may be our most powerful weapon in everyday speech: a device for concealing our true intentions, for avoiding responsibility for what we say, or *for turning the world or oneself inside out* (Muecke, 1969: 13). Like ironic nonverbal acts, most verbal instances of irony have overtones of mockery. Consider these exchanges between the husband, George, and his wife, Martha, in Edward Albee's play *Who's Afraid of Virginia Woolf?* (Bollobas, 1981).

Martha: Why don't you want to kiss me?

George: Well dear, if I kissed you, I'd get all excited. . . . I'd get beside myself, and I'd take you, by force, right here on the living room rug, and then our little guests would walk in, and . . . well, just think what your father would say about that.

. . .

Martha: It's the most . . . life you've shown in a long time.

George: You bring out the best in me, baby.

. . .

Martha: . . . You have a poetic nature, George . . . a Dylan Thomas-y quality that gets me right where I live.

These statements mock the addressee by expressing the opposite of what is meant (e.g., "Martha brings out the worst in George," "Kissing Martha would not get George excited," and "George does not have a poetic nature."). The ancient Greeks were masters of irony, often using mockery to achieve important philosophical ends. Socrates pretended to be ignorant, as in *Come now, my dear Euthyphro, inform me, that I may be wise,* and under the pretense of seeking to learn, he taught others. He ironically asserted that he was *never anyone's teacher. . . . I ask questions, and whoever wishes may answer and hear what I say.* Yet as Socrates ultimately discovered, irony can indeed be costly. Found guilty of the crime of *investigating the things between heaven and earth* and *making the weaker arguments stronger* and encouraging others to do likewise, Socrates chose death for his own punishment.

One of the most famous examples of irony comes from Jonathan Swift, who in *A Modest Proposal* (1729) contended that the English Protestant landlords in Ireland should restore the country to economic health by buying and eating the babies of the destitute unemployed Catholics.

> I have been assured by a very knowing American of my acquaintance in London, that a young healthy child well nursed is at a year old a most delicious, nourishing, and wholesome food, whether stewed, roasted, baked, or boiled, and I make no doubt that it will serve in a fricassee, or a ragout.

Swift uses *A Modest Proposal* to chastise the complacency of wealthy citizens by making an absurd suggestion with apparent sincerity. Despite Swift's ironic intentions, he was widely criticized for his unthinkable idea. Even today, one school system in New York State failed to appreciate the irony in *A Modest Proposal* and banned it for classroom use on the ground that it was "in bad taste."

Even brief ironic remarks can cause public turmoil. When the Beatles were at the peak of their popularity in 1964, John Lennon made the statement *The Beatles are more popular than Jesus Christ*. Lennon meant his comment not as a boast but to convey something like "Isn't this attention somewhat ridiculous? We really aren't in the same class as Jesus at all, but people [including the press to whom Lennon made his statement] are acting as if we were" (R. Lakoff, 1990). Lennon's remark was taken as intended without a great deal of attention in England. Yet there was tremendous consternation in the United States as civic and religious leaders condemned Lennon for his apparent belief that the Beatles were more important than the spiritual leader of Christianity. Radio stations stopped playing Beatles music, there were public burnings of Beatles records, and widespread protests greeted the Beatles when they toured the United States in 1965.

Another frequently misinterpreted case of irony came from the songwriter and performer Randy Newman, who recorded a song in the late 1970s called "Short People" (Fish, 1983). The song began by stating *Short people got no reason to live, short people got no reason, short people got no reason to live* and went on to detail the inadequacies of short people, including their small voices, beady little eyes, and the inconvenience of having to pick them up simply in order to say hello. Soon after its release, various groups organized to lobby against the song, even though Newman repeatedly stated that it was not his intention to ridicule short people but rather to comment on a subject of prejudice so absurd that it might expose the absurdity of all prejudice, whether against women, Jews, blacks, homosexuals, or whomever. Newman claimed that he was simply being ironic. After all, Newman himself, as he pointed out, was a short individual.

Notable instances of irony gone awry highlight the risks in using irony to mock or disparage particular audiences and their beliefs (many women criticized Kaufman for his wrestling matches even though they acknowledged the possibility of irony in what he intended). Many of us as ordinary speakers have been taken to task for ironic or sarcastic remarks. Although irony can easily be understood in most conversational contexts (Gibbs, 1986c, 1986d), understanding verbal irony requires that speakers and listeners share certain sensibilities about the subject being referred to. Irony can be recognized as a playful gambit, as opposed to a lie or an absurd statement, only when participants are sure they share the same beliefs and knowledge. If someone intends *John's a real Einstein* to mean "John's stupid," then both speaker and addressee must already share a low opinion of John's intelligence. Irony both makes use of presumptive homogeneity and reinforces it. Understanding irony communicates the attitude "You and I understand each other" (R. Lakoff, 1990).

Verbal irony is recognized by literary scholars as a technique of using incongruity to suggest a distinction between reality and expectation – saying one thing and meaning another – with the audience aware of both. But many kinds of irony have been identified (Booth, 1974; Muecke, 1969) – tragic irony, comic irony, rhetorical irony, practical irony, dramatic irony, double irony, situational irony, verbal irony, philosophical irony, self-irony, the irony of fate, and so on. At the very least, it is useful to distinguish between verbal irony and irony that arises from situations. Verbal irony implies that someone consciously and intentionally employs a technique. Situational irony reveals worldly events that are ironic by nature. Both verbal and situational irony involve a confrontation or juxtaposition of incompatibles, but in verbal irony an individual presents or evokes such a confrontation by his or her utterance(s), whereas situational irony is something that just happens to be noticed as ironic. An example of situational irony would be a pickpocket's having his own pocket picked while busy picking other people's pockets. When we report the irony of Oedipus's unknowingly pledging his own destruction, we cannot say *Oedipus is being ironic when he pledges his own destruction* but only *It is ironic that Oedipus . . .* By the same token, in reporting the intentional irony of Socrates, we cannot say *It is ironic that Socrates would insist on his ignorance* but only *Socrates is being ironic when he insists on his ignorance.* Most generally, one can intend to say something ironic (verbal irony), but one cannot intend to do something ironic (situational irony). I cannot say that I will perform three ironic acts today (situational irony), because when I say that some act is ironic, I am asserting that it is somehow unexpected or inconsistent from my point of view, and I cannot claim this with respect to my own intentions. Yet I can say of my past actions that it was ironic that I did such-and-such, or I could say of some hypothetical action that were I to do such-and-such, it would be ironic (Booth, 1974). Perhaps Kaufman's wrestling matches were intended to be seen by audiences in just this way.

Dramatic irony is the theatrical device of having a speaker utter words that have a meaning intelligible to the audience but of which the speaker is unaware. This kind of irony is quite complex, containing elements of both verbal and situational irony. There is an ironist (the author) being intentionally ironic by presenting ironic events. For instance, Oedipus, in Sophocles' *Oedipus Tyrannus,* at one point calls down curses upon the slayer of Laius, not knowing that they will fall upon his own head. Oedipus's statement is unintentionally ironic, a situation that the audience immediately recognizes but one that Sophocles specifically intends the audience to understand. The drama in this situation at times becomes almost unbearable for the audience as it anguishes over Oedipus's continued ignorance. Most generally, dramatic irony assumes that (a) the audience knows more than the protagonist, (b) the character reacts in a way contrary to that which is appropriate or wise, (c) characters or situations are contrasted for such ironic effects as parody, satire, or tragedy, and (d) there is a marked contrast between what the character understands about his or her acts and what the play demonstrates about them. This kind of irony, where the false images characters have formed of themselves clash with the meanings the audience forms, is common in novels and plays.

Early Greek comedies are also the source for understanding the concept of irony. The word *irony* comes from the Greek term *eironia,* which describes the main characteristic of of the stock characters (the "ironical man") in these plays. These comedies present the conflict between two characters, one being the "imposter," the other, the "ironical man." The imposter is the pompous fool who pretends to be more than he actually is. His antagonist is the shrewd dissembler who poses as less than he is. The conflict ends, of course, when the ironical man defeats the imposter. Our appreciation of the comedy and the irony in these situations comes from our knowledge of which character is the imposter and which the ironical man and how the conflict will undoubtedly conclude. Irony begins, then, in a conflict marked by the perception of distance between pretense and reality (Gerrig, 1993). We conceptualize Oedipus's situation as ironic because of the discrepancy between reality and Oedipus's own beliefs about his situation.

Irony

Verbal and situational irony, although mostly distinct, are related in one important way, in that speakers' intentional use of verbal irony reflects their conceptualizations of situations as ironic. When someone says *What lovely weather* in the midst of a rainstorm, this statement reflects the speaker's conceptualization of the incongruity between certain expectations that the day would be nice and the reality of rain. We judge events as ironic because of an awareness of the incongruity between expectation and reality, even though, in some cases, other participants in the situation appear to be blind to what is really happening. This awareness suggests that irony is not merely a matter of rhetoric or of language but is a fundamental figure in the poetics of mind. We conceptualize events, experiences, and ourselves as ironic, and our language often reflects this figurative mode of thinking.

There are famous examples from history and mythology in which our recognition of situational irony demonstrates an ironical mode of thought. In ancient Greece, Clisthenes introduced the punishment of ostracism, which banished offenders from their native land. Shortly afterwards, Clisthenes was ostracized. In the Bible, Haman is hanged on the same gallows he ordered built to hang Mordecai. The man who invented the guillotine was executed by it. The man who built the Bastille was imprisoned in it, and the bishop who invented the iron cage, a torture chamber so small that the victim could neither stand nor lie in it comfortably, was the first person confined in it.

Literature contains wonderful examples of situations that scream out as ironic. Stephen Crane's *The Red Badge of Courage* is full of ironies. Henry Fleming's wound is inflicted by a soldier in his own army, not by the enemy, when Henry is fleeing, not charging. But Fleming's wound is subsequently interpreted as a sign of heroism instead of cowardice.

Maupassant's most famous story, "The Necklace," is about two people who slave for 15 years to replace a necklace they borrowed and then lost, only to find that the original necklace was worthless. The columnist in West's *Miss Lonelyhearts* originally took the job of newspaper columnist to the lovelorn out of a cynical desire for professional advancement. However, the pathetic letters he receives so affect him that he decides he is Christ and becomes obsessively involved in the lives of the people who write him seeking advice. In the end, trying to perform a miracle, he rushes toward the cripple whose wife he has earlier seduced and is accidentally shot to death.

In one form or another, almost all comedy contains irony. Charlie Chaplin was a wonderful ironist – a little flat-footed man, apparently at the mercy of people who sought control over him, but in the end the unaccountable victor over everyone. Irony provides a way of seeing as comic certain events that might otherwise be seen as tragic. In the movie *Dr. Strangelove*, the loyal officer, who has finally located the security code for recalling the ill-fated bomber, is unable to telephone Washington because he does not have enough coins and cannot persuade the telephone operator that this is an emergency. One episode of the television comedy "Cheers" has the leading character, Sam, a notorious lady's man, dating this young, energetic woman, Jenny, who appears to love outdoor life. Sam and Jenny's dates are full of strenuous outdoor activity like running and backpacking, events that are taking a toll on the somewhat older Sam. Eventually Sam decides that he simply has to tell Jenny that he just can't keep up with her and that maybe they should break off the relationship. But when he confronts her, Sam tells Jenny, in an effort to save face, that Jenny is the one slowing him down and that he really wants to be with someone even more active. Jenny is relieved to hear this, because what she really wanted was a relationship with a man who liked to drink Champagne while sitting in a hot tub, the kind of thing that Sam, unbeknownst to her, wanted to do in the first place. As one overhearer, Frasier Crane, comments to a disconsolate Sam after witnessing his farewell chat with Jenny, I think that's what they call ironic!

Irony is not found only in special situations or events but is often evident in the way we think of and define various people, objects, and feelings. Many wonderful examples of irony are captured in *The Devil's Dictionary*, by Ambrose Bierce (first published in Bierce's newspaper columns from 1881 to 1906; collected in 1958). Consider the following examples of definitions given to various common words:

Abstainer: A weak person who yields to the temptation of denying himself a pleasure.

Beauty: The power by which a woman charms a lover and terrifies a husband.

Education: That which discloses to the wise and disguises from the foolish their lack of understanding.

Idiot: A member of a large and powerful tribe whose influence in human affairs has always been dominant and controlling.

Intimacy: A relation into which fools are providentially drawn to their mutual destruction.

Lawyer: One skilled in circumvention of the law.

Self-Esteem: An erroneous self-appraisement.

These irreverent, bitter, and clever definitions reveal an ironic understanding of common people and experiences where it is ironic to think of someone who abstains as yielding to temptation, and where it is ironic to view education as hiding from people what they don't know. We appreciate the cynical humor in these definitions because we share with Bierce an understanding of life's many ironies.

Self-reflection often leads individuals to adopt an ironic stance or ironic detachment regarding their everyday lives. Such anxious self-scrutiny not only serves to regulate the information communicated to others, it also establishes an ironic distance from the routine daily living. Mocking our plight in life, taking a cynical attitude toward many of the meaningless social routines we find ourselves engaged in, makes us less vulnerable to the pressures of such situations. By demystifying life, irony helps to convey to others the impression that we have somehow risen above its absurdity even as we continue to do what is expected of us in our jobs and personal lives. This ironic posture is seen by many as a fundamental style of everyday discourse.

Many popular forms of art offer parodies of familiar roles

and themes, inviting the audience to consider itself superior to its surroundings. Television programs in the 1970s and 1980s like *Soap, Moonlighting,* and *Mary Hartman, Mary Hartman* assured viewers of their own sophistication by mocking the conventions of soap operas and dramatic series. *Moonlighting* did this to an extreme when the actors came out of character to address the audience directly about the absurdity of the characters' actions. Novelists and playwrights call attention to the artificiality of their own creations and discourage readers from identifying with the characters. By means of irony and eclecticism, writers withdraw from their subjects but at the same time become so conscious of these distancing techniques that they find it more and more difficult to write about anything except the difficulty of writing. Writing about writing then becomes in itself an object of self-parody, as seen in the fiction of John Barth, Donald Barthelme, and Italo Calvino. Many social critics condemn these kinds of ironic detachment in the belief that such detachment cripples the will to change social conditions (Lasch, 1978). Yet irony is not simply a rhetorical choice we make but a natural mode of thinking about the world and our experience.

Many nonlinguistic acts also convey individuals' ironic understanding of situations. A perfect analogue to heavy sarcasm in conversation exists in *ironic applause.* The clapping is loud, but the beat is slow and measured. Another nonverbal gesture in the vocabulary of many American speakers is the ironic use of "airquotes." Airquotes are when the speaker's hands go up and a pair of fingers mark the invisible quotation marks around what is spoken. For instance, a co-worker may ironically say to friend that he's got to get home to (insert airquotes here) *the wife and kids* or to *the little woman,* as if to say he doesn't really view his wife in such a traditional manner. A political activist might refer to Ronald Reagan's use of the term (insert airquotes here) *freedom fighters* as a label for the Nicaraguan Contra forces. Or a young businesswoman might tell a friend that she is (insert airquotes here) a *yuppie woman* so the friend won't think she really enjoys her 12-hour days at work.

Even clothing fashions quote styles from previous periods

in an ironic manner. College students often wear outfits that mock some segment of society. During the 1960s and 1970s college students often wore military clothing (e.g., fatigues, army jackets and hats) as an ironic comment on the U.S. military involvement in the Vietnam War. College fashions today include conservative baggy pants and jackets (1930s) as well as tie-dyed shirts, peasant dresses, fishnet stockings, and hot pants straight from Carnaby Street (1960s). Adoption of these earlier styles is intended to be playful and an ironic comment on the fashions of previous generations. Popular films like *Bill and Ted's Bogus Journey* mock the high seriousness of films like Ingmar Bergman's *The Seventh Seal*. Adopting these ironic styles in clothing, film, and art provides a way for young people to define their own identity within the complex culture at large. The message young people convey with their Karen Carpenter theme parties and lava lamp parties that have become a college fad in Los Angeles is *Hey, I'm cool, you're cool, and we won't endanger our coolness by ever admitting to a genuine emotion or serious ambition. We won't try to come up with an alternative to the trashy culture we see around us; we'll simply make fun of it by showing we can be trashy, too.* Like people's use of airquotes, adopting certain ironic fashions does not necessarily remove people from responsibility for what they say or do. Instead, the ironic use of clothing, music, or film might better be viewed as a way of adjusting to complex circumstances in life.

Descriptions of ironic situations in everyday life are endless, yet each one reflects a pervasive, fundamental ability of people to conceptualize experience as ironic. Irony helps us cope with the inchoate in our everyday lives. We inescapably turn to figurative means when faced with the madness of our everyday existence. For this reason, irony has historically been referred to as a figure of thought (Quintilian, 1953; written in the first century B.C.), a great principle of human affairs (Vico, 1744/1952), the highest stage in the evolution of consciousness (ibid.), the endpoint of culture, and the reflective mode in which modern science and history must be written (H. White, 1973, 1978). Irony is now especially prevalent in the "play of tropes" in contemporary culture (Fernandez, 1986).

We live in a postmodern period, dubbed by some theorists the age of irony, where many of our most accepted truths have been tossed out in favor of a pluralistic world that acknowledges no universal truths (W. Anderson, 1990). This period is often referred to as the *age of irony* precisely because irony becomes one of the ways in which we think about our lives and the world we live in. Irony, under this guise, is a reasonable way for us to conceive of the disparities in our experience. Both individuals and communities adopt ironic stances or poses that reflect their ironic understanding of world events.

Irony helps define contemporary cultural identity. Consider one analysis of the irony in an international kayak festival and race held each year in the seaside mountains of Spain (Fernandez, 1986). A parade held in the nearby town just before the start of the kayaking competition is intended to provide a historical overview of the local province. Various local groups are left to themselves to decide what images (by means of floats, music, dancers, costumes) they wish to convey to the tens of thousands of onlookers who attend the event each year. The first entry in this historical review one year was a float representing the Stone Age ancestors of the Asturians (the local province) by 15 or 20 men dressed in caveman outfits and carrying plastic billy clubs as well as some rough-hewn hand axes. A large papier-mâché hand ax covered with tinfoil towered over the float. The men staged a mock battle, sometimes taunting the bystanders along the parade route. Note the emphasis on mock weaponry in this float in playful relation to the real instruments of violence in traditional military parades. One can't help noticing the contrast between the calculatedly brutish cavemen with their mock weapons and the serious image of paleolithic Asturian forebears.

One of the local canoe clubs followed the Stone Age float with its members dressed in Roman togas, led by one monarchical figure wearing a tin crown. At various points along the parade route, this group knelt down before the monarch as he delivered a peroration praising Asturia, its people, and its climate while the famous Asturian rain poured down in ironic contrast upon them. Following the canoe club came a group dressed as Arabs, and immediately after them was a group of men dressed as capitalists in black suits and stove-pipe hats, scattering play money to the crowd. The Arabs harassed the Romans with large clubs and were eventually engulfed by the capitalists while the play money floated down upon them all.

The festivities in this annual parade stand in playful counterstatement to the succession of military regimes that ruled Spain beginning in the mid 19th century. These authoritarian regimes sought to consolidate and manifest their power by frequent displays of the instruments of violence. The motivation for the ironic images in the parade stem from the people's resistance to the domination of the military in their lives, and their ironic statements help reestablish local claims to their own cultural identity. Yet the irony witnessed in the parade is not strictly political in the sense of presenting an alternative ideology to the sincerity of military parades in Spanish history. Rather the parade's message lies in an ironic detachment from the national culture, a reflexive irony that allows individuals and cultures to affirm and celebrate their own identity and humanity. The parade also contextualizes, and to some degree undermines, the seriousness of the ensuing international kayak competition. Not all of the festival participants or bystanders interpret the parade's images before them in ironic terms. But many elements in the parade suggest how people's recognition of the inchoateness of the human condition requires that we suspend belief in ourselves and celebrate incongruities. This kind of ironic leveling is at the core of how people conceive of their lives in a complex world (Fernandez, 1986).

IRONY AND SOCIAL SITUATIONS

The ironic nature of everyday thought allows us to say one thing but mean something different. Speakers use irony to fulfill communicative goals – to be witty, to put someone at ease, to save face more effectively than does the use of literal statement (Kreuz, Long, & Church, 1991). Irony serves an important social function in helping people maintain social relationships between family members, friends, and co-workers. Two prominent kinds of irony that serve these social functions are jocularity and sarcasm. Jocular statements are playful remarks used to chide others in a jesting manner. Sarcastic language refers to irony that is especially bitter and caustic. Jocular and sarcastic social acts are intertwined in contextualizing solidarity and authority relationships (Sechman & Couch, 1989). Jocularity is most often associated with solidarity moves that invite or affirm social relationships. Sarcasm is associated with either solidarity or authority relationships between speakers and addressees.

Scholars rarely distinguish between jocularity and sarcasm in theories of ironic discourse. Failure to distinguish between these two social acts probably stems from the fact that the forms are frequently combined to produce composite acts. Humorous acts often elicit solidarity among some participants and distress and distance among others. For example, if some member of one group in the presence of outsiders makes a bitter remark, such as *That's beyond the comprehension of us pinheads*, it may evoke amusement and affiliation among the group members but distance among the outsiders. Examples like this show how the same utterance can be jocular to some listeners and sarcastic to others.

One study of the conversations between co-workers and their bosses at a factory illustrates how jocularity and sarcasm can define social relationships (ibid.). A typical example of jocularity contextualized by a solidarity statement is the following brief exchange between male and female factory workers who were also close friends. The woman was walking past the man just as he dropped a piece of freshly cut metal. As their eyes met, this exchange occurred:

Man: This fucker is hot.

Woman: Piss on it.

Both workers laughed after the woman's comment. Although she did not seriously intend her co-worker to do what she said, something that the man clearly understood, her jocular remark affirmed an existing camaraderie.

Sarcastic comments among the factory workers ranged from mild put-downs to clearly hostile attacks. Sarcasm directed at other workers was invariably mild, with victims often acknowledging such comments by making their own jocular comments in return. For instance, one worker commented *Nice job, Joe* after another had dropped a tool, upon which the second worker responded *I couldn't have done it without your bumping my arm.*

Bitter sarcasm was rarely observed between people with a solidarity relationship. The few instances of hostile sarcasm between workers commented on violations of presumed relationships. The following exchange between two workers took place after one person had reported the other for some infraction (ibid.; p. 337).

A: Doesn't it make you feel good when you report others off?
   (*Delivered with a biting tone of voice while glaring at B. B made eye contact and again quickly broke it*)

B: Fuck you. I'm here to work.
   (*Who then looked down at his machine and began tinkering with it*)

A: (Continued to glare at worker B)
   No! Fuck you! You fun loving son of a bitch!
   (*The* Fuck you *was delivered as a challenge, the* fun loving *was sarcastic*)

As a result of this incident, Worker B was excluded from the solidarity network that existed among most workers at the factory.

Self-directed sarcasm was common among the workers, such as when one person uttered to himself *Nice job, Greg* after failing to adjust a machine properly. This self-directed sarcasm informed overhearers that the speaker recognized his or her error, much the way people utter *Whoops* and *Uh-oh* after committing some social gaffe (Goffman, 1976).

Foremen in the factory, who had positions of authority, often directed sarcastic comments to workers when their performance was unsatisfactory. These sarcastic remarks affirmed the presumption of an asymmetry in the relationship. Workers rarely used sarcasm with their bosses. One notable exception occurred when a long-time employee and a newly appointed foreman saw each other on a special Saturday morning shift. The foreman wore kneepads such as those used in laying linoleum. The worker and foreman acknowledged each other, and the following occurred (Sechman & Couch, 1989: 339).

Worker: Is Johnson (*the plant manager*) in the plant today?

Foreman: No. Why? (*Puzzled expression*)

Worker: I noticed you had your knee pads on. I thought maybe you were there dirtying your knees for him. (*The implication was that the foreman was currying favor with the manager*)

Foreman: (*While laughing and shaking his head*) Fuck you, you little son of a bitch! You ain't working any more goddamn Saturdays.

The foreman and worker's past relationship as co-workers suggest that this worker-initiated transaction implicitly called for an egalitarian relationship. When asked by another fellow why he talked to the boss in that manner, the worker responded *He's just Bruce*, again affirming the idea that they were equals as friends and not just superordinate and subordinate.

Sarcasm and jocularity transactions like these witnessed in a work environment appear inconsequential, but such talk has an important function in the way social relations are constructed, maintained, and modified. They are *nonserious acts that have serious consequences* (ibid., p. 342).

One area where irony profoundly affects social relationships is family discourse. Family conversations exhibit social processes by which individuals assert independence from and solidarity with other family members. Family talk also reveals how conflict arises through divergent perspectives on what constitutes certain explanations of behavior.

Consider the following conversation taken from the film

series *An American Family*. This cinema vérité–style 12-hour program, first broadcast in 1973 on public television, followed the ordinary events in the lives of individuals from one family living in southern California. A camera was always present in the house and followed family members outside the home (e.g., at school, at work, on vacation). The drama that unfolded in the series clearly suggested that the family members were acting as if the camera wasn't there. Irony and sarcasm fill many parts of the conversations among family members, again showing aspects of individuals' attempts to establish individuality and solidarity. More interesting, though, is the way irony marks how individuals conceptualize their situations as ironic. Both of these qualities are seen in one scene where the father (Bill) and mother (Pat) summon their teenage son (Grant) over to discuss his current summer activities. The episode begins with the parents sitting by their backyard swimming pool as the son approaches.

(1) *Bill*:   Come over here a little closer . . . I think

(2) *Grant*:   Well, I'd rather stay out of this

(3) *Bill*:   You . . . want to stay out of swinging distance

(4) *Grant*:   Yeah, I don't want to hurt you

(5) *Bill*:   Well . . . I mean. . . . I was talking with your mother, ya know, and I told her that you weren't interested in doing any more work, ya see . . . and I don't blame you . . . I think that's a very honest reaction, there's nothing wrong with . . . with that kind of feeling, umm . . . it's a natural thing to do not wanting to work.

(6) *Grant*:   No, ah . . . it's not that I don't want to work, it's just ah. . .

(7) *Pat*:   What kind of work did you have in mind Grant? Watching the television, and listening to records

(8) *Grant*:   I don't need your help mom

(9) *Pat*:   Playing the guitar, driving the car

(10) *Grant*:   Ah . . .

(11) *Pat*: Eating, sleeping

(12) *Bill*: No, ah, listen Grant, you are a very good boy, we're very proud of you

(13) *Grant*: Yeah, I know you are

(14) *Bill*: No, we are . . . you don't give us any trouble ya know

(15) *Grant*: Well, you sure are giving me a hell of a lot

(16) *Bill*: Well that's my job I think . . . if, ah, I don't why nobody else will and that's what I'm here for you . . . is to kind of see that you get off to a good start . . . lucky you may be with the deal, that's my job is to see that you get to see how life's going to be

(17) *Grant*: Yeah

(18) *Bill*: And, ah, if I don't then nobody else will . . . a lot of kids go around don't ever have that privilege of having a mean old man

(19) *Grant*: Yeah, sure is a privilege too

This conversation is not atypical of how many American families talk, particularly when parents converse with their teenage children. These participants employ irony/sarcasm to great effect not only to criticize but also to assert their own understanding of situations as ironic. For example, Grant says in (4) that he doesn't want to hurt his father, and he means this literally but intends in a jocular way to convey the pretense that he *could* hurt his father should they get into a physical fight. This utterance fulfills the need for father and son to lighten what must be mutually recognized as a potentially uncomfortable situation of the parents criticizing Grant for his unwillingness to work.

Later, in (7), (9), and (11), Pat sarcastically echoes Grant's putative belief that watching television, listening to records, playing the guitar, and so on constitute meaningful work activities. Grant is clearly disturbed by his mother's accusation and in (8) tells her to stop. Immediately after this, Bill steps in and attempts to get the conversation back on a less hostile track by asserting in (12) that both he and Pat are proud of Grant, a point not entirely obvious, given Pat's previous outburst. When Grant acknowledges his father's attempt to defuse the situation by agreeing with him in (13), Bill mistakenly understands Grant's comment as sarcasm and tries to set the record straight about this in (14) by reaffirming his opinion that Grant is a very good boy. Grant then emphatically points out in (15) the irony in his parents' hassling him about not working while at the same time telling him, as Bill does, that he never gives them any trouble. Later, in (18), Bill goes on to state, in a kind of parody of what his son might say, that most kids don't even have the *privilege of having a mean old man* like him to help them *see how life's going to be.* Finally, Grant sarcastically echoes his father when he says in (19) *Yeah, sure is a privilege too.*

The dialogue in this scene from *An American Family* illustrates just how facile people can be with irony and sarcasm. These speakers use irony to such a large extent because they conceptualize each others' behavior in terms of irony. Pat sees it as ironic that Grant *thinks* he wants to work while all he apparently does is play the guitar, watch tv, drive the car, and so on. The way she communicates, this imposes distance between herself and Grant and reveals hostility on her part toward Grant, a point Pat later acknowledges in the conversation. Pat's conceptualization of Grant's professed beliefs as ironic, given his behavior, leads her to speak of Grant in an ironic/sarcastic manner. Grant also perceives the irony in his parents' saying that they think he's a good boy, since they are expressing such hostility toward him. This sets the stage for Grant's later sarcastic comment *Sure is a privilege too.*

This dialogue illustrates how people's ironic conceptualization of each other and their social interactions affects the way they talk to one another. As this dialogue demonstrates, a speaker's direct quotation of another person allows him or her to imitate what are (or might be) another person's words rather than merely report them (cf. Clark & Gerrig, 1990; Haiman, 1989; Wierzbicka, 1974). A folk recognition of this mimicking aspect of direct quotation to achieve sarcastic effects is seen in the way many American teenage and college

age students talk using the word *like*, as in *So John says to me,
like "When are you going to go with me sometime?"* The word *like*
introduces a *mimetic performance* (Haiman, 1989): The speaker
announces that he or she is going to imitate the speech or state
of mind of the person being quoted, often to achieve a sarcastic effect.

Even the imitation of just a few words can have a sarcastic
effect. Consider this brief exchange.

A: Those friends of mine didn't know that.

B: One of these days, you are going to have to face up to the
fact that "those friends of yours" know nothing about everything. (Haiman, 1989: 149, quoting Deighton, *Funeral in
Berlin*).

The failure to substitute an anaphor (i.e., *they*) for the full noun
phrase *those friends of yours* conveys the speaker's sarcastic
disparagement of *those friends*.

The example considered above focuses on repetition or quotation of other speakers' actual words for sarcastic effect. Some
experimental work indicates that speakers will often quote
another person directly, especially in situations where the
quoted individual has made some sort of exaggerated statement or claim (M. D. Johnson, Gibbs, & Pfaff, 1992).

Sarcasm can also be conveyed in conversation by mocking
the kind of speech act a speaker utters. Consider these min-
dialogues.

A: Is she still mad at me?
B: Do birds fly? (*mocks the act of interrogation*)

A: I have a national reputation.
B: And I'm the Queen of England. (*mocks a claim*)

A: I promise this won't hurt.
B: And the check is in the mail. (*mocks a promise*).

Each sarcastic retort takes issue with the kind of speech act
uttered by the first speaker. The kind of quotation here where
Speaker B echoes some well-known utterance is particularly

suited to express the speaker's alienation from a message, because the echo or quote essentially acts out another person's words or actions.

Just as people speak ironically in conversation with specific addressees in mind, they may also make specific ironic comments in written discourse that are intended to injure particular individuals or these individuals' ideas. Academic writing, although generally seen as containing few instances of irony and humor, actually contains many examples where writers express certain beliefs by ironically disparaging some other writer(s). Most scholars comment on the tone, or tones, of voice associated with verbal irony (e.g., nasalization). Yet any written text can be read with a whole range of possible tones suggesting irony. Devices that signal the possibility of irony in print and academic writing involve the rich use of typographical indices, such as quotation marks, footnotes, italics, and special titles and headings, and heavy-handed disclaimers like [sic] and [?!] (Myers, 1990). The setting of words in "scare quotes," for example, is a common device to indicate that the quoting writer does not accept the words. One debate on irony, somewhat ironically, gives a good example of this. Sperber (1984: 134) quotes ironically some key terms from Clark and Gerrig (1984) when he asks the following rhetorical question: *If one says* What lovely weather! *when the weather is miserable, is it usually the case that the speaker is making fun of some "injudicious person" and of some "uncomprehending audience"?* Sperber clearly intends readers to recognize his belief that the terms *injudicious person* and *uncomprehending audience* carry little theoretical weight.

None of these devices are exclusive clues to irony, but all can be used to help signal a writer's ironic intentions. A related way for writers to convey their ironic intentions is through quotation. The ironic writer intends readers to recognize an intention in the use of these quoted words different from the one meant originally. This strategy is particularly effective in the rhetorical situation of academic controversies, because it relies on readers' assumptions about the intentions of writers and the appropriate forms of texts (Myers, 1990).

One academic debate between several linguists and computer scientists illustrates the use of quotation in conveying irony (ibid.). This debate started with Dresher and Hornstein's (1976) challenge to the claims of artificial intelligence (AI) in the 1970s to offer a model of language that was a reasonable alternative to the traditional view of generative grammar as suggested by linguistic theory. Schank and Wilensky (1977) responded to Dresher and Hornstein by defending their own model of natural language processing based on conceptual dependency (or CD, a system of semantic primitives) and by reasserting their support for a computational approach to linguistic theory. Readers generally expect responses in academic debates to refute specific claims made in the original attack, but look at how Schank and Wilensky responded to one of Dresher and Hornstein's criticisms.

> A large part of the remainder of the critique addresses the concern that "there is no principled way to expand any CD diagram into a more complex CD diagram. Each step requires new information to be brought in" (p. 369). Interestingly enough, this is precisely the point that we are trying to make. (p. 143)

Instead of arguing with the original criticism, Schank and Wilensky took Dresher and Hornstein's assertion as support for their own position. Certainly this is not what Dresher and Hornstein intended originally when they criticized Schank and Wilensky for not providing a principled way to expand CD diagrams. Somewhat ironically, Dresher and Hornstein's own words have been used against them to make a point that would not have been as forceful had Schank and Wilensky protested directly about Dresher and Hornstein's misunderstanding.

Other ironic remarks in academic debates simply quote previous work without comment, and the irony results from juxtaposition of the quoted passage with some other passage in the text. For instance, in a footnote Dresher and Hornstein (1976) quoted without comment something from Winograd (1974), one of the people whose work they were attacking, in their discussion of practical issues in building computational models of natural language understanding. Below is the relevant text of the Dresher and Hornstein article, followed by their quotation from Winograd.

Thus, one could start with fairly simple components (a small number of syntactic components, a small lexicon, etc.) which could be improved indefinitely (by adding more syntactic patterns, more lexical items) according to practical considerations such as time, money and computer space (p. 330)

If someone is trying to build the best robot which can be completed by the next year, he will avoid any really hard problems that come up, rather than accepting them as a challenge to look at a new area. There will be pressure from the organization of the projects and funding agencies to get results at the expense of avoiding hard problems. (Winograd, 1974: 93)

By quoting him directly, Dresher and Hornstein use Winograd's own words to support their contention about the implausibility of AI models given the practical limitations faced by computer scientists. Again, simply quoting someone else's words allows writers to convey ironic intentions about the quoted work and author(s). None of these examples of ironic quotation simply conveys the opposite of the quoted writer's literal statement. How people come to process these quoted statement as ironic must be complex. Readers do not simply establish ironic intentions by recognizing certain textual features that conventionally mark irony. Instead, readers enter texts uncertain and use several possible relations among the reader, the writer, and another writer to establish several intentions, some of which might be ironic. Readers look for intentions consistent with the new relations proposed among the reader, the ironic writer, and the victimized writer. We assume that the quoted writers believe their original assertions as they are quoted. Irony arises, however, because we assume that the statement was made with a different intention in the original text (Myers, 1990).

HOW IS IRONY UNDERSTOOD?

How do people arrive at the meaning of ironic statements? The variety of ways that irony appears in conversational and written discourse suggests that our quick ability to conceptualize and speak of many situations as ironic must in some way enable us to comprehend irony without great difficulty. As discussed in Chapter 3, however, the common view of irony states that people detect ironic meaning by assuming the opposite of an utterance's literal meaning after the literal meaning is seen as a violation of the Truthfulness maxims (Grice, 1975, 1978). Ironic statements are seen as deliberately intended by speakers and, unlike metaphor, do not invite further elaboration of their meaning once understood, because only the overt words in some local discourse have been violated (Booth, 1974).

According to the traditional view of irony, speakers often call attention to their sarcastic or ironic intentions by altering their tone or intonation when speaking. Consider a case where someone does something stupid and an observer comments *Clever* (Couthard, 1985). The context makes the remark ironic, but the speaker's articulation of the word *clever* makes the irony unmistakable. Of course, if the irony is missed and the initiator of the stupid act does not recognize its stupidity, the intelligence and keenness of the observer become questionable. But the sarcasm becomes even more pointed here through use of a tone indicating that the observer was truly impressed by the cleverness of the act.

To take another example, a cab driver who has not been tipped may feel hostile toward a passenger and may say *Thanks for the tip* with a soft, modulated intonation with no rises or falls. Such a tone of voice conveys calm, which, although it does not capture what the cab driver feels given that no tip was offered, achieves a sense of control and calm. In other circumstances, the act of irony calls for more forceful prosodic techniques which call the listener's attention to certain words and phrases by stressing them in one of many ways. This can be done by altering the pitch, length, or volume of the ironic phrase, thereby signaling certain qualifications to the words' usual meanings.

This traditional view attempts to limit how irony works so that the undermining of overt or literal meaning will have a fixed and specifiable shape, with special intonation cues providing the key for listeners to what speakers really mean. As discussed at some length in Chapter 3, the experimental evidence in psycholinguistics does not support the traditional view, in that (a) listeners need not analyze the literal meaning of a statement before deriving its ironic interpretation, and (b) people can understand irony quite easily even when there are no special intonation cues. Research has shown that readers take no longer to interpret ironic – or specifically, sarcastic – remarks, such as *He's a fine friend*, than they do to interpret the same sentences in literal contexts or to read nonsarcastic equivalent sentences, such as *He's a bad friend* (Gibbs, 1986c). Similar findings have been reported for understanding sarcastic indirect requests (e.g., *Why don't you take your time washing the dishes?*, meaning "Hurry up and wash the dishes") (Gibbs, 1986d). Thus, people do not normally go through some process of analyzing the context-free, literal meanings of ironic utterances before recognizing that such meanings violate Truthfulness maxims. People appear to quickly comprehend the irony in certain utterances from their understanding of irony in some situation (e.g., see that it is ironic to tell someone to take his or her time washing the dishes when it is commonly assumed that the dishes are to be washed promptly).

Various other attempts have been made to capture what goes on psychologically in understanding irony. One proposal, called the *echoic mention theory*, states that irony involves the distinction between use and mention rather than the distinction between literal and nonliteral meaning (Jorgensen, Miller, & Sperber, 1984; Sperber & Wilson, 1981). The sentence *Please be quiet*, for example, can be *used* to tell people to be quiet, but it is only *mentioned* in *The sign says "Please be quiet."* This distinction is useful because the truth value of the mentioned expression is irrelevant to the truth of the proposition it specifies. According to the echoic mention theory, there is no nonliteral proposition that hearers must substitute for the literal proposition. Rather the listener is *reminded* echoically of some familiar proposition (whose truth value is irrelevant) and of the speaker's attitude toward it. Consider this example: Charles says to Bob *You're a big help* when Bob has not assisted Charles in doing some task. The irony here comes from the fact that Charles has echoed some previously mentioned statement or belief, or perhaps some unspoken agreement between Charles and Bob. That is, Bob might earlier have offered to help Charles, or it might be Bob's job to do so. When Charles says *You're a big help* he is, in a sense, quoting this previous statement or verbalizing a shared belief that Bob is supposed to help Charles as a part of his job.

Various research demonstrates that people judge ironic utterances with explicit echoic mentions as being more ironic than statements that do not have such mentions (Gibbs, 1986c; Jorgensen et al., 1984). For instance, participants in one study read sarcastic remarks, such as *This sure is an exciting life* (meaning "This is very boring"). In one case the story context contained an explicit mention of some idea or belief that the subsequent sarcastic expression explicitly echoed. Other story contexts contained no such antecedent. Presented below is an example of these two types of story context.

Echoic Story

Gus just graduated from high school and he didn't know what to do with his life. One day he saw an ad about the Navy. It said that the Navy was not just a job, but an adventure. So Gus joined. Soon he was aboard a ship doing all sorts of boring things. One day as he was peeling potatoes, he said to his buddy,

This sure is an exciting life.

Nonechoic Story

Gus just graduated from high school and he didn't know what to do with his life. So Gus went out and joined the Navy. Soon he was aboard a ship doing all sorts of boring things. One day as he was peeling potatoes, he said to his buddy,

This sure is an exciting life.

People took less time to read these sarcastic statements in echoic contexts than in nonechoic ones. People also process sarcasm (an especially negative form of irony) that explicitly echoes an earlier stated utterance faster than they do sarcastic expressions based on less explicit or nonexistent echoes (Gibbs,

1986c). For example, in this study participants read stories like the following:

Normative (Negative) Context

Billy and Joe were long-time pals. But one time when Billy was away on a business trip, Joe slept with Billy's wife, Lynn. When Billy found out about it afterwards, he was upset. He confronted Joe and said to him,

You're a fine friend. (*Sarcastic target*)

You're a terrible friend. (*Nonsarcastic target*)

Nonnormative (Positive) Context

Billy and Joe were long-time pals. One time Billy was in desperate need of money. His car had broken down and he needed $300 to fix it. So he asked Joe for a loan. Joe said he could lend Billy the money. This made Billy quite happy and he said to Joe,

You're a terrible friend. (*Sarcastic target*)

You're a fine friend. (*Nonsarcastic target*)

Readers comprehend the sarcastic comments in the normative (negative) contexts more quickly than they do in the nonnormative contexts. These normative contexts are viewed as normative because of various social norms, including the adage *If you don't have anything good to say, then don't say anything at all.* Kreuz and Glucksberg (1989) extend the echoic mention theory to emphasize the reminding function of irony based on the shared attitudes and expectations of conversational participants. Most ironic utterances accomplish their communicative intent by reminding listeners of some antecedent event, but not all such reminders are echoic or refer to actual or implied utterances. For example, the utterance *Another gorgeous day!* made when it has been gray and raining for over two weeks need not echo anyone's utterance, thought, or opinion. It simply alludes to a generalized expectation or desire for good weather and in doing so expresses the speaker's disappointment at the actual weather. Swift's essay on the eating of small children also appears not to involve mention.

The echoic reminder theory explains why positive state-ments, such as *You're a fine friend*, are used sarcastically so much better than negative statements, such as *You're a terrible friend* (Gibbs, 1986c; Kreuz & Glucksberg, 1989). Positive state-ments do not require explicit antecedents, because these ex-pressions implicitly allude to societal norms and expectations that are invariably positive (e.g., if you don't have anything nice to say, then don't say anything). Negative statements, however, do not implicitly allude to these positive norms and require explicit antecedents if they are to be understood (Kreuz & Glucksberg, 1989). Echoic mention may well be a special case of reminders that allude to prior occurrences or states of affairs.

An alternative view of irony suggests that verbal irony in-volves pretense rather than echoic mention or reminding (Clark & Gerrig, 1984; Fowler, 1965). For example, a speaker who says in the context of a rainstorm *What lovely weather we're having* pretends to be an unseeing person, perhaps a weather forecaster exclaiming about the beautiful weather to an un-known audience. If pretense required only the appearance of asserting the opposite of what clearly is the case, then pre-tense theory would be a notational variant of the echoic men-tion theory (Clark & Gerrig, 1984). But pretense goes beyond this, because the speaker is pretending to be someone else (the unseeing person) and is also pretending to be talking to some person other than the listener. When listeners recognize this pretense, they should understand that the speaker is express-ing a derogatory attitude toward the idea expressed, the imagi-nary speaker, and the imaginary listener. These imaginary speakers and listeners may be recognizable individuals (like some specific weather forecaster) or people of recognizable type, such as inaccurate weather forecasters in general. Both Swift's essay *A Modest Proposal* and Newman's song, "Short People" can be treated as pretense in which the authors are pretending to be someone else speaking to an imaginary au-dience that might accept their ideas in all seriousness.

Although there is no experimental evidence to support the claims of the pretense theory of irony, both pretense theory and reminder theory suggest that the communicative purpose of irony is to call attention to some idea or attitude that both speaker and listener can derogate (Kreuz & Glucksberg, 1989; Williams, 1984). The special communicative purpose irony serves in discourse is the reason why listeners generally remember ironic statements better than they do literal ones (Gibbs, 1986c, 1986d; Kreuz et al., 1991). As Wilson and Sperber (1992) recently argued within the framework of relevance theory (see Chapter 5), irony communicates a wide range of contextual effects that are relatively weak. Consider this example. Several years ago there was a referendum in Great Britain on whether Britain should enter the Common Market. During the campaign, television and radio programs, newspapers, and magazines devoted a great deal of attention to the debate. At one point before the vote, the satirical magazine *Private Eye* appeared with a cover that showed a crowd of spectators at a village cricket match, sprawled on deckchairs, fast asleep and snoring. Beneath the photograph was the caption *The Common Market – The Great Debate.*

How did this caption communicate an ironic message? The photograph conveyed an impression of stupefied boredom on the part of the typical British citizen. Given the assumption that the Common Market debate resembled in some respects a village cricket match, to call the referendum issue a *Great Debate* is ridiculous, for the debate over Britain's entry into the Common Market may not have been all that important to most citizens. Beyond the clearly intended strong implicatures here about the real lack of interest in the debate, the ironic message in this magazine cover also weakly implicated a variety of contextual effects. Among these might be whatever assumptions readers create for themselves about the relationship between local cricket matches and the referendum issue, how the media's excessive attention to the debate was both ridiculous and boring, and so forth. It is communication of these vague impressions and attitudes that makes verbal irony so notable and such an effective way of expressing our complex conceptualizations of incongruous events.

Most instances of verbal irony are specifically intended to be understood as such by speakers. Yet many instances of conversation and literature convey irony that arises apart from anything specifically intended by speakers (a kind of dramatic irony). One scene in the movie *Married to the Mob* provides a good example of unintended verbal irony. An FBI agent is giving the heroine the third degree, and she exclaims *You're no different from the mob!* The FBI agent responds:

> Oh, there's a big difference, Mrs. De Marco. The mob is run by murdering thieving psychopathic killers. We work for the President of the United States.

It seems certain that the screenwriter intended these words ironically, and the audience's response suggests that the irony was appreciated, but the FBI agent did not mean what he said ironically or sarcastically.

One scene in *An American Family* has another example of unintended irony, where an utterance is understood as ironic despite the clear recognition that the comment was not intended by the speaker to be understood as such. This scene occurs fairly late in the series after Bill and Pat have separated because of, among many other things, Bill's infidelity. In this scene, Bill's teenage daughter, Delilah, visits him, and he begins the conversation by asking her about one of her brothers, Kevin.

(1) *Bill*: What's Kevin doing?

(2) *Delilah*: He studies a lot

(3) *Bill*: Is he

(4) *Delilah*: Yeah

(5) *Bill*: working pretty hard? . . . Got any girl friend? . . .

(6) *Delilah*: A lot of girls like him though

(7) *Bill*: Yeah, Kevin's got that irresistible charm. He wants to get back to Hong Kong

(8) *Delilah*: Takes after Dad

(9) *Bill*: Yeah, isn't that the truth

Delilah's comment in (8) that Kevin takes after his father in having irresistible charm is clearly a jocular remark, but what

is truly ironic is that Bill has been accused in a previous episode of having irresistible charm by his wife, Pat, leading to
his numerous affairs. Delilah seems unaware of this and
doesn't recognize the true irony in what she says in (8). But
Bill recognizes the ironic truthfulness in what Delilah says and
becomes noticeably embarrassed, and he then mumbles with
intended irony *Yeah, isn't that the truth*.

One experiment has investigated readers' processing of intended and unintended verbal irony (Gibbs & O'Brien, 1991).
Consider the following two situations:

John and Bill were taking a statistics class together.
Before the final exam, they decided to cooperate during the test.
So they worked out a system so they could secretly share
answers.
After the exam John and Bill were really pleased with themselves.
They thought they were pretty clever for beating the system.
Later that night, a friend happened to ask them if they ever
tried to cheat.
John and Bill looked at each other and laughed, then John said,
"I would never be involved in any cheating."

John and Bill were taking a statistics class together.
They studied hard together, but John was clearly better prepared
than Bill.
During the exam, Bill panicked and started to copy answers
from John.
John didn't see Bill do this and so didn't know he was actually
helping Bill.
John took the school's honor code very seriously.
Later that night, a friend happened to ask them if they ever
tried to cheat.
John and Bill looked at each other, then John said,
"I would never be involved in any cheating."

Both of these situations end with the identical statement, which
in each case is understood as verbal irony. The speaker in the
first story specifically intends his audience to understand what
is said as ironic, but the speaker in the second situation does
not intend his utterance to be understood ironically. In the
second story, only the addressees and overhearers see the

irony in what the speaker actually said. It is quite possible for people to understand a speaker's utterance as irony even though the speaker did not intend the utterance to be understood as irony.

Is it more difficult to understand unintended verbal irony than intended irony? Participants in this study read a series of stories like the ones above on a computer terminal. They read each story one line at a time, pushing a button on an accompanying keyboard to indicate that they had understood each sentence. The data of interest concerned the amount of time it took participants to read the last line of each story. The experiment was designed so that each participant saw only one story from each pair of stories (i.e., either the intentional or the unintentional story).

The results showed that people took much less time to read unintentionally ironic statements than to process intentionally ironic statements. No existing theory of irony provides a ready account for this difference. It appears that people find it easier to comprehend verbal ironies that spontaneously *create* ironic situations than it is to make sense of ironies that *remind* listeners of speakers' attitudes or beliefs. Of course, one could argue that participants in this study may not have understood the unintentionally ironic statements as being all that ironic. Yet these same participants rated the unintentionally ironic statements as being *more* ironic than were the intentionally ironic statements. So it appears that people did in fact see the final statements in the unintentional stories as being even more ironic than the intentionally ironic statements.

The data from this study clearly show that people can be sensitive to the presence of ironic situations and find it easier to understand statements that create those situations even when the irony is not intended to be communicated, or even recognized, by the speaker. In contrast, ironic statements that are specifically intended to remind listeners of some previous utterance, event, or expectation are more difficult to interpret than utterances that immediately and unintentionally create an ironic situation. Thus, although irony often reflects a speaker's communicative goal of identifying aspects of ironic situations (Littman & Mey, 1991), speakers may unintentionally create irony by what they say. These data most generally point to the necessity of including in theories of irony the fact that listeners/readers are able to monitor the distribution of what is known and not known by speakers and their audiences and between fictional characters in narratives (Gerrig, 1993).

In classical rhetoric, hyperbole and understatement are closely related to irony in that each misrepresents the truth. Hyperbole distorts the truth in that speakers assert more than is objectively warranted, as when Professor Smith says to Professor Jones *I have ten thousand papers to grade before noon*. Hyperbole should be contrasted with simple overstatement, by which a person unconsciously or unintentionally expresses a proposition that is stronger than the evidence warrants. The same proposition can be overstatement in one person's mouth and hyperbole in another's. A person who states *All Americans can attain their dreams of success* without realizing that the circumstances of nature and society prevent some people from achieving their full potential has simply overstated the truth. However, a person who realizes the truth might intend the listener to understand the same proposition as hyperbole for rhetorical effect. Many hyperboles are apparent because they are patently absurd, such as the idiomatic expressions *It makes my blood boil* and *It is raining cats and dogs* (both phrases are partly motivated by metaphor as well).

Understatement also distorts the truth because speakers say less than is objectively warranted, as when someone comments about a very drunk person *He seems to have had a bit too much to drink*. The term *litote* is reserved for a particular kind of understatement in which the speaker uses a negative expression where a positive one would have been more forceful and direct. Litotes express an overt lack of commitment and so imply a desire to suppress or conceal one's true attitude. Paradoxically litotes, like hyperbole, seem to involve intensification, suggesting that the speaker's feelings are too deep for plain expression (e.g., *It's not bad, He's no Hercules, She's no beauty, He's not exactly a pauper*). A famous example of understatement from Shakespeare is found in *Romeo and Juliet* in the scene where Romeo has just wounded – as it turns out, fatally – Mercutio. The following exchange occurs as Mercutio falls dramatically to the ground:

> *Romeo*:　　Courage, man. The hurt cannot be much.
>
> *Mercutio*:　No, 'tis not so deep as a well, nor so wide as a church door; but 'tis enough, 'twill serve (III.. i. 91–3)

The expressed meaning here is mild and the intended meaning intense as Mercutio ironically mocks Romeo for claiming that his deed is insignificant.

Because they express superficial indifference and underlying commitment, litotes are often treated as a category of irony. In everyday speech, hyperbole and litote represent antithetical postures and tend to correspond to contrasting philosophical attitudes: optimism and idealism in the case of hyperbole, pessimism and cynicism in the case of litote. Both hyperbole and understatement are traditionally viewed, then, as violations of Grice's maxims, with hyperbole violating the maxim of Quality (say what you believe to be true) and understatement violating the maxim of Quantity (contribute as much to the conversation as is required). In both cases, according to the Gricean framework, the speaker urges the addressee to seek an implicature beyond the straightforward literal interpretation of what is said.

However, hyperbole and understatement violate Truthfulness maxims only if one assumes that a speaker's utterance must be identical to his or her beliefs. These tropes do not violate or flout Truthfulness maxims when one assumes that speakers' utterances need to resemble their beliefs only in the sense of sharing some logical and contextual implications with what the speakers believe (Wilson & Sperber, 1990). For example, when Jane says *My boyfriend is the strongest man in the world*, she tries to convey some set of implications about her boyfriend, but not all of these need be identical with the proposition stated. Only some implications from her utterance need mirror what Jane truly believes. Like the case of irony, when people use hyperbole and understatement, they pretend that some state of affairs holds in the world in order to communicate ideas or attitudes regarding their stated propositions. When Jane goes on to say *My boyfriend is almost ten feet tall*, she is adopting the pretense of her boyfriend's being close to 10 feet tall to express the idea that he is tall. Of course with both hyperbole and understatement, the speaker's meaning is always somewhat indeterminate because there is only a resemblance between what someone says and what that person really believes to be true. Thus, we recognize by Jane's statement that she believes her boyfriend to be quite tall, but we never know for sure exactly how tall he is. Similarly, when Bob says of his wife's special apple pie *It's not bad*, we recognize that Bob thinks positively of his wife's pie, but we are somewhat unsure exactly how good he believes the pie to be.

The indeterminacy associated with understanding many tropes, such as irony, hyperbole, and understatement, shows exactly how important it is to specify the time course of understanding in theories of figurative language use. Listeners may comprehend a hyperbolic statement like *I've got ten thousand papers to grade before noon* in the sense of immediately recognizing the speaker's belief that she has many papers to grade before noon. But upon further processing or conscious reflection, the listener may, perhaps through his knowledge of the speaker, realize that the speaker probably has only four or five papers to grade and is so slow in grading them that she feels enormous pressure and conveys this through hyperbole. This elucidation of the speaker's intention and the true state of affairs requires a different theoretical description than the one needed to explain what goes on in the first few moments of trope comprehension.

There is no published experimental research in understanding hyperbole and understatement. My discussion of irony, hyperbole, and understatement, however, suggests that these tropes do not necessarily violate a maxim of Truthfulness. People's understanding of these tropes may be readily explained by weakening the traditional Truthfulness maxims in two ways. When making some statement, speakers (a) want to attribute belief in the proposition they express not necessarily to themselves but to someone or some cultural norm, and (b) speakers' statements need not be identical to their own beliefs but need only resemble their beliefs (ibid.). These alternative conceptions of Grice's maxims provide for a more accurate picture of the complexity of irony, hyperbole, and understatement as well as of the pragmatic information used when people make sense of these tropes in conversation.

OXYMORA

One of the most visible figures of thought and speech that reflect our incongruous understanding of experience is the oxymoron. Consider the following poem, "Defining Love," written in the 17th century by the Spanish poet Francisco de Quevedo:

> It's ice that burns, it is a frozen fire,
> it's a wound that hurts and is not felt,
> it's something well dreamt, an evil present,
> it's a brief retiring, that quickly tires.
>
> It's a carelessness that makes us care,
> a walk alone among the crowd,
> a loving only of being loved,
> a coward, with a brave man's name.
>
> It's a liberty locked up in prison,
> that lasts until the last convulsion;
> an illness which spreads if it's cured.
>
> This is young Cupid, this his abyss.
> Just see what friends he'll make with nothing,
> who's in all things against himself!

This poem describes the conflicting, contradictory thoughts and feelings that constitute some experiences of love. Poetry often expresses figurative impossibility where the contradictions of life are exposed. These oxymoronic comments about love reflect our understanding of experience of things that cannot to the will be settled (as the poet John Keats put it) – that life, when thought about, gives rise to the ultimately frustrating belief that things are and are not, can and cannot be, must and must not be. It is for this reason that oxymoron is *the show-off among figures of speech* (Vendler, 1988: 242) and some of the best evidence for the figurative processes that make up the poetics of mind.

Oxymora are traditionally defined as figures of speech that combine two seemingly contradictory elements, as in Shakespeare's *O heavy lightness! serious vanity! / Mis-shapen chaos of well-seeming forms! / Feather of lead, bright smoke, cold fire, sick health! (Romeo and Juliet, I. i. 172–4).* Literally speaking, these statements seem nonsensical in that smoke isn't bright, fire isn't cold, and to be healthy isn't to be sick. Of course, we do have an ability to take contradictory, even paradoxical, stances toward people and events. This ability is more than just seeing alternative sides of some person or situation that cannot be grasped at the same time (in a way we see ambiguous figures). Rather we seem able to grasp conceptually in a single instance two things that are apparently contradictory. George Bernard Shaw's quip *America and England are two countries separated by a common language* makes immediate sense to us through our cultural understanding of these two nations, despite the contradiction of two entities being divided by something in common.

Oxymora like *bright smoke, lead feathers,* and *sick health,* do not simply represent figures of speech but also reflect poetic schemes for conceptualizing human experience and the external world. Developments in the history of science have often been characterized as expressing oxymoronic thought. For instance, the transition from Ptolemy and Copernicus to Kepler implies a shift from thinking in terms of antithesis to thinking in terms of oxymoron: Celestial motion came to be seen as composed of both curves and straight lines (Hallyn, 1990). More generally, oxymora are frequently found in everyday speech, and many are barely noticed as such, as in *intense apathy, internal exile, man child, loyal opposition, pretty ugly, guest host,* and so on. The ubiquity of these figures suggests some underlying ability to conceive of ideas, objects, and events in oxymoronic terms.

A brief look at how people conceive of academic issues in possible oxymoronic terms is seen in these titles of recently published scientific articles:

Sexual science – Emerging discipline or oxymoron (*Journal of Sex Research*)
Is normative naturalism an oxymoron? (*Philosophical Psychology*)
Library simplification – An oxymoron (*Journal of Academic Librarianship*)
Noncoercive psychiatry – An oxymoron (*Journal of Humanistic Psychology*)
Sustainable growth – A bad oxymoron (*Journal of Environmental Science and Health*)
Is conservation education an oxymoron? (*Conservation Biology*)
Academically successful drug users – An oxymoron (*Journal of Drug Education*)

But how do people normally understand oxymora like those seen in Shakespeare (e.g., *sick health*) and in everyday speech (e.g., *pretty ugly*)? What makes some contradictory statements more meaningful to us than others? There appear to be two types of oxymoron (Shen, 1987). Direct oxymora consist of two terms that are antonyms or two terms whose only difference consists of a change in the plus or minus sign of their lowest distinctive feature, all other features being identical (e.g., *a feminine man* and *living death*). Indirect oxymora consist of two terms that are not direct antonyms of each other but have one term that is a hyponym of the first term's antonym. Consider the example *the silence whistles* (taken from the Hebrew poet Nathan Altherman's "Summer Night"). The antonym of *silence* is lexically realized by the word *sound*, whose semantic specification consists of the same features as *silence* except for the replacement of the plus sign of the distinctive feature "silence" ("−sound") by the minus sign. However, the second term of the oxymoron *the silence whistles* is not *sound*, but its hyponym *whistle*, which also shares the feature list of *sound* with the additional feature of +sharpness. Other indirect oxymora include *sacred garbage, bright smoke*, and *sweet sorrow*, all cases in which the second term is a hyponym of the first term's antonym.

One empirical analysis of the oxymora found in modern Israeli poetry and in classical literary dictionaries indicated that only 16% of oxymora were of the direct type, whereas 84% were indirect (Shen, 1987). Most of the common examples of oxymora found in everyday speech also appear to be indirect cases (e.g., *intense apathy*). Recent psycholinguistic research indicates that people found indirect oxymora more poetic and easier to understand than direct oxymora (Gibbs & Kearney, 1994). Moreover, understanding oxymora creates novel features that are not associated with either the adjective or noun terms in these figurative phrases (e.g., *clever imbecile* means more than the simple combination of the semantic properties of *clever* and *imbecile*). It appears that people access relevant knowledge to constrain their creative understanding of seemingly contradictory concepts. Most generally, the psychological evidence shows that people can make immediate sense out of novel oxymoronic statements. We easily interpret these contradictory phrases because of our conceptual ability to understand incongruent events and experiences.

CONCLUSION

The presence of irony, hyperbole, understatement, and oxymora in the way we speak about our common experiences points toward the conclusion that these figures provide part of the figurative foundation for everyday thought. These figures specifically illustrate how our conceptualization of incongruous situations motivates the need for speech that reflects these figurative schemes of thinking. We can maintain and modify social relationships by recognizing incongruous situations and then commenting on them directly in ironic terms that include figurative language, such as sarcasm, hyperbole, understatement, and oxymora.

Chapter 9

The poetic minds
of children

How good are children at figurative thinking? Is figurative thought a special skill, or is it a significant part of children's everyday cognition? Children frequently produce utterances that appear to have figurative meaning. For example, an 18-month-old child called a toy car *a snake* while twisting it up his mother's arm (Winner, McCarthy, Kleinman, & Gardner, 1979). A 24-month-old boy said *Cup swimming* while pushing a cup along the surface of the bath water and *I'm a big waterfall* while sliding down from his father's arms (Carlson & Anisfeld, 1969). At ages 3 and 4, Piaget's daughter Jacqueline said of a bent twig *It's like a machine for putting in petrol*, of a caddis fly in a stream *It's an insect in its cage*, and of a winding river *It's like a snake* (Piaget, 1962). She would even giggle as she rocked a spoon in her arms as if it were a baby. Other children also exhibit novel word usage, as in these examples: *Oh look he's barefoot all over*, *The chimney is a house-hat*, *The bad just crawls right out of me* (P. Harris, 1982). These young speakers show no hesitation in transferring words from one domain to another, for example, seeing a horse as wearing clothes, regarding an inanimate quality as animate, or using a restricted term like *barefoot* in a more general sense.

 These spontaneous utterances and actions suggest the possibility that even young children can perceive various similarities between disparate domains of experience, the very mark of metaphor. Educators often expect children to understand novel lexical usage. The Suzuki music method designed for preschoolers, for example, routinely personifies the violin, and the child is urged to treat the strings as hot or cold or sometimes fragile. Mother Goose describes a candle that wears a petticoat and the month of March as having the attributes of two different animals (*coming in like a lion and going out like a lamb*). Teachers often encourage school-age children to explore their poetic abilities by asking them to write poetry. Consider this poem written by a 7-year-old girl from California (Simon & Kennedy, 1979).

> I am a raindrop
> Right now I am falling.
> I am falling in a chimney
> And into the fire in the fireplace.
> I am making a fire flood.
> People are mad at me.
> I am ashamed of myself
> But I can't help it.
> A raindrop has to do her work
> And be ashamed of herself.

This composition shows how children think metaphorically about their own experiences, in this case elaborating on the comparison between a physical object and the poet's psychological experience. Although children do not frequently comment on resemblances between physical and psychological domains, they sometimes report dreams or stories that suggest their recognition of metaphorical resemblances. Consider a story written by a young girl, Mary, who had a troubled life and experienced much difficulty being close to other people (Bettelheim, 1955: 326). One day at school, Mary sat down at a typewriter and composed the following story, titled "The Lonely Cactus":

> Once upon a time there lived a little cactus plant and his name was Prickly. One day he said to his friend who was very old: I want a friend to play with. And the old cactus said, why can't you play with me? Because you are too old. If that is the reason it is very silly said the cactus. I will find you a friend, and he found a cactus just like himself.

Mary appears to personify herself as the cactus because she feels psychologically "prickly." The case study of a young girl aged 4 years 6 months provides another example of how children understand physical–psychological metaphor (B. Moore, 1988). One day soon after the death of her father, this girl was walking home with a helium balloon when it suddenly blew out of her hand. As the balloon rose irretrievably out of her reach, the young child began to call out for her father. One interpretation of this event is that the child recognized the loss of the balloon as the ground for an important insight into the irreversibility of death.

Over the next few months, the young girl seemed afraid of balloons, often breaking into tears at the mere sight of them. Six months after her father's death, the girl commented that she did not remember much about her father. Her mother then talked with her about some of the enjoyable experiences she and her father had shared. The next morning the girl awoke and immediately drew a picture with crayons of little girl grasping several colored balloons. Perhaps the previous evening's conversation temporarily brought this girl closer to her father's memory, something that could be expressed in the drawing of her holding onto the balloons. Over time she became less fearful of balloons and at age 6 even drew a picture of a boat with people on it accompanied by balloons. She also seemed more comfortable playing with balloons and would inflate them and then gradually let the air out. These observations make it difficult to avoid concluding that this child had come upon a metaphorical way of understanding a difficult, even abstract, experience of death.

It should not surprise us to hear that children possess figurative thought, given their fascination with fairy tales. Children appear quite capable of interpreting fairy tales as metaphorically related to their individual concerns (Bettelheim, 1976). Fairy stories are like myths in that both guide our thinking about some eternal questions: What is the world really like? How am I to live my life in it? How can I be true to myself? However, most myths give definite answers to these questions, whereas fairy tales are only suggestive of a message. Fairy tales speak to the child in demonstrating that a struggle against severe difficulties in life is unavoidable and is really an intrinsic part of human existence. But if we do not shy away from such struggles and steadfastly meet unexpected and often unjust hardships, we can overcome these obstacles to emerge victorious. Children hear stories like "Snow White," "The Three Little Pigs," "Hansel and Gretel," and "Rapunzel" and appear to make connections between the characters and events in these tales and their own lives. Part of the delight children take in hearing certain stories repeatedly stems not only from the enchantment these tales have as works of art but also from the psychological meaning children will continue to extract from these stories at different points in their lives, depending on their individual needs and interests. *These are not far-out stories appealing only to the aesthetically sensitive child: these are the basic texts of childhood* (B. Pearson, 1990: 186).

The miscellaneous anecdotal evidence on children's figurative ability is sometimes held in suspicion by experimental child psychologists, who argue that children's production of figurative language is nothing more than linguistic accident, errors of categorization, or the result of imagistic thinking that is typical of very young children. During the last 15 years, a tremendous amount of research has examined children's figurative competence, particularly with regard to how well they understand metaphor and reason analogically. This work provides good evidence that, contrary to the traditional view, children possess significant ability to engage in figurative modes of thought. My aim in this chapter is to review briefly some of the evidence on how children's use and understanding of metaphor, idioms, metonymy, and irony illustrate the developing poetic minds of children.

UNDERSTANDING METAPHOR

Among the empirical studies in children's use and understanding of figurative language, the vast majority focus on metaphor. The question of whether children can really produce and comprehend metaphorical language centers on conflicting views about the nature and definition of metaphor, the criteria for defining children's utterances as metaphorical, and young children's classification abilities (Vosniadou, 1987).

These issues arise for each of the studies that examined children's metaphoric competence.

How often do young children produce genuine metaphors? One study observed 73 children between 2.7 and 6.0 years of age during their regular school day and recorded all utterances that referred to an object, feeling, or event by a term that would not ordinarily be used for that referent (Billow, 1981). An utterance was scored as metaphorical if it was based on one perceptual similarity. For instance, if the child used the word *grass* to refer to green carpet, she was credited with the production of a metaphor based on the perceptual similarity between grass and green carpets. Most of the utterances (94%) that appeared metaphorical were based on such similarity.

However, the perception of similarity alone does not justify calling an utterance metaphorical. Noticing similarity between superficially dissimilar objects, such as between grass and green carpet, might have little to do with the mastery of metaphor. Children might in such cases be overextending the use of a word in order to refer to an object whose conventional name the child does not yet know (e.g., calling *carpet* by the label *grass*). These utterances do not necessarily indicate an intention to violate established categories and may not be metaphors.

Several studies attempted to distinguish between children's overextensions and their metaphoric renamings (Winner et al., 1979; Winner, McCarthy, & Gardner, 1980). Children are quite adept at engaging in renaming games with experimenters, replicating a skill they perform spontaneously in symbolic play (Hudson & Nelson, 1984; Winner, McCarthy, & Gardner, 1980): A block becomes a car and is called one, a hat an umbrella, and so on. Renaming things may indicate metaphoric intentions, since the child already knows how an object is named but chooses to call it something else.

These criteria were applied to one child's spontaneous speech between 27 and 58 months of age and to the elicited speech of children 3 to 10 years of age. An utterance was called a renaming if the experimenter knew that the child knew the literal name of the item but referred to it metaphorically or if the child indicated that she was in a pretend mode and intended to speak nonliterally. All other utterances were considered nonmetaphorical overextensions. With these criteria, 72% of the spontaneous apparent metaphors and 68% of the elicited ones were judged as renamings or pretend comparisons and therefore were to be judged as genuine metaphors (Winner, McCarthy, & Gardner, 1980).

One problem with these data is that renamings may not qualify as metaphors if the child only sees the two objects being compared as being literally similar. Pretend renamings may best be conceptualized as precursors of metaphor because, like metaphors, they are based on children's tendencies to impose a familiar schema on the object word. For instance, when a child calls a block a *cup*, he or she does not refer to conceptual similarities between the two objects but only indicates that the block represents something that can be used for drinking. Various aspects of pretend play involve certain objects' taking on properties of other objects, but these pretend actions do not necessarily indicate any particular metaphoric ability (Vosniadou, 1987). A necessary aspect of metaphor competence is that children recognize the nonliteral similarity between the objects and events being compared.

Do young children distinguish between literal and nonliteral similarity? There is some evidence that by age 4 children are capable of making such a distinction. One study presented 3- to 6-year-old children with two similarity tasks (Vosniadou & Ortony, 1983). For the *comparison* task, children completed statements of the form *A is like X*, choosing one of two words from (a) a metaphorical–literal pair (e.g., *rain is like tears* vs. *rain is like snow*), (b) a literal–anomalous pair (e.g., *rain is like snow* vs. *rain is like chair*), or (c) a metaphorical–anomalous pair (e.g., *rain is like tears* vs. *rain is like chair*). For the *categorization* task, children completed statements of the form *A is the same kind of thing as X*, choosing only from a metaphorical–literal pair.

Children showed no preference between literal and metaphorical alternatives in the comparison task but a clear preference for literal alternatives in the categorization task. For example, the metaphorical comparison *rain is like tears* was often the preferred one in the comparison task, but most children selected the literal comparison *rain is the same kind of thing as snow* in the comparison task. The 3-year-old children did not prefer literal alternatives in the categorization task, whereas 4-year-olds did. The younger children's lack of preference for literal alternatives argues against the idea that children first understand literal similarity and only later on, based on that, metaphoric similarity. By age 4, children know that some similarity statements come from the same conventional categories and other meaningful similarity comparisons come from different categories.

A few studies show that preschoolers can see similarity between items belonging to different adult categories. Four-year-old children can match pairs of polar adjectives (e.g., *loud–quiet*) not only to literal alternatives (e.g., loud and quiet sounds) but also to metaphorical ones (pairs of colors, faces, etc.) (Gardner, 1974). Similarly, preschoolers act just like adults when answering questions like *If a tree had a knee, where would it be?* by correctly locating the imaginary knee on a picture of a tree (Gentner, 1977). On the other hand, children below the age of 10 to 12 are unable to explain verbally or paraphrase metaphorical sentences (Asch & Nerlove, 1960; Cometa & Eson, 1978; J. Smith, 1976; Winner, Rosentiel, & Gardner, 1976). For example, children under 14 could not explain the metaphorical meaning of the sentence *The prison guard was a hard rock* (Winner et al., 1976). These results might be interpreted as evidence that metaphor comprehension is a complex ability emerging late in childhood.

The failure of many young children to interpret metaphor verbally has been explained in two ways. Some researchers argue that children go through a literal stage in their metaphor comprehension development during which they are unable to interpret language nonliterally (Asch & Nerlove, 1960; Demorest, Silberstein, Gardner, & Winner, 1983; H. Pollio et al., 1977; Winner et al., 1976). Just as it is often assumed that adults process figurative language by first analyzing literal meaning, children are seen as first going through a stage where all meaning is understood literally. Only later do children enter a second stage at which they clearly recognize the nonliteral meanings of metaphors.

There is actually little evidence in favor of the view that the development of children's metaphor comprehension begins at a literal stage. The same children who can understand metaphorical expressions under one condition where the context is quite predictable are unable to comprehend metaphors in less predictable circumstances (Vosniadou, Ortony, Reynolds, & Wilson, 1984). Similarly, children who can interpret the metaphorical meaning of an expression like *The car was dead* cannot comprehend *The idea bloomed* (Keil, 1986). These findings indicate that metaphor comprehension cannot proceed according to such stages, because a child would have to be in both the literal and nonliteral stages of metaphor comprehension at the same time.

Another reason for children's failure to explain metaphor lies in their particular level of cognitive development. Piaget and his associates have argued that children develop the ability to make classifications based on similarity during the concrete stages of cognitive development (ages 7–11), whereas the ability to make classifications based on proportionality develops during a later stage of formal operations (ages 11 and above) (Inhelder & Piaget, 1964). To the extent that metaphor comprehension is a type of classification behavior, there should be a correlation between comprehension of metaphor based on similarity (e.g., *my hair is spaghetti*) and concrete operational thought and between understanding of metaphor based on proportionality (e.g., *my head is an apple without a core*) and formal operational thinking. Both of these hypotheses find some empirical support in a study examining the ability of children aged 5–13 to explain various metaphors and proverbs (Billow, 1975).

Piaget's view has come under attack in recent years. First, adult concepts cannot be defined in terms of objective qualities of the objects themselves but only in terms of family resemblances (Rosch & Mervis, 1975, and see Chapter 2). Many developmental psychologists now embrace the view that concepts are ideas about kinds or are theories, as opposed to a view of concepts as lists of features or properties (Carey, 1985; Keil, 1989). Second, the ability to classify objects hierarchically seems to emerge much earlier than Piaget originally thought

(Rosch, Mervis, Gray, Johnson, & Boyes-Braem, 1976; G. Ross, 1980; Sugarman, 1983, 1987). The development of classification skills quite early in life suggests that preschool children may be aware that some comparison statements violate category boundaries and are metaphorical.

Of course, young children do have a tendency in many situations to interpret metaphors literally, but the reason they do this has little to do with these young children's being in a literal stage of processing. Instead, young children either may not possess sufficient real-world knowledge or may be limited in their ability to distinguish reality and pretense. A variety of research demonstrates that very young children will often believe implausible ideas, such as that a prison guard can turn into stone or that sweet people actually taste sweet (Winner et al., 1976). Children will also interpret metaphorical utterances like *The little girl was a bird flying to her nest* to mean that the girl pretended to act like a bird by flapping her arms up and down (Vosniadou, 1987). The point here is that the child's ability to engage in pretend play may tap into a cognitive ability different from that required for metaphor comprehension.

Part of the difficulty children face in many experimental tasks assessing metaphor comprehension is that they are often asked to explain the meanings of metaphorical sentences in the absence of linguistic or situational context (Pollio & Pickens, 1980; Vonsiadou et al., 1984). Children below the age of 10 exhibit fairly good metaphor comprehension when the task and materials are appropriate to what they know. Context obviously plays an important role in language comprehension, particularly in the understanding of nonliteral speech. Because young children have limited conceptual and linguistic knowledge, they may rely heavily on contextual information to interpret metaphors. Metaphorical sentences that represent relatively predictable story endings are easier for young children to comprehend than are metaphorical sentences representing unpredictable story endings (Vosniadou, 1987). Seven-year-old children understand proverbs in a task where they match a proverb with one of two pictures – a nonliteral correct interpretation and a foil (Honeck, Sowry, & Voegstle,

1978). Seven-year-olds can also read stories containing metaphors and correctly choose the most appropriate of four possible continuation sentences (Reynolds & Ortony, 1980). Six-
year-olds can comprehend metaphorical sentences based on
physical/perceptual similarity when tested in both explica-
tion and multiple-choice tasks (Winner, McCarthy, & Gardner,
1980). Even 4-year-olds show evidence of metaphor comprehension in a task where they enact metaphorical interpretations with toys in a toy-world environment (Vosniadou et al.,
1984).

One method that has recently been employed to investigate
metaphor comprehension in young children is the elicited repetition task (B. Pearson, 1990). This task simply requires children repeat a sentence that has just been read to them. Previous research indicates that correct imitation of sentences implies understanding of the material repeated (Slobin & Welch,
1973). For example, it is well established that anomalous sentences are repeated less accurately than are semantically well-
formed sentences (Eilers, 1975). If children do not understand
metaphor, then they should immediately repeat metaphor sentences less accurately than literal sentences, perhaps as poorly
as they repeat anomalous ones. Children aged 3 to 5 years
were asked to repeat different metaphoric (e.g., *The stars are
the moon's children*), literal (e.g., *The fog comes in after the rainstorm*), and anomalous (e.g., *Newspapers are stars wearing the
bath*) sentences. But even 3-year-olds repeated metaphor sentences as well as they did literal ones (Pearson, 1990). This
demonstration that metaphors are comprehended as well as
equivalent literal sentences and better than anomalies strengthens the case that asking children to explain metaphor verbally
vastly underestimates their true metaphoric abilities.

Another difficulty children face with metaphor is that their
conceptual system is less developed than that of adults. Young
children find metaphors based on physical or perceptual similarity easier to understand than metaphors based on abstract
or complex relations or metaphors that use physical terms to
describe psychological states (Billow, 1975; Gentner, 1988;
Winner et al., 1976). The perceptual properties of objects appear more salient for children and in many cases constitute

most of their knowledge of objects. At the same time, at least some of the developmental evidence shows that preschool children can notice similarity between stories that are related analogically in relational, not perceptual, terms (A. Brown, Kane, & Echols, 1986; Holyoke, Junn, & Billman, 1984). One theory to account for this finding proposes that young children may possess some fundamental ability to infer metaphorical mappings but do not draw such mappings with any consistency (Gentner, 1988, 1989). This *structure mapping theory* of analogical reasoning (see Chapter 5) holds that the key to successful analogical thinking lies in noticing relational commonalities between the base (or source) and target domains independent of the objects in which these relations are embedded. For example, the analogy between the solar system and the atom relationally maps the planets and the sun onto the electrons and the nucleus, so that electrons are considered to revolve around the nucleus in a manner similar to the planets' revolution around the sun. The structure mapping theory maintains that people seek to maximize systems of predicates linked by higher-order relations (e.g., *cause*) in preference to lower-order relations (e.g., *larger than*) or isolated predicates (e.g., *red*). Yet younger children do not necessarily show the same relational focus as adults and instead focus on object similarities when solving analogies or interpreting metaphors. Only later does a "relational shift" occur, when children maximize relational correspondences.

One study provided evidence in support of the relational shift hypothesis (Gentner, 1988). Children aged 5–6 and 9–10 and adults were asked to rephrase different kinds of metaphor as similes (e.g., *X is like Y because . . .*). The metaphors presented included relational metaphors based on relational similarities (e.g., *A cloud is like a sponge*), attributive metaphors based on surface or attribute similarities (e.g., *Soapsuds are like whipped cream*), and double metaphors that shared both relational and attribute similarities (e.g., *Plant stems are like drinking straws*). As expected, there was a developmental increase in the participants' ability to interpret metaphors based on relational similarities. Younger children interpreted the double metaphors primarily in terms of similar attributes, and older children and adults mostly gave relational interpretations. A second study, in which children were asked to select attributional and relational interpretations of these metaphors instead of producing paraphrases, obtained identical results.

These findings support the idea that children's increasing ability to interpret metaphors is due in part to their developing ability to focus on relational mappings from source to target domains. Younger children's inability to focus on relational similarities in metaphors may not reflect a structural deficit but can be explained, again, by their lack of specific background knowledge. Studies that control for the specific knowledge children possess show that relational metaphors are not harder to comprehend than attributive metaphors (Dent, 1984). For example, 5-, 7-, and 10-year-old children perceive metaphoric similarity between moving objects, such as a ballerina dancing and a top spinning, more readily than between stationary objects, such as a curvy river and a curvy snake.

Because metaphor understanding requires the mapping of knowledge from a source domain onto a target domain, children have an easier time understanding metaphors containing familiar terms (Billow, 1975; Keil, 1986; Malgady, 1977; Winner, McCarthy, & Gardner, 1980). Another proposal suggests that children are capable of understanding metaphor to the extent that they possess well-formed conceptual domains upon which any given metaphor is based (Keil, 1986). Metaphor comprehension emerges on a domain-by-domain basis, so that if one member of a conceptual domain (or semantic field) is understood, so too are the other members of the same domain. For this reason, the conceptual domains acquired first by children should be seen in the first metaphors used and understood by them. Because young children distinguish between animate and inanimate objects before they do between physical and nonphysical objects, metaphors based on the animate–inanimate distinction should be easiest for young children to comprehend.

A test of this hypothesis addressed the ability of kindergartners and second and fourth grade children to explain the meanings of metaphorical utterances from different conceptual domains (Keil, 1986). The findings showed that children who understood one metaphor from a given conceptual domain (e.g., animals, people, ideas) generally understood all the other members from that same domain. Thus, children who comprehended a metaphor from the domain of cars, such as *The car was thirsty*, also understood other car-domain metaphors, such as *The car was tired*. Furthermore, metaphors based on an animate–inanimate distinction (e.g., *The car was thirsty*) were understood by the younger children before metaphorical utterances referring to the physical–nonphysical object distinction (e.g., *The idea was not yet ripe*). These data demonstrate how children's metaphor comprehension depends critically on their conceptual knowledge.

A different study revealed a specific developmental progression in children's differentiation of conceptual domains (Vosniadou & Ortony, 1986). First and third grade children listened to stories containing analogies from a more to a less familiar domain (e.g., the healing of an infection was described in terms of winning a war) and answered questions about these stories. Six conceptual relations were identified as possible areas of transfer from the familiar source domain to the unfamiliar target domain: (a) descriptive properties, (b) characteristic activities, (c) emotions and thoughts, (d) structural and functional characteristics, (e) causal properties, and (f) plans and goals.

Children's answers to questions about these analogies indicated that they were willing to attribute human emotions and thought to inanimate things, but they did not transfer descriptive properties and characteristics from one domain to another. For example, one story that the children read described white blood cells as being like soldiers. Although the children did not conclude that white blood cells wore uniforms or ate breakfast, they did infer that white blood cells "think" that germs are "bad" and "feel" frightened when fighting germs.

Distinguishing one conceptual domain from another is a process that occurs over time, with some distinctions (e.g., descriptive properties and characteristics) being mastered long before others (e.g., emotions and thoughts). It is also clear from children's answers to questions about analogical stories that the source-to-target-domain mappings children draw are, at least, appropriately partial. The transfer of properties from source to target domains tends to be asymmetrical, as when aspects of humans were mapped onto animals and blood cells but not vice versa. These results show that children can map knowledge from source to target domains in the way adults do. Although children may not recognize the full range of differences between source and target domains, it is clear that they are capable of making metaphorical mappings.

The work discussed so far examined relatively young children's ability to comprehend different kinds of metaphorical statements in different contexts. Young children can under the right circumstances understand metaphor, a conclusion consistent with the claim that even young children possess the capacity to think metaphorically. A different line of developmental research indicates that even infants possess some metaphoric competence.

In one early study, infants were challenged to construct a similarity relationship between two events that shared no physical features or history of co-occurrence (e.g., a pulsing tone and paired slides of a dotted line and a solid line). Infants aged 9 to 12 months looked longer at the dotted line than at the solid line in the presence of a pulsing tone, suggesting that a metaphorical match was construed (Wagner, Winner, Cicchetti, & Gardner, 1981). Similarly, they looked more at an arrow pointing upward when listening to an ascending tone and to a downward arrow when listening to a descending tone. The infants were thus able to recognize an abstract dimension that underlies two physically and temporally dissimilar events (e.g., discontinuity in the pulsing tone and discontinuity in the dotted line). These findings are especially important because they parallel the idea that adults project image schemas from one domain onto another, for example, conceptualizing quantity in terms of verticality (MORE IS UP and LESS IS DOWN).

More recent research examined whether infants can construe an abstract unity between a facial expression of emotion (e.g., joy) and an auditory event (e.g., an ascending tone), events that also share no physical features or history of co-occurrence (Phillips, Wagner, Fells, & Lynch, 1990). The 7-month-old infants in this study did not categorize different facial expressions of joy and anger. The infants did look significantly longer at joy, surprise, and sadness when these facial expressions were matched with ascending, pulsing, and descending tones, respectively. Because the auditory and visual events in this experimental task were substantially different, infants had to act on the events within a short period of time to bring meaning (i.e., determine equivalences) to the disparity. Thus, infants had to determine the equivalence between both of a pair of facial expressions in concert with the auditory event. This is a striking demonstration of how infants metaphorically match disparate events to construe some meaning in facial expressions of emotion.

Work with young children also demonstrates their ability to perceive resemblances between related abstract properties of visual and auditory experiences (Marks, Hammeal, & Bornstein, 1987). Four-year-olds already perceive and conceive of similarities between pitch and brightness (low pitch equals dim; high pitch equals bright) and between loudness and brightness (soft equals dim; loud equals bright). Young children can also transfer the meanings of words and phrases from either modality to the other. For instance, children rate the adjective *bright* as higher in both pitch and loudness than the adjective *dim*. Similarly, young children rate the adjectives *loud and high-pitched* as being brighter than the adjectives *soft* and *low-pitched*. Yet some cross-modal resemblances evident to adults and older children are not easily recognized by younger children. For example, the cross-modal relation between pitch and size (low pitch equals large; high pitch equals small) does not appear with any regularity until around age 11.

The evidence on younger children's cross-modal matching ability provides additional weight to the argument that young children possess significant metaphoric ability (Shannon, 1992). Of course, recognizing the similarity or resemblance inherent in a synesthetic (or "cross-sensory") metaphor (e.g., *bright sound*) does not necessarily mean that children understand such phrases as metaphors. Infants may not necessarily be capable of metaphorically mapping when they appear to match certain sounds with facial expressions. Perhaps such mappings become truly metaphorical whenever the modalities become independent perceptual categories (Marks et al., 1987). Most theorists assume that the metaphor user must be aware that normally estranged domains have come joined and conventional meanings overridden. Children at play, dreamers, and poets should be aware of a tension between separate domains before we credit them with metaphoric thought. Four-year-old children clearly distinguish between different levels of perceptual dimensions (e.g., brightness is a perceptual dimension of things seen, and loudness a perceptual dimension of things heard). Thus, age 4 might be the latest at which children's understanding of cross-modal experiences is viewed as metaphoric.

Where does the ability to think metaphorically come from? Consider the following speculative answer to this question. Metaphorical thinking is not an innate property of the mind but arises from children's bodily experiences. For example, infants' direct experience of their bodies and of space, such as the dimensions up and down, is often correlated with various emotional experiences and comes to form the grounding of such basic metaphorical concepts as WELL-BEING or HAPPINESS IS UP. Caretakers who provide food, warmth, caresses, and soft voices are spatially above the child. All the child's energy is directed toward faces and voices that are up, and the child is often lifted up to receive special care and attention. In this way, the young child gradually learns the fundamental spatial–emotional concept HAPPINESS IS UP (Tolaas, 1991). This metaphorical mapping organizes many conventional expressions that we use to speak of our emotional experiences (*I'm uplifted, He is in high spirits, My mood rose, Cheer up*).

During the first few months of life, being down is a natural state serving maturational purposes, but later in life, when we grow up, being down is associated with all aspects of babyhood, such as dependence, helplessness, and inferiority. These relationships become another significant source of metaphor, as in DOWN IS SAD (*I'm in low spirits, He's down and out, I am down in the dumps*). Being in a subordinate spatial position is also linked to inferiority, as in DOWN IN INFERIORITY (*A major is below a colonel, He is the underdog, This is typical of lower forms of life*). Just as being spatially up is to be in control, being down is being controlled (*He had 50 men under him*).

With continued growth, infants are eventually able to stand erect. As babies first stand, they experience both success (standing/walking) and failure (stumbling/falling). Once infants begin to stand, they have a means of control over their own behavior, an opportunity to imitate and master the behavior of adults. This is the foundation for the basic metaphorical concepts UNSTEADINESS IS NEAR FAILURE (*He stumbled through his oral exams, The government is tottering*) and FALLING IS FAILURE (*His jokes fell flat, The scheme fell through, The government has fallen*). To be erect and straight represents moral qualities of straightforwardness, uprightness, and respectability. Stooping and bent body positions are associated with debasement and failure (*They hung their heads in shame, Her spirits drooped, They were weighed down with grief*). To be crooked is to be dishonest (*That man is a crook*).

In general, young children's early physical, sensorimotor experiences form the basis for more complex thoughts that are constituted by metaphor. This idea is evident in the writings of G. Lakoff and Johnson (1980; elaborated on in Tolaas, 1991). Even more recently, developmental psychologists have argued that early sensorimotor schemas in children, as first described by Piaget (1952), give rise to image schemas that form the significant link in the transition from perception to concepts (Mandler, 1992). To take just one example, the image schema of containment (M. Johnson, 1987) is important because of its relevance to preverbal thinking. Babies experience many kinds of containment, as when they eat and drink, spit things out, feel their bodies being clothed and unclothed, are taken in and out of rooms, and so on. Infants also see many visible containers, such as bottles, cups, and dishes, and notice the acts that make things disappear into and reappear out of these containers. Some concept of containment seems to be responsible for the better performance 9-month-old infants show on an object-hiding task when the occluder consists of an upright container rather than an inverted container or a screen (Freeman, Lloyd, & Sinha, 1980; Lloyd, Sinha, & Freeman, 1981). Infants of 5½ months are surprised when containers without bottoms appear to hold things (Kolstad, 1991). Finally, 9- to 12-month-old infants often open and close their mouths, open and close their hands, or cover and uncover their eyes with a pillow when they try to imitate acts that they cannot see themselves perform, such as blinking or opening their mouths (Piaget, 1952). These infants appear to engage in analogical understanding of the behavior they are trying to imitate. Mandler (1992) argues that these infants' understanding "seems a clear case of an image schema of the spatial movement involved when anything opens or closes, regardless of the particulars of the thing itself" (ibid.: 598).

The claim that young infants possess image schematic structures shows how preverbal concepts can be grounded in early perceptual–body experiences. These image schemas also provide the foundation for later language learning and reasoning. For example, it should not be difficult for the child to learn that *in* expresses a containment relation. When a 20-month-old child hears the phrase *The spoon is in the cup*, he or she already has more than a year's experience in analyzing one thing as being in another (ibid.). A single image schema can be used to join the two objects in a familiar relationship. Even though the preposition *in* cannot be pointed to, it is one of the earliest locative terms acquired in almost all languages.

Although there is no empirical work in developmental psychology that specifically links image schemas to children's understanding of metaphorical language, it is not unreasonable to assume that metaphor acquisition depends on early image schematic structures. Children's understanding of conventional expressions might very well be motivated by metaphoric schemes of thought that arise from early image schemas. In the same way, children's ability to produce and comprehend novel metaphorical expressions might also depend on their projections of image schemas onto more abstract knowledge domains. Metaphor understanding does not require that children have complete nonmetaphorical knowledge of different source and target domains, because many target domains are themselves constituted by metaphor (e.g., the abstract domains of anger, time, and causation). Determining the extent to which various concepts are metaphorically understood by children is a key challenge for developmental psychologists. Most generally, though, the development of metaphor comprehension appears to be constrained by limitations in children's conceptual knowledge, linguistic skills, and information processing abilities. Yet there is good evidence that young children can comprehend verbal metaphors if they are simple and used in appropriate contexts.

UNDERSTANDING IDIOMS

Children's learning of idioms is generally thought to depend on their ability to associate a given sequence of words with an arbitrary figurative meaning (e.g., *kick the bucket* means "to die"). As was discussed in Chapter 6, idioms are mostly assumed to be dead metaphors whose relatively fixed figurative meanings cannot be determined by combining the meanings of their individual words (see Strassler, 1982). Unlike novel metaphors, idiomatic expressions are generally thought to have fairly arbitrary nonliteral interpretations, with loss of their original metaphoric qualities. Adults may explicitly teach children the nonliteral meanings of idioms, or children may eventually recognize the incongruity between contextual information and the literal analysis of idiomatic phrases. What traditional accounts do *not* suggest is that children may learn the figurative meanings of idioms through some sort of compositional analysis or through an ability to draw metaphorical connections between the parts of idioms and their figurative referents.

Most experimental studies have focused on children's ability to recognize when idiomatic expressions are intended either literally or figuratively (Ackerman, 1982; Cacciari & Levorato, 1989; Gibbs, 1987c, 1991; L. Lodge & Leech, 1975; Nippold & Rudzinski, in press; Prinz, 1983). Generally, there is a developmental increase in children's correct interpretation of idioms. When children have either to explain verbally or choose the appropriate pictorial meaning of such idioms as *kick the bucket*, they tend to give literal interpretations, and it is only later on, around the age of 8 or 9, that children consis-

417

tently view idiomatic expressions as having figurative meanings. One reason for younger children's difficulty in understanding idioms is that they lack concrete referents for idiomatic meanings (Cacciari & Levorato, 1989). Idiomatic phrases
often refer to abstract concepts or mental states, such as intentions, feelings, and emotions, that children often find difficult to conceptualize (Flavell & Ross, 1981).

Other studies show that younger children can grasp the figurative sense of idioms if these phrases are presented in an in-
formation-rich context. One study presented first and third
graders with narratives biased to either the figurative or literal meanings of idioms (Cacciari & Levorato, 1989). An example of a story that biases toward a figurative interpretation
is presented below.

> One winter a little boy named Paul went to the mountains with
> his parents. They were staying at a hotel. The first day his
> mother told him that there were other children in the hotel
> and that he should try to meet them. He went to play on a
> frozen lake where there were other children, and he broke the
> ice.

The experimenter read each story to the child and then asked
a question concerning what the character did, such as when
he *broke the ice*. Here are the questions and possible answers
given to each child for the story presented above.

> What did Paul do when he broke the ice?
>
> (a) *he made friends with the other children*
> (b) *he broke a piece of ice*
> (c) *he told his mummy everything*

Answer (a) is the correct idiomatic interpretation of *broke the
ice*, choice (b) is a literal paraphrase of the idiom, and response
(c) is a plausible choice in the context of the story that differs
from both choices (a) and (b).

Other children in this study were presented with just the
idioms and the questions without any contextual information.
Children in both age groups were equally good at recogniz-

ing the figurative meanings of an idiom when it was embedded in a rich context. When idioms were presented out of context, children, especially the first graders, preferred literal interpretations.

Another study examined children's production of idioms (ibid.). Children were presented with the same stories used earlier, with the last word of the last sentence deleted (e.g., *He went to play on a frozen lake where there were other children and he broke the . . .*). The ends of the narratives were open to only to a small set of completions, among which the idiom completion was the most adequate. The children's task was to complete the story with the word they thought most appropriate. Although the children did not often give idiomatic completions (e.g., *broke the ice*), they did in many instances provide completions that were figurative, such as when the character in the story above *broke the problem*. These newly created phrases illustrate that even young children are sometimes aware that language can be used to convey nonliteral meaning.

Some research demonstrates that children's comprehension of idioms depends on their intuitions about the internal semantics of these figurative phrases (Gibbs, 1987c, 1991; Nippold & Rudzinski, in press). Simply viewing idioms as dead metaphors that form a unique class of lexical items vastly underestimates the dynamic properties of idioms. Just as metaphorical expressions differ in their conceptual complexity (see Chapter 5), idiomatic phrases also differ along a variety of linguistic and pragmatic dimensions (see Chapter 6). These differences could influence children's understanding of idioms.

In one study, kindergartners and first, third, and fourth graders listened to idiomatic expressions either alone or at the ends of short stories (Gibbs, 1991). Their task was to explain verbally the intended meanings of these phrases and then to choose the correct idiomatic interpretation, given several alternatives. The idioms presented to the children differed in their degree of analyzability. Some idioms were highly analyzable or decomposable (*make up your mind*), other idioms were nondecomposable (*beat around the bush*). The results

showed that younger children (kindergartners and first graders) understood decomposable idioms better than they did
nondecomposable phrases. Older children (third and fourth
graders) understood both kinds of idiom equally well in supporting contexts but were better at interpreting decomposable
idioms than they were at understanding nondecomposable
idioms without contextual information. Further analyses
showed that children did not understood idioms with well-
formed literal meanings any better than they did ill-formed
idioms.

Consequently, it is unlikely that young children find decomposable idioms easier to comprehend simply because these
phrases possess well-formed literal meanings. Instead, the
younger children find it easier to assign figurative meanings
to the parts of decomposable idioms and do not simply analyze each expression according to its literal interpretation.

When an idiom is analyzable, children can assign independent meanings to its individual parts and will relatively
quickly learn how these meaningful parts combine to form
the overall nonliteral interpretation of the phrase. For example,
when children encounter *lay down the law*, they recognize that
each component is independently meaningful, so that *lay down*
refers to the act of invoking and *law* refers to a set of rules
governing conduct. Learning the meanings of semantically
nondecomposable idioms is more difficult, precisely because
their overall figurative interpretations cannot be determined
through analyses of their individual parts. Children must learn
the nonliteral meanings of these nondecomposable phrases
by creating some arbitrary association between the word string
and its figurative meaning (e.g., between *beat around the bush*
and "to delay action"). Of course, there is some relationship
between *beat around the bush* and "to delay action" and *kick the
bucket* and "to die," but these relations are historical and/or
arbitrary, and it is difficult for children and adults to assign
the individual components of these idioms to particular parts
of their overall figurative meanings. With appropriate context, older children do quite well at explaining the figurative
meanings of nondecomposable phrases. But without contextual support, third and fourth graders still have a good deal

of difficulty explaining the meanings of all types of idiom. Thus, it is fairly safe to say that children still have much to learn about the exact meanings of all types of idiom after the age of 8 or 9 (see also Nippold & Martin, 1989, for similar conclusions).

The results of this study highlight the importance of semantic analyzabilty in idiom comprehension in children. Idiomatic expressions differ in the degree to which their individual parts contribute to these phrases' overall figurative meanings. Younger children learn the meanings of normally decomposable idioms earlier than they do either abnormally decomposable or semantically nondecomposable idioms.

One significant implication of some of the developmental research concerns how idiom acquisition compares with the learning of literal language. Children's understanding of idioms seems to be explained by the same rationale used to account for the comprehension of more literal, generative kinds of word strings. This is an important idea, because it supports a view of grammar and language use in which the idiomatic and generative components are not two autonomous domains of natural language but extreme points on a continuum. Idioms do not form a unique class of linguistic item (e.g., as dead metaphors) but share many of the compositional properties normally associated with more literal language (Gibbs & Nayak, 1989). Although most models of children's idiom acquisition and comprehension suggest that all idioms are "lexicalized" or "word-like" (i.e., noncompositional) (Lodge & Leech, 1975; Prinz, 1983), it is clear that younger children's intuitions as to how the parts of idioms contribute to their overall figurative meanings have a great influence on the course of idiom learning, a finding that might extend to learners of a second language. Furthermore, the focus here on the analyzability of idioms can be extended to children's learning and understanding of other types of nonliteral discourse. Proverbs, slang metaphors, and other types of conventional speech formula also exhibit differences in their degree of analyzability. It would not be surprising to see developmental differences in the rates of acquisition for these other kinds of figurative formula based on people's perceptions of their analyzability.

The developmental research on idioms suggests that children have the ability to draw metaphorical connections between idiomatic phrases and what these expressions mean figuratively. When children hear phrases like *blow off steam*, they appear able to recognize that the individual parts of these expressions relate metaphorically to the ideas "releasing" and "anger." Children also form metaphorical connections between idiomatic phrases and different discourse situations to infer the figurative meanings of idioms. These claims do not directly imply that children *must* draw explicit metaphorical mappings between idioms and their figurative meanings for them to learn the meanings of all idioms. In many cases, children will learn idioms without determining the metaphorical link between phrases and their figurative interpretations. Even so, children are generally much better at learning the meanings of analyzable idioms – phrases that are more clearly motivated by conceptual metaphors (e.g., ANGER IS HEATED FLUID IN A CONTAINER for *blow off steam*) – than unanalyzable expressions. Children learn at least to recognize that many analyzable idioms make sense in having the meanings they do because of their developing metaphorical knowledge.

UNDERSTANDING METONYMY

Children clearly hear various kinds of metonymic expression in daily conversation. Parents, in speaking to children, might use metonymic utterances like *The buses are on strike*, tautological phrases like *Boys will be boys*, and many indirect requests like *Can you pick up the doll?*, and children appear to comprehend these expressions. No empirical research has specifically investigated children's ability to understand such conventional metonymic utterances as *The buses are on strike*. Yet there is evidence on children's production of novel lexical items and on their understanding of indirect speech acts that suggests they possess some ability to think metonymically.

Children frequently create new words as they learn language. Consider the following innovative uses of nouns as verbs by some very young children (E. Clark, 1982):

Child age 2 years 4 months wanting to have some cheese weighed:
You have to scale it first.

Child age 2 years 7 months not wanting his mother to sweep his room:
Don't broom my mess.

Child age 2 years 11 months telling his father that his mother nursed the baby:
Mommy nippled Anna.

Child age 3 years 2 months pretending to shoot his mother with a stick:
I'm going to gun you.

Child age 3 years 2 months asking if the pants his mother is mending are fixed:
Is it all needled?

Child age 3 years 10 months taking spaghetti out of a pan with tongs:
I'm going to pliars this out.

These innovations are illegitimate for adults, even though most are understandable in context. Adults use other words to express the same meanings, such as *weigh* for *scale*, *sweep* for *broom*, *shoot* for *gun*, and so on. Two questions arise about young children's lexical innovations. First, why do children create new words? Children appear to create new words to fill gaps in their lexicon in particular communicative situations. Second, how do they do it?

One difficulty children face is that their vocabulary for actions is generally behind their vocabulary for objects. Verb meanings typically take a long time to work out (Gentner, 1978). For this reason, children create new verbs to meet the demands of particular communicative situations. The best way of doing this is to follow the rule that any noun denoting a concrete entity can be used as a verb for talking about a state, process, or activity associated with that entity (E. Clark, 1982). This rule for forming innovative denominalized verbs essentially captures a fundamental aspect of metonymic reasoning, where a part of something can stand for a whole activity or event. Thus, referring to *scale* in *You have to scale it first* represents a "stands for" relationship in the entire action sequence of weighing something. Similarly, *needled* in *Is it needled yet?* functions in a "stands for" relationship in the entire sequence of actions in mending something. These innovative denominalized verbs are simply not seen with any regularity in adult speech. Moreover, it is unlikely that children produce innovative denominalized verbs because of any confusion in their part-of-speech assignments for particular words. If this were the case, then young children should also use verbs as nouns, something that is rarely seen (ibid.). Instead, using a noun to act as a verb represents a precise means for children to talk about actions. The ubiquity with which young children create innovative denominalized verbs implies an ability to reason metonymically. Such linguistic evidence gives additional weight to the claim that children possess various kinds of figurative thought.

Children's creation and understanding of indirect requests also requires metonymic thought in that speakers make mention of a salient part of request transactions (e.g., *I need a drink of water*). Children's earliest requests are performed with gestures alone (Bates, 1976); somewhat later, via the combination of gestures and the names of desired objects (Carter, 1974; Dore, 1974; Ervin-Tripp, 1977; Halliday, 1977). Both observational and experimental studies report evidence of children's comprehension of direct and indirect requests at very early ages. Very young children with minimal linguistic skills do well in request transactions in which the roles of both participants are familiar and well understood. Children's experience with these transactions results in some request forms becoming conventionally situated, with children understanding these requests as wholes (Ervin-Tripp, 1977). In situations with unfamiliar partners, children's knowledge of conventional social routines allows them to respond appropriately in most cases, even though these children's ability to focus on specific grammatical nuances of the language is limited.

When children's linguistic knowledge is minimal, they make full use of contextual information and successfully respond to many action requests, regardless of their syntactical form. As children grow, their comprehension of requests becomes more dependent upon the grammatical structure of these utterances (Reeder, Wakefield, & Shapiro, 1988). This greater sensitivity to linguistic structure may result in increased misunderstanding of certain request forms that are particularly ambiguous or complex. However, the fact that young children formulate indirect speech acts and understand them in context suggests some ability to see how the mention of an object or some salient action can stand for an entire series of events that constitute the transaction of goods in request situations.

Many experimental studies support this claim about the link between metonymic thought and children's use and understanding of indirect speech acts. One study required 4-, 5-, and 6-year-old children to judge the appropriateness of a listener's response to three types of indirect requests differing only in their syntactic structure (ibid.). Some requests were affirmative syntactic constructions (e.g., *Can you shut the door?*), some contained a negative component (e.g., *Can't you answer the phone?*), and others requested the state of affairs presented in the predicate to be changed (e.g., *Must you play the piano?*). Children responded appropriately at the same level to indirect requests in the form of negative and affirmative constructions. Children at all three ages experienced some difficulty with requests containing modals *should* and *must* and did not always see that the behavior specified in the predicate must or must not be performed.

The findings of these studies demonstrate that children as young as 2 to 3 years of age develop appropriate strategies to respond to direct and indirect requests. However, what is still unclear is the extent to which children rely on contextual information to disambiguate the linguistic structure of requests. Children aged 1 and 2 show no difference in their appropriate responses to their mothers' direct (e.g., *Move the chair*) and indirect (e.g., *Can you move the chair?*) requests, regardless of whether the desired action is made explicit or not (Shatz, 1978). Older children, aged 3 years 6 months to 5 years 6 months, respond appropriately to indirect action requests with equal success, but older children (4- and 5-year-olds) did so about twice as often as did the younger children (Carrell, 1981; Garvey, 1975). Children sometimes produce yes–no answers to indirect action requests (e.g., *Can you put this where the dog is standing?*), indicating a reliance on the literal meaning of the embedded form. In other cases children recognize an intended request but misinterpret what exactly is being requested. For instance, to the indirect request *Can you put this where the dog is standing?* children will sometimes move the dog to the object, and to the information request *Can you tell me where the coat hanger belongs?* children respond *It's for hanging up coats* (Ledbetter & Dent, 1988). Preschoolers respond to indirect requests for action, such as *I need a wheel now*, with justification or noncompliance that makes reference to their inability to do the requested act, the lack of availability to comply, and so on (Garvey, 1975). Children seem to reply on the basis of appropriate conditions just the way adults judge certain directives as appropriate.

Children also seem biased to focus first on the implications of a message rather than on the specific propositional content or literal meaning of an utterance (Ackerman, 1986). Thus, children's successful responding to indirect requests may be a consequence of their *performative bias* and not a function of fully analyzing the propositional content and relating it to a list of contextually appropriate conditions in order to derive an indirect implication (Shatz, 1985).

One study showed that even 2-year-olds demonstrate some ability to adjust their behavior according to linguistic context. However, all the children, and especially younger ones, showed a bias to act in response to utterances, regardless of context. This action bias is a different strategy that diminishes as the child learns more about contextual or linguistic markings that indicate what sort of response is appropriate.

Young children's seemingly appropriate response behavior should not necessarily be taken as evidence that they share with adults the rather sophisticated speech act knowledge or inferential processes that have been associated with adults' indirect language use. Children as young as 2½ years old chose different paraphrases of the utterance *Would you like to play on the train?*, depending on whether the nonlinguistic context supported a request interpretation (the paraphrase "I want you to play on the train") or an offer interpretation (the paraphrase "I'll let you play on the train"). Yet one doesn't want to argue that children have an understanding that *Would you . . .?* sentences can be used in two ways. Some other sentence forms were not used in the initial sentence position, so children could very well have selected the utterance most appropriate to their interactional understanding without reference to the earlier statement uttered. Thus, it remains unclear whether they have demonstrated a sophisticated knowledge of the form–function relationship or just an understanding of two different situations primarily on nonlinguistic grounds.

Nevertheless, the ability of even young children to respond appropriately to many forms of indirect request illustrates their ability to use what is said and the context at hand to metonymically infer an entire request transaction. Even though children do not possess enough knowledge of form–function relationships to be completely accurate in making and understanding indirect speech acts, it is clear that they possess enough metonymic ability to act appropriately in many discourse situations.

UNDERSTANDING IRONY

Although developmental psychologists have studied metaphor and indirect speech act understanding in some detail, there have been far fewer empirical investigations of children's comprehension of irony and sarcasm. Following traditional approaches to figurative language, many developmental researchers assume that irony serves different cognitive and social functions than does metaphor. Metaphor highlights specific attributes of an object, person, or event and communicates new information about it (serving a cognitive function). Irony highlights the speaker's attitude toward the subject and presupposes an appreciation of that attitude by the listener (serving a social function). Children's acquisition of these two types of figurative speech supposedly differs because of the different function each serves (Winner, 1988).

A variety of empirical evidence suggests that children acquire a facility for metaphor before they use and understand ironic speech. Metaphor is more easily recognized as nonliteral than irony, because metaphor taken literally makes a highly implausible statement. For instance, Hamlet's metaphoric comment that the world is an unweeded garden is literally quite implausible. In contrast, an ironic statement like *This is what I call a peaceful way to spend the evening* is a fairly plausible statement; listeners could easily misinterpret this remark as a positive evaluation even when the speaker intends it ironically. Because the degree of implausibility serves as a cue to a speakers' nonliteral intentions, children are more likely to avoid a literal interpretation of metaphoric than of ironic statements.

On the other hand, it is easier to detect the relation between what is said and what is meant in irony than in metaphor, because what is meant ironically always refers to some aspect of the context in which it is said. As long as children recognize a speaker's reason to be critical, as when a speaker says *You're a fine friend*, they should have little difficulty realizing that what is meant is roughly the opposite of what was said. In the case of metaphor, however, even if the listener realizes that the speaker means to convey something similar to what was said, there are still many possible interpretations that could lead to misunderstanding. The world is truly like an unweeded garden in many ways (both share physical elements of soil, grass, plants, and general disorderliness), but the specific set of attributes meant to be highlighted must still be figured out.

These observations generally indicate that errors in understanding metaphor occur at the point at which children must discover the relations between what is said and what is meant, whereas errors in irony comprehension are most often seen at an earlier stage, in which children must recognize that an utterance is intended nonliterally, in that the speaker does not mean what he or she literally says (ibid.).

One of the earliest studies on irony comprehension looked at children's ability to detect the intentional falsity of ironic utterances (Ackerman, 1982). Children in the first and third grades were presented with stories ending in statements that were true, ironic, erroneous, or deceptive. One story described a boy named Billy whose brother ran in a race. There was a true version and an ironic version, in which Billy said *I see you won again*, even though his brother lost the race. Another version was written so that when Billy said *I see you won again*, he had mistakenly assumed that his brother had won the race. Finally, a deceptive version of the story had Billy clearly lying when he said *I see you won again*.

These stories were read to the children with appropriate intonation, including an ironic tone of voice when Billy spoke sarcastically. Each child was asked three questions about the final statement in each story: (1) *Did Billy's brother run well?* (a fact question), (2) *Did Billy know how well his brother had run?* (a belief question), and (3) *Was Billy pleased with his brother's performance?* (an intent question).

The 6-year-olds were not as good as the 8-year-olds or a group of adults at noting inconsistencies between the facts and the final statements, but they were able to detect that the various ironic and deceptive utterances were false. The 6-year-olds responded to the belief questions incorrectly much more often than did the 8-year-olds or the adults, and both 6- and 8-year-old children gave far fewer correct answers to the intent questions than did the adults when they heard ironic or deceptive statements. Yet the children experienced little difficulty inferring the speakers' intentions when they heard literally erroneous or literally true utterances. These findings suggest that children have trouble explaining why a speaker would say something false.

Distinguishing irony from deception is critical, because children tend to confuse the two. Various empirical studies explicitly distinguish between children's interpretations of intentional falsehoods as irony and as lies. One study presented children with stories that ended in sarcastic, deceptive, neutral, or sincere remarks (Demorest, Meyer, Phelps, Gardner, & Winner, 1984). In one story, a boy named Jay was embarrassed because he got a haircut that made his ears stick out. As Jay left the barbershop, he encountered his friend Mike. The story ended with the remark by Mike *Your haircut looks really terrific*. In the deception version, Mike spoke with a sincere intonation, put his arm on Jay's shoulder, and smiled. In the sarcastic version, Mike spoke with a sneer in his voice (sarcastic intonation) and laughed at Jay as he pointed at the hair-

cut. No intonational or behavior cues were present in the neutral story. Neutral items were included to determine whether,
given a false remark, children are more likely to infer deceptive than sarcastic intent. Finally, the story was altered in the
sincere–true version so that the statement was true: Jay's haircut was good. This sincere–true statement was uttered with
the same intonation as in the deception version.

The children were questioned about the truth (e.g., *Was Jay's
haircut good or bad?*), belief (e.g., *Did Mike think Jay's haircut
was good or bad?*), and literalness (e.g., *Did Mike want Jay to
think his haircut was good or bad?*) of each story. Each of these
questions reflected Grice's (1975) conversational maxims.
Children aged between 6 and 13 tended to ignore the literalness violation in the case of sarcasm and hence mistook sarcasm as deception. Understanding deception proved much
easier than understanding sarcasm. Only 6-year-olds had difficulty with deception, often interpreting it as either sincere
and true or sincere but wrong.

Why should children be biased to interpret irony as deception? Children might expect utterances to obey ordinary conversational maxims and consequently have trouble noticing
violations of these maxims. When several violations occur at
once, as in the case of irony, children are likely to note only
some of them and therefore to confuse irony with deception.
Children may also have difficulty with the idea of deliberately
saying one thing but meaning the opposite. Just as, at a perceptual level, young children have difficulty reconciling appearance and reality (Flavell & Taylor, 1984), on a verbal level
children have difficulty reconciling sentence and speaker
meaning.

However, there are other data showing that even 6-year-
olds possess some ability to distinguish irony and deception.
One study timed children as they decided whether a speaker
was making a mistake, telling a lie, or teasing (the term used
for irony) (Winner, 1988). Children took less time to decide
that an ironic remark was a lie than to decide that a lie was a
lie. At some level, children appear to discern that irony and
deception have different communicative functions, even if
these children often think of both as deception. Misunder-

standing irony appears to reflect a genuine conceptual confusion about why someone would knowingly say something false and not intend to deceive the listener (ibid.).

Other studies investigated young children's understanding of hyperbole and understatement (Winner, Windmueller, Rosenblatt, Bosco & Best, 1987). Children viewed videotapes of characters interacting, each ending with an understatement or a sarcastic or hyperbolic remark. In the sarcastic scene, two children were discussing the newspaper's weather forecast, which predicted sunshine. One child insisted that the paper was always right. Later, when it started to rain, the other child said *Your paper sure was right about the weather*. In an understatement episode, a girl returned from the grocery store with twenty bags of groceries. Her sister, noticing the number of bags, remarked *You bought a few too many groceries*. In a hyperbolic story, a child lay sick in bed, sneezing and surrounded by many used tissues. Her brother came into the room and exclaimed *You've used up enough tissues to fill the ocean*. After each episode, the children were asked questions about the truth, literalness, and intent of the final statement in each scene.

Overall, children had significantly more trouble understanding hyperbole and understatement than they did sarcasm. Sarcasm, once again, was often misunderstood as deception. Hyperbole, when misunderstood, was seen as either deception or error. Understatement, when misunderstood, was taken as sincere and true. In other words, children tended to ignore one violation for sarcasm (literalness), one or two violations for hyperbole (literalness and/or belief), and all three for understatement.

Many studies demonstrate that young children are much more successful at understanding sarcasm when there is strong linguistic and situational context for speakers' utterances (Vosniadou, 1989). Contextual information is particularly important in helping children recognize that a sarcastic remark is to be interpreted nonliterally. One reason why children detect sarcasm more readily than either hyperbole or understatement is that the discrepancy between sentence meaning and the facts of the situation is greater for sarcasm. Some scholars contend that context is, for this reason, a far more important cue for children to rely on when understanding sarcasm than are intonational cues (Winner, 1988).

There is other evidence, however, to suggest that children rely more on intonation than on the discrepancy between context and literal meaning. Some studies show that younger children do not recognize literal meaning as being potentially distinct from speaker intended meaning (Beal & Flavell, 1984; Bonitatibus, 1988). Not until around the age of 7 or 8 do children appear to consider literal meaning to be a unique form of meaning. At the same time, even babies are attuned to intonation and can use it to differentiate between vocal expressions of different emotions (Fernald & Kuhl, 1987; Mehler, Jusczyk, Lambertz, Halsted, Bertoncini, & Amiel-Tison, 1988).

One study demonstrated the significance of intonation in how children recognize sarcasm (Capelli, Nakagawa, & Madden, 1990). Third and sixth graders were presented with stories containing sarcastic dialogue and were later questioned about the speakers' intentions. The sarcasm in these dialogues was made apparent through the context in which the remark was uttered, the intonation the speaker used, or both. Children in both grades were very good at recognizing sarcasm when the speaker used sarcastic intonation, whether or not the context suggested a nonliteral meaning. Yet these same children had great difficulty detecting sarcasm when no special intonation was used, even though the context clearly supported a nonliteral interpretation of the speakers' remarks.

Intonation provides the primary clue to children that an utterance has sarcastic meaning. In many instances, children recognize a speaker's sarcastic intention through intonation alone. For example, if Dick hears Wendy say *Nice catch* with a sarcastic intonation, he will realize right away that she is insulting him. After noting that Wendy's comment refers to his catch, Dick will infer that she is disparaging his catching abilities. Neither the literal meaning of words nor the specific context plays any role in children's comprehension of sarcasm. Children need not detect any discontinuity between literal meaning and context to recognize people's sarcastic intentions. Without sarcastic intonation, children will often misunderstand speakers' sarcastic remarks (Capelli et al., 1990). Speakers often communicate sarcasm and irony without any special tone of voice, and so young children should experience some difficulty comprehending irony in these situations. However, the fact that even preschool children possess some ability to interpret ironic utterances, as well as to talk in a sarcastic manner, supports the notion that children can often conceptualize situations and speech events in ironic terms.

CONCLUSION

The evidence from developmental psychology does not support the traditional idea that the ability to use and understand figurative language develops late. Instead, young children possess significant ability to think in figurative terms as long as they possess the domain-specific knowledge needed to solve problems and understand linguistic expressions. Development of figurative language understanding may have more to do with the acquisition of various metacognitive and metalinguistic skills than with development of the ability to think figuratively per se. This conclusion is consistent with the growing body of literature demonstrating that analogical reasoning may lie at the core of development, as children learn to represent the world around them using mental models that are structurally similar to the real world (Goswami, 1991; Halford, 1991). Although figurative thinking has its limitations for both children and adults, it seems abundantly clear that young children have some ability to think figuratively and do so spontaneously and without undue effort.

Chapter 10

Implications and future directions

It is nearly impossible to think about the mind and how it works without using our poetic imagination. Consider the opening lines of "The Mind Is an Ancient and Famous Capital," by Delmore Schwartz:

> The mind is a city like London,
> Smoky and populous: it is a capital
> Like Rome, ruined and eternal,
> Marked by the monuments which no one
> Now remembers. For the mind, like Rome, contains
> Catacombs, aqueducts, amphitheatres, palaces,
> Churches, and equestrian statues, fallen, broken, or soiled,
> The mind possesses and is possessed by all the ruins
> Of every haunted, hunted generation's celebration.

We can't help thinking about the mind in figurative terms, because the mind itself is primarily structured out of various tropes. These figures of thought arise naturally from our ordinary, unconscious attempts to make sense of ourselves and the physical world. We admire the special talents of poets like Schwartz to express in words how we often think, yet all of us have as a significant part of our intellectual makeup the ability to think and express ourselves figuratively.

This book has described the various arguments and empirical evidence from recent work in the cognitive sciences on the pervasiveness of poetic thinking in everyday life. My working assumption has been that language is not independent of the mind but reflects our perceptual and conceptual understanding of experience. Figuration is not merely a matter of language but provides much of the foundation for thought, reason, and imagination. My examination of a wide-ranging body of work in cognitive science suggests a number of specific conclusions about the poetics of mind.

First, the assumption that people possess literal thoughts and literal meanings for words and sentences clearly requires dismantling. Our judgment that a particular word or sentence has a literal meaning is actually composed of a complex set of tacit knowledge that, among other things, is highly dependent on the context in which such judgments are made. One of the significant challenges for the cognitive sciences is to define clearly the circumstances under which different judgments of literality are made and to demonstrate how intuitions about literality reflect underlying theories of meaning and conceptual content. Another challenge is to explore in greater detail the extent to which "literal" concepts and meanings are motivated by figurative schemes of thought, such as metaphor and metonymy.

Despite my conclusion that literal meanings are not well defined, it was important to consider whether figurative language requires special cognitive processes in order to be understood. The evidence on this question is overwhelming: Similar cognitive mechanisms drive our understanding of both literal and figurative speech. This does not mean that figurative language is always understood in exactly the same way as nonfigurative language or that all types of figurative language are processed similarly. There may be many occasions when we encounter figurative discourse, especially in reading literary texts, that require additional mental effort to be understood. But the experimental evidence shows that people need not recognize figurative utterances as violating communicative norms or maxims in order to understand what these expressions figuratively mean.

A third conclusion about the poetics of mind is that a great deal of our knowledge and thinking is constituted by metaphorical mappings from dissimilar source and target domains. Many of our most basic concepts (e.g., causation, time, love, anger) are, at the very least, partly constituted by metaphor.

Scientific theories, legal reasoning, myths, art, and a variety of cultural practices exemplify many of the same figurative schemes found in everyday thought and language. We must not overextend this conclusion to assume that all aspects of thinking are metaphorical or even that many metaphorical concepts have no nonmetaphorical parts. A challenge for cognitive scientists is to conduct detailed analyses of different conceptual domains to determine the extent to which concepts, and the language that reflects these concepts, are and are not metaphorical. In the same way, metaphor scholars should continue to see how pervasiveness of metaphor in everyday thought constrains theories of verbal metaphor understanding. We should acknowledge that there are important differences between the *processes* and the *products* of linguistic understanding in formulating accounts of metaphor use. Theorists should be careful not to draw unwarranted conclusions about the processes of metaphor understanding from an examination of metaphor products, and vice versa.

Some of the best evidence about the figurative nature of ordinary thought is found in the work on the idiomatic language that makes up a large part of our everyday speech. Contrary to the traditional view that idioms, cliches, and proverbs are frozen semantic units or dead metaphors, the evidence from cognitive linguistics and psycholinguistics indicates that many of these conventional expressions reflect metaphorical thought that is very much alive and part of our everyday conceptual systems. People tacitly understand that many idiomatic phrases and conventional expressions have the particular meanings they do because such language arises from common metaphorical mappings in everyday thought.

Far less attention has been paid to metonymy and irony than to the master trope, metaphor. Yet there exists significant evidence that our ability to think metonymically and ironically motivates our using and easily understanding metonymic and ironic language. Metonymy constrains many kinds of reasoning and the inferences that establish coherence in discourse. Metonymy also underlies our use and understanding of other types of nonliteral language, such as indirect speech acts and tautological expressions. Irony is also a pervasive mode of thought that is evident not only in the way we speak but in the way we act in a variety of social/cultural situations. Hyperbole, understatement, and oxymora also reflect our conceptual ability to understand and speak about incongruous situations.

A final conclusion from the evidence in this book is that children's emerging ability to think figuratively motivates their use and understanding of many types of figurative speech. Earlier studies suggested that children's ability to understand nonliteral discourse is a late-emerging competence. But more recent research that employs sensitive experimental tasks and that tests understanding in more realistic social contexts shows that even young children possess some ability to comprehend figurative utterances. A challenge for developmental research is to explore in greater detail the relationship of children's conceptual knowledge to their understanding of figurative language. Part of this direction for future research is to study the extent to which children think of themselves and their social and physical worlds in figurative terms.

LANGUAGE, THOUGHT, AND THE BODY

Many of these conclusions about the poetics of mind are not commonly held by contemporary cognitive scientists. Cognitive scientists miss these important conclusions about the figurative nature of everyday thought because they fail to adhere to two primary commitments: (a) a commitment to seek general principles governing all aspects of human language (the generalization commitment) and (b) a commitment to make their account of human language consistent with what is generally known about human cognition (the cognitive commitment) (G. Lakoff, 1990). As outlined in the introduction, many language scholars in the cognitive sciences who seek generalizations that are often thought to reflect underlying linguistic universals work from what can be called the *generative wager* (cf. H. Clark & Malt, 1984).

It is highly likely that most aspects of language that are universal are a result not of general cognitive constraints, but of constraints specific to language functions – specific to an autonomous language faculty. It is therefore appropriate a priori to assume autonomous psychological constraints and to leave it to others to prove otherwise.

On the other hand, some cognitive scientists make the opposite bet, which might be called the *cognitive wager* (cf. Clark & Malt), 1984):

> It is highly likely that most language universals are a result not of linguistically autonomous constraints, but of constraints general to other cognitive functions. It is therefore appropriate a priori to assume that language universals are derived from general cognitive constraints and to leave it to others to prove otherwise.

Scholars who bet on the cognitive wager open themselves up to a whole new range of theoretical explanations that are rarely considered by those adhering to the generativist assumptions. This is not to say that *all* aspects of language reflect conceptual structure, because there is probably a fair amount of linguistic knowledge that is indeed autonomous of general cognitive mechanisms. The advantage of the cognitive approach is that it explicitly looks for possible links between cognition and language. Much of the evidence presented in this book suggests that explicitly studying the links between cognition and language reveals significant aspects of the poetic mind.

Failure to adopt the cognitive wager can lead to some mistaken impressions about the interaction of mind and language. Briefly consider one of the notable instances of the failure to consider cognitive explanations for linguistic structure. This example comes from Benjamin Lee Whorf's (1956) classic work on linguistic determinism. The hypothesis of linguistic determinism holds that the grammatical and categorical patterns of language embody a cultural world view and guide habitual thought. According to this idea, language contains an implicit classification of experience, and the language system as a whole embodies a world view that speakers of a language accept and project onto reality. The language speakers use does not make them blind to obvious facts of the world, but rather suggests associations that are not necessarily part of reality.

Whorf offered an analysis of time nomenclature in English to describe a habitual association of ideas not connected in reality that linguistic categories have engendered. English pluralizes nouns that denote concrete bounded objects, such as *pencils* and *apples*. The plurals of these words have a clear physical meaning of a group of more than one simultaneously present member of the category. However, English also uses the same grammatical pattern to refer to intervals of time that can be experienced only successively. For instance, we say *ten hours* and *ten apples*, yet only apples can be experienced simultaneously as a group of 10. It is just not physically possible to experience successive hours simultaneously. But English-speakers do not find it at all unusual to think of 10 hours as a group of hours. If we think 10 hours is too long for some task, it is not by thinking of a particular individual hour that was the last hour that we couldn't stand but by thinking of all the hours as a whole as too large (McNeil, 1987). This way of thinking follows the associated meaning of the plural pattern, as if hours could be simultaneously present in numbers greater than one.

Referring to 10 hours as a group is not a direct entailment of the experience of time, because speakers of other languages categorize their experiences of time differently. According to Whorf, time in Hopi is not seen as a collection of objects but rather as repeated appearances, similar to the idea of a person's coming to visit over and over. For Hopi-speakers, there is no sense in which successive time intervals can form a group any more than there is a sense in which two visits by the same person constitute a group of two people. This scheme is reflected in the linguistic patterns that the Hopi use to talk about time. For example, the words for *come* and *go* in Hopi refer to a process of "eventuating." *Come* translates into Hopi as *pew'i*, meaning "to eventuate here." *Go* translates as *anggo*, which implies "eventuate from it" (Whorf, 1956). These verbs signify not motion but manifestation. A time interval in the Hopi cultural model eventuates, but it does not move like a physical object in the way time does as part of the cultural model embodied by English verbs. For example, in English we use the TIME IS A MOVING OBJECT model, as when the future approaches us (*The time will come*), when time has moved ahead of us (*The time has long since passed*), or when we face in the direction of time (*Coming up in the weeks ahead* or *Looking forward to the trip*).

Hopi-speakers talk of time intervals using ordinal number terms, so that instead of saying *ten hours*, the Hopi say the equivalent of the 11th hour, meaning the 11th manifestation of an hour. This pattern avoids the individual meaning of a group and specifies a succession. Whorf concluded from this that the Hopi have no concept of time. He commented:

> After long and careful study and analysis, the Hopi language is seen to contain no words, grammatical forms, constructions or expressions that refer directly to what we call "time," or to past, present, or future, or to enduring or lasting. (1956: 57)

Whorf's analysis of Hopi time nomenclature nicely illustrates the generative wager, because it assumes that linguistic patterns arise autonomously from our conceptual system but can subsequently influence how we think about concepts. As he expressed it:

> We cut up and organize the spread and flow of events as we do, largely because, through our mother tongue, we are parties to an agreement to do so, not because nature itself is segmented in exactly the same way for all to see. (1956: 240)

If we accept this analysis and the resulting thesis of linguistic determinism, a very different picture emerges about the relation between figurative thought and everyday language than would be formulated from a cognitive point of view. According to the Whorfian view, instead of language's reflecting different schemes of figurative thought, language itself actually imposes its structure on thought and helps induce people to think figuratively, in some cases, about their experiences and the physical world. Although our everyday conceptual system is inherently not figurative, the figurative patterns of linguistic expression to which we are exposed would actually induce, for example, certain metaphorical mappings in which we partly conceptualize one domain of knowledge in terms of a dissimilar domain.

Even though we presumably have some conceptual notion of time that is not figurative, our exposure to these different linguistic expressions, such as *You're wasting my time, This gadget will save time, You're running out of time,* and *I've invested a lot of time in her,* highlights the possibility that time *can be* understood metaphorically as being like money. Many speakers will deduce the conceptual metaphor TIME IS MONEY not through any automatic conceptual mappings that arise from their everyday nonlinguistic experience but through knowing the various linguistic expressions American English has for speaking about time.

Of course, there is no doubt that people's experience with language enables them to recognize certain conceptual distinctions (cf. Lucy, 1992, for the most recent review of the extensive literature on this topic). For example, people may indeed learn to understand the idea that time can be thought of as money simply through some tacit awareness that English talks about time in the way it does. Yet the deeper question is *why* we speak about time, for instance, in the ways we do. There appears to be a conceptual motivation for why English-speakers see time as being like money. It is not just an arbitrary fact of English that we, unlike the Hopi, just happen to speak of time as money, because we actually *think* of time as money. Because time is an abstract concept, we automatically attempt to make sense of our experience of time via metaphor. At one level, we cannot really be said to have a concept of time apart from metaphor. We certainly have an *experience* of time that is nonmetaphorical, but we *conceptualize* time via metaphor, and the resulting metaphorical knowledge partly explains why we speak of time in the ways we do.

One important examination of time nomenclature in Hopi, following up on Whorf's preliminary observations, found, contrary to Whorf's conclusions, that Hopi-speakers also conceptualize time in various metaphorical ways (Malotki, 1983).

Different spatiotemporal metaphors motivate many of the ways Hopi-speakers express their conceptions of time. For example, the term *hayingwna* ("he approached it") is used spatially, as in *nu' put a-ngk hayingw-na* ("I got close behind him"). This spatial term is used metaphorically to express the idea of "getting closer to a point in time," as in *taawa-na-sa-mi ha-hayingw-na* ("It's getting closer to noon") or *tal'angw-mi hayingw-ti* ("It has gotten close to summer"). Similarly, the noun *qeni* ("space" or "an area void of physical objects") is metaphorically used to talk of time in the sense of free time to pursue a certain activity, as in *ya pay uu-pe qeni?* ("Do you have time?"). These examples illustrate how a systematic analysis that looks for possible links between spatiotemporal metaphors and time nomenclature shows that Hopi's talk of time is partly motivated by figurative thought.

There is an important lesson to be learned from this discussion of Whorf and linguistic determinism, a lesson that cognitive scientists should heed in their research on the relationship between thought and language. Most generally, it seems impossible a priori to distinguish between those universals whose explanations probably lie within an autonomous language faculty, if there is one, and those whose explanations lie outside this faculty. Really to demonstrate some aspects of linguistic structure are autonomous, one must show how this idea contrasts with cognitive explanations. Embracing the generative view simply doesn't allow for such contrasts; cognitive science theories of linguistic structure have suffered as a result.

My belief is that much of the research discussed in this book actually contributes to a deeper understanding of the conceptual contents of the human mind than is normally found in contemporary cognitive science precisely because this work embraces the cognitive wager. For instance, many analyses of systematic patterns in language suggest a variety of conceptual and preconceptual structures that make up the poetic mind, including idealized cognitive models, image schemas, metaphoric and metonymic mappings, mental spaces, and radial structures. This emphasis on the *content* of what people know and the bodily experiences that give rise to such knowledge is quite different from the major focus in cognitive science on the general *architectural form* of human thought and language.

For example, cognitive psychologists historically attempt to characterize the different structural stores through which information is processed and transformed from input (i.e., when information enters the system from the environment) to output (i.e., behavioral response). Psychologists work on identifying such information processing stores as sensory, short-term, and long-term memory or try to distinguish between different systems within long-term memory, such as semantic and episodic memory stores. Most recently, cognitive psychologists have been arguing about whether human cognition is best characterized as a symbolic or subsymbolic (e.g., neural network) system. In most cases, cognitive psychologists focus on the architecture of mind and on the mental processes that operate within this representational system. They do not worry about the kind of knowledge people have or how people come to know what they do about themselves and the world.

Consistent with this information processing approach to the study of mind in cognitive psychology, psycholinguists traditionally concentrate on specifying the general architecture of the language processor. For example, do people possess separate linguistic processors representing their knowledge of phonology, morphology, the lexicon, syntax, semantics, and pragmatics? This theoretical concern with general architectural features of the human language processor and the processes that operate on these linguistic representations has provided cognitive science with a rich array of insights into the structure of mind. But, as in the case of cognitive psychology in general, there is very little impetus in psycholinguistics to study the contents of the mind in terms of the actual beliefs and conceptions that people have of themselves and the world around them or how such knowledge specifically motivates linguistic behavior. Understanding what people actually know and what motivates how they know what they do is viewed as less theoretically interesting than being able to characterize the overall architecture of the mind. For this reason, psycholinguists, and cognitive scientists in general, tend not to focus on the cognitive motivation for linguistic structures, even though examining the cognitive bases of language reveals the fundamental poetic nature of everyday thought and language.

Looking at the actual content of what people know and its relation to everyday language also suggests specific links between language, mind, and the body. A great deal of our conceptual and linguistic knowledge arises from our bodily interactions with the world. Such knowledge is not static, propositional, and sentential, but grounded in recurring patterns of bodily experience. These patterns emerge throughout sensorimotor activity as we manipulate objects, orient ourselves spatially or temporally, and direct our perceptual focus for various purposes (M. Johnson, 1991). As was described earlier in regard to young children's acquisition of concepts, for example, we have a SOURCE–PATH–GOAL schema that develops as we learn to focus our eyes and track forms as they move through our visual field. From such experiences, a recurring pattern becomes manifest in tracking a trajector from Point A to another point, B. The pattern itself may vary considerably (many, e.g., objects, shapes, types of paths), but the emergent image schematic structure SOURCE–PATH–GOAL can be projected onto more abstract domains of understanding and reasoning (M. Johnson, 1987). Thus, the SOURCE–PATH–GOAL schema gives rise to conceptual metaphors, such as PURPOSES ARE DESTINATIONS. English is replete with systematic expressions that illustrate this underlying metaphorical conceptualization. For instance, we start off to get our Ph.D.s, but along the way we get sidetracked or led astray and are diverted from our original goal. We try to get back on the right path and to keep the end in view as we move along. Eventually we may come a long way and reach our goal (M. Johnson, 1991). This way of talking about experience shows how the PURPOSES ARE DESTINATIONS metaphor resulting from a very basic image schematic structure is constitutive of our understanding of intentional action.

It is not simply an arbitrary fact of English that we talk about our lives and careers in terms of sources, paths, and goals; rather we metaphorically conceptualize our experiences through very basic sensory experiences that are abstracted to form figurative thought. The SOURCE–PATH–GOAL schema is just one of many image schemas that structure a great deal of our understanding in its bodily and abstract dimensions (M. Johnson, 1987, 1991; G. Lakoff, 1987). Other prominent image schemas used in reasoning and knowledge include OBJECT, FIGURE–GROUND, CONTAINER, CYCLE, FORCE, BALANCE, ITERATION, and CENTER–PERIPHERY (M. Johnson, 1987). These image schemas are not merely discrete mental images, similar to those studied by cognitive psychologists, but reflect recurring overlapping patterns in the continuous flow of our subjective experiences in the world.

The work demonstrating explicit links between bodily experience and the actual content of what people know and understand is unique in the cognitive sciences. Looking for the conceptual and bodily foundations of knowledge through systematic analyses of linguistic expressions provides for a comprehensive understanding of both thought and language. Many cognitive linguists are constructing theories of language around bodily/perceptual representations (Jackendoff, 1987; G. Lakoff, 1987; G. Lakoff & Johnson, 1980; Langacker, 1986; Talmy, 1988). It is likely that adopting a bodily/perceptual view of concepts will better explain the structure and flexibility of concepts and many aspects of linguistic vagary (Barsalou, in press; see Chapter 2). Most generally, linking linguistic symbols with bodily/perceptual image schemas provides a natural solution to the symbols grounding problem often discussed in the cognitive sciences (Harnad, 1987, 1990; M. Johnson, 1987; G. Lakoff, 1987; Searle, 1980).

FIGURATIVE THOUGHT AND LINGUISTIC UNDERSTANDING

One reason why figurative thought is not traditionally seen as an important part of ordinary language use and understanding stems from the failure to distinguish between different levels at which cognition and language may interact. The five possible hypotheses considered in this book about how figurative thought may influence ordinary language use and understanding were:

1. Figurative thought has *nothing* to do with either the historical evolution of linguistic meaning or speakers' ordinary understanding of everyday language.

2. Figurative thought plays some role in changing the meanings of words and expressions over time but does not motivate ordinary speakers' contemporary use and understanding of language.

3. Figurative thought motivates the linguistic meanings that have currency within linguistic communities or may have some role in an *idealized* speaker's/hearer's understanding of language. But figurative thought does not actually play any part in individual speakers' cognitive systems to facilitate their ordinary understanding of language.

4. Figurative thought motivates an individual speaker's use and understanding of why various words and expressions mean what they do but does not play any role in people's ordinary on-line production or comprehension of everyday language.

5. Figurative thought is an essential part of our cognitive systems and functions automatically in people's on-line use and understanding of linguistic meaning.

Testing the validity of these hypotheses requires that scholars adhere to a commitment to look for possible effects of figurative thought on language change and ordinary language use and processing. Yet many cognitive scientists interested in capturing generalizations about linguistic structures fail to study or even acknowledge the hypothesis that figurative thought is a fundamental aspect of everyday thinking that potentially has many links to how people use and understand language. Much of the work described in this book has explicitly adopted the cognitive wager and has sought to explore the possible relations between figurative thought and language. This evidence clearly rejects possibility (1) and supports the claim that figurative thought motivates semantic change, the linguistic meanings that have currency in a language, how speakers make sense of why various expressions mean what they do, and possibly people's on-line production and processing of language. It is especially important to distinguish among these different possibilities for the relation between thought and language, because many cognitive scientists play fast and loose among these possibilities when they claim that figurative cognition either does or does not play a role in language use and understanding. For example, the evidence from cognitive linguistics and psycholinguistics that supports possibilities (2), (3), and (4) does not necessarily indicate that possibility (5) is true. It is incorrect to suppose that figurative knowledge has an automatic, immediate role in people's on-line processing of language until further on-line experiments have been conducted.

Of course, the fact that few on-line studies have explored the possible use of figurative concepts in immediate utterance interpretation should not lead cognitive scientists to dismiss the idea that figurative thought influences language understanding. Psycholinguistic research primarily focuses on very fast, unconscious mental processes that occur when people first read or hear language material. Yet this emphasis captures only a small part of what it means to understand language. The extensive evidence discussed in this book certainly points to different levels of understanding, such as that associated with how people make sense of what linguistic expressions mean. People have conceptual knowledge, much of which is figuratively based, that allows them to understand why it just makes sense to talk, for instance, of arguments as wars, anger as heated fluid in a container, time as money, and love as a journey. It is not just an arbitrary fact of the language that English-speakers, for example, talk about anger in terms of stacks being blown, ceilings being hit, or steam being released. Instead, people's bodily, real-world experiences help motivate such talk, and we use this knowledge to make sense of various linguistic expressions in the language. We may not necessarily tap into this deeper conceptual knowledge each and every time we encounter language, especially if such language is highly conventional. Even so, we clearly use such conceptual knowledge to make sense of why the language is the way it is. Psycholinguistic research needs to focus on these different aspects of what it means to understand language and not concentrate exclusively on those mental processes that operate in the first few hundred milliseconds of comprehension. Most generally, figurative language scholars must be careful not to generalize conclusions about one aspect of the temporal course of understanding in making claims about all aspects of linguistic understanding.

The empirical analysis of figurative thought has focused primarily on metaphor, with significantly less attention being paid to other tropes, such as metonymy and irony. One large-scale analysis by cognitive linguists at the University of California at Berkeley reveals that there are at least several hundred interrelated conceptual metaphors underlying everyday thinking and language (G. Lakoff, Espenson, Goldberg, & Schwartz, 1992). Many, but not all, of these conceptual metaphors are evident in languages other than English. Similar analyses suggest that there may be several dozen conceptual metonymies. Much additional work needs to be done to flesh out the major conceptual metaphors and metonymies in many world cultures. At the same time, there has been no empirical work in identifying conceptual ironies or oxymora other than to note, as I have done in this book, that these tropes provide distinct conceptual stances that individuals adopt to interpret their everyday experiences. No work has yet been done to answer the question of whether different kinds of conceptual metonymies and ironies play any role in how people make sense of or comprehend metonymic and ironic statements. Future work must explore the extent to which people use figurative knowledge in making sense of and immediately processing conventional expressions that for the most part seem quite literal. This work would be especially important because it could point the way to a better integration of ideas about sentence processing as studied by most psycholinguists with the growing body of research on figurative language understanding. In summary, the empirical examination of figurative thought and its role in linguistic understanding is still very much in its infancy.

A final aspect of figurative thought and linguistic understanding that deserves further attention is the distinction between *figurative processing* as a general mode of understanding that can be applied to any kind of situation or language and *processing figurative language*. The empirical studies on figurative discourse have predominantly examined how different aspects of language – metaphor, metonymy, irony, and so on – are understood. But there are many instances, especially in reading literature, when a specific figurative type of processing is given to a particular text. Figurative processing, as opposed to processing figurative language, may be distinguished as an intentionally selected strategy for reading (Steen, 1993). When readers adopt such strategies, the processing that occurs is figurative, even though there is no special linguistic or textual material that is either figurative or motivated by figurative modes of thought. Various literary theorists have noted how it is possible to produce a highly poetic reading of a poem or text because of a reader's explicit literary way of interpreting it (D. Lodge, 1977; Steen, 1993; Wellek & Warren, 1949). In this way, metaphor, metonymy, irony, and so on can legitimately be viewed as types of literary strategies that color people's imaginative understanding of texts and real-world situations. We must be careful to distinguish figurative processing from processing figurative language and turn some of our attention to what figurative processing strategies reveal about the ordinary poetic character of human cognition.

INTERACTION OF TROPES

This book has primarily investigated how different tropes reflect distinct cognitive processes of the poetic mind. Yet figures of thought do not exist in isolation from one another. Although metaphor and metonymy, for instance, individually motivate different kinds of linguistic expression, there are many cases where these tropes are combined in natural language. One analysis of the interaction of metaphor and metonymy in expressions of linguistic actions observed instances of both metaphor arising from metonymy and metonymy within metaphor (Goossens, 1990).

Consider first how we get metaphors for which there is a link with their metonymic origins. One instance is the phrase *to be close-lipped*, meaning "to be silent or to say little." *Close-*

lipped can be paraphrased literally as "having the lips close together" or as "having the lips closed." When *close-lipped* is used to indicate that a person is literally silent, we need the metonymic reading. If, on the other hand, we describe as *close-lipped* someone who is actually talking a lot but does not give away what we really want to hear from him or her, we have a metaphor. (Given the saliency of the metonymic reading, we have a metaphor from metonymy.)

Another example of metaphor from metonymy is to *speak tongue in cheek* ("to say something and mean the opposite, especially in an ironic way"). The metonymic motivation for this phrase comes from the scene in which you literally push your tongue into your cheek while saying something you do not really mean. In this metonymic reading, the tongue in the cheek is taken to be intentionally linked up with the ironic impact of what the speaker says. More generally, though, we use the phrase *tongue in cheek* to express that the primary speaker says something *as if* he or she had the tongue literally in the cheek – where there is a metaphorical mapping between two dissimilar domains (the domain of a tongue literally in the cheek and the domain of saying something ironic).

The other kind of interaction noted in this analysis is metonymy within metaphor. Consider the phrase *shoot off your mouth* ("to talk foolishly about something that one doesn't know much about or should not talk about"). The source domain in this metaphorical mapping is a foolish use of firearms, and it is mapped onto the target domain of unthoughtful linguistic action. When the word *mouth* is integrated into a scene relating to the use of firearms, it must be reinterpreted as having the properties of the gun alluded to in the phrase *shoot off your mouth*. In the target domain, however, there is a first level of interpretation that amounts to something like "to use your mouth foolishly," in which *mouth* metonymically stands for the speech faculty. This interaction of metonymy with metaphor motivates why *Don't shoot off your mouth* means "Don't say anything rash." A similar type of analysis can be given to other expressions about linguistic action, such as *catch someone's eye*.

These analyses of the interaction of metaphor and metonymy

in expressions of linguistic action illustrate how tropes are frequently combined to give rise to ordinary linguistic expressions. I mention this work because our poetic imagination is probably more complex and organized than a mere collection of individual tropes (see Chapter 4 for some preliminary attempts to elucidate these complex structures). Significant research remains to be done on the extent to which different tropes interact in everyday thought and ordinary linguistic use.

One of the unexplored properties of tropes is their multiplicity of function. Tropes are not frozen into objects and beings or into the linguistic expressions of the language. Individual symbols may take on different tropical meanings or functions depending on their use in particular social and historical contexts. Cultural anthropologists recognize the complex nature of polytropic symbols, or symbols whose multiple meanings in various contexts function as different types of trope (Fernandez, 1986, 1991; Friedrich, 1991; Ohnuki-Tierney, 1991).

One examination of the monkey in Japanese culture nicely demonstrates how polytropic symbols function in a culture. The monkey has served throughout history as the dominant verbal and visual metaphor of the self for the Japanese. At one level, the physiological parts of the monkey have simple equivalents to human parts. Each part constitutes a metonym for the monkey, but these metonymic forms are chosen to represent the monkey because of their metaphorical ability to link monkeys with humans. For example, the concept "monkey eyes" often stands for an entire monkey or the concept of monkey. But "monkey eyes" more generally represents for the Japanese a physiological part, the behavioral function of vision, the perceptual/intellectual capacity of humans to perceive reality, and the aesthetic/moral capacity of humans to feel emotion, especially sadness. Monkey eyes, therefore, simultaneously serve metonymically in relation to the whole monkey and metaphorically in relation to human body parts and significant human experiences. In this way, the phrase *monkey eyes* acts as a polytropic symbol in the poetic construction of the Japanese self. Most generally, anthropological research has begun to identify some of the ways that polytropic symbols function in different cultural experiences. This work should guide researchers in other fields in thinking about how the interactions of tropes are constitutive of human thought and language.

A final example of how tropes interact is an examination of the ways that authors frequently intertwine tropes in narratives. Authors combine tropes in narratives in subtle ways, often shifting between tropes as they shift points of view. One wonderful example of this narrative strategy is seen in a passage from Marcel Proust's *Remembrance of Things Past* (H. White, 1988). The passage relates four successive characterizations of a fountain by the narrator, Marcel, as he walks toward it in a garden of the Guermantes' palace where he has been attending a soiree. Presented below is the passage (Proust 1927/1981: 680–81).

It could be seen from a distance, slender, motionless, rigid, set apart in a clearing surrounded by fine trees, several of which were as old as itself, only the lighter fall of its pale and quivering plume stirring in the breeze. The eighteenth century had refined the elegance of its lines, but, by fixing its style of the jet, seemed to have arrested its life; at this distance one had the impression of art rather than the sensation of water. Even the moist cloud that was perpetually gathering at the summit preserved the character of the period like those that assemble in the sky round the palace of Versailles. But from a closer view one realized that, while it respected, like the stones of an ancient palace, the design traced for it beforehand, it was a constantly changing stream of water that, springing upwards and seeking to obey the architect's original orders, performed them to the letter only by seeming to infringe them, its thousand separate bursts succeeding only from afar in giving the impression of a single thrust. This was reality as often interrupted as the scattering of the fall, whereas from a distance it had appeared to me dense, inflexible, unbroken in its continuity. From a little nearer, one saw that this continuity, apparently complete, was assured, at every point in the ascent of the jet where it must otherwise have been broken, by the entering into line, by the lateral incorporation of a parallel jet which mounted higher than the first and was itself, at a greater altitude which was however already a strain upon its endurance, relieved by a third. From close to, exhausted drops could be seen falling back from the column of water, passing their sisters on the way up, and at times, torn and scattered, caught in an eddy of the night air, disturbed by this unremitting surge, floating awhile before being drowned in the basin. They teased with their hesitations, with their journey in the opposite direction, and blurred with their soft vapour the vertical tension of the shaft that bore aloft an oblong cloud composed of countless tiny drops but seemingly painted in an unchanging golden brown which rose, unbreakable, fixed, slender, swift, to mingle with the clouds in the sky. Unfortunately, a gust of wind was enough to scatter it obliquely on the ground; at times indeed a single disobedient jet swerved and, had they not kept a respectful distance, would have drenched to their skins the incautious crowd of gazers.

This passage is organized in a manner that is *more tropical than logical* (H. White, 1988: 256). That is, the narrative is organized in terms of the meanings and functions of the different tropes and their relations to each other rather than by a series of propositions that are logically or causally connected. In particular, the passage presents the narrator's movement successively through the four tropes of metaphor, metonymy, synecdoche, and irony as alternative descriptions of the fountain. This "movement" through the four tropes parallels the actual movement of the narrator toward the fountain from an initial *metaphoric apprehension* of it, through a metonymic characterization as a *dispersion of its attributes*, to a *synecdochic comprehension of its possible nature*, to, finally, *an ironic distancing of the process of narration itself* (ibid., p. 258).

For example, from a distance, the narrator's impression of the fountain is captured in a metaphor as a *pale and quivering plume*. Closer, the fountain is metonymically described as *scattering of the fall*, with new jets of water producing the effect of a *single thrust*. Even closer, the fountain is understood in a synecdochic manner in which the form and content of the spray are grasped together. Finally, the fountain is seen in ironic terms in the contrast between the various figures of speech and the reminder from the unfortunate *gust of wind* that the fountain is, after all, only a fountain. None of these tropical modes of description is better than any other, but the end of the passage gives us the critical information needed to grasp *the point of it all*: that the events in this story are of a particular kind, specifically an *ironic story* (ibid, p. 263).

The sequence of tropes in this passage constitutes a narrative structure and a mode of interpretation. The individual tropes do not work independently but are functionally related to each other to provide figurative coherence to the text that cannot be explained merely in logical or causal terms. This kind of narrative strategy reflects the fundamental impulse of authors to construe events in figurative ways that involve the complex interaction of different tropes.

CODA

What does our poetic imagination matter to cognitive science? My response to this question is that cognitive science cannot approach adequate explanations of human mind and behavior until it comes to terms with the fundamental poetic character of everyday thought. This argument is not similar to the Romantics' heralding of the imagination over rationality in which, as Shelley claimed, *poets are the unacknowledged legislators of the world*. Figurative language is not the novel creation of unconstrained imaginative thinking, because the evidence presented in this book clearly indicates a picture of figurative imagination as a systematic and orderly part of human cognitive processes. My plea is for a greater recognition of the poet in each one of us – to recognize that figuration is not an escape from reality but constitutes the way we ordinarily understand ourselves and the world in which we live.

References

Abbott, V., Black, J., & Smith, E. (1985). The representation of scripts in memory. *Journal of Memory and Language, 24,* 179–199.

Abrahams, R. (1962). Playing the dozens. *Journal of American Folklore, 75,* 207–218.

Abrahams, R. (1968). A rhetoric of everyday life: Traditional conversational genres. *Southern Folklore Quarterly, 32,* 44–59.

Ackerman, B. (1982). Contextual integration and utterance interpretation: The ability of children and adults to interpret sarcastic utterances. *Child Development, 53,* 1075–1083.

Ackerman, B. (1986). Children's sensitivity to comprehension failure in interpreting a nonliteral use of an utterance. *Child Development, 57,* 485–497.

Aitchison, J. (1987). *Words in the mind: An introduction to the mental lexicon.* Oxford: Blackwell Publisher.

Aleksandrowicz, D. (1962). The meaning of metaphor. *Bulletin of the Menninger Clinic, 26,* 92–101.

Allbritton, D. (1992). *The use of metaphor to structure text representations: Evidence for metaphor-based schemas.* Unpublished doctoral dissertation, Yale University.

Alston, W. (1964). *Philosophy of language.* Englewood Cliffs, NJ: Prentice-Hall.

Anderson, R., & Ortony, A. (1975). On putting apples into bottles: A problem of polysemy. *Cognitive Psychology, 7,* 167–180.

Anderson, R., Pichert, J., Goetz, E., Schallert, D., Stevens, K., & Trollip, S. (1976). Instantiation of general terms. *Journal of Verbal Learning and Verbal Behavior, 15,* 667–679.

Anderson, W. (1990). *Reality isn't what it used to be: Theatrical politics, ready-to wear religion, global myths, primitive chic, and other wonders of the postmodern world.* San Francisco: Harper & Row.

References

Apter, M. (1982). Metaphor as synergy. In D. Miall (Ed.), *Metaphor: Problems and perspectives* (pp. 77–91). Brighton: Harvest Park.

Arbib, M., & Hesse, M. (1986). *The construction of reality.* Cambridge: Cambridge University Press.

Arewa, E., & Dundes, A. (1964). Proverbs and the enthnography of speaking folklore. *American Anthropologist, 66,* 70–85.

Arkes, N., & Harkness, A. (1980). Effect of making a diagnosis on subsequent recognition of symptoms. *Journal of Experimental Psychology: Human Learning and Memory, 6,* 568–575.

Arlow, J. (1979). Metaphor and the analytic situation. *Psychoanalytic Quarterly, 48,* 363–385.

Armstrong, S., Gleitman, L., & Gleitman, H. (1983). What some concepts might not be. *Cognition, 13,* 263–308.

Arnheim, R. (1933). *Film.* London: Faber & Faber.

Asch, S., & Nerlove, H. (1960). The development of double function terms in children: An exploratory investigation. In B. Kaplan & S. Wapner (Eds.), *Perspectives in psychological theory: Essays in honor of Heinz Werner* (pp. 47–60). New York: International Universities Press.

Austin, J. (1962). *How to do things with words.* Oxford: Oxford University Press.

Ayer, A. (1936). *Language, truth and logic.* London: Gollancz.

Bach, K., & Harnish, R. (1979). *Linguistic communication and speech acts.* Cambridge, MA: MIT Press.

Barclay, J., Bransford, J., Franks, J., McCarrell, N., & Nitsch, K. (1974). Comprehension and semantic flexibility. *Journal of Verbal Learning and Verbal Behavior, 13,* 471–481.

Barley, N. (1972). A structural approach to the proverb and maxim with special reference to the Anglo-Saxon corpus. *Proverbium, 20,* 737–750.

Barsalou, L. (1982). Context-independent and context-dependent information in concepts. *Memory & Cognition, 10,* 82–93.

Barsalou, L. (1983). Ad hoc categories. *Memory & Cognition, 11,* 211–227.

Barsalou, L. (1985). Ideals, central tendency, and frequency of instantiation as determinants of graded structure in categories. *Journal of Experimental Psychology: Learning, Memory, and Cognition, 11,* 629–654.

Barsalou, L. (1987). The instability of graded structure in concepts. In U. Neisser (Ed.), *Concepts and conceptual development: Ecological and intellectual factors in categorization* (pp. 101–140). New York: Cambridge University Press.

References

Barsalou, L. (1989). Intra-concept similarity and its implications for inter-concept similarity. In S. Vosniadou & A. Ortony (Eds.), *Similarity and analogical reasoning* (pp. 76–121). New York: Cambridge University Press.

Barsalou, L. (1991). Deriving categories to achieve goals. In G. H. Bower (Ed.), *The psychology of learning and motivation: Advances in research and theory* (Vol. 27, pp. 1–64). New York: Academic Press.

Barsalou, L. (in press). Flexibility, structure, and linguistic vagary in concepts: Manifestations of a compositional system of perceptual symbols. In A. Collins, S. Gathercole, M. Conway, & P. Morris (Eds.), *Theories of memory*. Hillsdale, NJ: Erlbaum.

Barsalou, L., & Medin, D. (1986). Concepts: Fixed definitions or dynamic context-dependent representations? *Cahiers de Psychologie Cognitive, 6,* 187–202.

Bates, E. (1976). *Language and context: Studies in the acquisition of pragmatics.* New York: Academic Press.

Bates, E., & MacWhinney, B. (1982). Functionalist approaches to grammar. In E. Wanner & L. Gleitman (Eds.), *Language acquisition: The state of the art* (pp. 173–218). New York: Cambridge University Press.

Beal, C., & Flavell, J. (1984). Development of the ability to distinguish communicative intention and literal message meaning. *Child Development, 55,* 920–928.

Beardsley, M. (1962). The metaphorical twist. *Philosophy and Phenomenological Research, 22,* 293–307.

Beardsley, M. (1976). Metaphor and falsity. *Journal of Aesthetics and Art Criticism, 35,* 218–222.

Beattie, G. (1979). Planning units in spontaneous speech: Some evidence from hesitation in speech and speaker gaze direction in conversation. *Linguistics, 17,* 61–78.

Becker, J. (1975). The phrasal lexicon. In B. Webber & R. Schank (Eds.), *Theoretical issues in natural language processing* (pp. 70–73). Cambridge, MA: Association for Computational Linguistics.

Bennet, D. (1975). *Spatial and temporal uses of English prepositions.* London: Longman Group.

Bettelheim, B. (1955). *Symbolic wounds: Puberty rites and the envious male.* London: Thames & Hudson.

Bettelheim, B. (1976). *The uses of enchantment: The meaning and importance of fairy tales.* New York: Random House.

Bicchieri, C. (1988). Should a scientist abstain from metaphor? In

References

A. Klamer, D. McCloskey, & R. Solow (Eds.), *The consequences of economic rhetoric* (pp. 100–116). New York: Cambridge University Press.

Bickerton, D. (1969). Prolegomena to a linguistic theory of metaphor. *Foundations of Language, 5,* 34–52.

Bierce, A. (1958). *The devil's dictionary.* Mount Vernon, NY: Peter Pauper Press.

Bierwisch, M. (1967). Some semantic universals of German adjectivals. *Foundations of Language, 3,* 1–36.

Billow, R. (1975). A cognitive developmental study of metaphor comprehension. *Developmental Psychology, 11,* 415–423.

Billow, R. (1981). Observing spontaneous metaphor in children. *Journal of Experimental Child Psychology, 31,* 430–445.

Binkley, T. (1974). On the truth and probity of metaphor. *Journal of Aesthetics and Art Criticism, 33,* 171–180.

Binkley, T. (1979). The principle of expressibility. *Philosophy and Phenomenological Research, 39,* 307–325.

Bird-David, N. (1990). The giving environment: Another perspective on the economic system of gatherer-hunters. *Current Anthropology, 31,* 183–196.

Bird-David, N. (1992). Beyond the hunting and gathering mode of subsistence: Observations on Nayaka and other modern hunter gatherers. *Man, 27,* 19–45.

Black, M. (1955). Metaphor. *Proceedings of the Aristotelian Society, 55,* 273–294.

Black, M. (1962). *Models and metaphors.* Ithaca, NY: Cornell University Press.

Black, M. (1979). More on metaphor. In A. Ortony (Ed.), *Metaphor and thought* (pp. 1–18). Cambridge: Cambridge University Press.

Black, M. (1981). Metaphor. In M. Johnson (Ed.), *Philosophical perspectives on metaphor* (pp. 63–82). Minneapolis: University of Minnesota Press.

Blakemore, D. (1992). *Understanding utterances: An introduction to pragmatics.* Oxford: Blackwell Publisher.

Blasko, D., & Connine, C. (1993). Effects of familiarity and aptness on metaphor processing. *Journal of Experimental Psychology: Learning, Memory, and Cognition, 19,* 295–308.

Boatner, M., Gates, J., Makkai, A. (1975). *A dictionary of American idioms.* Woodbury, NY: Barron.

Bobrow, S., & Bell, S. (1973). On catching on to idiomatic expressions. *Memory & Cognition, 1,* 343–346.

References

Bock, K., & Brewer, W. (1980). Comprehension and memory of the literal and figurative meaning of proverbs. *Journal of Psycholinguistic Research, 9,* 59–72.

Bogen, D. (1991). Linguistic forms and social obligations: A critique of the doctrine of literal expression in Searle. *Journal for the Theory of Social Behavior, 21,* 31–62.

Bolinger, D. (1965). The atomization of meaning. *Language, 41,* 555–573.

Bolinger, D. (1971). *The phrasal verb in English.* Cambridge, MA: Harvard University Press.

Bollobas, E. (1981). Who's afraid of irony? An analysis of uncooperative behavior in Edward Albee's *Who's Afraid of Virginia Woolf? Journal of Pragmatics, 5,* 323–334.

Bonitatibus, G. (1988). Comprehension monitoring and the apprehension of literal meaning. *Child Development, 59,* 60–70.

Bono, J. (1990). Science, discourse, and literature. The role/rule of metaphor in science. In S. Petterfreund (Ed.), *Literature and science: Theory and practice* (pp. 59–90). Boston: Northeastern University Press.

Booth, W. (1974). *A rhetoric of irony.* Chicago: University of Chicago Press.

Bosman, J. (1987). Persuasive effects of political metaphors. *Metaphor and Symbolic Activity, 2,* 97–113.

Boswell, D. (1986). Speaker's intentions: Constraints on metaphor comprehension. *Metaphor and Symbolic Activity, 1,* 153–170.

Bower, G., Black, J., & Turner, T. (1979). Scripts in memory for text. *Cognitive Psychology, 11,* 177–220.

Bowers, J., & Osborn, M. (1966). Attitudinal effects of selected types of concluding metaphors in persuasive speeches. *Speech Monographs, 33,* 147–155.

Boyd, R. (1979). Metaphor and theory change: What is "metaphor" a metaphor for? In A. Ortony (Ed.), *Metaphor and thought* (pp. 356–408). Cambridge: Cambridge University Press.

Bredin, H. (1984). Metonymy. *Poetics Today, 5,* 45–48.

Bresnan, J., & Kaplan, R. (1982). Grammars as mental representations of language. In J. Bresnan (Ed.), *The mental representation of grammatical relations* (pp. xvii–lii). Cambridge, MA: MIT Press.

Brewer, W., Harris, R., & Brewer, M. (1977). *Comprehension of literal and figurative meaning.* Unpublished manuscript, Department of Psychology, University of Illinois, Urbana-Champaign.

Brooke-Rose, C. (1958). *A grammar of metaphor.* London: Mercury.

References

Brown, A. (1989). Analogical learning and transfer: What develops? In S. Vosniadou & A. Ortony (Eds.), *Similarity and analogical reasoning* (pp. 369–412). New York: Cambridge University Press.

Brown, A., Kane, M., & Echols, C. (1986). Young children's mental models determine analogical transfer across problems with a common goal structure. *Cognitive Development, 1,* 103–122.

Brown, P., & Levinson, S. (1978). Universals in language usage: Politeness phenomena. In E. Goody (Ed.), *Questions and politeness* (pp. 56–311). Cambridge: Cambridge University Press.

Brown, P., & Levinson, S. (1987). *Politeness.* Cambridge: Cambridge University Press.

Brown, R. (1973). *A first language: The early stages.* Cambridge, MA: Harvard University Press.

Brown, R. H. (1976). Social theory as metaphor: On the logic of discovery for the sciences of conduct. *Theory and Society, 3,* 169–197.

Brown, R. H. (1987). *Society as text: Essays on rhetoric, reason, and reality.* Chicago: University of Chicago Press.

Brugman, C. (1981). *The story of "over."* New York: Garland.

Brugman, C. (1983). The use of body-part terms as locatives in Chalcatongo Mixtec. In *The survey of California and other Indian languages* (Rep. No. 4, pp. 235–290). University of California, Berkeley.

Brugman C. (1984). *Metaphor in the elaboration of grammatical categories in Mixtec.* Linguistics Department, University of California, Berkeley.

Brugman, C., & Lakoff, G. (1988). Cognitive topology and lexical networks. In S. Small, G. Cotrell, & M. Tannenhaus (Eds.), *Lexical ambiguity resolution* (pp. 477–508). Palo Alto, CA: Morgan Kaufman.

Bruner, J., & Feldman, C. (1990). Metaphors of consciousness and cognition in the history of psychology. In D. Leary (Ed.), *Metaphors in the history of psychology* (pp. 230–238). New York: Cambridge University Press.

Bühler, K. (1908). Über gedankenerinnerungen. *Archiv für die Gesamte Psychologie, 12,* 24–92.

Burke, K. (1969). *A grammar of motives.* Berkeley and Los Angeles: University of California Press.

Burt, J. (1992). Against the lexical representation of idioms. *Canadian Journal of Psychology, 46,* 582–605.

Butterworth, B. (1975). Hesitation and semantic planning in speech. *Journal of Psycholinguistic Research, 3,* 75–87.

References

Bybee, J., & Moder, C. (1983). Morphological classes as natural categories. *Language, 59,* 251–270.

Cacciari, C., & Glucksberg, S. (1991). Understanding idiomatic expressions: The contribution of word meanings. In G. Simpson (Ed.), *Understanding word and sentence* (pp. 217–240). The Hague: North Holland.

Cacciari, C., & Levorato, M. (1989). How children understand idioms in discourse. *Journal of Child Language, 16,* 387–405.

Cacciari, C., & Tabossi, P. (1988). The comprehension of idioms. *Journal of Memory and Language, 27,* 668–683.

Camac, M., & Glucksberg, S. (1984). Metaphors do not use associations between concepts, they create them. *Journal of Psycholinguistic Research, 13,* 443–445.

Campbell, J. (1972). *Myths to live by.* New York: Bantam.

Cantor, N., & Mischel, W. (1977). Traits as prototypes: Effects on recognition memory. *Journal of Personality and Social Psychology, 35,* 38–48.

Capelli, C., Nakagawa, N., & Madden, C. (1990). How children understand sarcasm: The role of context and intonation. *Child Development, 61,* 1824–1841.

Caramazza, A., & Grober, E. (1976). Polysemy and the structure of the subjective lexicon. In C. Rameh (Ed.), *Semantics: Theory and application* (pp. 181–206). Washington, DC: Georgetown University Press.

Carbonell, J. (1981). Invariance hierarchies in metaphor interpretation. In *Proceedings of the Third Meeting of the Cognitive Science Society* (pp. 292–295). Cognitive Science Society.

Carey, S. (1985). *Conceptual change in childhood.* Cambridge, MA: MIT Press.

Carlson, P., & Anisfeld, M. (1969). Some observations on the linguistic competence of a two-year-old child. *Child Development, 40,* 565–575.

Carnap, R. (1956). *Meaning and necessity* (2nd ed.). Chicago: University of Chicago Press.

Carpenter, P., & Just, M. (1975). Sentence comprehension: A psycholinguistic processing model of verification. *Psychological Review, 82,* 45–73.

Carrell, P. (1981). Children's understanding of indirect requests: Comparing child and adult comprehension. *Journal of Child Language, 8,* 320–345.

Carroll, J., & Mack, R. (1985). Metaphor, computing systems, and active learning. *International Journal of Man–Machine Studies, 22,* 39–57.

Carter, A. (1974). *Communication in the sensorimotor period.* Unpublished doctoral dissertation, University of California, Berkeley.

Caruth, E., & Ekstein, R. (1966). Interpretation within the metaphor: Further considerations. *Journal of the American Academy of Child Psychiatry, 5,* 35–45.

Caton, S. (1985). The poetic construction of self. *Anthropological Quarterly, 58,* 141–151.

Caton, S. (1990). *Peaks of Yemen I summon: Poetry as cultural practice in a northern Yemeni tribe.* Berkeley and Los Angeles: University of California Press.

Chafe, W. (1968). Idiomaticity as an anomaly in the Chomskyan paradigm. *Foundations of Language, 4,* 109–127.

Chafe, W. (1970). *Meaning and the structure of language.* Chicago: University of Chicago Press.

Chomsky, N. (1965). *Aspects of the theory of syntax.* Cambridge: MA: MIT Press.

Chomsky, N. (1980). *Rules and representations.* New York: Columbia University Press.

Clark, E. (1982). The young word maker: A case study of innovation in the child's lexicon. In E. Wanner & L. Gleitman (Eds.), *Language acquisition: The state of the art* (pp. 390–425). Cambridge: Cambridge University Press.

Clark, E. (1987). The principle of contrast: A constraint on language acquisition. In B. MacWhinney (Ed.), *Mechanisms of language acquisition* (pp. 1–33). Hillsdale, NJ: Erlbaum.

Clark, E., & Clark, H. (1979). When nouns surface as verbs. *Language, 55,* 767–811.

Clark, H. (1969). Linguistic processes in deductive reasoning. *Psychological Review, 76,* 387–404.

Clark, H. (1974). Semantics and comprehension. In T. Sebeok (Ed.), *Current trends in linguistics: Vol. 12. Linguistics and adjacent arts and sciences* (pp. 1291–1498). The Hague: Mouton.

Clark, H. (1979). Responding to indirect speech acts. *Cognitive Psychology, 11,* 430–477.

Clark, H. (1983). Making sense of nonce sense. In G. Flores d'Arcais & R. Jarvella (Eds.), *The process of understanding language* (pp. 297–332). New York: Wiley.

Clark, H. (1991). Words, the world, and their possibilities. In G.

References

Lockhead & J. Pomerantz (Eds.), *The perception of structure: Essays in honor of Wendell Garner* (pp. 263–277). Washington, DC: American Psychological Association.

Clark, H., & Carlson, T. (1982). Context for comprehension. In J. Long & A. Baddeley (Eds.), *Attention and performance XI* (pp. 313–330). Hillsdale, NJ: Erlbaum.

Clark, H., & Chase, W. (1972). On the process of comparing sentences against pictures. *Cognitive Psychology, 3*, 472–517.

Clark, H., & Clark, E. (1977). *Psychology and language: An introduction to psycholinguistics.* New York: Harcourt Brace Jovanovich.

Clark, H., & Gerrig, R. (1983). Understanding old words with new meaning. *Journal of Verbal Learning and Verbal Behavior, 22*, 591–608.

Clark, H., & Gerrig, R. (1984). On the pretense theory of irony. *Journal of Experimental Psychology: General, 113*, 121–126.

Clark, H., & Gerrig, R. (1990). Quotations as demonstrations. *Language, 66*, 764–805.

Clark, H., & Lucy, P. (1975). Understanding what is meant from what is said: A study in conversationally conveyed requests. *Journal of Verbal Learning and Verbal Behavior, 14*, 56–72.

Clark, H., & Malt, B. (1984). Psychological constraints on language: A commentary on Bresnan, Kaplan, and on Givon. In W. Kintsch, J. Miller, & P. Paulson (Eds.), *Methods and tactics in cognitive science* (pp. 191–216). Hillsdale, NJ: Erlbaum.

Clark, H., & Marshall, C. (1981). Definite reference and mutual knowledge. In A. Joshi, B. Webber, & I. Sag (Eds.), *Elements of discourse understanding* (pp. 10–63). Cambridge: Cambridge University Press.

Clark, H., & Schunk, D. (1980). Polite responses to polite requests. *Cognition, 8*, 111–143.

Cohen, L. (1979). The semantics of metaphor. In A. Ortony (Ed.), *Metaphor and thought* (pp. 64–77). Cambridge: Cambridge University Press.

Cohen, T. (1975). Figurative speech and figurative acts. *Journal of Philosophy, 72*, 669–684.

Cohen, T. (1976). Notes on metaphor. *Journal of Aesthetics and Art Criticism, 34*, 249–259.

Cohen, T. (1978). Metaphor and the cultivation of intimacy. *Critical Inquiry, 5*, 3–12.

Coleman, L., & Kay, P. (1981). Prototype semantics: The English verb *lie. Language, 57*, 26–44.

References

Colombo, L., & Flores d'Arcais, G. (1984). The meaning of Dutch prepositions: A psycholinguistic study of polysemy. *Linguistics, 22,* 51–98.

Cometa, M., & Eson, M. (1978). Logical operations and metaphor interpretation: A Piagetian model. *Child Development, 49,* 649–659.

Connor, K., & Kogan, N. (1980). Topic–vehicle relations in metaphor: The issue of asymmetry. In R. Honeck & R. Hoffman (Eds.), *Cognition and figurative language* (pp. 283–310). Hillsdale, NJ: Erlbaum.

Conrad, C. (1978). Some factors involved in the recognition of words. In J. Cotton & R. Klatsky (Eds.), *Semantic factors in cognition* (pp. 78–99). Hillsdale, NJ: Erlbaum.

Cooper, D. (1986). *Metaphor.* London: Blackwell Publisher.

Couthard, M. (1985). *An introduction to discourse analysis.* London: Longman Group.

Crews, F. (1984). *The Random House handbook* (4th ed.). New York: Random House.

Cruse, D. (1986). *Lexical semantics.* Cambridge: Cambridge University Press.

Cutler, A. (1982). Idioms: The older the colder. *Linguistic Inquiry, 13,* 317–320.

Cutler, A. (1983). Lexical complexity and sentence processing. In G. Flores d'Arcais & R. Jarvella (Eds.), *The process of understanding language* (pp. 42–80). New York: Wiley.

Dahlgren, K. (1985). The cognitive structure of social categories. *Cognitive Science, 9,* 379–398.

Dascal, M. (1987). Defending literal meaning. *Cognitive Science, 11,* 259–281.

Dascal, V. (1990). Walking the tightrope: The psychotherapeutic potential of enacting a movement metaphor. *Assaph, C, 7,* 103–112.

Dascal, V. (1992). Movement metaphors: Linking theory and therapeutic practice. In M. Stanenov (Ed.), *Current advances in semantic theory* (pp. 151–157). Amsterdam: John Benjamins.

Dashiell, J. (1925). A physiological-behaviorist's description of thinking. *Psychological Review, 32,* 54–73.

Davidson, D. (1979). What metaphors mean. In S. Sacks (Ed.), *On metaphor* (pp. 29–46). Chicago: University of Chicago Press.

Davitz, J. (1969). *The language of emotion.* New York: Academic Press.

Davitz, J., & Mattis, S. (1964). The communication of emotional meaning by metaphor. In J. R. Davitz (Ed.), *The communication of emotional meaning* (pp. 157–176). New York: McGraw-Hill.

References

Deese, J. (1965). *The structure of associations in language and thought.* Baltimore: Johns Hopkins University.

Demorest, A., Meyer, C., Phelps, E., Gardner, H., & Winner, E. (1984). Words speak louder than actions: Understanding deliberately false remarks. *Child Development, 55,* 1527–1534.

Demorest, A., Silberstein, L., Gardner, H., & Winner, E. (1983). Telling it as it isn't: Children's understanding of figurative language. *British Journal of Developmental Psychology, 1,* 121–130.

Dent, C. (1984). The developmental importance of notion information in perceiving and describing metaphoric similarity. *Child Development, 55,* 1607–1613.

Dewey, J. (1894). Psychological literature: Ethical. *Psychological Review, 1,* 109–113.

Dong, P. (1971). The applicability of transformations to idioms. In *Papers from the Seventh Regional Meeting of the Chicago Linguistic Society* (pp. 198–205). Chicago: The Society.

Dore, J. (1974). A pragmatic description of early language development. *Journal of Psycholinguistic Research, 3,* 343–350.

Dorfmueller, M., & Honeck, R. (1981). Centrality and generativity within a linguistic family: Toward a conceptual base theory of groups. *Psychological Record, 30,* 95–109.

Douglas, M. (1973). *Natural symbols: Explorations in cosmology.* New York: Random House.

Dowty, D., Wall, R., & Peters, S. (1981). *An introduction to Montague semantics.* Dordrecht: Reidel.

Dresher, E., & Hornstein, N. (1976). On some supposed contributions of artificial intelligence to the scientific study of language. *Cognition, 4,* 321–398.

Dresher, E., & Hornstein, N. (1977). Reply to Schank and Wilensky. *Cognition, 5,* 147–150.

Dubnick, R. (1980). Visible poetry: Metaphor and metonymy in the paintings of René Magritte. *Contemporary Literature, 21,* 407–419.

Dupre, J. (1981). Natural kinds and biological taxa. *Philological Review, 40,* 66–90.

Durkin, K., & Manning, J. (1989). Polysemy and the subjective lexicon: Semantic relatedness and the salience of intraword senses. *Journal of Psycholinguistic Research, 18,* 577–612.

Eilers, S. (1975). Suprasegmental and grammatical control over telegraphic speech in young children. *Journal of Psycholinguistic Research, 4,* 227–239.

Ekstein, R. (1966). Interpretation within the metaphor. In R. Ekstein

(Ed.), *Children of time and space, of action and impulse* (pp. 158–165). East Norwalk, CT: Appleton-Century-Crofts.

Endicott, K. (1979). *Batek negrito religion: The world view and rituals of a hunting and gathering people of peninsular Malaysia.* Oxford: Clarendon Press.

Ervin-Tripp, S. (1976). Is Sybil there? The structure of some American directives. *Language in Society, 4,* 25–66.

Ervin-Tripp, S. (1977). Wait for me, roller skate. In S. Ervin-Tripp & C. Mitchell-Kernan (Eds.), *Child discourse* (pp. 165–188). New York: Academic Press.

Estes, W. (1986). Array models for category learning. *Cognitive Psychology, 18,* 500–549.

Estill, R., & Kemper, S. (1982). Interpreting idioms. *Journal of Psycholinguistic Research, 11,* 559–568.

Fainsilber, L., & Ortony, A. (1987). Metaphorical uses of language in the expression of emotion. *Metaphor and Symbolic Activity, 2,* 239–250.

Fehr, B. (1988). Prototype analysis of the concepts of love and commitment. *Journal of Personality and Social Psychology, 35,* 557–579.

Fehr, B., & Russell, J. (1984). Concepts of emotions viewed from a prototype perspective. *Journal of Experimental Psychology: General, 113,* 464–486.

Fernald, A., & Kuhl, P. (1987). Acoustic determinants of infant preference for motherese speech. *Infant Behavior and Development, 10,* 279–293.

Fernandez, J. (1986). *Persuasion and performance: The play of tropes in culture.* Bloomington: Indiana University Press.

Fernandez, J. (Ed.) (1991). *Beyond metaphor: The theory of tropes in anthropology.* Stanford, CA: Stanford University Press.

Fillmore, C. (1975). An alternative to checklist theories of meaning. *Proceedings of the Berkeley Linguistics Society, 1,* 123–131.

Fillmore, C. (1982). Frame semantics. In Linguistic Society of Korea (Ed.), *Linguistics in the morning calm* (pp. 111–138). Seoul: Hanshin.

Fillmore, C., Kay, P., & O'Conner, M. (1988). Regularity and idiomaticity in grammatical constructions: The case of *let alone. Language, 64,* 501–538.

Fish, S. (1980). *Is there a text in this class?* Cambridge, MA: Harvard University Press.

Fish, S. (1983). Short people got no reason to live: Reading irony. *Daedalus, 112,* 175–191.

References

Flavell, J., & Ross, L. (1981). *Cognitive social development.* New York: Cambridge University Press.

Flavell, J., & Taylor, M. (1984). Seeing and believing: Children's understanding of the distinction between appearance and reality. *Child Development, 55,* 1710–1720.

Fodor, J. A. (1983). *The modularity of mind: An essay on faculty psychology.* Cambridge, MA: Bradford.

Fodor, J. A., Garrett, M., Walker, E., & Parkes, C. (1980). Against definitions. *Cognition, 8,* 263–367.

Fodor, J. D., Fodor, J. A., & Garrett, M. (1975). The psychological unreality of semantic representations. *Linguistic Inquiry, 6,* 515–531.

Foerster, N., & Steadman, J. (1941). *Writing and thinking: A handbook of composition and revision.* Boston: Houghton-Mifflin.

Fowler, H. (1965). *A dictionary of modern English usage* (2nd ed.; revised by E. Gowers.). Oxford: Oxford University Press.

Fox, H. (1982). *Metaphor: New projects by contemporary sculptors.* Washington, DC: Smithsonian Institution Press.

Francik, E., & Clark, H. (1985). How to make requests that overcome obstacles to compliance. *Journal of Memory and Language, 24,* 560–568.

Fraser, B. (1970). Idioms within a transformational grammar. *Foundations of Language, 6,* 22–42.

Fraser, B. (1988). Motor oil is motor oil: An account of English nominal tautologies. *Journal of Pragmatics, 12,* 215–220.

Freeman, S., Lloyd, G., & Sinha, G. (1980). Infant search tasks reveal early concepts of containment and canonical usage of objects. *Cognition, 8,* 243–262.

Frege, G. (1952). On sense and reference. In P. T. Geach & M. Black (Eds.), *Philosophical writings of Gottlob Frege* (pp. 56–78). Oxford: Blackwell Publisher. (Original work published 1892).

Freud, S. (1900). *The interpretation of dreams.* London: Allen & Unwin.

Friedrich, P. (1991). Trope as cognition and poetic discovery. In J. Fernandez (Ed.), *Beyond metaphor: The theory of tropes in anthropology* (pp. 17–55). Stanford, CA: Stanford University Press.

Frye, N. (1990). *Myth and metaphor.* Charlottesville: University of Virginia Press.

Furbank, P. (1978). *E. M. Forster: A life.* New York: Harcourt Brace Jovanovich.

Gablik, S. (1970). *Magritte.* Greenwich, CT: New York Graphic Society.

Gardner, H. (1974). Metaphors and modalities: How children project polar adjectives onto diverse domains. *Child Development, 45,* 84–91.

References

Garnham, A. (1979). Instantiation of verbs. *Quarterly Journal of Experimental Psychology, 31,* 207–214.

Garrod, S., & Sanford, A. (1985). On the real-time character of interpretation during reading. *Language and Cognitive Processes, 1,* 43–61.

Garvey, C. (1975). Requests and responses in children's speech. *Journal of Child Language, 2,* 41–63.

Gasser, M., & Dyer, M. (1986). Speak of the devil: Representing deictic and speech act knowledge in an integrated memory. In *Proceedings of the Sixth Annual Meeting of the Cognitive Science Society* (pp. 388–398). Hillsdale, NJ: Erlbaum.

Gazdar, G., Pullum, G., Klein, E., & Sag, I. (1985). *Generalized phrase structure grammar.* Cambridge, MA: Harvard University Press.

Geeraerts, D. (1989). Types of meaning in idioms. In M. Evarert & E. van der Linden (Eds.), *Proceedings of the First Tilburg Workshop on Idioms* (pp. 39–61). Tilburg: ITK.

Gelman, S. (1988). The development of induction within natural and artificial categories. *Cognitive Psychology, 20,* 65–95.

Genette, G. (1980). *Narrative discourse: An essay on method* (J. Lewin, Trans.). Ithaca, NY: Cornell University Press.

Gentner, D. (1977). Children's performance on a spatial analogies task. *Child Development, 48,* 1034–1039.

Gentner, D. (1978). On relational meaning: The acquisition of verb meaning. *Child Development, 49,* 988–998.

Gentner, D. (1981). Verb semantic structures in memory for sentences: Evidence for componential representation. *Cognitive Psychology, 13,* 56–83.

Gentner, D. (1982). Are scientific analogies metaphors? In D. Miall (Ed.), *Metaphor: Problems and perspectives* (pp. 106–132). Brighton: Harvest Press.

Gentner, D. (1983). Structure-mapping: A theoretical framework for analogy. *Cognitive Science, 7,* 155–170.

Gentner, D. (1988). Structure-mapping in analogical development: The relational shift. *Child Development, 59,* 47–59.

Gentner, D. (1989). The mechanisms of analogical reasoning. In S. Vosniadou & A. Ortony (Eds.), *Similarity and analogical reasoning* (pp. 199–241). Cambridge: Cambridge University Press.

Gentner, D., & Clements, C. (1988). Evidence for relational selectivity in the interpretation of analogy and metaphor. In G. Bower (Ed.), *The psychology of learning and motivation* (Vol. 22, pp. 307–358). Orlando, FL: Academic Press.

Gentner, D., Falkenhainer, B., & Skorstad, J. (1988). Viewing metaphor as analogy. In D. Helman (Ed.), *Analogical reasoning* (pp. 171–177). Dordrecht: Kluwer.

Gentner, D., & Gentner, D. R. (1983). Flowing waters or teeming crowds: Mental models of electricity. In D. Gentner & A. Stevens (Eds.), *Mental models* (pp. 99–129). Hillsdale, NJ: Erlbaum.

Gentner, D., & Grudin, J. (1985). The evolution of mental metaphors in psychology: A 90-year retrospective. *American Psychologist, 40*, 181–192.

Genung, J. (1893). *Outlines of rhetoric*. Boston: Ginn.

George, V., & Dundes, A. (1978). The Gomer: A figure of American hospital folk speech. *Journal of American Folklore, 91*, 568–581.

Gernsbacher, M. (1991). Comprehending conceptual anaphors. *Language and Cognitive Processes, 6*, 81–105.

Gerrig, R. (1986). Process models and pragmatics. In N. Sharkey (Ed.), *Advances in cognitive science 1* (pp. 23–42). Chichester: Wiley.

Gerrig, R. (1989a). The time-course of sense creation. *Memory & Cognition, 17*, 194–207.

Gerrig, R. (1989b). Empirical constraints on computational theories of metaphor: Comments on Indurkhya. *Cognitive Science, 13*, 235–241.

Gerrig, R. (1993). *Experiencing narrative worlds*. New Haven, CT: Yale University Press.

Gerrig, R., & Gibbs, R. (1988). Beyond the lexicon: Creativity in language production. *Metaphor and Symbolic Activity, 4*, 1–19.

Gerrig, R., & Healey, A. (1983). Dual processes in metaphor understanding: Comprehension and appreciation. *Journal of Experimental Psychology: Learning, Memory, and Cognition, 9*, 667–675.

Gibbs, R. (1979). Contextual effects in understanding indirect requests. *Discourse Processes, 2*, 1–10.

Gibbs, R. (1980). Spilling the beans on understanding and memory for idioms in conversation. *Memory & Cognition, 8*, 449–456.

Gibbs, R. (1981a). Your wish is my command: Convention and context in interpreting indirect requests. *Journal of Verbal Learning and Verbal Behavior, 20*, 431–444.

Gibbs, R. (1981b). Memory for requests in conversation. *Journal of Verbal Learning and Verbal Behavior, 20*, 630–640.

Gibbs, R. (1982). A critical examination of the contribution of literal meaning to understanding nonliteral discourse. *Text, 2*, 9–27.

Gibbs, R. (1983). Do people always process the literal meanings of indirect requests? *Journal of Experimental Psychology: Learning, Memory, and Cognition, 9*, 524–533.

Gibbs, R. (1984). Literal meaning and psychological theory. *Cognitive Science, 8*, 275–304.

Gibbs, R. (1985a). On the process of understanding idioms. *Journal of Psycholinguistic Research, 14*, 465–472.

Gibbs, R. (1985b). Situational conventions and requests. In J. Forgas (Ed.), *Language and social situations* (pp. 197–211). New York: Springer-Verlag.

Gibbs, R. (1986a). Skating on thin ice: Literal meaning and understanding idioms in conversation. *Discourse Processes, 9*, 17–30.

Gibbs, R. (1986b). On the psycholinguistics of sarcasm. *Journal of Experimental Psychology: General, 115*, 1–13.

Gibbs, R. (1986c). Comprehension and memory for nonliteral utterances: The problem of sarcastic indirect requests. *Acta Psychologica, 62*, 41–57.

Gibbs, R. (1986d). What makes some indirect speech acts conventional? *Journal of Memory and Language, 25*, 181–196.

Gibbs, R. (1987a). What does it mean to say that a metaphor has been understood? In R. Haskell (Ed.), *Cognition and symbolic structures: The psychology of metaphoric transformation* (pp. 31–48). Norwood, NJ: Ablex.

Gibbs, R. (1987b). Mutual knowledge and the psychology of conversational inference. *Journal of Pragmatics, 11*, 561–588.

Gibbs, R. (1987c). Linguistic factors in children's understanding of idioms. *Journal of Child Language, 14*, 569–586.

Gibbs, R. (1989). Understanding and literal meaning. *Cognitive Science, 13*, 243–251.

Gibbs, R. (1990a). Psycholinguistic studies on the conceptual basis of idiomaticity. *Cognitive Linguistics, 1*, 417–451.

Gibbs, R. (1990b). Comprehending figurative referential descriptions. *Journal of Experimental Psychology: Learning, Memory, and Cognition, 16*, 56–66.

Gibbs, R. (1990c). The process of understanding literary metaphor. *Journal of Literary Semantics, 19*, 65–79.

Gibbs, R. (1991). Semantic analyzability in children's understanding of idioms. *Journal of Speech and Hearing Research, 34*, 613–620.

Gibbs, R. (1992a). Categorization and metaphor understanding. *Psychological Review, 99*, 572–577.

Gibbs, R. (1992b). When is metaphor: The idea of understanding in theories of metaphor. *Poetics Today, 13*, 575–606.

Gibbs, R. (1992c). What do idioms really mean? *Journal of Memory and Language, 31*, 485–506.

References

Gibbs, R. (1993a). Process and products in making sense of tropes. In A. Ortony (Ed.), *Metaphor and thought* (2nd ed.) (pp. 252–276). New York: Cambridge University Press.

Gibbs, R. (1993b). Why idioms are not dead metaphors. In C. Cacciari & P. Tabossi (Eds.), *Idioms: Processing, structure and interpretation* (pp. 57–78). Hillsdale, NJ: Erlbaum.

Gibbs, R. (in press). What's cognitive about cognitive linguistics? In E. Casad (Ed.), *Cognitive linguistics in the redwoods*. The Hague: Mouton.

Gibbs, R., Buchalter, D., Moise, J., & Farrar, W. (1993). Literal meaning and figurative language. *Discourse Processes, 16* 387–403.

Gibbs, R., & Delaney, S. (1987). Pragmatic factors in making and understanding promises. *Discourse Processes, 10,* 107–126.

Gibbs, R., & Gerrig, R. (1989). How context makes metaphor comprehension seem "special." *Metaphor and Symbolic Activity, 4,* 154–158.

Gibbs, R., & Gonzales, G. (1985). Syntactic frozenness in processing and remembering idioms. *Cognition, 20,* 243–259.

Gibbs, R., & Kearney, L. (1994). When parting is such sweet sorrow: Understanding and appreciating oxymora. *Journal of Psycholinguistic Research, 23,* 75–89.

Gibbs, R., Kushner, J., & Mills, R. (1991). Authorial intentions and metaphor comprehension. *Journal of Psycholinguistic Research, 20,* 11–30.

Gibbs, R., & McCarrell, N. (1990). Why boys will be boys and girls will be girls: Understanding colloquial tautologies. *Journal of Psycholinguistic Research, 19,* 125–145.

Gibbs, R., & Mueller, R. (1988). Conversational sequences and preference for indirect speech acts. *Discourse Processes, 11,* 101–116.

Gibbs, R., Mueller, R., & Cox, R. (1988). Common ground in asking and understanding questions. *Language and Speech, 31,* 321–335.

Gibbs, R. & Nagaoka, A. (1985). Getting the hang of American slang: Studies on understanding and remembering slang metaphors. *Language and Speech, 28,* 177–194.

Gibbs, R., & Nascimento, S. (1993). How we talk when we talk about love: Metaphorical concepts and understanding love poetry. In R. Kreuz & M. MacNulty (Eds.), *Empirical and aesthetic approaches to literature.* Norwood, NJ: Ablex.

Gibbs, R., & Nayak, N. (1989). Psycholinguistic studies on the syntactic behavior of idioms. *Cognitive Psychology, 21,* 100–138.

Gibbs, R., & Nayak, N. (1991). Why idioms mean what they do. *Journal of Experimental Psychology: General, 120,* 93–95.

References

Gibbs, R., Nayak, N., Bolton, J., & Keppel, M. (1989). Speakers' assumptions about the lexical flexibility of idioms. *Memory & Cognition, 17,* 58–68.

Gibbs, R., Nayak, N., & Cutting, C. (1989). How to kick the bucket and not decompose: Analyzability and idiom processing. *Journal of Memory and Language, 28,* 576–593.

Gibbs, R., & O'Brien, J. (1990). Idioms and mental imagery: The metaphorical motivation for idiomatic meaning. *Cognition, 36,* 35–68.

Gibbs, R., & O'Brien, J. (1991). Psychological aspects of irony understanding. *Journal of Pragmatics, 16,* 523–530.

Gibbs, R., Strom, L., & Spivey, M. (1993). *The metaphorical motivation for proverbial meaning.* Manuscript in preparation.

Gibbs, R., & Tenney, Y. (1980). The concept of scripts in understanding stories. *Journal of Psycholinguistic Research, 9,* 275–284.

Gigerenzer, G. (1991). From tools to theories: A heuristic of discovery in cognitive psychology. *Psychological Review, 98,* 254–267.

Gigerenzer, G., & Murray, D. (1987). *Cognition as intuitive statistics.* Chicago: University of Chicago Press.

Gildea, P., & Glucksberg, S. (1983). On understanding metaphor: The role of context. *Journal of Verbal Learning and Verbal Behavior, 22,* 577–590.

Glass, A. (1983). The comprehension of idioms. *Journal of Psycholinguistic Research, 12,* 429–442.

Gleason, H. (1961). *An introduction to descriptive linguistics.* New York: Holt, Rinehart & Winston.

Glucksberg, S. (1989). Metaphors in conversation: How are they understood? Why are they used? *Metaphor and Symbolic Activity, 4,* 125–144.

Glucksberg, S. (1991). Beyond literal meanings: The psychology of allusion. *Psychological Science, 2,* 146–152.

Glucksberg, S., Brown, M., & McGlone, M. (1993). Conceptual metaphors are not automatically accessed during idiom comprehension. *Memory & Cognition, 21,* 711–719.

Glucksberg, S., Gildea, P., & Bookin, H. (1982). On understanding nonliteral speech: Can people ignore metaphors? *Journal of Verbal Learning and Verbal Behavior, 21,* 85–98.

Glucksberg, S., & Keysar, B. (1990). Understanding metaphorical comparisons: Beyond similarity. *Psychological Review, 97,* 3–18.

Goffman, E. (1967). *Interaction ritual.* New York: Doubleday.

Goffman, E. (1971). *Relations in public: Microstudies of the public order.* New York: Basic.

References

Goffman, E. (1976). Replies and responses. *Language in Society, 5,* 257–313.

Goldin, S. (1978). Memory for the ordinary: Typicality effects in chess memory. *Journal of Experimental Psychology: Human Learning and Memory, 4,* 605–616.

Goldman-Eisler, F. (1968). *Psycholinguistics: Experiments in spontaneous speech.* London: Academic Press.

Goodman, N. (1968). *Languages of art.* Indianapolis: Bobbs-Merrill.

Goodman, N. (1972). Seven strictures on similarity. In N. Goodman (Ed.), *Problems and projects* (pp. 437–447). New York: Bobbs-Merrill.

Goossens, L. (1990). Metaphtonymy: The interaction of metaphor and metonymy in expressions for linguistic action. *Cognitive Linguistics, 1,* 323–340.

Gordon, D. (1978). *Therapeutic metaphors.* Cupertino, CA: META Publishers.

Gordon, D. (1983). Hospital slang for patients: Crocks, gomers, gorks, and others. *Language in Society, 12,* 173–185.

Gordon, D., & Lakoff, G. (1975). Conversational postulates. In P. Cole & J. Morgan (Eds.), *Syntax and semantics: Vol. 3. Speech acts* (pp. 107–142). New York: Academic Press.

Goswami, U. (1991). Analogical reasoning: What develops? A review of research and theory. *Child Development, 62,* 1–22.

Gould, S. (1977a). *Ontogeny and phylogeny.* Cambridge, MA: Harvard University Press.

Gould, S. (1977b). Eternal metaphors of paleontology. In A. Hallam (Ed.), *Patterns of evolution* (pp. 1–26). Amsterdam: Elsevier.

Gould, S. (1983). For want of metaphor. *Natural History, 92,* 14–93.

Graesser, A., Mio, J., & Millis, K. (1989). Metaphors in persuasive communication. In D. Meutsch & R. Viehoff (Eds.), *Comprehension and literary discourse: Results and problems of interdisciplinary approaches* (pp. 131–154). Berlin: De Gruyter.

Graesser, A., Woll, S., Kowalski, D., & Smith, D. (1980). Memory for typical and atypical actions in scripted activities. *Journal of Experimental Psychology: Human Learning and Memory, 6,* 503–515.

Gray, J. (1935). An objective theory of emotion. *Psychological Review, 42,* 108–116.

Green, G. (1989). *Pragmatics and natural language understanding.* Hillsdale, NJ: Erlbaum.

Greenspan, S. (1986). Semantic flexibility and referential specificity of concrete nouns. *Journal of Memory and Language, 25,* 539–557.

References

Grice, H. P. (1957). Meaning. *Philosophical Review, 64,* 377–388.

Grice, H. P. (1975). Logic and conversation. In P. Cole & J. Morgan (Eds.), *Syntax and semantics: Vol 3. Speech acts* (pp. 41–58). New York: Academic Press.

Grice, H. P. (1978). Further notes on logic and conversation. In P. Cole (Ed.), *Syntax and semantics: Vol. 9. Pragmatics* (pp. 113–127). New York: Academic Press.

Gruber, H. (1974). A psychological study of scientific creativity: Charles Darwin's early thought. In H. Gruber & P. Barrett (Eds.), *Darwin on man* (pp. 1–257). New York: Dutton.

Guenther, F. (1975). On the semantics of metaphor. *Poetics, 4,* 199–220.

Hackman, W. (1979). The relationship between concept and instrument design in eighteenth-century experimental science. *Annals of Science, 36,* 205–224.

Haiman, J. (1980). Dictionaries and encyclopedias. *Lingua, 50,* 329–357.

Haiman, J. (1989). Alienation in grammar. *Studies in Language, 13,* 129–170.

Halford, G. (1991). *Children's understanding: The development of mental models.* Hillsdale, NJ: Erlbaum.

Halliday, M. (1977). *The meaning of modern English.* Oxford: Oxford University Press.

Hallyn, F. (1990). *The poetic structure of the world: Copernicus and Kepler.* Cambridge, MA: Zone.

Hampton, J. (1987). Inheritance of attributes in natural concept conjunctions. *Memory & Cognition, 15,* 55–71.

Harnad, S. (1987). Category induction and representation. In S. Harnad (Ed.), *Categorical perception: The groundwork of cognition* (pp. 535–565). New York: Cambridge University Press.

Harnad, S. (1990). The symbol grounding problem. *Physica D, 42,* 335–346.

Harre, R. (1970). *The principles of scientific thinking.* Chicago: University of Chicago Press.

Harris, P. (1982). Cognitive prerequisites to language? *British Journal of Psychology, 73,* 187–195.

Harris, R. (1976). Comprehension of metaphors: A test of the two-stage processing model. *Bulletin of the Psychonomics Society, 8,* 312–314.

Harris, R. (1979a). Memory of metaphors. *Journal of Psycholinguistic Research, 8,* 61–71.

Harris, R. (1979b). Memory for literary metaphors. *Bulletin of the Psychonomics Society, 13,* 246–249.

References

Harris, R., Lahey, M., & Marsalek, F. (1980). Metaphors and images: Rating, reporting, and remembering. In R. Honeck & R. Hoffman (Eds.), *Cognition and figurative language* (pp. 163–182). Hillsdale, NJ: Erlbaum.

Hartley, J., & Homa, D. (1981). Abstraction of stylistic concepts. *Journal of Experimental Psychology: Human Learning and Memory, 7,* 33–46.

Hausman, C. (1989). *Metaphor and art.* New York: Cambridge University Press.

Hayakawa, S. (1941). *Language in action.* New York: Harcourt Brace.

Hedley, J. (1988). *Power in verse: Metaphor and metonymy in the Renaissance lyric.* University Park: Pennsylvania State University Press.

Henle, P. (1958). *Language, thought, and culture.* Ann Arbor: University of Michigan Press.

Heringer, J. (1976). Idioms and lexicalization in English. In M. Shibtani (Ed.), *Syntax and semantics: Vol. 6. The grammar of causative constructions* (pp. 205–216). New York: Academic Press.

Hesse, M. (1966). *Models and analogies in science.* Notre Dame, IN: University of Notre Dame Press.

Hjelmslev, L. (1953). *Prolegomena to a theory of language.* Baltimore: Waverly Press.

Hodges, J. (1967). *Harbrace college handbook.* New York: Harcourt Brace & World.

Hoffman, R. (1980). Metaphors in science. In R. Honeck & R. Hoffman (Eds.), *Cognition and figurative language* (pp. 393–423). Hillsdale, NJ: Erlbaum.

Hoffman, R., Cochran, E., & Nead, J. (1990). Cognitive metaphors in experimental psychology. In D. Leary (Ed.), *Metaphors in the history of psychology* (pp. 173–229). New York: Cambridge University Press.

Hoffman, R., & Honeck, R. (1987). Proverbs, pragmatics, and the ecology of abstract categories. In R. Haskell (Ed.), *Cognition and symbolic structures* (pp. 121–140). Norwood, NJ: Ablex.

Hoffman, R., & Kemper, S. (1987). What could reaction time studies be telling us about metaphor comprehension? *Metaphor and Symbolic Activity, 2,* 149–186.

Holyoke, K., Junn, E., & Billman, D. (1984). Development of analogical problem-solving. *Child Development, 55,* 2042–2055.

Homa, D. (1984). On the nature of categories. In G. H. Bower (Ed.), *The psychology of learning and motivation: Advances in research and theory* (Vol. 18, pp. 49–94). New York: Academic Press.

References

Honeck, R., Kibler, C., & Firment, M. (1987). Figurative language and psychological views of categorization: Two ships in the night. In R. Haskell (Ed.), *Cognition and symbolic structures* (pp. 103–120). Norwood, NJ: Ablex.

Honeck, R., Reichmann, P., & Hoffman, R. (1975). Semantic memory for metaphor: The conceptual base hypothesis. *Memory & Cognition, 3,* 409–415.

Honeck, R., Sowry, B., & Voegstle, K. (1978). Proverbial understanding in pictorial context. *Child Development, 49,* 327–331.

Honeck, R., Voegstle, M., Dorfmueller, A., & Hoffman, R. (1980). Proverbs, meaning, and group structure. In R. Honeck & R. Hoffman (Eds.), *Cognition and figurative language* (pp. 127–162). Hillsdale, NJ: Erlbaum.

Hormann, H. (1983). The calculating listener or how many are *einige, mehrere,* and *ein paar* (some, several, and a few). In R. Bauerke, C. Schwarze, & A. van Strechan (Eds.), *Meaning, use, and interpretation of language* (pp. 221–234). Berlin: De Gruyter.

Howe, J. (1977). Carrying the village: Cuna political metaphors. In D. Sapir & C. Crocker (Eds.), *The social use of metaphor* (pp. 132–163). Philadelphia: University of Pennsylvania Press.

Howe, N. (1988). Metaphor in contemporary American political discourse. *Metaphor and Symbolic Activity, 3,* 87–104.

Hudson, J., & Nelson, K. (1984). Play with language: Overextensions as analogies. *Journal of Child Language, 11,* 337–346.

Indurkhya, B. (1987). Approximate semantic transference: A computational theory of metaphors and analogy. *Cognitive Science, 11,* 445–480.

Inhelder, B., & Piaget, J. (1964). *The early growth of logic in the child.* London: Routledge & Kegan Paul.

Inhoff, A., Lima, S., & Carroll, P. (1984). Contextual effects on metaphor comprehension in reading. *Memory & Cognition, 12,* 558–567.

Jackendoff, R. (1975). Morphological and semantic regularity in the lexicon. *Language, 51,* 639–671.

Jackendoff, R. (1983). *Semantics and cognition.* Cambridge, MA: MIT Press.

Jackendoff, R. (1987). On beyond zebra: The relation of linguistic and visual information. *Cognition, 26,* 89–114.

Jackendoff, R. (1990). *Semantic structures.* Cambridge, MA: MIT Press.

Jackendoff, R., & Aaron, D. (1991). Review of G. Lakoff & M. Turner, *More than cool reason: A field guide to poetic metaphor. Language, 67,* 320–338.

References

Jaeger, J. (1980). *Categorization in phonology: An experimental approach.* Unpublished doctoral dissertation, University of California, Berkeley.

Jakobson, R. (1960). Closing statement: Linguistics and poetics. In T. Sebeok (Ed.), *Style in language* (pp. 350–377). Cambridge, MA: MIT Press.

Jakobson, R. (1971). Two types of language and two types of aphasic disturbances. In R. Jakobson (Ed.), *Selected writings* (Vol. 2, pp. 239–259). Cambridge, MA: MIT Press.

James, W. (1905). President's address: The experience of activity. *Psychological Review, 1,* 1–17.

Janus, R., & Bever, T. (1985). Processing metaphoric language: An investigation of the three-stage model of metaphor comprehension. *Journal of Psycholinguistic Research, 14,* 473–487.

Johnson, J., & Taylor, S. (1981). The effect of metaphor on political attitudes. *Basic and Applied Social Psychology, 2,* 305–316.

Johnson, M. (1987). *The body in the mind: The bodily basis of reason and imagination.* Chicago: University of Chicago Press.

Johnson, M. (1991). Knowing through the body. *Philosophical Psychology, 4,* 3–20.

Johnson, M. D., Gibbs, R., & Pfaff, K. (1992). *How to speak with tongue in cheek.* Manuscript in preparation.

Johnson, M. G., & Malgady, R. (1979). Some cognitive aspects of figurative language: Association and metaphor. *Journal of Psycholinguistic Research, 8,* 249–265.

Johnson, M. G., & Malgady, R. (1980). Toward a perceptual theory of metaphoric comprehension. In R. Honeck & R. Hoffman (Eds.), *Cognition and figurative language* (pp. 259–282). Hillsdale, NJ: Erlbaum.

Johnson-Laird, P. (1983). *Mental models: Towards a cognitive science of language, inference, and consciousness.* Cambridge: Cambridge University Press.

Johnson-Laird, P., & Quinn, R. (1976). To define true meaning. *Nature, 264,* 635–636.

Jones, R. (1982). *Physics as metaphor.* Minneapolis: University of Minnesota Press.

Jorgensen, J. (1990). Definitions as theories of word meaning. *Journal of Psycholinguistic Research, 19,* 293–316.

Jorgensen, J., Miller, G., & Sperber, D. (1984). Test of the mention theory of irony. *Journal of Experimental Psychology: General, 113,* 112–120.

Kanouse, D. (1972). Verbs as implicit quantifiers. *Journal of Verbal Learning and Verbal Behavior, 11,* 141–147.

References

Kardon, J. (1981). Metaphorical machinery. In *Machineworks: Vito Acconci, Alice Aycock, Dennis Oppenheim* (Exhibition catalog, pp. 6–15). Philadelphia: Institute of Contemporary Art.

Katz, A. (1982). Metaphoric relationships: The role of feature saliency. *Journal of Psycholinguistic Research, 11*, 283–296.

Katz, A. (1989). On choosing the vehicles of metaphors: Referential concreteness, semantic distances, and individual differences. *Journal of Memory and Language, 28*, 486–499.

Katz, A. (1992). Psychological studies in metaphor processing: Extensions in the placement of terms in semantic space. *Poetics Today, 13*, 607–632.

Katz, J. (1972). *Semantic theory.* New York: Harper & Row.

Katz, J. (1973). Compositionality, idiomaticity, and lexical substitution. In S. Anderson & P. Kiparsky (Eds.), *A Festschrift for Morris Halle* (pp. 357–376). New York: Holt, Rinehart & Winston.

Katz, J. (1977). *Propositional structure and illocutionary force.* New York: Crowell.

Katz, J. (1981). Literal meaning and logical theory. *Journal of Philosophy, 78*, 203–234.

Katz, J., & Fodor, J. (1963). The structure of semantic theory. *Language, 39*, 170–210.

Keil, F. (1986). Conceptual domains and the acquisition of metaphor. *Cognitive Development, 1*, 73–96.

Keil, F. (1989). *Constraints on cognitive development.* Cambridge, MA: MIT Press.

Kelly, M., & Keil, F. (1987). Metaphor comprehension and knowledge of semantic domains. *Metaphor and Symbolic Activity, 2*, 33–52.

Kemper, S. (1981). Comprehension and the interpretation of proverbs. *Journal of Psycholinguistic Research, 10*, 179–198.

Kemper, S. (1989). Priming the comprehension of metaphors. *Metaphor and Symbolic Activity, 4*, 1–18.

Kempson, R. (1977). *Semantic theory.* Cambridge: Cambridge University Press.

Keysar, B. (1989). On the functional equivalence of literal and metaphorical interpretations in discourse. *Journal of Memory and Language, 28*, 375–385.

Kierkegaard, S. (1965). *The concept of irony.* Bloomington: Indiana University Press.

Kintsch, W. (1974). *The representation of meaning in memory.* Hillsdale, NJ: Erlbaum.

Kittay, E. (1987). *Metaphor: Its cognitive force and linguistic structure.* Oxford: Clarendon Press.

References

Kockman, T. (1983). The boundary between play and nonplay in Black verbal dueling. *Language in Society, 12,* 329–337.

Kolstad, V. (1991, June). *Understanding containment in 5.5-month-old infants.* Poster presented at the meeting of the Society for Research in Child Development, Seattle.

Kovecses, Z. (1986). *Metaphors of anger, pride, and love.* Philadelphia: John Benjamins.

Kovecses, Z. (1988). *The language of love.* Lewisburg, PA: Bucknell University Press.

Kreuz, R., & Glucksberg, S. (1989). How to be sarcastic: The echoic reminder theory of verbal irony. *Journal of Experimental Psychology: General, 118,* 374–386.

Kreuz, R., & Graesser, A. (1991). Aspects of idiom comprehension: Comment on Nayak and Gibbs. *Journal of Experimental Psychology: General, 120,* 90–92.

Kreuz, R., Long, D., Church, M. (1991). On being ironic: Pragmatic and mnemonic implications. *Metaphor and Symbolic Activity, 6,* 149–162.

Kronfeld, X. (1980). Novel and conventional metaphors: A matter of methodology. *Poetics Today, 2,* 13–24.

Kuhn, T. (1979). Metaphor in science. In A. Ortony (Ed.), *Metaphor and thought* (pp. 409–419). Cambridge: Cambridge University Press.

Kukla, A. (1980). The modern language of consciousness. In L. Michaels & C. Ricks (Eds.), *The state of the language* (pp. 516–523). Berkeley and Los Angeles: University of California Press.

Labov, W. (1972). *Language in the inner city: Studies in Black English vernacular.* Philadelphia: University of Pennsylvania Press.

Labov, W. (1973). The boundaries of words and their meanings. In C. Bailey & R. Shuy (Eds.), *New ways of analyzing variation in English* (Vol. 1, pp. 340–373). Washington, DC: Georgetown University Press.

Lakoff, G. (1986). The meanings of literal. *Metaphor and Symbolic Activity, 1,* 291–296.

Lakoff, G. (1987). *Women, fire, and dangerous things: What categories reveal about the mind.* Chicago: University of Chicago Press.

Lakoff, G. (1990). The invariance hypothesis: Is abstract reason based on image-schemas? *Cognitive Linguistics, 1,* 39–74.

Lakoff, G. (1991a). Metaphor and war: The metaphor system used to justify war in the Gulf. In B. Hallet (Ed.), *Engulfed in war: Just war and the Persian Gulf.* Honolulu: Matsunaga Institute for Peace.

References

Lakoff, G. (1991b). *Comments on Jackendoff and Aaron*. Unpublished manuscript, Dept. of Linguistics, University of California, Berkeley.

Lakoff, G. (1993). The contemporary theory of metaphor. In A. Ortony (Ed.), *Metaphor and thought* (2nd ed.). (pp. 202–251). New York: Cambridge University Press.

Lakoff, G., Espenson, J., Goldberg, A., & Schwartz, A. (1992). *Master metaphor list*. Unpublished manuscript, University of California, Berkeley.

Lakoff, G., & Johnson, M. (1980). *Metaphors we live by*. Chicago: University of Chicago Press.

Lakoff, G., & Turner, M. (1989). *More than cool reason: A field guide to poetic metaphor*. Chicago: University of Chicago Press.

Lakoff, R. (1973). The logic of politeness: Or minding your p's and q's. In *Papers from the Ninth Regional Meeting, Chicago Linguistic Society* (pp. 292–305). Chicago: The Society.

Lakoff, R. (1990). *Talking power: The politics of language*. New York: Basic.

Lambrecht, K. (1984). Formulaicity, frame semantics, and pragmatics in German binomial expressions. *Language, 60,* 753–796.

Langacker, R. (1986). *Foundations of cognitive grammar*. Stanford, CA: Stanford University Press.

Lanham, R. (1969). *A handlist of rhetorical terms*. Berkeley and Los Angeles: University of California Press.

Lasch, C. (1978). *The culture of narcissism*. New York: Norton.

Leary, D. (Ed.) (1990). *Metaphors in the history of psychology*. New York: Cambridge University Press.

Ledbetter, P., & Dent, K. (1988). Young children's sensitivity to direct and indirect request structure. *First Language, 8,* 227–246.

Lee, C. (1990). Some hypotheses concerning the evolution of polysemous words. *Journal of Psycholinguistic Research, 19,* 211–220.

Leedy, J. (1969). *Poetry therapy*. Philadelphia: Lippincott.

Leeming, D. (1990). *The world of myth*. New York: Oxford University Press.

Leezenberg, M. (1991, April). *Tropical fruits, figurative language, context, and cognitive content*. Paper presented at the International Conference on Style in Philosophy and the Arts, Amsterdam.

Lenoir, T. (1988). Practice, reason, context: The dialogue between theory and experiment. *Science in Context, 2,* 3–22.

Letherdale, W. (1974). *The role of analogy, model and metaphor in science*. Amsterdam: North Holland.

Levin, S. (1977). *The semantics of metaphor*. Baltimore: Johns Hopkins University Press.

Levinson, S. (1983). *Pragmatics*. Cambridge: Cambridge University Press.

Lewis, D. (1969). *Convention*. Cambridge, MA: Harvard University Press.

Lewis, D. (1972). General semantics. In D. Davidson & G. Harman (Eds.), *Semantics of natural language* (pp. 169–218). Cambridge: Cambridge University Press.

Lindner, S. (1983). *A lexico-semantic analysis of verb-particle constructions with "up" and "out."* Bloomington: Indiana University Linguistics Club.

Lindsay, P., & Norman, D. (1977). *Human information processing*. New York: Academic Press.

Littman, D., & Mey, J. (1991). The nature of irony: Toward a computational model of irony. *Journal of Pragmatics, 15*, 131–152.

Lloyd, S., Sinha, G., & Freeman, N. (1981). Spatial reference systems and the canonicality effect in infant search. *Journal of Experimental Child Psychology, 32*, 1–10.

Lodge, D. (1977). *The modes of modern writing*. London: Arnold.

Lodge, L., & Leech, E. (1975). Children's acquisition of idioms in the English language. *Journal of Speech and Hearing Research, 18*, 521–529.

Loewenberg, I. (1973). Truth and consequences of metaphor. *Philosophy and Rhetoric, 6*, 30–46.

Loewenberg, I. (1975). Identifying metaphors. *Foundations of Language, 12*, 315–338.

Long, D., & Summers, M. (1979). *Longman dictionary of English idioms*. London: Longman Group.

Lucy, J. (1992). *Language diversity and thought: A reformulation of the linguistic relativity hypothesis*. New York: Cambridge University Press.

Lyons, J. (1968). *Introduction to theoretical linguistics*. Cambridge: Cambridge University Press.

MacCormac, E. (1976). *Metaphor and myth in science and religion*. Durham, NC: Duke University Press.

MacCormac, E. (1985). *A cognitive theory of metaphor*. Cambridge, MA: MIT Press.

Mack, D. (1975). Metaphoring as speech act: Some happiness conditions for implicit similes and simple metaphors. *Poetics, 4*, 221–256.

MacWhinney, B. (1987). The competition model. In B. MacWhinney

(Ed.), *Mechanisms of language acquisition* (pp. 249–308). Hillsdale, NJ: Erlbaum.

MacWhinney, B. (1989). Competition and lexical categorization. In R. Corrigan, F. Eckman, & M. Noonan (Eds.), *Linguistic categorization* (pp. 195–241). Philadelphia: John Benjamins.

Makkai, A. (1972). *Idiom structure in English*. The Hague: Mouton.

Malgady, R. (1977). Children's interpretation and appreciation of similes. *Child Development, 48,* 1734–1738.

Malgady, R., & Johnson, M. (1976). Modifiers in metaphors: Effects of constituent phrase similarity on the interpretation of figurative sentences. *Journal of Psycholinguistic Research, 5,* 43–52.

Malgady, R., & Johnson, M. (1980). Measurement of figurative language: Semantic feature models of comprehension and appreciation. In R. Honeck & R. Hoffman (Eds.), *Cognition and figurative language* (pp. 239–258). Hillsdale, NJ: Erlbaum.

Malotki, E. (1983). *Hopi time*. Berlin: Mouton.

Malt, B. (1990). Features and beliefs in the mental representation of categories. *Journal of Memory and Language, 29,* 289–315.

Malt, B., & Smith, E. (1983). Correlated properties in natural categories. *Journal of Verbal Learning and Verbal Behavior, 23,* 828–835.

Mandler, J. (1992). How to build a baby – 2. *Psychological Review, 99,* 587–604.

Markman, E. (1989). *Categorization and naming in children: Problems in induction*. Cambridge, MA: MIT Press.

Marks, L., Hammeal, R., & Bornstein, M. (1987). Perceiving similarity and comprehending metaphor. *Monographs of the Society for Research in Child Development, 32,* 1–93.

Márquez, G. (1988). *Love in the time of cholera*. New York: Knopf.

Marschark, M., & Hunt, R. (1985). On memory for metaphor. *Memory & Cognition, 13,* 193–201.

Marschark, M., Katz, A., & Paivio, A. (1983). Dimensions of metaphor. *Journal of Psycholinguistic Research, 12,* 17–40.

Martin, J. (1992). Computer understanding of conventional metaphoric language. *Cognitive Science, 16,* 233–270.

Matthews, R. (1971). Concerning a linguistic theory of metaphor. *Foundations of Language, 7,* 413–425.

Mayer, R. (1975). Different problem solving competencies established in learning computer programming with and without meaningful models. *Journal of Educational Psychology, 67,* 725–734.

Mayer, R. (1978). Advanced organizers that compensate for the organization of text. *Journal of Educational Psychology, 70,* 880–886.

References

Mayer, R. (1980). Elaborate techniques that increase the meaningfulness of technical text: An experimental test of the learning strategy hypothesis. *Journal of Educational Psychology, 72*, 770–784.

McCabe, A. (1983). Conceptual similarity and the quality of metaphor in isolated sentences vs. extended contexts. *Journal of Psycholinguistic Research, 12*, 41–68.

McCabe, A. (1988). Effect of different contexts on memory for metaphor. *Metaphor and Symbolic Activity, 3*, 105–132.

McGlone, M., Glucksberg, S., & Cacciari, C. (in press). Semantic productivity and idiom comprehension. *Discourse Processes.*

McMullen, L. (1989). Use of figurative language in successful and unsuccessful cases of psychotherapy: Three comparisons. *Metaphor and Symbolic Activity, 4*, 203–226.

McNamara, T., & Sternberg, R. (1983). Mental models of word meaning. *Journal of Verbal Learning and Verbal Behavior, 22*, 449–474.

McNeil, D. (1987). *Psycholinguistics: A new approach.* New York: Harper & Row.

McNeil, D. (1992). *Hand and mind.* Chicago: University of Chicago Press.

Medin, D. (1989). Concepts and conceptual structure. *American Psychologist, 44*, 1469–1481.

Medin, D., & Ortony, A. (1989). Psychological essentialism. In S. Vosniadou & A. Ortony (Eds.), *Similarity and analogical reasoning* (pp. 179–195). Cambridge: Cambridge University Press.

Medin, D., & Ross, B. (1992). *Cognitive psychology.* San Diego: Harcourt Brace Jovanovich.

Medin, D., & Schaffer, M. (1978). A context theory of classification learning. *Psychological Review, 85*, 207–238.

Medin, D. & Shoben, E. (1988). Context and structure in conceptual combination. *Cognitive Psychology, 20*, 158–190.

Medin, D., & Smith, E. (1981). *Concepts and categories.* Cambridge, MA: Harvard University Press.

Mehler, J., Jusczyk, P., Lambertz, G., Halsted, N., Bertoncini, J., & Amiel-Tison, C. (1988). A precursor of language acquisition in young infants. *Cognition, 29*, 143–178.

Merritt, M. (1976). On questions following questions in service encounters. *Language in Society, 4*, 315–357.

Merwin, W. (1973). *Asian figures.* New York: Atheneum.

Messenger, J. (1959). The role of proverbs in a Nigerian judicial system. *Southwestern Journal of Anthropology, 15*, 64–73.

Miller, G. (1962). Some psychological studies in grammar. *American Psychologist, 17*, 748–762.

References

Miller, G. (1979). Images and models, similes and metaphors. In A. Ortony (Ed.), *Metaphor and thought* (pp. 203–253). Cambridge: Cambridge University Press.

Miller, G., & Gildea, P. (1987). How children learn words. *Scientific American, 257*, 94–99.

Miller, G., & Johnson-Laird, P. (1976). *Language and perception.* Cambridge, MA: Harvard University Press.

Miller, R. (1976). The dubious case for metaphors in educational writing. *Educational Theory, 26*, 174–181.

Milton, J. (1967). Areopagitica: A speech for the liberty of unlicensed printing to the parliament of England. In J. Patrick (Ed.), *The prose of John Milton* (pp. 264–310). New York: New York University Press. (Originally published 1644).

Minard, J. (1965). Response-bias interpretation of "perceptual defense": A review and evaluation of recent research. *Psychological Review, 72*, 74–88.

Moltz, H. (1965). Contemporary instinct theory and the fixed action pattern. *Psychological Review, 72*, 27–47.

Moore, B. (1988). A young child's use of a physical–psychological metaphor. *Metaphor and Symbolic Activity, 3*, 223–232.

Moore, T., & Carling, C. (1982). *Understanding language: Toward a post-Chompskyan linguistics.* London: Macmillan.

Morgan, J. (1978). Two types of convention in indirect speech acts. In P. Cole & J. Morgan (Eds.), *Syntax and semantics: Vol. 3. Speech acts* (pp. 45–61). New York: Academic Press.

Muecke, D. (1969). *The compass of irony.* London: Methuen.

Mueller, R., & Gibbs, R. (1987). Processing idioms with multiple meanings. *Journal of Psycholinguistic Research, 16*, 63–81.

Munro, A. (1979). Indirect speech acts are not strictly conventional. *Linguistic Inquiry, 10*, 353–356.

Munro, P. (1989). *Slang U: The official dictionary of college slang.* New York: Crown.

Murphy, G. (1988). Comprehending complex concepts. *Cognitive Science, 12*, 529–562.

Murphy, G. (1990). Noun phrase interpretation and conceptual combination. *Journal of Memory and Language, 29*, 259–288.

Murphy, G., & Medin, D. (1985). The role of theories in conceptual coherence. *Psychological Review, 92*, 289–316.

Myers, G. (1990). The rhetoric of irony in academic writing. *Written Communication, 7*, 419–455.

Nayak, N., & Gibbs, R. (1990). Conceptual knowledge in idiom interpretation. *Journal of Experimental Psychology: General, 116*, 315–330.

References

Needham, W. (1992). Limits on literal processing during idiom interpretation. *Journal of Psycholinguistic Research, 21,* 1–16.

Newmeyer, F. (1972). The insertion of idioms. In *Papers from the Eighth Regional Meeting, Chicago Linguistics Society* (pp. 78–92). Chicago: The Society.

Newmeyer, F. (1974). The regularity of idiom behavior. *Lingua, 34,* 327–342.

Nietzsche, F. (1974). On truth and falsity in their ultramoral sense. In O. Levy (Ed. and Trans.), *The complete works of Frederick Neitzsche.* New York: Gordon Press. (Original work published 1873)

Nippold, M., & Martin, S. (1989). Idiom interpretation in isolation versus context: A developmental study with adolescents. *Journal of Speech and Hearing Research, 32,* 59–66.

Nippold, M., & Rudzinski, M. (in press). Familiarity and transparency in idiom explanation: A developmental study of children and adolescents. *Journal of Speech and Hearing Research, 36.*

Norman, D., & Rumelhart, D. (1975). *Explorations in cognition.* San Francisco: Freeman.

Norton, C. (1989). *Life metaphors: Stories of ordinary survival.* Carbondale, IL: Southern Illinois University Press.

Nosofsky, R. (1988). Exemplar-based accounts of relations between classification, recognition, and typicality. *Journal of Experimental Psychology: Learning, Memory, and Cognition, 14,* 700–708.

Nosofsky, R. (1991). Tests of an exemplar model for relating perceptual classification and recognition in memory. *Journal of Experimental Psychology: Human Perception and Performance, 17,* 3–27.

Nunberg, G. (1978). *The pragmatics of reference.* Bloomington: Indiana University Linguistics Club.

Nunberg, G. (1979). The non-uniqueness of semantic solutions: Polysemy. *Linguistics and Philosophy, 3,* 143–184.

Oden, G. (1987). Concept, knowledge, and thought. In M. Rosenzweig & L. Porter (Eds.), *Annual Review of Psychology, 38,* 203–227.

Ohnuki-Tierney, E. (1991). Embedding and transforming polytrope: The monkey as self in Japanese culture. In J. Fernandez (Ed.), *Beyond metaphor: The theory of tropes in anthropology* (pp. 159–189). Stanford, CA: Stanford University Press.

Olson, D. (1977). From utterance to text: The bias of language in speech and writing. *Harvard Educational Review, 47,* 254–279.

Ong, W. (1982). *Orality and literacy: The technologizing of the word.* London: Methuen.

References

Ortony, A. (1975). Why metaphors are necessary and not just nice. *Educational Theory, 25,* 45–53.

Ortony, A. (1976). On the nature and value of metaphor: A reply to my critics. *Educational Theory, 26,* 395–398.

Ortony, A. (1979a). Beyond literal similarity. *Psychological Review, 86,* 161–180.

Ortony, A. (1979b). The role of similarity in similes and metaphors. In A. Ortony (Ed.), *Metaphor and thought* (pp. 186–201). Cambridge: Cambridge University Press.

Ortony, A. (1988). Are emotion metaphors conceptual or lexical? *Cognition and Emotion, 2,* 95–103.

Ortony, A., Reynolds, R., & Arter, J. (1978). Metaphor: Theoretical and empirical research. *Psychological Bulletin, 85,* 919–943.

Ortony, A., Schallert, D., Reynolds, R., & Antos, S. (1978). Interpreting metaphors and idioms: Some effects of context on comprehension. *Journal of Verbal Learning and Verbal Behavior, 17,* 465–477.

Ortony, A., Vondruska, R., Foss, M., & Jones, L. (1985). Salience, similes, and the asymmetry of similarity. *Journal of Memory and Language, 24,* 569–594.

Paivio, A. (1971). *Imagery and verbal processes.* Hillsdale, NJ: Erlbaum.

Paivio, A. (1979). Psychological processes in the comprehension of metaphor. In A. Ortony (Ed.), *Metaphor and thought* (pp. 150–171). Cambridge: Cambridge University Press.

Palmer, F. (1981). *Semantics.* Cambridge: Cambridge University Press.

Partridge, E. (1935). *Slang today and yesterday.* London: Macmillan.

Payne, S. (1988). Metaphorical instructions and the early learning of an abbreviated-command computer system. *Acta Psychologica, 69,* 207–230.

Pearson, B. (1990). The comprehension of metaphor by preschool children. *Journal of Child Language, 17,* 185–203.

Pearson, P., Raphael, R., TePaske, R., & Hyser, H. (1981). The function of metaphor in children's recall of expository passages. *Journal of Reading Behavior, 13,* 249–261.

Peterson, J. (1935). Aspects of learning. *Psychological Review, 42,* 1–27.

Petrie, H. (1979). Metaphor and learning. In A. Ortony (Ed.), *Metaphor and thought* (pp. 438–461). Cambridge: Cambridge University Press.

Pfaff, K., Gibbs, R., & Johnson, M. (1993). *Metaphorical knowledge in understanding euphemism.* Manuscript in preparation.

References

Phillips, R., Wagner, S., Fells, C., & Lynch, M. (1990). Do infants recognize emotion in facial expressions? Categorical and metaphorical evidence. *Infant Behavior and Development, 13,* 71–84.

Piaget, J. (1952). *Origins of intelligence in children.* Madison, CT: International Universities Press.

Piaget, J. (1962). *Play, dreams, and imitation in childhood.* New York: Norton.

Pollio, H., Barlow, J., Fine, H., & Pollio, M. (1977). *Psychology and the poetics of growth: Figurative language in psychology, psychotherapy, and education.* Hillsdale, NJ: Erlbaum.

Pollio, H., & Burns, B. (1977). The anomaly of anomaly. *Journal of Psycholinguistic Research, 6,* 247–260.

Pollio, H., Fabrizi, M., & Weedle, H. (1982). A note on pauses in spontaneous speech as a test of the derived process theory of metaphor. *Linguistics, 20,* 431–444.

Pollio, H., & Pickens, J. (1980). The developmental structure of figurative competence. In R. Honeck & R. Hoffman (Eds.), *Cognition and figurative language* (pp. 311–340). Hillsdale, NJ: Erlbaum.

Pollio, H., & Smith, M. (1980). Metaphoric competence and complex human problem solving. In R. Honeck & R. Hoffman (Eds.), *Cognition and figurative language* (pp. 365–392). Hillsdale, NJ: Erlbaum.

Popiel, S., & McRae, K. (1988). The figurative and literal senses of idioms, or all idioms are not equal. *Journal of Psycholinguistic Research, 17,* 475–487.

Potter, M., Kroll, J., Yachzel, B., Carpenter, E., & Sherman, J. (1986). Pictures in sentences: Understanding without words. *Journal of Experimental Psychology: General, 115,* 281–294.

Powell, M. J. (1985). Conceptions of literal meaning in speech act theory. *Philosophy and Rhetoric, 18,* 133–157.

Prinz, P. (1983). The development of idiomatic meaning in children. *Language and Speech, 36,* 263–272.

Proust, M. (1981). *Remembrance of things past: Cities of the plain* (C. Moncrieff & T. Kilmartin, Trans.). New York: Random House. (Original work published 1927)

Pryluck, C. (1975). The film metaphor: The use of language-based models in film study. *Literature/Film Quarterly, 3,* 117–123.

Pulman, S. (1982). Are metaphors creative? *Journal of Literary Semantics, 11,* 78–89.

Pulman, S. (1983). *Word meaning and belief.* Norwood, NJ: Ablex.

Putnam, H. (1975). The meaning of "meaning." In *Philosophical papers: Vol. 2. Mind, language, and reality* (pp. 215–271). Cambridge: Cambridge University Press.

References

Quine, W. (1960). *Word and object*. Cambridge, MA: MIT Press.

Quine, W. (1966). *The ways of paradox and other essays*. New York: Random House.

Quine, W. (1979). A postscript on metaphor. In S. Sacks (Ed.), *On metaphor* (pp. 159–160). Chicago: University of Chicago Press.

Quinn, N. (1987). Convergent evidence for a cultural model of American marriage. In D. Holland & N. Quinn (Eds.), *Cultural models in language and thought* (pp. 173–194). New York: Cambridge University Press.

Quinn, N. (1991). The cultural basis of metaphor. In J. Fernandez (Ed.), *Beyond metaphor: The theory of tropes in anthropology* (pp. 56–93). Stanford, CA: Stanford University Press.

Quintilian (1953). *The Institutio oratoria* (H. Butler, Trans.). Cambridge, MA: Harvard University Press. (Originally published 1891).

Read, S., Cesa, I., Jones, D., & Collins, N. (1990). When is the federal budget like a baby? Metaphor in political rhetoric. *Metaphor and Symbolic Activity, 5,* 125–149.

Reagan, R. (1987). The syntax of English idioms: Can the dog be put on? *Journal of Psycholinguistic Research, 16,* 417–441.

Reddy, M. (1969). A semantic approach to metaphor. In R. Binnick et al. (Eds.), *Papers from the Fifth Regional Meeting of the Chicago Linguistics Society* (pp. 240–251). University of Chicago.

Reddy, M. (1979). The conduit metaphor. In A. Ortony (Ed.), *Metaphor and thought* (pp. 284–324). Cambridge: Cambridge University Press.

Reeder, K., Wakefield, J., & Shapiro, J. (1988). Children's speech act comprehension strategies and early literacy experiences. *First Language, 8,* 29–48.

Reichmann, P. (1975, April). *Does imagery facilitate memory for conceptual information?* Paper presented at the meeting of the Eastern Psychological Association, New York.

Reider, N. (1972). Metaphor as interpretation. *International Journal of Psychoanalysis, 53,* 463–469.

Reinsch, N. (1971). An investigation of the effects of metaphor and simile in persuasive discourse. *Speech Monographs, 38,* 142–145.

Reiser, B., Black, J., & Lehnert, W. (1985). Thematic knowledge structures in the understanding and generation of narratives. *Discourse Processes, 8,* 357–389.

Reynolds, R., & Ortony, A. (1980). Some issues in the measurement of children's comprehension of metaphorical language. *Child Development, 51,* 1110–1119.

References

Reynolds, R., & Schwartz, R. (1983). Relation of metaphor processing to comprehension and memory. *Journal of Educational Psychology*, 75, 450–459.

Richards, I. A. (1936). *The philosophy of rhetoric*. New York: Oxford University Press.

Ricoeur, P. (1977). *The rule of metaphor*. Toronto: University of Toronto Press.

Ricoeur, P. (1978). The metaphorical process as cognition, imagination, and feeling. In S. Sacks (Ed.), *On metaphor* (pp. 141–158). Chicago: University of Chicago Press.

Rips, L. (1975). Inductive judgments about natural categories. *Journal of Verbal Learning and Verbal Behavior*, 14, 665–681.

Rips, L. (1989). Similarity, typicality, and categorization. In S. Vosniadou & A. Ortony (Eds.), *Similarity and analogical reasoning* (pp. 21–59). Cambridge: Cambridge University Press.

Roediger, H. (1980). Memory metaphors in cognitive psychology. *Memory & Cognition*, 8, 231–246.

Rogers, R. (1978). *Metaphor: A psychoanalytic view*. Berkeley and Los Angeles: University of California Press.

Rommetveit, R. (1983). In search of a truly interdisciplinary semantics: A sermon on hopes of salvation from hereditary sins. *Journal of Semantics*, 2, 1–28.

Rommetveit, R. (1988). On literacy and the myth of literal meaning. In R. Saljo (Ed.), *The written word* (pp. 13–40). New York: Springer-Verlag.

Rorty, R. (1979). *Philosophy and the mirror of nature*. Princeton, NJ: Princeton University Press.

Rorty, R. (1989). *Contingency, irony, and solidarity*. New York: Cambridge University Press.

Rosch, E. (1975). Cognitive reference points. *Cognitive Psychology*, 7, 532–547.

Rosch, E. (1978). Principles of categorization. In E. Rosch & B. Lloyd (Eds.), *Cognition and categorization* (pp. 28–49). Hillsdale, NJ: Erlbaum.

Rosch, E., Mervis, C. (1975). Family resemblances: Studies in the internal structure of categories. *Cognitive Psychology*, 7, 573–605.

Rosch, E., Mervis, C., Gray, W., Johnson, D., & Boyes-Braem, P. (1976). Basic objects in natural categories. *Cognitive Psychology*, 8, 382–439.

Rosen, R. (1977). *Psychobabble: Fast talk and quick cure in the era of feeling*. New York: Atheneum.

Ross, G. (1980). Categorization in 1- to 2-year olds. *Developmental Psychology, 16*, 391–396.

Ross, J. (1981). *Portraying analogy.* Cambridge: Cambridge University Press.

Roth, E., & Shoben, E. (1983). The effect of context on the structure of categories. *Cognitive Psychology, 15*, 346–378.

Ruhl, C. (1989). *Monosemy: A study in linguistic semantics.* Albany: State University of New York Press.

Rumelhart, D. (1979). Some problems with the notion of literal meanings. In A. Ortony (Ed.), *Metaphor and thought* (pp. 78–90). Cambridge: Cambridge University Press.

Rumelhart, D., & McClelland, J. (1986). *Parallel distributed processing* (Vol. 1). Cambridge, MA: MIT Press.

Rumelhart, D., & Norman, D. (1981). Analogical processes in learning. In J. Anderson (Ed.), *Cognitive skills and their acquisition* (pp. 335–360). Hillsdale, NJ: Erlbaum.

Salamone, F. (1976). The arrow and the bird: Proverbs in the solution of Hausa conjugal conflicts. *Journal of Anthropological Research, 32*, 358–371.

Sampson, G. (1980). *Making sense.* New York: Oxford University Press.

Sanford, A., & Garrod, S. (1981). *Understanding written language.* Chichester: Wiley.

Sarbin, T. (1990). Metaphors of unwanted conduct: A historical sketch. In D. Leary (Ed.), *Metaphors in the history of psychology* (pp. 300–332). Cambridge: Cambridge University Press.

Schafer, R. (1976). *A new language for psychoanalysis,* New Haven, CT: Yale University Press.

Schank, R. (1972). Conceptual dependency: A theory of natural language understanding. *Cognitive Psychology, 3*, 552–631.

Schank, R. (1973). Identification of conceptualizations underlying natural language. In R. Schank & K. Colby (Eds.), *Computer models of thought and language* (pp. 187–248). San Francisco: Freeman.

Schank, R., & Abelson, R. (1977). *Scripts, plans, goals, and understanding: An inquiry into human knowledge structures.* Hillsdale, NJ: Erlbaum.

Schank, R., & Wilensky, R. (1977). Response to Dresher and Hornstein. *Cognition, 5*, 133–145.

Scheffler, I. (1979). *Beyond the letter: A philosophical inquiry into ambiguity, vagueness, and metaphor in language.* London: Routledge & Kegan Paul.

References

Schweigert, W. (1986). The comprehension of familiar and less familiar idioms. *Journal of Psycholinguistic Research, 15,* 33–45.

Schweigert, W. (1991). The muddy waters of idiom comprehension. *Journal of Psycholinguistic Research, 20,* 305–314.

Schweigert, W., & Moates, D. (1988). Familiar idiom comprehension. *Journal of Psycholinguistic Research, 17,* 281–296.

Scott, J. (1975). *Film: the medium and the maker.* New York: Holt, Rinehart & Winston.

Searle, J. (1969). *Speech acts: An essay on the philosophy of language.* New York: Cambridge University Press.

Searle, J. (1975). Indirect speech acts. In P. Cole & J. Morgan (Eds.), *Syntax and semantics: Vol. 3. Speech acts* (pp. 59–82). New York: Academic Press.

Searle, J. (1978). Literal meaning. *Erkenntnis, 13,* 207–224.

Searle, J. (1979). Metaphor. In A. Ortony (Ed.), *Metaphor and thought* (pp. 92–123). Cambridge: Cambridge University Press.

Searle, J. (1980). The background of meaning. In J. Searle, F. Kiefer, & M. Bierwisch (Eds.), *Speech act theory and pragmatics* (pp. 22–43). Dordrecht: Reidel.

Searle, J. (1983). *Intentionality.* Cambridge: Cambridge University Press.

Sechman, M., & Couch, C. (1989). Jocularity, sarcasm, and relationships: An empirical study. *Journal of Contemporary Ethnography, 18,* 327–344.

Seidenberg, M., Tannenhaus, M., Leiman, J., & Bienkowski, M. (1982). Automatic access of meanings of ambiguous words in context: Some limitations of knowledge-based processing. *Cognitive Psychology, 14,* 489–537.

Seifert, C., Robertson, S., & Black, J. (1985). Types of inferences generated during reading. *Journal of Memory and Language, 24,* 405–422.

Selfridge, O. (1966). Pandemonium: A paradigm for learning. In L. Uhr (Ed.), *Pattern recognition* (pp. 339–348). New York: Wiley.

Shannon, B. (1988). Semantic representation of meaning: A critique. *Psychological Bulletin, 104,* 70–83.

Shannon, B. (1990). Why are dreams cinematographic? *Metaphor and Symbolic Activity, 5,* 235–248.

Shannon, B. (1992). Metaphor: From fixedness and selection to differentiation and creation. *Poetics Today, 13,* 659–685.

Sharkey, N., & Sharkey, A. (1987). What is the point of integration? The loci of knowledge-based facilitation in sentence processing. *Journal of Memory and Language, 26,* 255–276.

Sharpe, E. (1940). Psychophysical problems revealed in language: An examination of metaphor. *International Journal of Psychoanalysis, 21,* 201–213.

Shatz, M. (1978). Children's comprehension of their mothers' question-directives. *Journal of Child Language, 5,* 39–41.

Shatz, M. (1985). Contributions of mother and mind to the development of communicative competence. In M. Perlmutter (Ed.), *Minnesota symposium on child development* (Vol. 17, pp. 33–59). Minneapolis: University of Minnesota Press.

Shaver, P., Schwartz, J., Kirson, D., & O'Connor, C. (1987). Emotional knowledge: Further exploration of a prototype approach. *Journal of Personality and Social Psychology, 52,* 1061–1086.

Shen, Y. (1987). On the structure and understanding of poetic oxymoron. *Poetics Today, 8,* 105–122.

Shen, Y. (1989). Symmetric and asymmetric comparisons. *Poetics, 18,* 517–536.

Shen, Y. (1992). Metaphors and categories. *Poetics Today, 13,* 771–794.

Sherman, M. (1973). Bound to be easier? The negative prefix and sentence comprehension. *Journal of Verbal Learning and Verbal Behavior, 12,* 76–84.

Shinjo, M., & Myers, J. (1987). The role of context in metaphor comprehension. *Journal of Memory and Language, 26,* 226–241.

Shore, B. (1991). Twice-born, once conceived: Meaning construction and cultural cognition. *American Anthropologist, 93,* 9–27.

Siegelman, E. (1990). *Metaphor and meaning in psychotherapy.* New York: Guilford Press.

Simon, J., & Kennedy, S. (Eds.) (1979). *A raindrop has to do her work.* Berkeley, CA: Aldebaran Review.

Slobin, D., & Welch, C. (1973). Elicited imitation as a research tool in developmental linguistics. In C. Ferguson & D. Slobin (Eds.), *Studies of child language development* (pp. 485–496). New York: Holt, Rinehart & Winston.

Smith, E., & Medin, D. (1981). *Categories and concepts.* Cambridge, MA: Harvard University Press.

Smith, J. (1976). Children's comprehension of metaphor: A Piagetian interpretation. *Language and Speech, 19,* 236–243.

Smith, M., Pollio, H., & Pitts, M. (1981). Metaphor as intellectual history: Concepts and categories underlying figurative usage in American English from 1675–1975. *Linguistics, 19,* 911–935.

Snyder, H. (1990). A case study in defining literacy: David Olson's journey from the great divide to the great beyond. *Interchange, 21,* 1–12.

References

Spears, R. (1982). *Slang and euphemism*. New York: New American Library.

Sperber, D. (1984). Verbal irony: Pretense or echoic mention? *Journal of Experimental Psychology: General, 113*, 130–136.

Sperber, D., & Wilson, D. (1981). Irony and the use–mention distinction. In P. Cole (Ed.), *Radical pragmatics* (pp. 295–318). New York: Academic Press.

Sperber, D., & Wilson, D. (1985/86). Loose talk. In *Proceedings of the Aristotelian Society* (pp. 153–172). Oxford: Blackwell Publisher.

Sperber, D., & Wilson, D. (1986). *Relevance: Communication and cognition*. Oxford: Blackwell Publisher.

Stanford, W. (1936). *Greek metaphor*. Oxford: Blackwell Publisher.

Steen, G. (1993). *Metaphor and literary reception*. London: Longman Group.

Stern, J. (1983). Metaphor and grammatical deviance. *Nous, 17*, 577–599.

Stern, J. (1985). Metaphor as demonstrative. *Journal of Philosophy, 82*, 677–710.

Stern, J. (1991). What metaphors do not mean. *Midwest Studies in Philosophy, 16*, 13–52.

Sternberg, R. (1990). *Metaphors of mind: Conceptions of the nature of intelligence*. New York: Cambridge University Press.

Sternberg, R., & Tourangeau, R. (1981). Aptness in metaphor. *Cognitive Psychology, 13*, 27–55.

Strassler, J. (1982). *Idioms in English*. Tübingen: Gunter Narr.

Stroop, J. (1935). Studies in interference in serial verbal reactions. *Journal of Experimental Psychology, 18*, 643–662.

Sugarman, S. (1983). *Children's early thought: Developments in classification*. New York: Cambridge University Press.

Sugarman, S. (1987). *Piaget's construction of the child's reality*. New York: Cambridge University Press.

Sweetser, E. (1987). The definition of "lie": An examination of the folk models underlying a semantic prototype. In D. Holland & N. Quinn (Eds.), *Cultural models in language and thought* (pp. 43–66). New York: Cambridge University Press.

Sweetser, E. (1990). *From etymology to pragmatics: The mind–body metaphor in semantic structure and semantic change*. Cambridge: Cambridge University Press.

Swinney, D. (1979). Lexical access during sentence comprehension: (Re)consideration of context effects. *Journal of Verbal Learning and Verbal Behavior, 18*, 545–569.

Swinney, D., & Cutler, A. (1979). The access and processing of idiomatic expressions. *Journal of Verbal Learning and Verbal Behavior, 18*, 523–534.

Tabossi, P., & Johnson-Laird, P. (1980). Linguistic context and the priming of semantic information. *Quarterly Journal of Experimental Psychology, 32*, 595–603.

Talmy, L. (1988). Force dynamics in language and cognition. *Cognitive Science, 12*, 49–100.

Tanner, W., & Swets, J. (1954). A decision-making theory of visual detection. *Psychological Review, 61*, 401–409.

Tarski, A. (1956). *Logic, semantics, and metamathematics.* Oxford: Oxford University Press.

Taylor, A. (1962). *The proverb and index to "The proverb."* Hasboro, PA: Folklore Associates.

Taylor, J. (1989). *Linguistic categorization.* Oxford: Oxford University Press.

Thompson, A., & Thompson, J. (1986). To look so low as where they are: Hand and heart synecdoches in *Othello. Southern Review, 19*, 29–44.

Thompson, A., & Thompson, J. (1987). *Shakespeare: Meaning and metaphor.* Brighton: Harvest Press.

Thorndyke, P. (1975). Conceptual complexity and imagery in comprehension. *Journal of Verbal Learning and Verbal Behavior, 14*, 359–371.

Tolaas, J. (1991). Notes on the origins of some spatialization metaphors. *Metaphor and Symbolic Activity, 6*, 203–218.

Tourangeau, R., & Sternberg, R. (1981). Aptness in metaphor. *Cognitive Psychology, 13*, 27–55.

Tourangeau, R., & Sternberg, R. (1982). Understanding and appreciating metaphors. *Cognition, 11*, 203–244.

Trick, L., & Katz, A. (1986). The domain interaction approach to metaphor processing: Relating individual differences and metaphor characteristics. *Metaphor and Symbolic Activity, 1*, 185–213.

Truffaut, F. (1969). *Hitchcock.* London: Panther Books.

Turbayne, C. (1962). *The myth of metaphor.* Columbia: University of South Carolina Press.

Turner, M. (1987). *Death is the mother of beauty.* Chicago: University of Chicago Press.

Turner, M. (1991). *Reading minds: The study of English in the age of cognitive science.* Princeton, NJ: Princeton University Press.

Tversky, A. (1977). Features of similarity. *Psychological Review, 84*, 327–352.

Tversky, A., & Kahneman, D. (1983). Probability, representativeness, and the conjunction fallacy. *Psychological Review, 90,* 293–315.

Ullmann, S. (1964). *Language and style.* Oxford: Blackwell Publisher.

Urdang, L. (1988). *The whole ball of wax and other colloquial phrases.* New York: Perigee Books.

Van Besien, F. (1989). Metaphors in scientific language. *Communication and Cognition, 22,* 5–22.

Vendler, H. (1988). *The music of what happens: Poems, poets, critics.* Cambridge, MA: Harvard University Press.

Verbrugge, R. (1977). Resemblances in language and perception. In R. Shaw & J. Bransford (Eds.), *Perceiving, acting, and knowing: Towards an ecological psychology* (pp. 365–392). Hillsdale, NJ: Erlbaum.

Verbrugge, R., & McCarrell, N. (1977). Metaphoric comprehension: Studies in reminding and resembling. *Cognitive Psychology, 9,* 494–533.

Vico, G. (1952). *The new science* (T. Bergin & M. Fisch, Trans.). Ithaca, NY: Cornell University Press. (Original work published 1744).

Voegstle, K. (1983). *Categorization of figurative concepts.* Unpublished doctoral dissertation, University of Cincinnati.

Vosniadou, S. (1987). Children and metaphors. *Child Development, 58,* 870–885.

Vosniadou, S. (1989). Analogical reasoning as a mechanism in knowledge acquisition: A developmental perspective. In S. Vosniadou & A. Ortony (Eds.), *Similarity and analogical reasoning* (pp. 413–437). Cambridge: Cambridge University Press.

Vosniadou, S., & Ortony, A. (1983). The emergence of the literal–metaphorical–anomalous distinction in young children. *Child Development, 54,* 154–161.

Vosniadou, S., & Ortony, A. (1986). Testing the metaphoric competence of the young child: Paraphrase vs. enactment. *Human Development, 29,* 223–224.

Vosniadou, S., Ortony, A., Reynolds, R., & Wilson, P. (1984). Sources of difficulty in children's comprehension of metaphorical language. *Child Development, 55,* 1588–1607.

Voss, J., Kennet, J., Wiley, J., & Engstler-Schooler, T. (1992). Experts at debates: The use of metaphor in the U.S. Senate debate on the Gulf Crisis. *Metaphor and Symbolic Activity, 7,* 197–214.

Wagner, S., Winner, E., Cicchetti, D., & Gardner, H. (1981). "Metaphorical" mappings in human infants. *Child Development, 52,* 728–731.

Wasow, T., Sag, I., & Nunberg, G. (1982). Idioms: An interim report. In *Proceedings of the XII International Congress of Linguistics, Tokyo* (pp. 87–96).

Weinreich, U. (1966). Explorations in semantic theory. In T. Sebeok (Ed.), *Current trends in linguistics* (Vol. 3, pp. 395–477). The Hague: Mouton.

Weinreich, U. (1969). Problems in the analysis of idioms. In J. Puhvel (Ed.), *Substance and structure of language* (pp. 23–81). Berkeley and Los Angeles: University of California Press.

Wellek, R., & Warren, A. (1949). *Theory of literature*. Harmondsworth: Penguin Books.

Wentworth, H., & Flexner, S. (1960). *Dictionary of American slang*. New York: Crowell.

White, G. (1987). Proverbs and cultural models: An American psychology of problem solving. In D. Holland & N. Quinn (Eds.), *Cultural models in language and thought* (pp. 151–172). New York: Cambridge University Press.

White, H. (1973). *Metahistory: The historical imagination in nineteenth-century Europe*. Baltimore: Johns Hopkins University Press.

White, H. (1978). *Tropics of discourse*. Baltimore: Johns Hopkins University Press.

White, H. (1988). The rhetoric of interpretation. *Poetics Today, 9,* 253–274.

Whitman, W. (1964). Slang in America. In F. Stovall (Ed.), *The collected writings of Walt Whitman: Prose works* (pp. 572–577). New York: New York University Press. (Originally published 1892).

Whitney, P., McKay, T., Kellas, G., & Emerson, W. (1985). Semantic activation of noun concepts in context. *Journal of Experimental Psychology: Learning, Memory, and Cognition, 11,* 126–135.

Whittock, T. (1990). *Metaphor and film*. New York: Cambridge University Press.

Whorf, B. (1956). *Language, thought, and reality: The selected writings of Benjamin Lee Whorf*. New York: Wiley.

Wierzbicka, A. (1974). The semantics of direct and indirect discourse. *Studies in Language, 3/4,* 267–307.

Wierzbicka, A. (1987). Boys will be boys: "Radical semantics" vs. "radical pragmatics." *Language, 63,* 95–114.

Wilensky, R., & Arens, Y. (1980). PHRAN – A knowledge-based approach to natural language analysis (Memorandum UCB/ERLM80/34). Electronics Research Laboratory, University of California at Berkeley.

Wilks, Y. (1972). *Grammar, meaning, and the machine analysis of natural language*. London: Routledge & Kegan Paul.

References

Wilks, Y. (1978). Good and bad arguments for semantic primitives. *Communication and Cognition, 10,* 181–221.

Williams, J. (1984). Does mention (or pretense) exhaust the concept of irony? *Journal of Experimental Psychology: General, 113,* 127–129.

Williams, J. (1992). Processing polysemous words in context: Evidence for interrelated meanings. *Journal of Psycholinguistic Research, 21,* 193–218.

Williams-Whitney, D., Mio, J., & Whitney, P. (1992). Metaphor production in creative writing. *Journal of Psycholinguistic Research, 21,* 497–509.

Willinsky, J. (1987). The paradox of text in the culture of literacy. *Interchange, 18,* 147–162.

Wilson, D., & Sperber, D. (1989). Representation and relevance. In R. Kempson (Ed.), *Mental representations: The interface between language and reality* (pp. 133–154). Cambridge: Cambridge University Press.

Wilson, D., & Sperber, D. (1990, July). *Is there a maxim of truthfulness?* Paper presented at the International Pragmatics Association Meetings, Barcelona.

Wilson, D., & Sperber, D. (1992). On verbal irony. *Lingua, 87,* 53–76.

Winner, E. (1979). New names for old things: The emergence of metaphoric language. *Journal of Child Language, 6,* 469–491.

Winner, E. (1988). *The point of words: Children's understanding of metaphor and irony.* Cambridge, MA: Harvard University Press.

Winner, E., McCarthy, M., & Gardner, H. (1980). The ontogenesis of metaphor. In R. Honeck & R. Hoffman (Eds.), *Cognition and figurative language* (pp. 341–361). Hillsdale, NJ: Erlbaum.

Winner, E., McCarthy, M., Kleinman, S., & Gardner, H. (1979). First metaphors. In D. Wolf (Ed.), *Early symbolization: New directions for child development* (pp. 29–41). Washington, DC: Jossey-Bass.

Winner, E., Rosenstiel, A., & Gardner, H. (1976). The development of metaphoric understanding. *Developmental Psychology, 12,* 289–297.

Winner, E., Windmueller, G., Rosenblatt, E., Bosco, L., & Best, E. (1987). Making sense of literal and nonliteral falsehood. *Metaphor and Symbolic Processes, 2,* 13–32.

Winograd, E. (1974). *Five lectures on artificial intelligence* (Memo AIM No. 246). AI Laboratory, Stanford University.

Winter, S. (1989). Transcendental nonsense, metaphoric reasoning, and the cognitive stakes for law. *University of Pennsylvania Law Review, 137,* 1105–1198.

References

Wise, M. (1988). Mediating machines. *Science in Context, 2,* 77–113.

Wisniewski, E., & Gentner, D. (1991). On the combinatorial semantics to noun pairs: Minor and major adjustments to meaning. In G. Simpson (Ed.), *Understanding word and sentence* (pp. 241–284). The Hague: North Holland.

Wittgenstein, L. (1953). *Philosophical investigations.* New York: Macmillan.

Zwicker, E., & Scharf, B. (1965). A model of loudness summation. *Psychological Review, 72,* 3–26.

Name Index

Aaron, D., 167, 168
Abbott, V., 296, 299, 330
Abelson, R., 296, 299, 329
Abrahams, R., 138, 139, 309
Acconci, Vito, 187
Ackerman, B., 271, 417, 426, 428
Aitchison, J., 38, 270
Albee, Edward, 360
Aleksandrowicz, D., 127
Allbritton, D., 256, 257
Alston, W., 275
Altherman, Nathan, 396
Amiel-Tison, C., 432
Anderson, R., 34
Anderson, W., 370
Anisfeld, M., 399
Antos, S., 99, 107, 338
Apter, M., 134
Arbib, M., 172
Arens, Y., 271
Arewa, E., 137
Aristotle, 61, 121, 122, 129, 169–70,
    208, 210–11, 212
Arkes, N., 50
Arlow, J., 127
Armstrong, S., 55
Arnheim, R., 184
Arter, J., 211, 212
Asch, S., 405
Austin, J., 64
Aycock, Alice, 187
Ayer, A., 61

Bach, K., 82, 352, 357
Bacon, Francis, 71
Barclay, J., 34
Barley, N., 137
Barlow, J., 123
Barsalou, L., 33, 34, 51, 52, 53, 54,
    247, 445
Barth, John, 368
Barthelme, Donald, 283, 284, 368
Bates, E., 50, 424
Beal, C., 432
Beardsley, M., 222, 223
Beatles, 361–2
Beattie, G., 105
Becker, J., 271
Bell, S., 92, 270, 271
Bennet, D., 43
Bergman, Ingmar, 369
Bertoncini, J., 432
Best, E., 431
Bettelheim, B., 400, 401
Bever, T., 100
Bicchieri, C., 170, 173
Bickerton, D., 218, 222
Bienkowski, M., 41
Bierce, Ambrose, 367
Bierwisch, M., 31
Billman, D., 409
Billow, R., 403, 406, 408, 410
Binkley, T., 222, 226
Bird-David, N., 192
Black, J., 296, 330

Name Index

Name Index

Name Index

Subject Index

Subject Index

contiguity relation, 324

contradictory concepts, understanding of, 395–6, 397

contrast, principle of, 29, 48

CONTROL IS UP: LACK OF CONTROL IS DOWN (conceptual metaphor), 46, 157–8

CONTROLLER FOR THE CONTROLLED, THE, (metonymy) 12

convention in indirect speech acts, 352–3, 354, 357, 358

conventional cultural associations, 324–5

conventional literality, 75, 76

conventional metaphors, 13, 22, 105–6, 206; dead metaphors and, 273–8; mind in, 177; novel extensions of, 154–7

conventional metonymies, 320, 324, 333, 336, 344

conventions of usage in comprehension of idioms, 274–5, 308

conversational implicature, theory of, 81–3, 327–8, 331, 347

conversational maxims, 430; alternatives to, 393–4; violation of, 109

"Convicted Minimalist Spills Bean" (Barthelme), 283, 284

cooperation, 346

cooperative communication, norms of, 229, 245

cooperative principle, 83, 113, 245; maxims of, 81–3

cosmic myths, 188

"Crazed Man, The" (Yeats), 214

creativity, 7, 8–9

cross-modal matching in children, 413–14

cultural anthropologists, 197, 202, 451

cultural identity, irony in, 370–1

cultural knowledge, 73, 311

cultural models, 203, 204, 205, 206

cultural world view in language, 438–42

culturally shared metaphors, 158–9, 183

culture, 17; journey metaphor in, 191–2; and literal meaning of concepts, 55, 78; and literalness, 27; metaphor in, 21, 122, 192–206; polytropic symbols in, 451–2

Cuna tribe, 193–4

dead metaphors, 10, 158, 273–4, 436; and conventional metaphors, 273–8; idioms as, 21–2, 91, 267–8, 275–8, 290, 292, 295, 303, 306, 308, 318, 417, 419, 421

death, myths about journey toward, 191

deception, distinguishing irony from, 429–31

decomposability of idioms, 278, 279, 281, 282–3, 284–5, 286, 289, 291, 419–21

"Defining Love" (Quevedo), 394–5

definition of words and concepts, 27–40, 49; possibility of, 35–40

deictic terms, 30

denotation, 30

detour transactions, 353–4

developmental psychology, 19, 416–17, 427, 433

Devil's Dictionary, The (Bierce), 367

diachronic semantics, 158

dictionary(ies), 27, 28, 31, 37, 39, 59

Dictionary of Contemporary English, 37

direct oxymora, 396–7

directionality (metaphor), 217

Dr. Strangelove (film), 366

domains interaction model, 239, 241–3, 246, 262

double-bind situations, proverbs in, 137

double metaphor, 245

DOWN IS INFERIORITY (metaphor), 414–15

513

Subject Index

dramatic irony, 363–4, 388
Durée poignardee, La (artwork), 186

echoic mention theory, 383–6
eclecticism, 368
economic theory, metaphor in, 170–1
educational theorists on metaphor, 129–30
effects = structures fallacy, 54–5
ELECTRICITY IS A FLOWING STREAM (metaphor), 162
ELECTRICITY IS A TEEMING CROWD (metaphor), 162
emotion, expression of, 50, 137
emotion concepts, 297, 298–300, 301–2; metaphorical, 149, 163–4
emotional experience, metaphor in, 125–7, 128
emotive meanings, 61, 64, 69
encyclopedia, 28
epistemic justification, 220
epistemic modal verbs, 159–61
eponyms, 339–43
error recovery model, 107, 337–8
essentialism, 59
essentialist heuristic, 57
Eurythmics, 14–15
event structure metaphor, 149–50, 152–4
everyday experience/life: cognition grounded in, 79; irony in, 359–60, 369–70; metaphor view of, 203; poetic thinking in, 434–5
everyday speech/discourse: figurative thought/language in, 3; irony in, 14, 367; metaphor in, 8–9, 122–4; oxymora in, 395, 396
everyday thought/language: figurative nature of, 3, 10, 11, 15–16, 18–19, 331, 397; figurative thought and, 440–1, 445–9; idiomaticity in, 268; ironic

nature of, 371–2; metaphoric structure of, 9, 21, 120–1, 122, 134, 146–67; metonymy in, 12–13, 324, 327, 330–1, 333; nature of, 437; poetic character of, 444, 454
exactness, literal meaning and, 62–3, 65–6
exemplar view, 50, 51, 52
expectation/reality incongruity in irony, 362–3, 365
experience: metaphorical structuring of, 146–54; myths as organizing principles for, 188; see also everyday experience/life
experiential gestalts, 203, 249
experimental psychology: idiom in, 268; metaphor in, 174–8; metonymy in, 324
explicitness, literal meaning and, 62, 63, 65–6
expository style (writing), 71–2
expressibility principle, 62, 226
extension, 30, 43
extensionalism, 29–30

face, 351–2, 371
fairy tales, 143, 401–2
FALLING IS FAILURE (metaphor), 415
familiarity: in comprehension of idioms, 96; and comprehension of metaphors, 104
family discourse, irony in, 374–7
family resemblance principle, 49–50
Fang people, 194–5
figuration, 16, 20, 435, 454
figurative language, 1–23, 454; context and, 216; in everyday speech, 16, 121; literal meaning and, 20, 25, 26, 75–8; production of, 104; in psychotherapy, 127; social functions of, 134–40; "specialness" of, 121, 132, 136, 435

514